THE HANDBOOK OF MANAGED FUTURES

Performance, Evaluation & Analysis

REVISED EDITION

THE HANDBOOK OF MANAGED FUTURES

Performance, Evaluation & Analysis

CARL PETERS

BEN WARWICK

Editors

IRWIN
Professional Publishing©
Chicago • London • Singapore

THE HANDBOOK OF MANAGED FUTURES: PERFORMANCE, EVALUATION, AND
ANALYSIS

1 2 3 4 5 6 7 8 9 0 DOC DOC 9 0 9 8 7 6

ISBN 1-55738-917-9

This publication is designed to provide accurate and
authoritative information in regard to the subject matter
covered. It is sold with the understanding that neither the
author or the publisher is engaged in rendering legal, accounting,
or other professional service. If legal advice or other expert
assistance is required, the services of a competent professional
person should be sought.

*From a Declaration of Principles jointly adopted by a Committee
of the American Bar Association and a Committee of Publishers.*

Library of Congress Cataloging-in-Publication Data

The handbook of managed futures : performance, evaluation & analysis / Carl
  Peters, Ben Warwick, editors. Rev. ed.
      p.   cm.
    Includes index.
    ISBN 1-55738-917-9
    1. Futures. I. Peters, Carl C. II. Warwick, Ben.
  HG6024.A3 H362 1996
  332.64/5—DC21   96-29592

http://www.mhcollege.com

Since the publication of the first edition of this book, the managed futures industry has changed considerably. Perhaps the biggest difference is the perception of futures as "alpha-providers" rather than the traditional view of a separate asset class. The second edition of *Managed Futures* attempts to address the latest issues in implementation, product development, and capital markets research.

Part I examines the role of managed futures in the asset allocation process. Futures are examined as a stand-alone investment, in combination with stocks and bonds, and as a tool in downside equity risk management. The performance of publicly offered commodity pools is also presented.

Part II highlights recent innovations in managed futures product development. Topics include the use of managed futures and currencies in an overlay strategy, managed futures structured notes, index-linked commodity funds, and the use of managed futures in emerging markets. Issues related to the selection and monitoring of commodity trading advisors (CTAs) are also presented by four well-known asset allocators.

Part III examines current research into the nature of market inefficiencies. Although most of the previous academic study generally supports the efficient market hypothesis (EMH), recent work using more robust methodologies has shown marked discrepancies with the EMH. But perhaps the greatest evidence regarding inefficiencies is the continuing viability of the managed futures industry, now over 20 years old.

It is hoped that the information presented in this book will help increase the knowledge base and awareness of our industry.

Carl Peters
Ben Warwick

CONTENTS

The Case for Managed Futures

CHAPTER 1

Managed Futures— An Overview

Carl C. Peters

This chapter begins with a description of the characteristics of futures, and managed futures investments. There are certain unique features, such as margin, leverage, and event sensitivity, which are part of futures products that need to be understood in order to correctly interpret performance. The remaining part of this chapter addresses the following main issues of performance:

1. Performance as a stand-alone investment
2. Potential as a hedge against inflation
3. Correlation to stock and bond performance
4. Effectiveness in portfolio diversification

DESCRIPTION OF MANAGED FUTURES INVESTMENTS

A futures contract is an agreement to deliver or accept a specified quantity of a commodity (or financial instrument) at a predetermined price at a designated time in the future. Futures contracts exist for a number of diverse commodity and financial instrument groups. Included are the grains, livestock, foods and fibers, petroleum and related products, metals, currencies, interest rate instruments, and indices for stocks and bonds. A buyer is said to have established a long position (i.e., agreed to accept delivery) and can profit if prices rise. A seller, on the other hand, has established a short position (i.e., agreed to deliver) and can profit if prices fall.

For most investors liquidation is done by selling or buying an equal number of contracts to offset their original positions. Because of the ease of entering or exiting, going long or short, relatively low costs per transaction, and liquidity of the futures markets, professional management generally consists of active buying and selling, frequently aided by technical analysis [Brorsen and Irwin (1985)] in an attempt to profit from both rising and falling prices.

Domestic futures markets operate under regulations of the Commodity Futures Trading Commission (CFTC), the commodities counterpart of the Securities Exchange Commission (SEC). Additionally, the National Futures Association (NFA) monitors, administers, and self-regulates the professional conduct and financial responsibility of its membership, as does the National Association of Security Dealers (NASD) for securities.

Futures investing involves putting up a "good faith" deposit (also called "margin") to ensure that an adverse price movement will be covered if a contract is liquidated at a loss. However, margin for futures investments is different from that required for stocks and bonds. Stock margins constitute a partial payment for the stock; the remainder or debit balance is usually kept in a margin account as a debt upon which interest is charged. Commodity margins, on the other hand, are good-faith deposits to ensure that adverse price movements are covered. Stock margin requirements fluctuate in a range from 50 to 90 percent of the stock purchased. Commodity margin requirements are usually only 5 to 10 percent of the face value of a contract. Whereas the purchaser of stock using a margin has to *pay* interest on the difference between his deposit and the value of the stock, the investor in commodities can *receive* interest on the money that is used as the "good-faith" deposit. It is common to use between 10 and 30 percent of investment funds to satisfy all margin requirements in managed futures accounts, with the remainder used as reserve. Since short-term instruments such as U.S. Treasury bills can be used for margin; it is not uncommon for an account to be able to earn interest on its entire investment capital while being used for margin and reserve.

Managed futures investments fall into three broad categories each with its own cost structure and capital requirements: individual accounts, private pools, and public commodity funds. Individual accounts generally have low costs and large minimum capital requirements. Public commodity funds, on the other hand, have higher costs but the lowest minimum investment requirements. Private commodity pools generally have the lowest costs, and investment minimums somewhere in between. These categorizations are not all-inclusive, and exceptions do exist. There can, however, be substantive differences in performance for each, so their identities should be kept distinct.

In addition to the above categories, institutions have further shaped the managed futures product line into more customized programs including structured notes and portfolio overlay strategies.

An important issue to be considered when analyzing performance is the time period selected for analysis. The inflationary era of the late 1970s caused commodity prices to move upward substantially. The decade of the 1980s, on the other hand, marked a return to lower inflation and relative price stability. The 1990s have seen very low inflation and a very strong appreciation in stocks and bonds relative to commodities. To the extent that performance of managed futures products is related to price trends in commodity prices (a subject addressed by some of the research herein) and that inflation is detrimental to stock and bond investments, periods of high and low inflation can have a significant impact on relative performance.

PERFORMANCE AS A STAND-ALONE INVESTMENT

Performance comparisons between investment alternatives necessarily include measures of both return and risk. Most researchers equate risk with variability of returns and its most popularized measure—standard deviation. The higher the standard deviation the larger the variability, and the lower the probability that the average rate of return will occur in any one period. Although standard deviation suffers from some shortcomings [see Strahm (1983), or Peters (1989)], it has found wide acceptance by both researchers and investors as a proxy for risk.

One measure of performance is the simple ratio of return-to-risk (typically the ratio of excess return [over and above the risk-free rate] to standard deviation—called the Sharpe Ratio). Maximizing these ratios (return-to-risk), while an intuitively appealing approach, does not take into account the investor's risk preferences [Reilly (1985)]. A proper and complete analysis would address the unique utility function of each investor. This of course is not possible except under the most general circumstances [see Fischmar and Peters (1990)], so we are left with simple comparisons of return and risk between alternatives.

Without exception, all researchers found managed futures products to have higher variability (as measured by variance or standard deviation) than stocks, bonds, or T-bills. The question then becomes whether returns were high enough to justify this additional risk. Researchers found that returns for CTAs [Lintner (1983), Baratz and Eresian (1985, 1989), Oberuc (1990)] and private pools [Orr, (1985, 1987)] were indeed higher than stocks, bonds, and T-bills. None of the research addressed the return-risk preferences of investors so the question if returns were high enough to overcome the increased variability remains unanswered.

Findings regarding public funds were somewhat different, however. Lintner (1983) found higher returns for public commodity funds than stocks, bonds, and T-bills. Brorsen and Irwin (1985) and Irwin and Landa (1987) also drew the same conclusion regarding bonds, and T-bills, but found returns approximately equal to stocks. Murphy (1986) found inferior returns compared to stocks and T-bills on a *net* basis, but higher returns on a *gross* basis (he did not examine bonds). Elton, Gruber, and Rentzler (1987, 1990) found inferior returns compared to traditional investments. These differences in findings show a deterioration in *relative* performance between public commodity funds and traditional investments over time, coincidental with the transition from the inflationary times of the late 1970s to the period of relative economic stability of the 1980s. That public funds lost their return advantage, while CTA and private pools did not, reflects in part their higher cost structure. Murphy (1986) and Irwin, Krukmeyer, and Zulaf (1992) showed how decreasing cost structures could have changed their conclusions regarding public funds.

Schneeweis (1996 A) found that the standard deviation of the "average" CTA from a sample of 68 CTAs for the period 1987–1995 was actually similar to the "average" stock out of a sample of 250 stocks listed in the S&P 500. He also points out that while recent stock and bond returns have exceeded those of CTAs, such returns were abnormally high (the highest in 10 years) whereas the returns from CTAs were much closer to their 10-year average (1995 returns were 14.1 percent versus their 10-year average of 15.8 percent).

POTENTIAL AS A HEDGE AGAINST INFLATION AND STOCK/BOND MARKET DECLINES

The likelihood that inflation can produce weakness in stock and bond markets probably needs no lengthy explanation. As prospects for inflation appear, interest rates rise, causing concerns that consumption and private domestic investment will fall, i.e., reduce aggregate demand for goods and services. The discounted present value of company earnings also drops and stocks in general become weak. On the other hand, inflation means a rise in prices. During inflation commodity prices generally trend upward over time [Bodie (1983)]. Commodity trading advisors, whether technicians or fundamentalists, are generally trend-followers, so it is expected that they would exploit inflation-generated trends. Have managed futures outperformed stocks and bonds during such periods?

Bodie and Rosansky (1980) examined quarterly prices for 27 years, 1950–1976, for stocks, bonds, bills, and a passive portfolio of all actively traded commodity futures. They found returns from futures positively correlated with inflation, but negatively correlated with stocks and bonds. Furthermore, they found that a hypothetical portfolio consisting of 60 percent stocks and 40 percent passive futures reduced variability of an all-stock portfolio without sacrificing return. In a follow-up study, Bodie (1983) examined annual prices for 29 years, 1953–1981, for stocks, bonds, bills, and a passive portfolio of commodity futures. He found real rates of return for commodity futures again to be positively correlated with inflation, while stocks, bonds, and bills were negatively correlated with inflation, but positively correlated with one another. These studies acknowledge the conservative approach of using a strict buy and hold strategy for futures, where the only hope for long-term positive nominal rates of return was through unanticipated inflation, but point out that even a passive strategy produces some improvements to the overall portfolio.

The question of how well managed futures did, compared to a passive portfolio of futures during periods of inflation, was addressed in a study by Irwin and Landa (1987). They examined, among other things, the performance of stocks, bonds, bills, a passive portfolio of all actively traded commodity futures, and performance of futures funds during the period 1975–1985. Their study showed that managed futures far outperformed their passive counterpart during the inflationary era of 1977–1981, in addition to showing significantly better performance during the entire 1975–1985 period.

Orr (1985, 1987) analyzed return patterns and showed that stock and bond returns were below their long-term trendlines, and managed futures above, during the period of higher inflation of the early 1980s.

Generally, most researchers found managed futures to be an effective hedge against inflation. An exception was Elton, Gruber, and Rentzler (1987, 1990), who found no indications of effectiveness. However, they used monthly data over a period that did not span a time of sustained inflation. They also used direct month-to-month comparisons and ignored possible lead-lag relationships between commodity prices and the measured rate of inflation. Other researchers who used quarterly or annual data and longer time frames reached opposite conclusions. The problems discussed above could account for these differences in findings.

With regard to hedging stock portfolios, Schneeweis (1996 B) found that managed futures may offer risk/return benefits when compared to a partially hedged position in the stock market. For example, it was shown that an equal weighted investment in the MAR CTA index and the S&P 500 outperformed a strategy consisting of investment in the S&P 500 plus a simulated at-the-money put option under most market conditions.

CORRELATION WITH STOCKS AND BONDS

Before discussing correlation, an important first step is to define the needs of the investor. It is assumed that the investor already has a portfolio of traditional assets including stocks and bonds. His needs are to earn a return large enough to meet the requirements of the beneficiaries of his portfolio, and to control risk to the lowest possible levels. Risk is assumed to be portfolio return variability; the higher the variability, the less likely that the average return will occur. Although this definition has its limitations and other measures may be more appropriate [Peters (1989)], [Fischmar and Peters (1990)], it has found wide use in modern portfolio management.

In the context of traditional modern portfolio theory [Markowitz (1959)] the objectives of the investor are first to use a portfolio on the so-called "efficient frontier,"[1] commensurate with his return/risk preferences, and second, to find ways to shift this efficient frontier toward more return and less risk. These objectives are illustrated in an example shown in Figure 1–1 using stock/bond portfolios with and without managed futures. A portfolio made up of stocks and bonds only (portfolio "A") can be improved by the addition of a third asset category (in this example, managed futures) if a favorable shift occurs in the efficient frontier as shown. The investor can reallocate units to achieve more return at the same risk (portfolio "B"), less risk for the same return (portfolio "C") or any combination in between.

Risk is measured by standard deviation. The higher the standard deviation, the greater the risk. The shift in efficient frontier upward (more return) and to the left (less risk) is accomplished by adding new asset classes with the correct characteristics to the portfolio. Correlation is an important dimension of performance because of the role it plays quantitatively and qualitatively in determining if portfolio enhancement can occur through diversification. Elton, Gruber, and Rentzler (1987) showed that a futures investment should be added to a portfolio if

$$
\begin{bmatrix} \text{Sharpe Ratio of} \\ \text{Candidate Asset} \end{bmatrix} \geq \begin{bmatrix} \text{Correlation} \\ \text{Coefficient} \end{bmatrix} \times \begin{bmatrix} \text{Sharpe Ratio} \\ \text{of Portfolio} \end{bmatrix}
$$

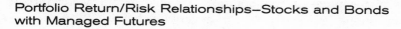

FIGURE 1–1

Portfolio Return/Risk Relationships—Stocks and Bonds
with Managed Futures

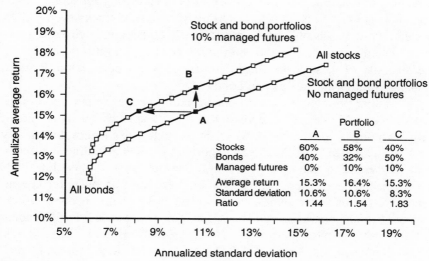

Annualized standard deviation

Notes:

1. The "efficient frontier" is defined mathematically as that combination of assets that have minimum combined variance at all possible levels of return.

2. Stocks are represented by the S&P 500 Index, bonds by the Shearson Lehman International Government Corporate Bond Index, and managed futures by the MAR Equal Weighted CTA Index.

The Sharpe Ratio is defined as the ratio of excess return (beyond the risk-free rate) to standard deviation. If the correlation coefficient is zero, the above condition reduces to

$$\left[\begin{array}{c} \text{Sharpe Ratio of} \\ \text{Candidate Asset} \end{array} \right] \geq 0$$

which can only occur if the rate of return exceeds the risk-free rate.

Therefore, if there is no significant correlation, a managed futures investment can enhance portfolio performance when its expected return is merely greater than the risk-free rate. And, all other things being the same, if correlation is negative, the "hurdle" rate of return becomes even less. Thus the correlation coefficient is an important determinant of the effectiveness of any asset used for diversification.

There are a number of reasons to expect little correlation between managed futures and stocks and bonds. Conditions that are not favorable to stocks and bonds usually are favorable for managed futures. Inflation, deflation, and times of economic and political uncertainty can cause major moves in the price of commodities. As an example, when inflation appeared during 1977–1981, the Consumer Price Index (CPI) rose over 60 percent. Futures funds averaged over 37 percent during the same 5-year period [Irwin and Landa (1987)]. On the other hand, stocks averaged 14 percent, while bonds only broke even. Nearly all economic circumstances are reflected somewhere in the commodity markets, and it is probable that the diversity of these forces helps contribute to noncorrelation between managed futures and stocks and bonds.

Another possible basis for noncorrelation between managed futures and stocks and bonds is the diversity of the markets traded. There are at least 30 futures contracts on U. S., CFTC regulated exchanges that qualify for large scale trading.[2] Market categories include agriculturals (wheat, corn, soybeans, soybean meal, and oil), livestock (hogs and cattle), foods and fibers (sugar, coffee, cotton, cocoa), petroleum products (crude oil, heating oil, unleaded gasoline), metals (silver, gold, platinum, copper), currencies (British pound, German mark, Japanese yen, Swiss franc, Canadian dollar), interest rate instruments (U.S. Treasury Bonds, Bills, Notes, Eurodollar Deposits, Municipal Bond Index), and stock indices (S & P 500). In addition, there are at least as many international financial and commodity markets representing countries such as Australia, Japan, Korea, the U.K., France, Germany, Spain, Italy, and others. The diversity of markets traded contributes to the noncorrelated nature in performance between managed futures and stocks and bonds.

Yet another factor contributing to noncorrelation is the structure of futures contracts themselves. When a position is taken in a futures contract it can be just as easily long (i.e., to profit from rising prices) or short (i.e., to profit from falling prices). There are no rules making it relatively more difficult to establish short as opposed to long positions as there are in the equity markets. If one has the ability to recognize trends, profits can be made either in rising or falling markets. The capability of profiting from declining markets can provide a significant degree of noncorrelation in return patterns. A clear example of the difference between managed futures and other asset management styles is to consider active management in the debt and equity markets. Most traditional investing by institutions is to buy and hold in these markets, and to retreat to cash when weakness occurs. The Commodity Trading Advisor, on the other hand, can be long or short (or neutral). It is not difficult to see how the latter strategy could be noncorrelated with the former.

With few exceptions researchers have found no significant correlation between futures products and stocks or bonds. And in no case did the correlation approach that found between stocks and bonds themselves. Lintner (1983) found small positive correlation between funds and stocks, but improvements from diversification were still possible. Orr (1985, 1987) showed small positive correlation was present between pools and stocks or bonds during a period of low inflation, but the reverse was true during a period of higher inflation. Irwin and Landa (1987) showed small positive correlation between stocks and passive futures portfolios, but strong negative correlation between stocks and public commodity funds over the same time period. Schneeweis (1996 A) found virtually no correlation with stocks and bonds overall. When the data were segmented according to periods when the stock market rose or fell, managed futures were found to be significantly *negatively* correlated with stocks/bonds during periods of weakness, and positively correlated during periods of strength. Other authors found no positive correlation, and some found evidence of significant negative correlation.

In summary, there is agreement that returns from managed futures products are independent or negatively correlated with those of stocks and bonds. Oberuc (1990) has extended these conclusions to include Eurostocks and Eurobonds as well.

PERFORMANCE IN PORTFOLIO DIVERSIFICATION

The results of the preceding section show that futures products appear to have little positive correlation to stocks and bonds, making them promising candidates for portfolio diversification. Improvement in portfolio performance can occur whenever the efficient frontier is shifted upward (toward more return) and/or to the left (less risk). If this occurs the investor can reallocate his asset mix to include the diversifying investment and a mix of original assets in order to obtain larger return for the same risk, less risk for the same return, or a combination of both.

With two exceptions, (both from the same authors), researchers found that futures products could have improved portfolio performance.

Bodie and Rosansky (1980), Bodie (1983), Herbst and McCormack (1986, 1988), and Irwin and Landa (1987) all examined passive futures investments in combination with stocks and/or bonds and concluded that enhancement would have occurred. Orr (1985, 1987) examined private pools in a similar manner, with the same conclusions. Lintner (1983), Baratz and Eresian (1985, 1989), Fischmar and Peters (1990), and Oberuc (1990) found that CTA performance would likewise have improved performance of stock and bond (and cash) portfolios.

The results for public commodity funds were not as clear. Lintner (1983), and Irwin and Brorsen (1985) found that improvement could occur by using public commodity funds for diversification. However, Murphy (1987) found that portfolio enhancement depended on costs associated with public commodity funds; improvement did occur when using returns on a *gross* basis (before costs) but not on a *net* basis (after costs). Elton, Gruber, and Rentzler (1987) concluded that public commodity funds were not attractive additions to portfolios of stocks and bonds. While Elton, Gruber, and Rentzler (1990) drew the same conclusion, they also found that public commodity funds with general partners with above-average performance in prior funds produced significantly better returns with new products—enough so as to have qualified them as attractive diversification assets for stock and bond portfolios. Irwin, Krukmeyer, and Zulaf (1992) showed that public commodity fund performance, when adjusted to reflect institutional level costs and fees, justified their inclusion in stock and bond portfolios. Schneeweis (1996 A) concluded that managed futures have unique properties that make them attractive in portfolio diversification.

SUMMARY

The purpose of this book was to review and summarize the findings of various researchers regarding the performance of managed futures. Performance was measured along the following lines:

1. As a stand-alone investment.
2. As a hedge against inflation and stock/bond market weakness.
3. Correlation with returns of traditional investments.
4. As a diversifying asset in stock and bond portfolios.

Results were categorized by type (Passive Futures Portfolios, Commodity Trading Advisors, Private Commodity Pools, and Public Commodity Funds) and time period analyzed.

Regarding stand-alone performance, results were mixed. Managed futures products have the same or higher variability than stocks or bonds (passive futures had comparable variability). Returns were also higher than stocks and bonds for CTAs and Private Commodity Pools, but results for Public Commodity funds were mixed. Studies that were conducted earlier in the 1980s tended to show funds having better returns, while those completed later (after taking into account more of the bull market of the 1980s) showed a deterioration in relative performance compared to stocks and bonds.

All studies were unanimous in their findings that futures products had no significant positive correlation to stocks or bonds. Many found no correlation and some found significantly negative correlation. These conclusions are particularly noteworthy when considering futures products for diversifying stock and bond portfolios.

Of the studies that examined the performance of futures products as a hedge against inflation, the majority found confirming evidence. The distinguishing characteristic of these studies is that they covered periods of sustained inflation and used longer time frames of measurement (i.e., quarterly or annual data). Orr (1987) specifically looked at performance around long-term trendlines as did Schneeweis (1996 A, B) during periods of stock market strength and weakness. In contrast, those studies that found inconclusive evidence neither completely spanned inflationary periods, nor used long time frames. Short-term, month-to-month comparisons were made without attempting to test for lead-lag relationships.

Finally, the large majority of the authors found futures products effective in diversifying stock and bond portfolios. An area of disagreement occurred in public commodity funds products; however, it was shown that conclusions were very sensitive to cost structures and time period analyzed. In summary, the weight of academic evidence seems to conclude that futures products have clearly no correlation with stocks and bonds and offer potentially attractive benefits in diversifying stock and bond portfolios. Research as well as methodological considerations also argue strongly for inflation hedging effectiveness. Performance as a stand-alone investment appears to be mixed, depending on the product and time period analyzed.

The evidence presented shows that investments in managed futures are well founded, both in financial theory and practical experience. Long-term positive performance has been generated in excess of the risk-free rate of return, and correlation to stock and bond portfolios has been low or nonexistent. As such, managed futures are finding a place in the investment portfolios of individuals, retirement plans, and institutional investors.

ENDNOTES

1. The "efficient frontier" is defined mathematically as that combination of assets that have minimum combined variance at all possible levels of return.
2. Additionally, there are a growing number of futures contracts traded on foreign futures exchanges as well as cash and forward contracts in currencies that can have significant liquidity.

BIBLIOGRAPHY

Baratz, Morton S., and Eresian, Warren. "The Role of Managed Futures Accounts in an Investment Portfolio." *MAR Mid-Year Conference on Futures Money Management,* Chicago: July 1986.

Baratz, Morton S., and Eresian, Warren. "The Role of Managed Futures Accounts in an Investment Portfolio." *MAR Conference on Futures Money Management,* January 1990.

Bodie, Zvi. "Commodity Futures as a Hedge against Inflation." *The Journal of Portfolio Management,* Spring 1983.

Bodie, Zvi and Rosansky, Victor. "Risk and Return in Commodity Futures." *Financial Analysts Journal,* May–June 1980.

Brorsen, B. Wade, and Irwin, Scott H. "Examination of Commodity Fund Performance." *Review of Research in the Futures Markets* 4, 1985.

Elton, Edwin J.; Gruber, Martin J.; and Rentzler, Joel C. "The Performance of Publicly Offered Commodity Funds." *Financial Analysts Journal,* July–August 1990.

Elton, Edwin J.; Gruber, Martin J.; and Rentzler, Joel C. "Professionally Managed, Publicly Traded Commodity Funds." *Journal of Business* 60, no. 2, 1987.

Fischmar, Daniel, and Peters, Carl C. "Portfolio of Stocks, Bonds and Managed Futures Using Compromise Stochastic Dominance." *The Journal of Futures Markets* II, no. 3, June 1991.

Herbst, Anthony F., and McCormack, Joseph P. "A Further Examination of the Risk-Return Characteristics of Portfolios Combining Commodity Futures Contracts with Common Stocks." *Working Paper Series, Center for the Study of Futures Markets,* Columbia University, February 1988.

Herbst, Anthony F., and McCormack, Joseph P. "An Examination of the Risk-Return Characteristics of Portfolios Combining Commodity Futures Contracts with Common Stocks." *Working Paper Series, Center for the Study of Futures Markets,* Columbia University, January 1986.

Irwin, Scott, and Brorsen, B. Wade. "Public Futures Funds." *The Journal of Futures Markets* 5, no. 2, 1985.

Irwin, Scott, and Landa, Diego. "Real Estate, Futures, and Gold as Portfolio Assets." *The Journal of Portfolio Management,* Fall 1987.

Irwin, Scott H.; Krukmeyer, Terry; and Zulauf, Carl R. "The Investment Performance of Public Commodity Pools over 1979–1989," submitted to *The Journal of Futures Markets,* and accepted for publication, 1992.

Lee, Chung F.; Leuthold, Raymond; and Cordier, Jean. "The Stock Market and Commodities Futures Market: Diversification and Arbitrage Potential." *Financial Analysts Journal,* July–August 1985.

Lintner, John. "The Potential Role of Managed Commodity—Financial Futures Accounts (and/or Funds) in Portfolios of Stocks and Bonds." *Presented at the Annual Conference of the Financial Analysts Federation,* May 1983; Toronto, Canada.

Markowitz, H. *Portfolio Selection: Efficient Diversification of Investments.* New York: Wiley, 1959.

Murphy, J. Austin. "Futures Fund Performance: A Test of the Effectiveness of Technical Analysis." *The Journal of Futures Markets,* Vol. 6, No. 2, 1986.

Oberuc, Richard E. "How to Diversify Portfolios of Euro-stocks and Bonds with Hedged

U.S. Managed Futures." First International Conference on Futures Money Management, Geneva, Switzerland: May 4, 1990.

Orr, Almer. "John Lintner and the Theory of Portfolio Management." *Presented at the Sixth Annual Managed Accounts Reports Conference,* Chicago: February 1985 (revised, 1987).

Peters, Carl C. "A Comparative Analysis of Portfolio Diversification Criteria Using Managed Futures." *Proceedings of the Fourth Annual Convention of the Pennsylvania Economic Association,* May 1989.

Peters, Carl C. "New Perspectives on Portfolio Risk Management." *Presented at the 10th Annual MAR Conference on Futures Money Management,* Scottsdale, Arizona: January 1989.

Schneeweis, Thomas. "The Benefits of Managed Futures." A paper commissioned by the European Managed Futures Association, 1996(A).

Schneeweis, Thomas. "Managed Futures and Hedge Fund Investment for Downside Equity Risk Management." 1996(B). *Derivatives Quarterly* 3, no. 1, 1996.

Strahm, N. "Preference Space Evaluation of Trading System Performance." *Journal of the Futures Markets* 3, no. 3, 1983.

CHAPTER 2

MANAGEMENT SUMMARY

Title: "The Benefits of Managed Futures"

Publication: Paper was commissioned by the European Managed Futures Association. The date of acceptance was June 1996.

Authors: Thomas Schneeweis, University of Massachusetts

                Richard Spurgin, Clark University

Data: Monthly return data for individual CTAs, commodity pools, the S&P 500, and bonds from 1985–1995.

Synopsis: The study supports the use of managed futures as a means to reduce portfolio volatility risk, enhance portfolio returns in environments in which traditional stock and bond investment media offer limited opportunities, and participate in a wide variety of new financial products and markets not available in traditional investor products.

The Benefits of
Managed Futures

SYNOPSIS OF MAIN CONCLUSIONS

During the past decades, the investment management industry has undergone numerous changes. New forms of investment products have come into existence to meet the needs of changing financial regulation, information technology, and investor demands. Today, while most investors concentrate on traditional investment vehicles such as stocks, bonds, and currencies, an increasing number of alternative investment products, such as managed futures (i.e., investment funds that use international futures and options markets as their primary investment vehicle), are becoming available which offer the investor new means of increasing return while reducing risk through diversification.

Many investors, however, are uncertain as to the value of many of these new investment vehicles. This is not unexpected. Financial instruments such as stocks, foreign securities, and mortgage-backed bonds existed for years before they were regarded as "suitable" investments. Today, every reasonable investor would have a portion of his or her wealth in such financial instruments. Similarly, while managed futures products have existed for over 30 years, they remain unfamiliar to some investors. Today, managed futures may be viewed as a "new alternative investment" for professional money managers as well as individual investors. Managed futures offer investors a means of investing in all major international markets and financial instruments through investment vehicles offered by *commodity trading advisors* (CTAs). CTAs use global futures/option markets

19

as their primary investment universe. There are three common methods of investment in managed futures products; publicly traded commodity pools (Funds), private commodity pools (Pools), and individually managed single or multiadvisor commodity trading accounts (CTAs). Another alternative investment is hedge funds, for which investment managers use futures and options markets as well as direct investment in traditional securities and physical commodities.

The benefits of investing in options, futures, or other derivative securities (e.g., exotic swaps and options) have been widely debated in the popular financial press. Unfortunately, much of this publicity, while good theater, is often bad economics. These discussions often focus on a few isolated cases in which investors misunderstood the risks of the investment, and rarely focus on the broader question of whether a diversified portfolio can benefit from properly managed exposure to futures and options markets. This chapter offers an updated analysis of the benefits of managed futures. Although previous studies (see Appendix IV) have also addressed the "portfolio diversification" advantages and economic basis for managed futures performance, in this study we review recent academic evidence of market trends and risk patterns that may offer opportunities for managed futures returns and provide further empirical evidence as to the benefits of managed futures. In comparison to previous studies, in this analysis the benefits of managed futures performance are reviewed as a stand-alone investment, as a multiple manager fund, and as an addition to existing investment portfolios. In contrast to previous studies, not only are comparisons made to traditional U.S. and international stock and bond indexes but also to actively managed stock and bond portfolios. Lastly, while results are presented in terms of traditional risk and return, results are also discussed in terms of the unique risk/return patterns (e.g., truncated return distributions) that can be achieved with the addition of managed futures to a stock and/or stock and bond portfolio.

GROWTH IN MANAGED FUTURES

Futures and options have been used for centuries both as a risk management tool and return enhancement vehicle, yet managed futures as an investment alternative have been available only since the late 1960s. More recently, institutional investors such as corporate and public pension funds, endowments and trusts, and bank trust departments have been including managed futures as one segment of a well-diversified portfolio. This report (as previous analyses) emphasizes the potential benefits of

managed futures (e.g., reduced portfolio risk, potential for enhanced portfolio returns, ability to profit in different economic environments, and the
ease of global diversification) as well as the special benefits that futures/
options traders have (e.g., lower transaction costs, lower market impact
costs, use of leverage, and trading in liquid markets). In addition, the market integrity and safety of trading in organized exchanges for futures/
options contracts provides further assurances of investor safety.

MANAGED FUTURES STAND-ALONE AND MULTI-CTA RISK ANALYSES

CTAs have often been regarded as a fundamentally riskier asset than many
traditional assets. Although individual CTAs may have large monthly variations in returns, over a common period (1987–1995), the stand-alone risk
(e.g., standard deviation) of the average CTA from a sample of 68 CTAs
(with consistent data from 1987–1995) was similar to that of the average
firm for a sample of 250 stocks listed in the S&P 500. Moreover, results
indicate that the benefits of creating a portfolio of equal weighted CTAs
over this period is similar to that of a similarly sized sample from stocks
listed in the S&P 500, that is, a reduction in risk of approximately 50 percent. Lastly, it is shown that the correlation between a portfolio of randomly selected CTAs and a typical representative managed futures benchmark
(e.g., the Managed Accounts Reports Dollar-Weighted CTA Index,
MAR$CTA) can be over .90. Thus although managed futures benchmarks
may not reflect the unique performance of individual CTA accounts, funds,
or pools, they play a similar role in managed futures performance analysis
that stock indexes play in evaluating mutual fund performance.

MANAGED FUTURES/TRADITIONAL ASSET: STAND-ALONE AND PORTFOLIO PERFORMANCE

CTA Performance

Modern portfolio theory emphasizes the importance of viewing the benefits
of investment in a particular asset class not as a stand-alone investment or a
stand-alone portfolio but the potential diversification benefits of combining
various asset classes. Over the past ten years (1985–1995), investment in a
portfolio of commodity trading advisors (e.g., MAR$CTA) provides risk
and return benefits when considered as an addition to existing passive and
actively managed stock and bond portfolios (e.g., S&P 500, Salomon

Brothers U.S. and World Government bond indexes, Fidelity Magellan Fund and Fidelity Intermediate bond fund, MSCI international and domestic stock indexes). In addition, managed futures offer increased investor return with reduced risk even when considered as an addition to widely diversified asset portfolios that include investment in passive and actively traded commodity indexes (e.g., JPMorgan commodity index, Goldman Sachs commodity index, MLM). In fact, a CTA-based portfolio (e.g., MAR$CTA) outperformed many traditional investment media even on a stand-alone basis when performance criteria such as minimum and maximum values are taken into account.

Fund/Pool Performance

Retail investors may not be able to invest directly with commodity trading advisors due to high minimum investments. Alternative managed futures products such as commodity funds and pools carry higher investor fees than direct CTA investment, yet even with the higher fees, these products offer the potential to improve the return of a portfolio for a given level of risk. As increased competition and a wider market for managed futures products reduces fees for managed futures products to levels similar to actively managed investment in traditional asset classes, the potential benefits of retail-managed futures products will increase further.

BASES FOR CTA/FUND/POOL RISK/RETURN BENEFITS

One major incentive for managed futures investment lies in their ability to offer risk reduction through diversification while still offering returns comparable to other traditional investments (e.g., domestic and international equity indexes). Results indicate that managed futures have historically low correlations with a wide range of national and international stock and bond indexes as well as commodity indexes.

The economic bases for the low correlation between managed futures investment and traditional stock and bond investment are extensive and varied. Research on traditional investment vehicles (e.g., stocks, bonds, and currency) indicate that investors underreact to information and, consequently, trends are present in security prices. Trading techniques designed to capture these trends may be profitable. In addition, research on traditional security markets also has shown that market prices react to unexpected changes in micro (e.g., earnings) or macro (e.g., interest rates,

GNP) information. Trading techniques based on forecasts of these fundamental variables likewise may result in positive return/risk tradeoffs. The
importance of this research is that profits from market trends or unexpected changes in information may only be available from managed
futures investment but not in other actively managed assets such as stock
mutual funds because cash market transaction costs and institutional
restrictions on short selling and leverage make it unprofitable for mutual
fund managers to engage in these strategies. Managed futures enable an
investor to capture those returns available in the spot market more cheaply (e.g., replicate cash indexes with lower transaction costs) and capture
opportunities not easily achieved in spot markets (e.g., the ability to sell
short and the ability to alter the degree of leverage in an asset position).
Lastly, to the degree that only margin positions are subject to overseas currency risks, the cost of hedging currency risk on one's market value is
reduced. Results show that:

- The differing investment styles and sector specialization of CTAs
enable investors to create portfolios that offer higher expected returns in
market cycles and market conditions when traditional stock or bond market investment has low expected returns. For instance, analysis of seasonal
patterns of managed futures as well as traditional investment media show
that managed futures products have the potential to offer return patterns
not available in traditional asset investment. For instance, managed futures
products may better capture seasonal returns due to liquidity problems in
energy and other commodity markets (e.g., convenience yield), trending
markets due to unexpected informational releases in markets with low liquidity (e.g., currency markets), or changes in expected volatility in months
with historically high informational uncertainty (e.g., summer agricultural
markets).

- Managed futures indexes (e.g., MAR$CTA index) produced con-
sistently higher returns in those months when the S&P 500 or a combined
S&P 500 and Salomon Brothers U.S. Government Bond portfolio had the
highest negative returns. Managed futures also achieve superior returns in
months when various traditional asset classes had their highest positive
returns. This is not true for other commodity-based investment products
such as JPMorgan or Goldman Sachs commodity indexes or even passive
technical trading commodity products such as the MLM index.

- Correlation tests comparing managed futures indexes with traditional assets reveal an interesting property of the relationship between managed futures returns and returns to traditional asset classes. Overall, the correlation between managed futures and stock portfolios is approximately

zero. However, when the data are segmented according to whether the stock market rose or fell, results indicate that managed futures are negatively correlated with traditional assets (e.g., stock and stock and bond portfolios) when these cash market portfolios posted significant negative returns, and are positively correlated when these portfolios report significant positive returns. Thus managed futures may offer unique asset allocation properties.

ALTERNATIVE RISK/RETURN OPPORTUNITIES

Although historical data indicate that adding managed futures to a stock and bond and/or combined equity and commodity portfolio would have increased the return for a given level of risk, it is possible that similar benefits could be obtained using other investment media (e.g., options, hedge funds). Results also show that:

■ Managed futures may offer risk/return benefits when compared to a partially hedged position in the stock market. For instance, it is shown that an equal weighted investment in the MAR$CTA index and the S&P 500 outperformed a comparison strategy consisting of investment in the S&P 500 plus a simulated at-the-money put under most market conditions. These results indicate that managed futures may offer some of the hedging properties of a put option at a lower cost.

■ The benefits of hedge funds, which invest directly in futures and options as well as direct investment in traditional securities and physical commodities, may offer an additional investment alternative. Unfortunately, historical index data on various hedge fund investment styles and trading strategies only exist for the past two years. Even over this time period, which corresponds to a historically poor risk/return period for managed futures, managed futures offer potential for risk/return improvement when considered as additions to existing hedge funds.

RECENT PERFORMANCE

It is important to note that neither this nor any study can capture or review all possible questions relating to the future or past performance of various investment products. Over the past two years, for instance, the S&P 500 as well as the Salomon Brothers U.S. government bond index have generally outperformed managed futures on a stand-alone basis. Moreover, results show that over this very recent time period, some managed futures investment styles or trading strategies failed to improve the risk/return tradeoff when added to existing traditional asset portfolios. However, investors must realize the uniqueness of the recent time period. Returns to the S&P 500 in 1995 (annualized returns over 35 percent) have not been repeated in any of the past 10 years while the annualized returns to the MAR$CTA index (14.1 percent) were similar to the 10-year average (15.8 percent).

CONCLUSION

Recent analyses of the benefits of managed futures have focused the potential benefits of managed futures in return enhancement and portfolio diversification. As noted in these studies, the ability of managed futures traders to trade a wide variety of international futures and options markets, which are often more liquid than traditional cash markets, and for which the transaction costs and market impact of trading are less than traditional cash markets, results in benefits to traders who can benefit from the structural efficiencies of futures and options markets. In addition, the ability of managed futures traders to trade primarily in regulated exchanges helps ensure investor safety. Lastly, the ability of managed futures traders to take unique leverage positions in both rising and falling markets results in unique return opportunities not easily found in either traditional stock and bond markets or commodity investments.

The failure of managed futures to grow in the recent market environment may be due to several factors. First, public perception of the risk of futures and option markets as stand-alone investments does not correspond to the actual risks of investing in managed futures products—especially when the risk is considered at the investor's portfolio level. Second, the unexpected recent performance of stock and bond markets may lead certain investors to expect similar returns in the near future. In fact, research has shown that for many individuals, future risk and return expectations are based on recent experience. Lastly, it is possible that, for many investors, the concerns over benefits of managed futures leads them to avoid managed futures. However, investors must realize that these concerns are not unique to managed futures. As shown in the studies listed in Appendix V, concerns over the use of managed futures benchmarks as indicators of actual investor performance also exist for more traditional benchmarks. As in all investment markets, investors must take time to analyze the actual performance of their potential investment with their existing or potential portfolio. However, as is true for managed futures, traditional stock indexes also have problems of survival bias and style or asset class consistency (only one firm of the original Dow Jones Industrial Average is still part of the index).

It is hoped that the results of this study will put to rest many of these concerns. Most traditional asset managers use futures and options markets in numerous ways (e.g., rebalance portfolios, manage currency risk, trade bonds with option features such as convertibility or callability). Most traditional money managers, however, are restricted by regulation or convention from using more actively traded futures and options contracts. Moreover, as new financial products come into existence, such as futures contracts traded on S&P 500 value or growth stocks, managed futures may provide the most logical means of quickly taking advantage of the potential returns from such new products. The logical extension of using investment managers with specialized knowledge of traditional markets is to add specialized managers who can obtain the unique returns in market conditions and types of securities not generally available to traditional asset managers; that is, managed futures.

SUMMARY EMPIRICAL SUPPORT

GROWTH OF MANAGED FUTURES

Summary: Futures and options have been used for centuries both as a risk management tool and return enhancement vehicle. However, managed futures as an investment alternative have been available only since the late 1960s. More recently, institutional investors such as corporate and public pension funds, endowments and trusts, and bank trust departments have been including managed futures as one segment of a well-diversified portfolio. As shown in Figure 2–1, the dollars under management in the Managed Futures industry have grown from less than $1 billion under management in 1980 to approximately $20 billion in 1994.

This growth reflects investor knowledge of the potential benefits of managed futures in return enhancement and portfolio diversification. As noted in this and other studies (see Appendix IV), managed futures traders have the ability to trade in a wide variety of international futures and options markets which are often more liquid than traditional cash markets and for which the transaction costs and market impact of trading are less than traditional cash markets. As a result, managed futures traders can benefit from the structural efficiencies of the futures and options markets. In addition, the ability of managed futures traders to trade primarily in

FIGURE 2–1

Managed Futures Assets under Management,
1980 to 1994

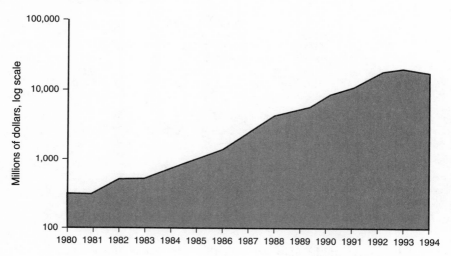

regulated exchanges helps ensure investor safety. Lastly, the ability of managed futures traders to take unique leverage positions in both rising and falling markets results in unique return opportunities not easily found in either traditional stock and bond markets or commodity investments

MANAGED FUTURES STAND-ALONE AND MULTI-CTA RISK ANALYSIS

Summary: The term *managed futures* represents an industry comprised of professional money managers known as *commodity trading advisors* (CTAs) who manage client assets on a discretionary basis, using global futures markets as an investment medium. CTAs have often been regarded as a high-risk investment. However, as shown in Table 2–1 for the period 1987-1995, the average monthly standard deviation of a sample of over 60 CTAs with complete data over the time period was not significantly different from the average monthly standard deviation derived from a random sample of over 250 stocks taken from the S&P 500. Thus, CTAs are on average not more risky than an equity security listed in the S&P 500.

TABLE 2-1

Average Monthly Standard Deviation

	Average CTAs*		Portfolio CTAs Equal Weight	MAR CTA Index Equal Weight	Equity†	Portfolio Equity Equal Weight	
	S.D	S.D of S.D.	S.D.	S.D	S.D	S.D. of S.D	S.D
Period 1987-1995	10.51	4.26	5.95	4.75	8.36	2.60	6.17
1987-1991	12.22	5.46	7.20	6.00	9.31	2.90	6.51
1992-1995	7.45	3.07	3.72	2.33	6.98	2.52	5.67

* CTAs drawn from a sample of 68 CTAs with consistent data from 1987-1995 (see EMFA Study)
† Equities are drawn from a sample of 250 equity issues drawn from the S&P 500

The above table also reflects the similarity of the risk pattern between the risk of the sample CTA portfolio and that of the MAR equal weighted CTA index. In addition, results indicate that as for stocks, over 50 percent of the average CTA standard deviation is reduced if held as part of a relatively large multi-CTA portfolio. This is similar to that reported for the sample of 250 stocks taken from the S&P 500, although the impact on risk reduction is greater for combining CTAs than equity issues. It is important to remember that while the impact on standard deviation of creating CTA portfolios is similar to that of creating portfolios of stocks, the variability of standard deviation around the average standard deviation is greater for CTA than stocks. Investors choosing individual CTAs should be aware of the greater heterogeneity of risk for individual CTAs as compared to individual stocks.

Multi-CTA Portfolio Risk

Summary: Modern portfolio theory points out that the true measure of risk for investors who hold portfolios of assets is the expected standard of a portfolio of investments. Past research has shown that an equally weighted diversified portfolio of 8 to 10 randomly selected equity securities will result in a portfolio standard deviation similar to that of the population from which it is drawn. As shown in Figure 2-2, similarly for managed futures, a

FIGURE 2–2

A. Standard Deviation of Returns

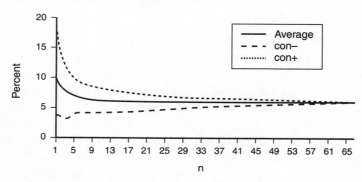

B. Correlation Portfolio, MAR$CTA

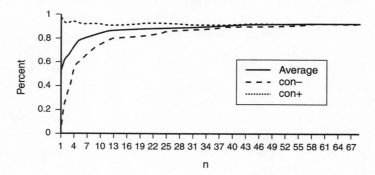

randomly equal weighted portfolio of 8 to 10 CTAs has a standard deviation similar to that of the population from which it is drawn. Thus, as for multifirm equity portfolios, multimanager CTA portfolios may have risk levels similar to that of a larger population of CTAs. As important, as shown in Figure 2–2, a portfolio of randomly selected CTAs may likewise have a correlation in excess of .90 with that of a typical benchmark for managed futures returns; that is, the dollar weighted MAR CTA portfolio. Confidence intervals are also given for respective standard deviation and correlations in Figure 2–2. Thus, the use of the MAR$CTA can represent the performance of the smaller subset (e.g., multi-CTA portfolios) of CTAs.

MANAGED FUTURES/TRADITIONAL ASSET: STAND-ALONE AND PORTFOLIO PERFORMANCE

CTA Performance

Summary: Over the past 11 years (1985-1995), investment in a portfolio of commodity trading advisors (e.g., MAR$CTA) provides risk and return benefits when considered as an addition to existing passive and actively managed stock and bond portfolios (e.g., S&P 500, Salomon Brothers U.S. Government bond indexes (USBI), Salomon Brothers World Government bond indexes (WGBI), Fidelity Magellan Fund and Fidelity Intermediate bond fund, and MSCI world, regional and domestic stock indexes). In addition, managed futures offer increased investor return with reduced risk even when considered as an addition to widely diversified asset portfolios, which include investment in passive and actively traded commodity indexes (e.g., JPMorgan commodity index, MLM).

Results in Table 2–2 show the ability of managed futures as represented by the MAR$CTA index to provide improved return/risk tradeoffs as stand-alone instruments as well as additions to existing stock and bond indexes and managed stock and bond funds as represented by the Excess Annual Break-even. The Excess Annual Break-even represents the degree to which the MAR$CTA actual return exceeded the return necessary for MAR$CTA inclusion with the comparison investment asset.

The ability of managed futures to improve the relative return/risk tradeoff is shown in Figure 2–3. The annualized mean return/standard deviation ratio is given for additions of MAR$CTA to the alternative investment. Results are presented which indicate the actual return and risk performance of including CTAs with alternative asset over a wide range of CTA weights for the period 1985-1995.

The improvement in return/standard deviation ratios from adding managed futures to existing stock, bond, and stock and bond positions as shown in Figure 2–3 is further reflected in Figure 2–4, which shows the risk and return frontier of S&P 500, Salomon Brothers U.S. government bond index, and portfolios containing the stock (55 percent) and bond (45 percent) indexes as managed futures are added to these existing asset portfolios. Results show that adding managed futures to these existing traditional asset positions results in risk and return alternatives not easily found in individual stock or bond portfolios or in combined stock and bond portfolios. In addition, for various borrowing/lending rates, the projected tangency points of the combined CTA/traditional asset portfolios dominate the non-CTA traditional single asset or combined stock and bond portfolios.

TABLE 2-2

Performance Measures for Managed Futures and Other Asset Classes
Eleven-Year Performance: January 1985 to December 1995

1/85 to 12/95	MAR$CTA	MLM	JPMCI	SP500	Salomon US Bond	MSCI	Salomon World Bond	Fidelity Magellan	Intermed. US Bond
Average Annual Return	15.81	9.83	10.34	15.11	9.89	14.86	12.17	17.96	9.03
Annual Standard Deviation	14.58	6.33	17.88	15.06	5.12	14.85	7.22	17.20	4.28
Avg. Ret./S.D.	1.08	1.55	0.58	1.00	1.93	1.00	1.68	1.04	2.11
Minimum Monthly Return	-6.37	-4.12	-14.53	-24.31	-2.42	-18.59	-4.07	-29.85	-2.67
Maximum Monthly Return	17.83	6.41	19.81	12.66	4.75	11.13	6.52	12.22	5.46
Correlation with MAR	1.00	0.43	-0.06	0.12	0.18	0.08	0.17	0.10	0.18
Excess Annual Breakeven	0.00	6.01	10.02	8.79	7.76	9.14	7.69	8.75	7.96

Eleven-Year Performance of Managed Futures and Asset Portfolios: January 1985 to December 1995

1/85 to 12/95	MAR$CTA	Port I US Equal Weighted	Port II US Equal No CTA	Port III US Stock and Bond	Port IV Fidelity Equal	Port V Fidelity No CTA	Port VI Fidelity Stock/Bond	Port VII World Equal	Port VIII World No CTA	Port IX World Stock/Bond
Average Annual Return	15.81	12.85	11.91	13.02	13.31	12.47	14.28	13.26	12.40	13.88
Annual Standard Deviation	14.58	5.79	5.50	9.17	5.81	5.55	10.06	6.20	6.20	9.89
Avg. Ret./S.D.	1.08	2.22	2.17	1.42	2.29	2.25	1.42	2.14	2.00	1.40
Minimum Monthly Return	-6.37	-2.88	-4.19	-10.76	-3.95	-5.66	-14.10	-2.38	-3.19	-6.51
Maximum Monthly Return	17.83	6.54	7.34	7.58	6.21	6.93	7.68	6.71	7.55	7.95
Correlation with MAR	1.00		0.21	0.15		0.20	0.14		0.17	0.12
Excess Annual Break-even			6.54	8.09		6.36	8.18		7.22	8.40

F I G U R E   2–3

Return/Risk Ratio of Stock, Bond, and Managed Futures

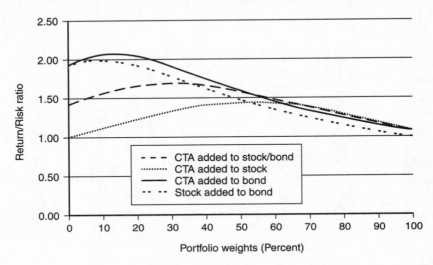

F I G U R E   2–4

Risk and Return of Stock, Bond, and Managed Futures

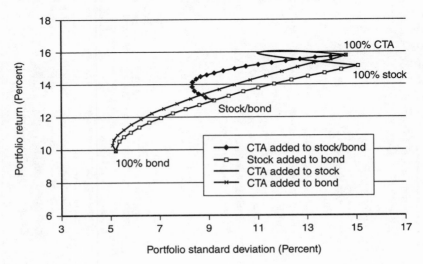

Fund/Pool Performance

Summary: For retail investors, who may not be able to invest directly with commodity trading advisors, alternative managed futures products such as commodity funds and pools, which carry higher investor fees than direct CTA investment, also offer the potential to improve the return of a portfolio for a given level of risk. As increased competition and a wider market for managed futures products reduces fees for managed futures products to levels similar to actively managed investment in traditional asset classes, the potential benefits of retail managed futures products will increase further.

Table 2–3 shows that the Excess Break-even Returns are generally positive when various managed futures funds/pools are considered as additions to existing stock and bond. The Excess Annual Break-even represents the degree to which the actual Fund/Pool return exceeded the return necessary for inclusion in the comparison investment asset.

BASES FOR CTA/FUND/POOL RISK/RETURN BENEFITS

Summary: Managed futures returns may be difficult if not impossible to achieve through other investment media. Futures may enable an investor to capture returns available in the spot market more cheaply (e.g., replicate cash indices with lower transactions costs) and capture opportunities not easily achieved in spot markets (e.g., the ability to sell short and the ability to alter the degree of leverage in an asset position). Managed futures indexes (e.g., MAR$CTA index) produced consistently higher returns in those months in which the S&P 500, Fidelity Magellan, or MSCI world equity indices; the Fidelity Intermediate bond fund, the Salomon Brothers U.S. and World Government bond indices, and U.S. and world active and passive stock/bond portfolios as well as combined stock, bond, and commodity portfolios had the highest negative returns. Managed futures also achieve superior returns in months when traditional asset classes and stock, bond, and combined stock, bond, and commodity portfolios had their highest positive returns. Correlation tests comparing managed futures indexes with traditional assets reveal an interesting property of the relationship between managed futures returns (MAR$CTA) and returns to traditional asset classes. Overall, as noted in Table 2–2, the correlation between managed futures and stock portfolios is approximately zero. However, when the data are segmented according to whether the stock

TABLE 2-3

MAR Fund/Pool Subindex Performance, January 1985 to December 1995

FP Index Performance	Dollar Weight	Equal Weight	Public	Single Advisor
Average Return	10.35	9.11	8.02	11.54
Standard Deviation	15.07	15.17	16.61	14.81
Avg. Ret./S.D.	0.69	0.60	0.48	0.78
Excess Break-even Return				
SP500 Composit	2.72	1.68	0.16	3.75
US Govt. Bond Index	1.92	1.09	−0.69	3.05
MSCI	2.88	1.89	0.40	3.85
SB World Govt Bond	1.62	1.09	−1.08	2.74
Fidelity Magellan	2.56	1.65	−0.11	3.57
Fid. Intermed. Bond	2.29	1.44	−0.29	3.44
US-NoCTA Equal	0.51	−0.62	−2.30	1.87
US Stock/Bond Port.	1.85	0.95	−0.81	2.84
World-NoCTA Equal.	0.96	−0.01	−1.75	2.23
MSCI/World Bond Port.	1.87	1.12	−0.73	2.80
Fidelity-NoCTA Equal	0.19	−0.76	−2.77	1.56
Magellan/Intermed Bond	1.86	1.09	−0.89	2.85

market rose or fell, results indicate that managed futures are negatively correlated with traditional asset class products (e.g., stock and stock and bond portfolio) when these cash market portfolios posted significant negative returns and are positively correlated when these portfolios report significant positive returns. Thus managed futures may offer unique asset allocation properties.

As important, relative return patterns between managed futures products and traditional financial investments may reflect the ability of various managed futures traders to obtain return in markets in which long positions in the underlying assets provide negative returns. Table 2–4 indicates that when traditional asset portfolios returns are ranked from low to high and divided into 11 twelve-month subperiods, the number of months in which the MAR$CTA index provides superior returns increases as the performance of the portfolio decreases.

TABLE 2–4

Relative Performance of CTA Index and U.S. Asset Indexes

Panel 4A. MAR CTA Index and SP500 Index

Group Rank	Avg. Return SP500	Avg. Return MAR$CTA	Number of Months MAR$>SP500
1	−7.06	2.65	12
2	−2.53	−0.34	8
3	−1.19	0.81	9
4	−0.09	1.12	7
5	0.91	1.36	7
6	1.59	0.09	4
7	2.40	0.69	3
8	3.21	0.35	1
9	4.13	1.31	3
10	5.12	2.62	3
11	8.47	4.84	1

Group 1 Correlation: −0.12

Group 11 Correlation: 0.46

Panel 4B. MAR CTA Index and SB Bond Index

Group Rank	Avg. Return US Bond Index	Avg. Return MAR$CTA	Number of Months MAR$>USBI
1	−1.82	0.87	11
2	−0.91	−0.50	9
3	−0.26	2.57	11
4	0.18	−0.54	4
5	0.56	2.17	7
6	0.90	1.16	5
7	1.19	1.22	4
8	1.53	0.36	2
9	1.91	2.78	4
10	2.30	2.38	2
11	3.64	3.03	1

Group 1 Correlation: 0.20

Group 11 Correlation: 0.39

Panel 4C. MAR CTA Index and Portfolio II

Group Rank	Avg. Return Port II	Avg. Return MAR$CTA	Number of Months MAR$>Port II
1	−2.03	0.34	12
2	−0.58	0.20	8
3	0.02	1.16	9
4	0.41	1.79	9
5	0.76	0.22	4
6	1.05	0.17	3
7	1.31	1.44	5
8	1.66	0.70	2
9	2.03	3.33	4
10	2.60	2.06	3
11	3.89	4.08	0

Group 1 Correlation: −0.12

Group 11 Correlation: 0.14

Panel 4D. MAR CTA Index and Portfolio III

Group Rank	Avg. Return Port III	Avg. Return MAR$CTA	Number of Months MAR$>Port III
1	−3.95	2.18	12
2	−1.66	−0.57	9
3	−0.52	2.21	8
4	0.26	0.96	6
5	0.78	0.58	7
6	1.26	−0.05	2
7	1.62	1.74	5
8	2.19	−0.55	1
9	2.88	0.62	2
10	3.75	2.51	3
11	5.78	5.88	2

Group 1 Correlation: −0.17

Group 11 Correlation: 0.39

In Table 2–4, for instance, results show that for 12 of the 12 worst S&P 500 return months and that for 11 of the 12 worst USBI months, the MAR$CTA outperformed the alternative index. Similar results are evident for the combined stock, bond, and commodity portfolio (portfolio II) and for the combined stock and bond portfolio (portfolio III). For instance, the graphical representations of the monthly return patterns for each of the comparison MAR$CTA and the S&P 500 are given in Figure 2–3. Similar tests were conducted for Fidelity Magellan and Intermediate bond fund, and MSCI equity and Salomon Brothers World government bond indexes as well as stock and bond portfolios and stock, bond, and commodity portfolios formed from these active U.S. investment vehicles and international investment vehicles. Results are similar to those presented here (see EMFA, "The Benefits of Managed Futures, Technical Report (1996)).

ALTERNATIVE RISK/RETURN OPPORTUNITIES

Summary: Although historical data indicate that including managed futures in a stock and bond and/or combined equity and commodity portfolio would have increased the return for a given level of risk, it is possible that similar benefits could be obtained using other investment media (e.g., options, hedge funds). Results also show that managed futures may offer risk/return benefits when compared to a partially hedged position in the stock market. For instance, it is shown in Figure 2–5 that the MAR$CTA index outperformed the S&P 500 in months in which the S&P 500 had its lowest returns. It is also shown in Figure 2–6, that an equal weighted investment in the MAR$CTA index and the S&P 500 outperformed investment in the S&P 500 plus a simulated at-the-money put under most market conditions. These results indicate that managed futures may offer some of the hedging properties of a put option at a lower cost. It is, of course, important to point out that the performance of the equity/protective put and the equity/managed futures position are not strictly comparable since the performance of the managed futures position is stochastic. The individual investor must determine whether the potential relative return compensates for the expected risk.

RECENT PERFORMANCE

Summary: Over the most recent 6-year period (1990-1995), the MAR CTA indexes have continued to provide benefits as additions to existing stock, bond, and stock/bond portfolios (Table 2–5). Over the past 2 years,

FIGURE 2–5

Performance of MAR$CTA Index Relative to SP500

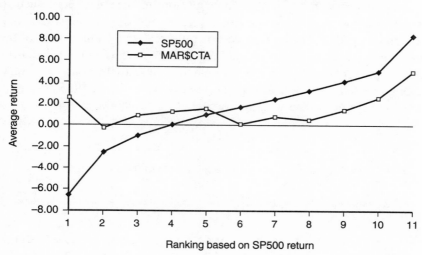

FIGURE 2–6

Performance of MAR$CTA and SP500 Protective Put Strategy

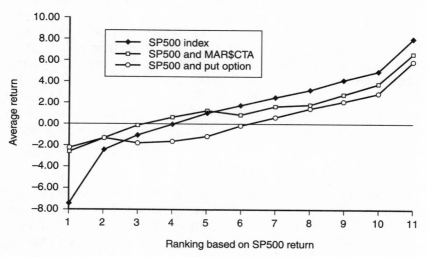

for instance, the S&P 500 as well as the Salomon Brothers U.S. government bond index have generally outperformed managed futures on a stand-alone basis, while various managed futures products continued to provide investor benefits when considered as additions to existing stock and bond portfolios. However, investors must realize the uniqueness of the recent time period. Returns to the S&P 500 in 1995 (annualized returns over 35 percent) have not been repeated in any of the past 11 years, although the annualized returns to the MAR$CTA index in 1995 (14.1 percent) were similar to the 11-year average (15.8 percent).

Panel 5. CTA Subindex Performance, January 1990 to December 1995

CTA Index Performance	Dollar Weight	Equal Weight	Currency	Discretionary	Diversified	Energy	Financial	Trend Follow
Average Return	13.43	9.46	13.09	14.31	10.30	7.32	13.38	12.19
Standard Deviation	11.49	10.12	16.60	8.19	12.87	10.75	13.85	18.09
Avg. Ret./S.D.	1.17	0.93	0.79	1.75	0.80	0.68	0.97	0.67
Excess Break-even Return								
SP500 Composite	8.39	4.58	7.46	9.28	5.41	2.91	7.65	7.45
US Govt. Bond Index	6.41	2.99	5.33	7.51	3.28	2.97	5.24	4.49
MSCI	7.52	3.54	7.09	8.35	4.36	1.40	7.39	6.31
SB World Govt. Bond	5.65	2.37	4.58	7.83	2.12	2.85	4.06	3.25
Fidelity Magellan	8.82	5.07	7.85	9.69	6.18	2.99	7.82	8.01
Fid. Intermed. Bond	6.07	2.75	5.12	7.36	2.95	2.79	4.90	4.01
US Equal Weight Port.	6.27	2.53	6.15	7.47	2.95	0.50	6.34	4.34
US Stock/Bond Port.	8.11	4.45	7.01	9.07	5.14	3.30	7.10	7.00
World Equal Weight Port.	6.85	2.92	6.40	7.81	3.42	0.79	6.70	5.25
MSCI/World Bond Port.	7.64	3.70	6.80	8.45	4.34	1.85	7.08	6.41
Magellan Equal Weight	6.29	2.66	6.24	7.60	3.19	0.29	6.20	4.28
Magellan/Intermed Bond	8.49	4.89	7.38	9.46	5.84	3.31	7.24	7.48

CONCLUSION

It is important to note that neither this nor any study can capture or review all possible questions relating to the future or past performance of various investment products. It is hoped that the results of this study will put to rest many of these concerns. Simply put, most traditional asset managers presently use futures and options markets in numerous ways (e.g., rebalance portfolios, manage currency risk, trade bonds with option features such as convertibility or callability). Most traditional money managers, however, are restricted by regulation or convention from using more actively traded futures and option contracts. Moreover, as new financial products come into existence, such as futures contracts traded on S&P 500 value or growth stocks, managed futures may provide the most logical means of quickly taking advantage of the potential returns from such new products. The logical extension of using investment managers with specialized knowledge of traditional markets to obtain maximum return/risk tradeoffs is to add specialized managers who can obtain the unique returns in market conditions and types of securities not generally available to traditional asset managers; that is, managed futures.

SELECTED REFERENCES

Chance, Don. *Managed Futures and Their Role in Investment Portfolios.* Charlottesville: AIMR, 1994.

Chandler, B. *Managed Futures: An Investor's Guide.* New York: John Wiley & Sons, 1994.

Elton, E.J.; M.J. Gruber; and J.C. Rentzler. "Professionally Managed, Publicly Traded Commodity Funds," *Journal of Business* (April 1987), pp. 177–199.

Elton, E.J.; M.J. Gruber; and J.C. Rentzler. "New Public Offerings, Information, and Investor Rationality: The Case of Publicly Offered Commodity Funds," *Journal of Business* 6, no. 1 (1989) pp. 1–15.

Elton, E.J.; M.J. Gruber; and J. Rentzler, "The Performance of Publicly Offered Commodity Funds," *Financial Analyst Journal* (July-August 1990), pp. 23–30.

Elton, E.J.; M.J. Gruber; and J. Rentzler, "The Performance of Publicly Offered Commodity Funds." In C. Peters ed. *Managed Futures.* Chicago: Probus Publishing, 1992, pp. 387–401.

Fox-Andrews, M., and Nicola Meaden. *Derivative Markets and Investment Management.* Englewood Cliffs, NJ: Prentice Hall: Hertfordshire, G.B., 1995.

Irwin, Scott. "Further Evidence on the Usefulness of CTA Performance Information in Public Commodity Pool Prospectuses and a Proposal for Reform." In *Advances in Futures and Options Research* 7 (1994), pp. 251–264.

Irwin, S., C. R. Zulauf, and Barry Ward. "The Predictability of Managed Futures Returns." *Journal of Derivatives* (Winter 1994), pp. 20–27.

Irwin, S., T. Krukemyer, and C. R. Zulauf. "Are Public Commodity Pools a Good Investment," in Peters, C.C., ed. *Managed Futures: Performance Evaluation and Analysis of Commodity Funds, Pools and Accounts.* Chicago: Probus Publishing, 1992, pp. 405–433.

Peck, A.E., ed., *Selected Writings on Futures Markets.* Vol. 1-5. Chicago Board of Trade., 1995.

Peters, C.C., ed. *Managed Futures: Performance Evaluation and Analysis of Commodity Funds, Pools and Accounts.* Chicago: Probus Publishing, 1992.

Schneeweis, T., U. Savanayana, and D. McCarthy. "Alternative Commodity Trading Vehicles: A Performance Analysis," *Journal of Futures Markets* (August 1991), pp. 475–490.

Schneeweis, T., U. Savanayana, and D. McCarthy. "Multi-Manager Commodity Portfolios: A Risk/Return Analysis," in C. Epstein, ed. *Managed Futures* (New York: John Wiley & Sons, 1992), pp. 81–102.

Schneeweis, T., R. Spurgin, and D. McCarthy. "Survivor Bias in Commodity Trading Advisor Performance." *Journal of Futures Markets*. Forthcoming.

Schneeweis, T., R. Spurgin, and D. McCarthy. "Informational Content in Historical CTA Performance." In *Journal of Futures Markets*. Forthcoming.

Sharpe, W. "The Sharpe Ratio." *Journal of Portfolio Management,*" Fall, 1994.

Thaler R., *The Winners Curse: Paradoxes and Anomalies of Economic Life*. New York: The Free Press, 1992.

APPENDIX I

Managed Futures

Individual Accounts represent about 30 percent of all managed accounts. They are usually opened by institutional investors or high-net-worth individuals. These funds usually require a substantial capital investment so that the advisor is able to diversify his trading among a large number of market positions. An individual account enables the institutional investor to customize the account to his own specifications.

Private Pools currently represent about 55 percent of all managed futures accounts. This type of account commingles money from several investors, usually into a limited partnership. Most of these pools have minimum investments ranging from approximately $25,000 to $250,000. These futures partnerships usually allow for admission/redemption on a monthly or quarterly basis. The main advantage of private pools is the economy of scale that can be achieved for middle-sized investors. A pool also may be structured with multiple trading advisors and trading approaches, providing the investor with maximum diversification. Because of the lower administrative and marketing costs, private pools have historically performed better than public funds.

Public Funds or Pools currently represent about 15 percent of all managed accounts. The advantage of public funds is that they provide a way for small investors to participate in an investment vehicle.

Commodity Trading Advisors (CTAs) are responsible for the actual trading of the managed account. The two major types of advisors are technical traders and fundamental traders. Technical traders may use computer software programs to follow pricing trends and perform quantitative analysis. Fundamental traders forecast prices by analysis of supply and demand factors and other market information.

Futures Commission Merchants (FCMs) are the brokerage firms that execute, clear, and carry CTA-directed trades on the various exchanges. Many of these firms also act as CPOs and trading managers, providing administrative reports on investment performance. Additionally, they may offer managed future funds as an alternative investment opportunity to their customers.

Commodity Pool Operators (CPOs) assemble public funds or private pools. There are approximately 1,215 registered with the NFA. In the United States, this is usually in the form of limited partnerships. Most commodity pool operators hire independent CTAs to make the daily trading decisions. The CPO may distribute the product directly or act as a wholesaler to the broker/dealer community.

Investment Consultants can be a valuable institutional investor resource for learning about managed futures alternatives and in helping to implement the managed fund program.

Trading Managers or "Manager of Managers" are available to assist institutional investors in selecting CTAs from the more than 2,500 registered with the National Futures Association (NFA). These managers have developed sophisticated methods of analyzing CTA performance records so that they can recommend and structure a portfolio of trading advisors.

[These descriptions are from the CBOT "Managed Futures: An Alternative Investment Opportunity" (1994).]

APPENDIX II

Alternative Commodity and Managed Futures Indexes

Dow Jones Futures and Spot Commodity Index is composed of 12 commodities: cattle, coffee, copper, corn, cotton, gold, hogs, lumber, silver, soybeans, sugar, and wheat. The weightings of the indexes are neutral; that is, each commodity's price on a given day is divided by its price on the base date and the results are totaled. The total is divided by 12 and multiplied by 100 to yield the index. To estimate the price of a commodity 5 months in the future, two contract months are used, one expiring in fewer than 150 days and one expiring in more than 150 days. It is assumed that each contract expires on the 15th of its delivery month. For each commodity, weights are assigned to the two contracts, based on the number of days between the 150th and the theoretical expiration date of the contract. Then the price of each contract is multiplied by its weight, the results are added, and the sum is divided by the number of days between the expiration dates of the two contracts. The result is the estimated price of the commodity for delivery in exactly five months, or 150 days.

Commodity Research Bureau Index (CRB) is a futures price index that represents an unweighted geometric average of 21 component commodity prices. Each of these 21 commodity prices has been arithmetically averaged for all actively traded contracts expiring on or before the end of the 9th calendar month from the current date, excluding noncycle months. After these two averaging techniques have been performed, the resulting value is converted to a percentage of the base year value.

Goldman Sachs Commodity Index (GSCI) is an arithmetic measure of the performance of actively traded, dollar-denominated nearby commodity futures contracts. As of January 9, 1995, there were 22 commodities in the index.

The weights assigned to individual commodities are based on a 5-year moving average of world production. Weights are determined each July and are made effective the following January. All contracts are rolled on the fifth business day of the month before the expiration month of the contract. Subindexes are calculated for agricultural, energy, industrial, livestock, and precious metals contracts. Two versions of the indexes are available: a total return version, which assumes that capital sufficient to purchase the basket of commodities is invested at the risk-free rate; and a spot version, which only tracks movements in the futures prices. This study uses the total return measure.

JPMorgan Commodity Index (JPMCI) is composed of 11 highly liquid industrial commodity futures contracts. It excludes "softs," relying exclusively on energy, precious metals, and industrial metals. The two nearby contracts for each commodity are used, and rolls are conducted over a 5-day period from the 5th to the 9th business day of the month. Component weights are rebalanced monthly according to a scoring system that seeks to maximize risk-return performance, track unexpected changes in inflation, provide a hedge against stock and bond investments, and correlate with economic growth measures. Subindexes for energy, precious metals, and industrial metals are also available. The JPMCI is published in both spot and total return formats. This study uses the total return measure. The JPMCI was officially launched on September 21, 1994.

Bankers Trust Commodity Index (BTCI) is based on spot rather than futures prices. It assumes ownership of a basket of five physical commodities: crude oil, gold, aluminum, heating oil, and silver. Fifty-five percent of the weight is given to energy components, and the remaining 45 percent to the three metals. The basket is priced daily using spot quotes such as the London gold fix. Front-month futures quotes, which are equivalent to cash market quotes, are used for energy prices. BTCI thus reproduces the price changes of a basket of physical assets without the storage and holding costs. The BTCI was launched on July 18, 1994.

Mount Lucas (MLM) Index differs from other indexes in two important ways. First, it allows both long and short positions in the underlying futures contracts. Second, it incorporates financial and currency futures (but not stock index futures) into the index, along with the commodities tracked by other indexes. The index is an equally weighted average of the monthly returns from 25 separate futures contracts. Within each market (e.g., corn futures), the index will be long or short depending on whether the contract is above or below its trailing 12-month moving average. MLM is a total-return index. It was launched in May 1989.

Managed Account Reports (MAR) tracks the performance of individual CTAs as well as CTA Funds and Pools that invest in individual CTAs. MAR produces several performance indexes, the dominant being the CTA equal-weighted and dollar-weighted indices. MAR classifies CTAs into a number of different groups, and publishes each group's performance index. These groups are currency, energy, financial, diversified, discretionary, and trend-following. MAR also reports the following subindexes for fund and pool performance: guaranteed, multi-advisor, single-advisor, private pools, and public pools.

Barclay Trading Group, publisher of the Barclay Managed Futures Report, also creates CTA performance indexes. Indexes are based on monthly returns of CTAs with established track records. Barclay publishes an equal weighted index of all CTAs as well as the following subindexes: agricultural, currency, diversified, energy, financial/metal, discretionary, and systematic.

TASS offers historical managed futures performance similar to MAR or Barclays. It publishes a dollar-weighted CTA index and one subindex of currency CTAs. Additional indexes and subindexes will be available in the future.

Hedge Fund Research, EACM, Van Hedge, and MAR offer historical managed futures/hedge fund performance on an array of indexes and subindexes designed to capture the return to unique managed futures/hedge fund strategies. These indexes include relative value, event-driven, equity hedge funds, global asset allocators, and short selling. Subindexes include long/short equity, convertible hedge, bond hedge, rotational, deal arbitrage, bankruptcy, and multievent. For managed futures, the principal subindexes reflect the trading style of the manager, usually broken down into discretionary and systematic groups.

Risk and Return Measures

The risk and return measures used in this analysis are consistent industry definitions for investment analysis for traditional and alternative investment media. The following return and risk measures are used to identify the risk factor for evaluating the risk/return benefit of managed futures performance:

Measure of Return:

Returns: Determined as the logarithmic monthly holding period returns and are presented as annualized logarithmic returns. For multiasset CTA portfolio, efficient frontier and relative return after ranking on traditional asset, arithmetic returns are used.

Measure of Volatility:

Standard Deviation: A measure of the dispersion (distance) of the observations (return performance) from the mean (or average) observation. This measure is expressed as a percentage on an annualized basis.

Return/Risk Ratio: A ratio that represents a rate of return adjusted for risk (standard deviation), as is generally calculated as [(Annual rate of return - Risk free rate of return)/Annualized Standard Deviation]. In this paper, except for excess break-even ratios, the Return/risk is given as a "return information ratio" that is, the Annualized rate of return/Annualized Standard Deviation. For a complete discussion of the return/risk ratio, see W. Sharpe, "The Sharpe Ratio," *JPM* (Fall 1994).

Minimum Monthly Return: The lowest return observed in any month over the time period analyzed and is expressed on an annualized basis.

Maximum Monthly Return: The highest return observed in any month over the time period analyzed and is expressed on an annualized basis.

Correlation: The standardized comovement of managed futures benchmark (e.g., MAR$CTA) and an alternative investment benchmark measured from their respective historical averages.

Excess Annual Break-even: Various models have been proposed to measure the possible impact of adding a security onto an existing portfolio and its impact on that portfolio's risk and return. For instance, simple break-even models have been suggested that indicate whether adding an asset to an existing portfolio increases its Sharpe ratio. The break-even (R_c) and excess break-even rate of return *(EBK)* is computed as follows:

$$R_c = \left(\frac{R_p - R_F}{\sigma_P}\right)(P_{CP})\,\sigma_C + R_F \qquad EBK = R_c - \left(\frac{R_p - R_F}{\sigma_P}\right)(P_{CP})\,\sigma_C + R_F$$

where, R_c = Break-even rate of return required for CTA index to improve Sharpe ratio of index p

R_f = Riskless rate of return

R_p = Rate of return on alternative index p

P_{cp} = Correlation coefficient between CTA index c and alternative benchmark index p

σ_c = Standard deviation of CTA index c

σ_p = Standard deviation of alternative index p

APPENDIX IV

Summary of Recent Articles on Managed Futures Performance and Benefits of Managed Futures

Portfolio Diversification Opportunities, CBOT (1996): This pamphlet updates the CBOTs review of the benefits of managed futures for the U.S. market. The report emphasizes the potential benefits of managed futures (e.g., reduced portfolio risk, potential for enhanced portfolio returns, ability to profit in different economic environments, and the ease of global diversification) as well as the special benefits that futures traders have (e.g., lower transaction costs, lower market impact costs, use of leverage, and liquid markets). In addition, the report emphasizes the market integrity and safety of trading in organized exchanges for futures contracts.

Managed Futures: An Investment Alternative for Australian Superannuation Funds? APMFA (October, 1995): This report updates the APMFA's review of the benefits of managed futures for the Australian market. The report gives an overview of futures markets and futures markets' pricing as well as an overview of past empirical research. Lastly, the paper provides empirical evidence on the diversification benefits of managed futures in investment from the viewpoint of an Australian investor and emphasizes the differential styles of various commodity trading advisors and the diversity of markets traded as reasons for the potential benefits.

Comparisons of Commodity and Managed Futures Benchmark Indexes, CISDM (April, 1996): Benchmark indexes are commonly used in studies of investment performance to provide a performance index that reflects the particular style of an investment manager. Although benchmark indexes are common in the areas of stock and bond investment, in recent years futures- and options-based commodity trading products have grown rapidly as alternative means of investing in cash market commodity and financial securities. Various commodity- and futures-market-based indexes have existed for years (e.g., CRB, Dow Jones futures index). However, indexes based on the performance of commodity futures traders (e.g., MAR, Barclay indexes) have only recently been used in discussions of benchmark performance or asset class determination. This paper reviews the risk/return performance and the relative tracking error of the principal commodity- and futures-based benchmark indexes as well as that of the indexes used to track various commodity trading advisors and managed-futures based trading products. Results indicate that although commonly used managed futures indexes are highly correlated, existing commodity and managed futures benchmark indexes have unique risk/return patterns and thus are of use to investors who wish to monitor these unique return patterns.

Comparison of Hedge Fund Benchmark Indexes CISDM (April 1996): Academic studies have contrasted the performance of various benchmark indexes for stock and investments. Recently, however, alternative asset security forms (real estate, mortgage-backed bond funds, convertible bond funds, distressed securities, etc.) have become increasingly commonplace in investor portfolios. As new investment alternatives (e.g., real estate, venture capital, international markets) have grown, benchmark indexes have been created that attempt to mimic the performance of investor performance in these investment areas. One area of dramatic investment growth is hedge fund investment. Although stock and bond funds invest primarily in cash markets and managed futures funds are restricted to futures and options markets, hedge funds invest in both cash and futures markets simultaneously. In addition, hedge funds may differ from traditional stock, bond, and public commodity funds in that they are structured primarily for pool investment and not for public sale. This paper reviews the risk/return performance and the relative tracking error of the principal hedge indexes and compares their performance with traditional stock, bond, commodity, and managed futures indexes. Results indicate that in contrast to results reported for commonly used managed futures indexes, existing hedge fund benchmark indexes differ in important ways (e.g., mean return versus median return). Thus, as for stock, bond, and managed-futures investment, one must understand the unique structural and computational differences in commonly used hedge fund benchmarks.

Informational Content in Historical CTA Performance, CISDM (January 1996, forthcoming in Journal of Futures Markets): The past decade has witnessed a dramatic increase in the use of public commodity funds as stand-alone investments or as additions to traditional stock and bond portfolios. For investors, as for traditional stock and bond mutual funds, investment in public commodity funds is often based on past performance. However, as for traditional stock and bond funds, controversy exists over the extent to which past performance of public commodity funds provides evidence as to future performance. As for stock and bond analysis, in which a greater consistency between ex ante risk measurement and ex post return performance is shown at the portfolio level than at the security level, results show evidence of a greater consistency between ex ante risk and ex post return performance when CTA portfolios are delineated by risk class. Thus past CTA performance is valuable in forecasting CTA and multiadvisor CTA portfolios return and risk parameters, especially at the portfolio level. In terms of public policy, public disclosure of individual CTA as well as relative benchmark information may be of benefit to potential investors who desire to forecast expected risk-adjusted public commodity fund performance.

Survivor Bias in Commodity Trading Advisor Performance, CISDM (October 1995, forthcoming in Journal of Futures Markets): The impact of survivorship bias on empirical studies of mutual fund performance has received considerable attention. Likewise, for managed futures, empirical studies have attempted to reduce the impact of survivorship bias on studies of commodity fund performance. In this paper, the differential performance of survivor and nonsurvivor CTA subsamples is analyzed. Pairwise comparison results indicate that significant return differences exist between the survivor and nonsurvivor samples (approximately 1.5 percent annually). However, since nonsurvivor CTAs comprise only 10 percent of the full sample (survivors and nonsurvivors), the annual return bias in analyzing only survivor firms is approximately 1.5 percent. Moreover, when held in a portfolio with other risky asset classes, this return bias may be offset by a lower correlation of a full sample of CTAs relative to a survivor sample.

Lastly, using traditional abnormal return methodology, we also show that the return differential between survivor and nonsurvivor samples (on an absolute and risk-adjusted basis) is due primarily to return performance in the months just prior to CTA dissolution and not necessarily due to differential returns over extended past investment periods.

Investment through CTAs: An Alternative Managed Futures Investment, CISDM (January 1996, forthcoming in The Journal of Derivatives): Previous analyses of managed futures (investment funds that use international futures and options markets as their primary investment vehicle in asset management) principally focus on public commodity funds and pools. Today, fund management in managed futures is not limited to investment in commodity funds and pools but has expanded to direct investment with commodity trading advisors (CTAs).The study of CTA investment performance, as for investment in most other investment areas, is hampered by the difficulty of controlling for survivor bias. The results of this study, largely free of survivor bias, indicate that on a stand-alone basis, a portfolio of CTAs underperformed the comparison asset classes (e.g., stocks and bonds) on a simple Sharpe ratio basis. However, results also show that the CTA portfolio had superior minimum/maximum return tradeoffs compared to other stand-alone stock and bond portfolios and provide risk/return benefits when considered as additions to existing stock and bond portfolios. This study also provides evidence that simple models of multiasset portfolio creation and CTA selection may improve the performance of multiasset or multiadvisor CTA portfolios.

CBOT (Chicago Board of Trade), Chicago, Ill., U.S.A.

APMFA (Asian Pacific Managed Futures Association), Sydney, Australia

CISDM (Center for International Security and Derivative Markets), SOM/UMASS, Amherst, Mass.

CHAPTER 3

MANAGEMENT SUMMARY

Title: "Investment Performance of Public Commodity Pools: 1979-1990"

Publication: The Journal of Futures Markets, Vol 13, No. 7, 799-820 (1993)

Authors: Scott Irwin, Ohio State University

Terry R. Krukemyer, Agricultural Economic Consultant with Sparks Commodities, Inc., and a graduate student at Memphis State University

Data: Monthly return data for individual CTAs and commodity pools from 1979 to 1990.

Synopsis: The study focused on three issues of investment in commodity pools. First, a market portfolio of pools performs better than an investment in a randomly selected pool. Second, compared with alternative stock and bond investments, the standalone investment performance of public commodity pools is poor. In only two cases is the Sharpe ratio of a public commodity pool higher than a stock or bond investment. Finally, the portfolio performance of public pools is neutral, neither improving nor worsening the return-risk trade-offs of stock and bond portfolios.

The study also indicated that if the cost structure of public pools were reduced to reflect the fees typically levied to institutional clients, the potential to make the pools a desirable addition to stock and bond portfolios was significant.

Investment Performance of Public Commodity Pools: 1979-1990

Scott H. Irwin
Associate Professor in the Department of Agricultural Economics at The Ohio State University

Terry R. Krukemyer
Agricultural Economic Consultant with Sparks Companies, Inc. and a graduate student in the Fogelman College of Business and Economics at Memphis State University

Carl R. Zulauf
Associate Professor in the Department of Agricultural Economics at The Ohio State University

INTRODUCTION

Several academic studies investigate the investment performance of public commodity pools.[1] The studies do not provide a consensus regarding their investment performance. One set of studies [Lintner (1983); Brorsen and Irwin (1985); Irwin and Brorsen (1985); Murphy (1986); Irwin and Landa (1987)] concludes that public commodity pools produce favorable or appropriate investment returns. In contrast, another set of studies [Elton, Gruber, and Rentzler (1987, 1990); Schneeweis, Savayana, and McCarthy (1991)] concludes that public commodity pools are inferior investment vehicles compared to other financial instruments.

The different findings of previous studies may be a function of the sample periods examined. Studies that find positive investment performance generally examine pool returns from the late 1970s and early

The authors acknowledge the helpful comments of Robert Strong, Francis Longstaff, and seminar participants at Georgetown University, The Ohio State University, and the Commodity Futures Trading Commission.

The Journal of Futures Markets 13, no. 7, 799–820 (1993)
© 1993 by John Wiley & Sons, Inc.

1980s. In contrast, studies that find inferior performance generally examine returns only from the 1980s. Another important difference is that some studies [Brorsen and Irwin (1985); Murphy (1986), Elton, Gruber, and Rentzler (1987, 1990)] assume investment in a single randomly selected pool, while others [Lintner (1983); Irwin and Brorsen (1985); Irwin and Landa (1987); Schneeweis, Savayana, and McCarthy (1991)] assume investment in a portfolio of pools.

This study investigates the impact of sample period and investment strategy on the investment performance of public commodity pools. The sample period for the study is January 1979 through December 1990. Compared with previous studies, the sample period is relatively long, and permits testing of whether performance is sensitive to the inclusion of returns from the late 1970s. In contrast to previous studies, investment in both a single randomly selected pool and a portfolio of pools is considered. This permits testing of whether performance is sensitive to the strategy assumed for investing in public commodity pools.

Three aspects of investment performance are examined. First, the attractiveness of public commodity pools as a stand-alone investment is evaluated. Second, the role of public commodity pools in investment portfolios is investigated. Third, the impact of costs on the portfolio performance of public commodity pools is analyzed.

In addition, these results are used to examine the efficiency of futures markets. Unique tests of efficiency are possible because: (1) pool returns represent actual trading experience in futures markets and (2) pool trading represents a non-trivial proportion of speculative trading in futures markets. Only one previous study (Murphy) analyzes the implications of public commodity pool returns for the efficiency of futures markets.

DATA

Data are collected for all public commodity pools trading during the period January 1979 through December 1990. The pools include domestic U.S. pools that collect money predominantly from U.S. citizens, as well as off-shore commodity pools that trade in U.S. futures markets but are open only to foreign investors. The initial year of 1979 is chosen because this is the first year in which 10 public commodity pools are active throughout the year.[2] By comparison, only three public commodity pools are active throughout 1978.

End-of-month net asset value per unit and distributions per unit are collected for each public commodity pool. The unit values are net of all costs for a given month. Costs include brokerage charges, management and incentive fees, and administrative charges.[3] Sources include: (1) the *Norwood Report* from January 1979 to April 1982, (2) the "Funds Review" section published monthly in *Futures* (formerly *Commodities*) magazine from May 1982 through December 1990,[4] (3) *Managed Accounts Reports* and 10-Q reports filed with the Securities and Exchange Commission, and (4) direct communication with commodity pool managers to obtain data otherwise unavailable.

Elton, Gruber, Rentzler's (1987) procedures are followed for pools entering the data set and for pools dissolving during a year.[5] A pool does not enter a calendar year's data set until its first January of trading. When a pool dissolves during a year, the dissolution value is reinvested in the market portfolio (average commodity pool) until the end of the calendar year of dissolution. This procedure allows the usually lower rate of return of a dissolving pool to be included in calculating average returns. Thus, a survivorship bias in average returns is avoided.

If a pool suspends trading, the unit value from the last month of trading is brought forward until trading resumes. This produces a zero percent monthly rate of return for as long as trading is suspended. Once trading begins again, the usual calculations are resumed.

Monthly returns of a broad range of financial investments are collected to provide comparisons with public commodity pools. They include buy-and-hold portfolios of common stocks, small stocks, U.S. Treasury bills, intermediate government bonds, long-term government bonds, and long-term corporate bonds. Data for these instruments are taken from Ibbotson Associates, Inc. (1991).

In addition, returns are calculated to a passive futures buy-and-hold strategy based on the Commodity Research Bureau (CRB) Composite Index of 27 commodity futures prices. Since futures margins may be deposited in the form of interest-bearing instruments, buy-and-hold futures returns are calculated as the sum of the change in the CRB Index and Treasury bill returns (Edwards and Ma (1988)].

Finally, returns for all of the alternative investments are on a gross rather than net basis. Because transactions costs generally are small relative to the returns of the alternative investments, comparison to net public commodity pool returns is appropriate.

CALCULATION OF PUBLIC COMMODITY POOL RETURN AND RISK

Consistent with earlier studies, the monthly set return of a public commodity pool is defined as

$$R_{c,t} = \frac{NAV_{c,t} - NAV_{c,t-1} + D_{c,t}}{NAV_{c,t-1}} \qquad (1)$$

where $R_{c,t}$ is the net return for commodity pool c in month t, $NAV_{c,t}$ is the net asset value per unit for commodity pool c at the end of month t, $NAV_{c,t-1}$ is the net asset value per unit for commodity pool c at the end of month $t-1$, and $D_{c,t}$ is the cash distribution made by commodity pool c in month t. The formula assumes cash distributions are reinvested in the pool at the end of the month of distribution.

Two different strategies for investing in public commodity pools are examined: (1) a single randomly selected pool and (2) a market portfolio of pools. The first strategy assumes that funds are invested in a *single* randomly selected pool, whereas the second strategy assumes an equally weighted investment is made in *all* pools.[6]

The two strategies may entail substantially different risks. If the "market" is defined as all public commodity pools, a randomly selected pool contains both the systematic (undiversifiable) market risk and the unsystematic (diversifiable) risk associated with holding only one pool. A market portfolio of pools contains only the systematic risk associated with holding all pools. If returns of individual commodity pools are less than perfectly correlated (positively), the risk of a randomly selected pool will exceed the risk of a market portfolio of pools.

Following Elton, Gruber, and Rentzler (1987), both monthly and annual holding period investment horizons are examined. The two holding periods are used to reflect different time horizons that investors may use when making investments. The rate of return for a monthly horizon is calculated as the average arithmetic rate of return. The rate of return for an annual horizon is calculated as the average geometric rate of return.[7]

For a given year, average monthly returns and standard deviation of monthly returns for a randomly selected pool are generated by a two-step procedure. First, the arithmetic average, geometric average, and standard deviation of the monthly returns during the year are calculated for each pool. Second, the individual average returns (arithmetic or geometric) and standard deviations are averaged.[8] If a pool ends trading in any month other than December, it is not included in calculating that year's average standard deviation. The reason is that lack of trading during part of the year could bias the average standard deviation downward.

Average monthly returns and standard deviation of the market portfolio for a given year also are generated by a two-step procedure. First, portfolio returns for each month during the year are calculated. Portfolio returns are generated by averaging the returns of all pools trading during a month. Second, the average and standard deviation of the 12 monthly portfolio returns is calculated.

Average returns for a monthly holding period will be identical for a randomly selected pool and the market portfolio of pools. The reason is that the average of the individual pools' average monthly returns equals the average of the monthly portfolio returns. This equality holds only when equal weighting of returns is assumed for the market portfolio.

Average returns for an annual holding period are not expected to be equal for a randomly selected pool and the market portfolio. This is due to the use of a geometric average to calculate average returns for the annual holding period. The larger the standard deviation of returns, the smaller will be the geometric average of returns. Since the standard deviation of a randomly selected pool is likely to be higher than that of the market portfolio, the average return of a randomly selected pool for an annual holding period is expected to be smaller than the average return of the market portfolio of pools.

Finally, to provide a check on the data and application of the methodology, returns and risk are calculated for the sample period examined by Elton, Gruber, and Rentzler (1987). The returns generated by this study closely replicate those reported by Elton, Gruber, and Rentzler. Results of the comparison are presented in Appendix A.

STAND-ALONE PERFORMANCE

As shown in Table 3–1, public commodity pool returns are highly variable across years. For example, monthly holding period returns for a randomly selected commodity pool range from a high of 4.221 percent per month in 1979 to a low of –0.876 percent in 1986. Furthermore, average returns are sensitive to the sample period selected, particularly to the inclusion of 1979. For a monthly holding period, randomly selected pool returns average 1.158 percent per month over 1979–1990, but decrease to 0.879 percent per month over 1980–1990, and 0.784 percent per month over 1986–1990.

A time series plot of annual holding period returns is shown in Figure 3–1. The plot suggests that the 1979 return may be an outlier.[9] Over 1980–1990, returns appear to follow a stationary pattern. It has been suggested that public commodity pool returns may diminish as the size of their trading increases [Irwin and Brorsen (1987)], but commodity pool returns exhibit no such downward trend after 1979.[10]

TABLE 3-1

Net Return and Standard Deviation for Public Commodity
Pools, 1979–1990

Year	Number of Pools	Randomly Selected Commodity Pool			Market Portfolio of Commodity Pools		
		Average Return		Standard Deviation	Average Return		Standard Deviation
		MHP[a]	AHP[b]		MHP[a]	AHP[b]	
		%/month			%/month		
1979	10	4.221	3.138	13.713	4.221	3.912	8.352
1980	15	2.520	1.728	15.015	2.520	2.284	7.320
1981	22	0.838	0.399	8.845	0.838	0.670	6.124
1982	43	0.518	0.053	9.436	0.518	0.327	6.450
1983	62	−0.577	−1.177	10.155	−0.577	−0.818	7.303
1984	78	1.098	0.585	9.741	1.098	0.863	7.381
1985	94	1.358	1.006	8.154	1.358	1.212	5.672
1986	98	−0.876	−1.350	9.299	−0.876	−1.066	6.498
1987	111	2.854	2.495	8.441	2.854	2.696	6.038
1988	128	0.715	0.202	9.482	0.715	0.481	7.415
1989	149	−0.297	−0.622	7.413	−0.297	−0.428	5.360
1990	186	1.522	1.340	5.611	1.522	1.479	3.059
Average:							
1979–1990		1.158	0.650	9.609	1.158	0.968	6.414
1980–1990		0.879	0.424	9.236	0.879	0.700	6.238
1986–1990		0.784	0.413	8.049	0.784	0.632	5.674

[a]Monthly holding period.
[b]Annual holding period.

A randomly selected commodity pool's monthly standard deviation ranges from 15.015 percent per month in 1980 to 5.611 percent per month in 1990 (Table 3–1). Over the entire 1979–1990 period, average monthly standard deviation of a randomly selected commodity pool is 9.609 percent. As expected, standard deviation for the market portfolio of commodity pools is substantially smaller. It averages 6.414 percent per month over 1979–1990, a one-third reduction in risk compared to holding a single randomly selected commodity pool.

For comparative purposes, average returns and standard deviations of the alternative investments over 1979–1990 are reported in Table 3–2.

FIGURE 3-1

Average Monthly Return of Public Commodity Pools, 1979–1990

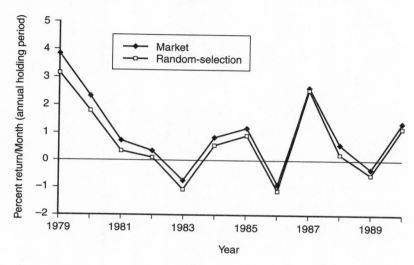

Several observations are noteworthy. First, the standard deviation of commodity pool returns is generally greater than the standard deviation of returns for alternative investments. This is especially true for a randomly selected pool, which has a standard deviation over one-and-a-half times that of common stocks. Second, over the entire 1979–1990 period, monthly and annual holding period returns for the market portfolio of pools, as well as the monthly holding period returns for a randomly selected pool, exceed returns for bills and bonds, but not for common and small stocks. In contrast, over both 1980–1990 and 1986–1990, returns for commodity pools are not favorable relative to both stocks and bond investments. This difference in results reinforces the previously noted importance of the data for 1979. Third, over none of the sample periods does the annual holding period return of a randomly selected commodity pool exceed the return of Treasury bills or of the passive buy-and-hold futures strategy. Fourth, the average return of the market portfolio of commodity pools exceeds the average return for the buy-and-hold futures strategy over both monthly and annual holding periods. This result suggests that the active trading strategies used by public pools as a group generate net returns that exceed the gross returns of a passive buy-and-hold strategy.

TABLE 3-2

Return and Standard Deviation for Alternative Investments, 1979–1990

Investment[a]	1979–1990			1980–1990			1986–1990		
	Average Return		Standard Deviation	Average Return		Standard Deviation	Average Return		Standard Deviation
	MHP[b]	AHP[c]		MHP[b]	AHP[c]		MHP[b]	AHP[c]	
RS comm. pool	1.158	0.650	9.609	0.879	0.424	9.236	0.784	0.413	8.049
MP comm. pools	1.158	0.968	6.414	0.879	0.700	6.238	0.784	0.632	5.674
B&H futures	0.753	0.702	3.209	0.579	0.530	3.165	0.542	0.504	2.787
Common stocks	1.337	1.225	4.711	1.323	1.208	4.793	1.185	1.034	5.418
Small stocks	1.280	1.108	5.748	1.099	0.933	5.623	0.235	0.048	5.849
T-bills	0.715	0.715	0.222	0.705	0.705	0.228	0.553	0.552	0.108
IT gov't bonds	0.901	0.877	2.181	0.950	0.927	2.195	0.757	0.746	1.445
LT gov't bonds	0.936	0.861	3.924	1.026	0.949	3.985	0.905	0.853	3.286
LT corp. bonds	0.933	0.870	3.592	1.046	0.982	3.622	0.856	0.830	2.284

[a]RS comm. pool: Randomly selected commodity pool; MP comm. pools: Market portfolio of commodity pools; B&H futures: Buy-and-Hold futures; T-bills: Treasury bills; IT gov't bonds: intermediate-term government bonds; LT gov't bonds: Long-term government bonds; LT corp. bonds: Long-term corporate bonds.

[b]Monthly holding period.

[c]Annual holding period.

Given the well-known trade-off between the return and risk of investments, a comprehensive measure of stand-alone investment performance is needed. A widely used method of ranking individual investment alternatives is the Sharpe ratio,

$$SR_i = \frac{R_i - r_f}{\sigma_i} \tag{2}$$

where SR_i is the Sharpe ratio of investment i, R_i is the expected return of investment i, r_f is the risk-free return, and σ_i is the standard deviation of investment i.

Sharpe ratios are calculated using Treasury bill returns as a proxy for the risk-free return. The calculated ratios and corresponding investment rankings are presented in Table 3–3. The rankings indicate that the stand-alone performance of public pools generally is poor. There are only two cases where a pool investment outranks a stock or bond investment: the market portfolio of pools is ranked higher than long-term government bonds for a monthly holding period over 1979–1990 and is ranked higher than small stocks for an annual holding period over 1986–1990. Among the alternative futures investments, the market portfolio of commodity pools always is the highest ranked investment.

PORTFOLIO PERFORMANCE

Although the stand-alone performance of public commodity pools is poor, this does not necessarily imply that investment in pools is without merit. It is possible that public pools may be an attractive addition to investment portfolios. Elton, Gruber, and Rentzler (1987) show that a commodity pool should be added to an existing portfolio if

$$\frac{R_c - r_f}{\sigma_c} > \frac{R_p - r_f}{\sigma_p} \cdot \rho_{c,p} \tag{3}$$

where R_c is the expected return of commodity pool c, r_f is the risk-free return, σ_c is the standard deviation of commodity pool c, R_p is the expected return of portfolio p, σ_p is the standard deviation of portfolio p, and $\rho_{c,p}$ is the correlation coefficient between the expected returns of commodity pool c and portfolio p.

Equation (3) is the condition commodity pools must meet to improve the return-risk trade-off of an existing portfolio of investments. The intuition behind the condition may be more evident if interpreted in terms of

TABLE 3-3

Sharpe Ratio and Rank for Alternative Investments, 1979–1990

Investment[a]	1979–1990		1980–1990		1986–1990	
	MHP[b]	AHP[c]	MHP[b]	AHP[c]	MHP[b]	AHP[c]
			Sharpe ratio			
RS comm. pool	0.046	−0.007	0.019	−0.031	0.029	−0.017
MP comm. pools	0.069	0.038	0.028	−0.002	0.040	0.012
B&H futures	0.012	−0.004	−0.040	−0.055	−0.004	−0.017
Common stocks	0.132	0.108	0.129	0.105	0.117	0.089
Small stocks	0.098	0.068	0.070	0.041	0.054	−0.086
IT gov't bonds	0.085	0.074	0.112	0.101	0.141	0.134
LT gov't bonds	0.056	0.037	0.081	0.061	0.107	0.092
LT corp. bonds	0.061	0.043	0.094	0.076	0.133	0.122
			Sharpe ratio rank			
RS comm. pool	7	8	7	7	7	7
MP comm. pools	5	6	6	6	6	5
B&H futures	8	7	8	8	8	6
Common stocks	1	1	1	1	3	4
Small stocks	2	3	5	5	5	8
IT gov't bonds	3	2	2	2	1	1
LT gov't bonds	6	5	4	4	4	3
LT corp. bonds	4	4	3	3	2	2

[a]RS comm. pool: Randomly selected commodity pool; MP comm. pools: Market portfolio of commodity pools; B&H futures: Buy-and-hold futures; IT gov't bonds: Intermediate-term government bonds; LT gov't bonds: Long-term government bonds; LT corp. bonds: Long-term corporate bonds.
[b]Monthly holding period.
[c]Annual holding period.

Sharpe ratios. For commodity pools to improve the return-risk trade-off of an investment portfolio, the Sharpe ratio of commodity pools must exceed the product of the Sharpe ratio of the existing investment portfolio and the correlation coefficient between commodity pools and the investment portfolio. It is important to note that the break-even condition is not based on an equilibrium asset pricing model. The condition is relevant only to a prespecified portfolio, which may or may not be an efficient or optimal portfolio.

A key component of the break-even condition is the correlation between commodity pool returns and portfolio returns. Correlation

TABLE 3–4

Correlation between Monthly Returns of a Randomly Selected Commodity Pool and Other Financial Investments, 1979–1990

Year	Number of Pools	Common Stocks	Small Stocks	T-Bills	IT Gov't Bonds	LT Gov't Bonds	LT Corp. Bonds	B&H Futures	MP of Comm. Pools	Inflation
1979	10	0.086	0.139	−0.144	0.319	0.379	0.357	0.395	0.641	0.094
1980	13	0.098	0.137	−0.217	−0.105	−0.265	−0.229	0.121	0.389	−0.056
1981	22	−0.056	−0.066	0.161	0.092	0.154	0.204	−0.359	0.624	0.091
1982	43	−0.115	−0.228	−0.027	−0.261	−0.067	−0.130	−0.287	0.676	0.145
1983	60	−0.120	−0.093	0.334	−0.193	−0.363	−0.257	0.389	0.708	0.176
1984	77	−0.320	−0.324	−0.073	0.153	0.140	0.203	−0.425	0.672	−0.110
1985	88	0.299	0.404	0.127	−0.120	−0.033	0.008	−0.155	0.635	−0.255
1986	94	0.310	0.305	0.343	0.385	0.462	0.485	−0.195	0.655	−0.378
1987	106	0.143	0.134	−0.309	−0.221	−0.192	−0.174	0.496	0.705	0.008
1988	124	0.240	0.071	0.085	0.156	0.172	0.239	0.486	0.744	0.019
1989	144	0.383	0.368	0.111	0.162	0.205	0.240	−0.334	0.622	0.143
1990	174	−0.364	−0.313	0.132	−0.313	−0.345	-0.373	0.165	0.492	0.179
Average:										
1979–1990		0.049	0.045	0.044	0.005	0.021	0.048	0.025	0.630	0.005
1980–1990		0.045	0.036	0.061	−0.024	−0.012	0.020	−0.009	0.629	−0.003
1986–1990		0.142	0.113	0.072	0.034	0.060	0.083	0.124	0.644	−0.006

[a]IT gov't bonds: Intermediate-term government bonds; LT gov't bonds: Long-term government bonds; LT corp. bonds: Long-term corporate bonds; B&H futures: Buy-and-hold futures; MP of comm. pools: Market portfolio of commodity pools.

coefficients between a randomly selected pool and the alternative investments are shown in Table 3–4. Monthly returns of the market portfolio of pools exhibit nearly identical correlations with the alternative investments. Hence, only correlations for a randomly selected pool are presented.

Although the correlations between commodity pool returns and stock and bond returns vary somewhat from year to year, the central tendency is toward zero correlation. Over the 1979–1990 sample period, the average correlation between monthly returns of a randomly selected commodity pool and stock and bond investments range from 0.005 for intermediate-term government bonds to 0.049 for common stocks. Monthly commodity pool returns also do not show any evidence of correlation with buy-and-hold futures or the rate of inflation. Finally, the correlation between returns to a randomly selected pool and returns to the market portfolio of commodity pools is relatively high, indicating that the degree of co-movement in individual commodity pool returns is substantial.

The correlation results suggest that it is reasonable to assume that public commodity pool returns are uncorrelated with the returns to any of the stock and bond investments. The assumption of zero correlation allows equation (3) to be simplified as follows:

$$R_c - r_f > 0 \tag{4}$$

Hence, if public commodity pools are to enter a portfolio of the stock and bond investments, the difference between pool returns and the risk-free rate (excess returns) must be greater than zero. The hypothesis that excess returns are greater than zero can be tested with the use of a t-statistic. Note that the break-even condition applies to any individual stock or bond investment as well as any portfolio of stock and bond investments. The reason is that the correlation between commodity pools and any portfolio of stock and bond investments (e.g., 60 percent common stocks and 40 percent corporate bonds) is zero if the correlation between pools and the individual stock and bond investments is zero.[11]

Excess net public pool returns are presented in Table 3–5.[12] Again, Treasury bill returns are used as a proxy for the risk-free rate of return. Consistent with the above described findings of this study, excess net returns are highest for the 1979–1990 period. Excess net returns for a randomly selected pool are positive over all three sample periods at the monthly holding period, but are negative over all three sample periods at the annual holding period. Excess net returns for the market portfolio of pools are positive for all holding periods and sample periods except for the annual holding period over the 1980–1990 sample period. However, based on t-statistics, none of the positive excess returns for a randomly selected pool or the market portfolio of pools are significantly different from zero.[13]

The results show that investment in public pools does not cause a statistically significant improvement in the performance of stock and bond portfolios. Therefore, the portfolio performance of pools is not superior. On the other hand, investment in public pools is not significantly detrimental to the performance of stock and bond portfolios. Hence, the portfolio performance of pools is not inferior. The most appropriate conclusion is that the portfolio performance of public pools is neutral, neither improving nor worsening the return-risk trade-offs of stock and bond portfolios.

Finally, it is useful to note that portfolio performance is ordinarily better when data from 1979 are included. This result is consistent with the different conclusions of earlier studies. Previous studies that include data

TABLE 3–5

Excess Net Returns for Public Commodity Pools, 1979–1990[a]

Sample Period	Randomly Selected Commodity Pool		Market Portfolio of Commodity Pools	
	MHP[b]	AHP[a]	MHP[b]	AHP[c]
	Percent per month			
1979–1990	0.443	−0.066	0.443	0.252
	(1.043)	(−0.165)	(1.042)	(0.601)
1980–1990	0.174	−0.282	0.174	−0.005
	(0.484)	(−0.772)	(0.484)	(−0.014)
1986–1990	0.231	−0.139	0.231	0.080
	(0.341)	(−0.199)	(0.341)	(0.116)

Note: The figure in parentheses is a t-statistic. One (two) star(s) indicates the average excess return of public commodity pools is significantly different from zero at the 10 (5)% level of significance. Two-tailed tests of significance are used.
[a]Excess net return = Net return − Treasury bill return.
[b]Monthly holding period.
[c]Annual holding period.

from the high return years of the late 1970s tend to find positive portfolio results [e.g., Lintner (1983)], while studies that use samples solely from the 1980s tend to report negative portfolio results [e.g., Elton, Gruber, and Rentzler (1990)].

THE IMPACT OF COST ON PORTFOLIO PERFORMANCE

Performance problems of public commodity pools frequently have been attributed to high operating costs [e.g., Elton, Gruber, and, Rentzler (1987)]. Estimates of the total operating costs of public commodity pools range from 17 to 19 percent of annual equity [Irwin and Brorsen (1985); Murphy (1986); Basso (1989)]. In contrast, Ippolito (1989) reports that costs of stock mutual funds are about 1 percent of annual equity.

The performance impacts of lower costs can be analyzed by using evidence from institutional pension fund investments in commodity pools. Costs for institutional commodity pools are 10 to 12 percent of annual equity, approximately seven percentage points less than costs for public commodity pools (Table 3–6).[14] The biggest reduction is in commissions, which are decreased from 9 to 2 percent of annual equity. This reflects a much lower brokerage charge per trade.[15] In addition, the usual management fee paid by institutional investors is half the usual management fee paid by public investors, 2.5 versus 5.0 percent of annual equity.

The potential impact of these lower costs is analyzed by adjusting the monthly returns on the market portfolio of pools to reflect the lower costs paid by institutional investors.[16] The adjustment requires two steps. First, gross trading returns of public commodity pools are estimated. This entails subtracting Treasury bill returns from net public pool returns and then adding back the public pool costs. Second, the net return to institutional commodity pools is estimated by subtracting the costs of institutional investors from the estimated gross trading returns and adding back Treasury bill returns. Details of the procedure are reported in Appendix B.

The lower costs negotiated by institutional investors substantially impacts the performance of commodity pools (Table 3–7). Average returns increase one-and-a-half to two times after the cost adjustment. For example, average returns for an annual holding period over 1980–1990 are 1.339 percent per month after the cost adjustment, compared to 0.700 percent per month before the cost adjustment. Standard deviation of returns is changed only slightly by the adjustment, while the correlation with other investments, as represented by the correlation with common stocks, remains near zero. In fact, the correlation with stocks is even closer to zero after the cost adjustment.

The portfolio break-even results stand in sharp contrast to the original break-even results. Average excess net returns after the cost adjustment are substantially positive in all six cases. Moreover, excess net returns are significantly different from zero and positive for the monthly and annual holding periods over 1979–1990 and for the monthly holding period over 1980–1990. Hence, using the typical cost structure negotiated by institutions, this analysis suggests that commodity pool investment may improve the return-risk trade-offs of stock and bond portfolios.

IMPLICATIONS FOR THE EFFICIENCY OF FUTURES MARKETS

The returns to public commodity pools provide a unique test of the efficiency of futures markets for two reasons. First, pool returns represent actual trading experience in futures markets. Most previous studies of market efficiency rely on simulated returns to trading strategies [e.g.,

TABLE 3–6

Costs of Commodity Pool Investments

Type of Commodity Pool	Cost Category			
	Commissions (Annual Percent of Equity	Management (Annual Percent of Equity)	Incentive (Annual Percent of Gross Trading Profts	Total (Annual Percent of Equity)
Public commodity pool	9.3	5.0	20.0	17–19
Institutional commodity pool	2.0	2.5	25.0	10–12

Sources: Irwin and Brorsen (1985); Murphy (1986); Basso (1989); Hecht (1989).

TABLE 3–7

Net Return Statistics for the Market Portfolio of Public Commodity Pools after Cost Adjustment for Institutional Investors, 1979–1990

Sample Period	Average Net Return		Standard Deviation	Correlation with Common Stocks	Excess Net Return[a]	
	MHP[b]	AHP[c]			MHP[b]	AHP[c]
	Percent per month				Percent per month	
1979–1990	1.767	1.593	6.151	0.010	1.051**	0.878*
					(2.582)	(2.172)
1980–1990	1.503	1.339	5.929	0.010	0.800**	0.634
					(2.287)	(1.796)
1986–1990	1.418	1.281	5.510	0.029	0.865	0.728
					(1.313)	(1.091)

Note: The figure in parentheses is a t-statistic. One (two) star(s) indicates the average excess return of public commodity pools is significantly different from zero at the 10 (5)% level of significance. Two-tailed tests of significance are used.
[a]Excess net return = net return − treasury bill return.
[b]Monthly holding period.
[c]Annual holding period.

Lukac, Brorsen, and Irwin (1988)] or statistical tests of the behavior of futures prices [e.g., Chowdhury (1991)]. Second, pool returns represent a nontrivial proportion of speculative trading in futures markets. While precise estimates are unavailable, public commodity pool positions may represent as much as 10 percent of the total open interest in some futures markets [Brorsen and Irwin (1987)]; Commodity Futures Trading Commission (1991)].

Market efficiency usually implies that prices reflect all available information [Fama (1970)]. If futures markets are fully efficient, then it is futile to expend resources in an effort to "beat the market." Since it is not possible to improve upon the information reflected in market prices, gross trading returns should equal zero, or equivalently, traders should experience losses equal to costs.

Applying Fama's definition of futures market efficiency to public commodity pools requires estimates of gross trading returns. Gross trading returns are estimated as a part of the cost analysis discussed in the previous section. The estimated average gross trading return (excluding interest earnings) for the market portfolio of public pools over 1979–1990, 1980–1990, and 1986–1990 is 1.696, 1.312, and 1.644 percent per month, respectively. The smallest t-statistic for the average gross trading returns is 2.28, and all gross returns are significantly different from zero at the 5 percent level.[17] Hence, Fama's definition of futures market efficiency is strongly rejected with respect to public commodity pool returns.[18]

The rejection of Fama's definition of market efficiency may not be as serious as appearances suggest. The reason is that Fama's depiction of equilibrium is based on the assumption that information is costless to collect and use. However, a full information equilibrium is impossible if information is costly [Grossman and Stiglitz (1980)]. Market participants have an incentive to collect and use costly information only if returns cover the cost of information. If returns do not cover the cost of information, rational participants will not trade based on the information, and market prices will not reflect the information. Hence, the impossibility of fully efficient markets when information is costly.

Jensen (1978) suggests a definition of market efficiency that is not subject to the aforementioned "impossibility" problem, and hence, is more economically sensible. According to Jensen, an efficient market is one in which prices reflect information to the point where the marginal benefits of collecting and using information equal the marginal costs. In other words, the returns to any trading strategy adjusted for costs and risk should equal zero in an efficient market.

Applying Jensen's definition of market efficiency to public commodity pool returns requires two steps. First, the returns must be net of all costs. Second, the returns must be adjusted for risk, which required the assumption of a particular equilibrium asset pricing model. While not universally accepted, the Capital Asset Pricing Model (CAPM) [Sharpe (1964); Lintner (1965)] is widely used to adjust returns for risk. If the "market return" is proxied by any linear combination of the stock and bond return series examined in this study, then the (near) zero correlations reported in Table 3–4 imply that the CAPM market beta of public commodity pools is approximately equal to zero. Under the CAPM, any investment with a zero beta, and hence no market risk, should earn the risk-free rate of return.

The above discussion suggests a relatively simple test of (Jensen) market efficiency in the case of public commodity pools; net returns should not be significantly different from the risk-free rate of return. In other words, the excess net return of public pools should not be significantly different from zero. None of the excess net returns for public commodity pools reported in Table 3–5 are significantly different from zero. Returns of public pools therefore, are consistent with market efficiency after adjusting for costs and risk. That is, pools earn a gross return just sufficient to offset the costs and risk involved in collecting and using information. It is interesting to note that a similar result is found for stock mutual funds [Ippolito (1989)].

The same efficiency test can be applied to the estimated returns to an institutional commodity pool. In contrast to the results for public pools, estimated excess returns to institutional commodity pools are positive and significantly different from zero for a monthly holding period over 1979–1990 and 1980–1990, as well as for the annual holding period over 1979–1990 (Table 3–7). Market efficiency is thus rejected with respect to the estimated returns for institutional commodity pools over some of the sample scenarios.

Several interpretations can be given to the rejections of market efficiency with respect to institutional commodity pools. First, the significant excess returns may reflect a return to risk, which the CAPM does not incorporate. The CAPM assumes a constant return to risk for all investments. The estimated returns for institutional commodity pools may reflect a time-varying return to risk. Second, the excess returns may represent a market inefficiency that is in the process of being eliminated. Institutional pension funds increasingly are investing in commodity pool programs [Angrist (1992)]. As this investment increases, the estimated excess returns may be eliminated. Third, the assumptions used to estimate institutional returns may not be representative of actual futures trading by institutions.

SUMMARY AND CONCLUSIONS

This study investigates the investment performance of public commodity pools over the sample period January 1979 through December 1990. The sample period is relatively long and permits testing of whether performance is sensitive to the inclusion of returns from the late 1970s. Investment in both a single randomly selected pool and a portfolio of pools is evaluated to determine if performance is sensitive to the investment strategy. Returns are calculated for both a monthly and an annual holding period.

Among the alternative futures investments, the market portfolio of commodity pools performs the best. The Sharpe ratio of the market portfolio of pools always exceeds the Sharpe ratio of a randomly selected pool and a passive buy-and-hold futures strategy. This result suggests: (1) that investment in public commodity pools should involve a portfolio of pools and (2) that the active trading strategies used by public pools as a group generate net returns that exceed the returns of a passive buy-and-hold strategy.

Compared with alternative stock and bond investments, the stand-alone investment performance of public commodity pools is poor. In only two cases is the Sharpe ratio of a public commodity pool higher than a stock or bond investment. The poor stand-alone performance is not particularly sensitive to the sample period or to whether the investment strategy involves a single randomly selected pool or a market portfolio of pools.

Investment in public pools does not cause a statistically significant improvement in the performance of stock and bond portfolios, and hence, the portfolio performance of pools is not superior. On the other hand, investment in public pools is not significantly detrimental to the performance of stock and bond portfolios, and therefore, the portfolio performance of pools is not inferior. The most appropriate conclusion is that the portfolio performance of public pools is neutral, neither improving nor worsening the return-risk trade-offs of stock and bond portfolios.

Portfolio performance is ordinarily better when data from 1979 are included in the analysis. This result is consistent with the conclusions of earlier studies. Previous studies that include data from the high return years of the late 1970s tend to find positive portfolio results [e.g., Lintner (1983)], whereas studies that use samples solely from the 1980s tend to report negative portfolio results [e.g., Elton, Gruber, and Rentzler (1990)].

The cost of investing in public commodity pools is often mentioned as a reason for their unattractive performance. When costs are reduced to the level that large institutional pension funds have been able to obtain, average returns to the market portfolio of pools exceed stock and bond portfolio break-even levels in all cases. Moreover, returns are significantly greater than break-even returns over 1979–1990 and 1980–1990. Therefore, reducing costs to investors has the potential to make a portfolio of public commodity pools a desirable addition to stock and bond portfolios.

Finally, the results provide unique evidence regarding futures market efficiency. Unique tests of efficiency are possible because: (1) pool returns represent actual trading experience in futures markets and (2) pool trading represents nontrivial proportion of speculative trading in futures markets. Returns of public commodity pools are consistent with market efficiency after adjusting for costs and risk. That is, public commodity pools earn a gross return just sufficient to offset the costs and risk of collecting and using information.

In contrast to the results for public pools, estimated returns to institutional commodity pools over some periods more than offset costs and risk. Market efficiency is therefore rejected for institutional commodity pools over some of the sample scenarios. Several interpretations can be given to the rejections of market efficiency. First, the estimated returns for institutional commodity pools may reflect a time-varying return to risk. Second, institutional returns may represent a market inefficiency that is in the process of being eliminated. Third, the assumptions used to estimate institutional returns may not be representative of actual futures trading by institutions.

ENDNOTES

1. Commodity pools also are known as commodity funds and futures funds. The official term in all regulatory matters is commodity pool, and hence, this term is used throughout the article.

2. Twelve pools report monthly public data in January 1979 to the *Norwood Report*. However, the Talisman Fund and The Dunn Corporation Limited Partnership ceased to report monthly data in April 1979 and January 1981, respectively, even though they continue to trade after these dates. The reason for the cessation of reporting is unknown. Hence, these two pools are not included in the data set.

3. Public commodity pool returns do not reflect initial sales (load) charges sometimes paid by investors. The effect of including load charges is relatively small. Consider the case of an investor who places funds in a pool for 5 years and pays a typical load charge of 8.5% of initial investment. The cost of the load charge over the 5 years is 0.142% per month.

4. Return data is provided to *Futures* by Managed Accounts Reports, Inc.

5. Most commodity pools are created to trade for a specific length of time [e.g., Merrill Lynch, Pierce, Fenner, and Smith (1989)]. However, a pool will cease trading before this specified time if the total equity or unit value falls below the prescribed minimum in the prospectus or an amount needed to trade effectively. The pool may also stop trading if performance is less than acceptable. In the 12-year period from 1979 through 1990, 56 pools ceased trading. Dissolution net asset values are obtained for 32 pools. The net asset value at the end of the last reported month of trading is used as the dissolution value for the remaining pools. For a detailed examination of commodity pool dissolution, see Elton, Gruber, and Rentzler (1990).

6. Equity-weighted returns also are calculated. They are not significantly different from equal-weighted returns, so only the latter are used in this study. See Appendix D in Krukemyer (1990) for results and further discussion.

7. Over the same period, the average return for monthly holding periods will be equal to or larger than the average return for an annual holding period. This occurs because an arithmetic average will always be equal to or larger than a geodetic average, assuming the variance of the series is greater than zero [Grossman (1987)].

8. It is not possible to directly calculate the average annual holding period returns for a randomly selected pool in 1980. The reason is that one pool (McClean I) had a −100 percent return in December 1980. Hence, the 1980 annual holding period return (geometric average) for this pool is not defined (it equals negative infinity). As a consequence, the average annual holding period return for all pools in 1980 also is undefined. Returns to an equally weighted portfolio of all 15 pools are substituted. Initial weights are determined by December 1979 net asset values. No rebalancing of the portfolio weights is allowed in the calculations.

9. The abnormal returns in 1979 appear to be related to market conditions rather than the particular pools trading in that year. The ten pools trading in 1979 produce returns and risks representative of all pools over the remainder of the sample period, despite the fact that 5 of the 10 pools dissolve between 1980 and 1985. (As before, when a pool dissolves, it is assumed that the dissolution value is reinvested in the remaining pools until the end of the year.) Over 1980–1990, the 10 pools generate average returns for a monthly holding period of 1.013 percent per month and a standard deviation of 8.456 percent per month. By comparison, average return and standard deviation of all pools over 1980 to 1990 equals 0.879 percent per month and 9.236 percent per month, respectively.

10. Linear time-trend regressions support this conclusion. Using annual observations over 1980–1990, public pool returns are regressed on time. Co-efficients for time are insignificantly different from zero for the randomly

selected pool regressions and the market portfolio regressions. The same result is found using monthly returns for the market portfolio of pools over 1980–1990.

11. This follows from the fact that

$$Cov(X, bY + cZ) = b \ Cov(X,Y) + c \ Cov(X,Z)$$

If $Cov(X,Y) = Cov(X,Z) = 0$, then $Cov(X, bY = cZ) = 0$.

12. Excess returns and t-statistics are calculated using annual observations. Hence, the t-statistics for 1979–1990, 1980–1990, and 1986–1990 are based on 12, 11, and 5 observations.

13. Note that a two-tailed test of significance is used. This is done for two reasons. First, a two-tailed test is more conservative. Second, a two-tailed test allows the hypothesis tests to be interpreted in the context of the Capital Asset Pricing Model. This latter issue will be considered in the section on market efficiency implications.

14. The term *institutional commodity pools* is used only in the descriptive sense. To date, there are no commodity pools created for and marketed to institutional investors. Instead, institutions directly employ commodity trading advisors and brokers who trade the institution's monies in a similar fashion to a public commodity pool.

15. Irwin and Brorsen (1985) report that investors in their sample of public commodity pools often are charged full retail commission rates. The data in Table 3-6 imply that institutional investors have negotiated for brokerage rates nearly 80 percent lower than those paid by public investors (assuming similar trading strategies across the two investments).

16. Related analysis is reported in Murphy (1986), Cornew (1988), and Edwards and Ma (1988).

17. The estimated gross trading returns of pools are of further interest in light of the trading strategies used by most public commodity pools. Previous researchers note that most pools base trading decisions on "trend-following" technical systems [Irwin and Brorsen (1985); Murphy (1986); Elton, Gruber, and Rentzler (1987)]. It is frequently argued that trend-following systems do not work [e.g., Elton, Gruber, and Rentzler (1987, p. 176)]. The gross trading returns of public commodity pools suggest that trend-following systems may have some value. Corroborating evidence is found in recent simulation studies of the profitability of technical trading systems [e.g., Lukac, Brorsen, and Irwin (1988); Lukac and Brorsen (1990)]. Lukas and Brorsen simulate trading of 23 technical systems on 30 futures markets over 1976–1985. Using leverage assumptions similar to that actually employed by public commodity pools, Lukac and Brorsen find that gross trading profits (before interest earnings) average 2.15 percent per month

across all systems and markets. Gross trading returns are positive and significantly different from zero for all 23 systems.

18. The general rejection of efficiency may reflect a mixture of inefficient and efficient futures markets. It is possible that all or most of the gross trading returns are earned in just a few futures markets. For example, anecdotal evidence suggests public commodity pools may have generated much of their profits during the 1980s in currency futures markets.

APPENDIX A

Returns to public commodity pools also are calculated for the sample period July 1979–June 1985, which is the sample period examined by Elton, Gruber, and Rentzler (1987). Both sets of returns are based on the strategy of investing in a single randomly selected pool. Returns and standard deviations differ only slightly over the entire sample (bottom row, Table A3–1). Furthermore, except for the first 2 years, returns and standard deviations are similar for each year. The differences for the first 2 years are likely due to the different sources of data for this earlier period. For this study, data over July 1979–April 1982 are collected from the *Norwood Report*. The remainder of the data are collected from *Managed Accounts Reports* (as reported in *Futures*). All of Elton, Gruber, and Rentzler's data are collected from *Managed Accounts Reports*.

APPENDIX B

Two steps are required to adjust public commodity pool returns for the lower costs of institutional investors. First, gross public commodity pool trading returns for month t are calculated as follows:

$$GPCP_t = (NPCP_t - TB_t + CCPCP_t = MMPCP_t)$$
$$\text{if } (NPCP_t - TB_i + CCPCP_t + MMPCP_t) \leq 0 \text{ (5a)}$$

$$GPCP_t = (NPCP_t - TB_t + CCPCP_t + MMPCP_t)/(1 - (IPCP_t/100))$$
$$\text{if } (NPCP_t - TB_t + CCPCP_t + MMPCP_t) > 0 \text{ (5b)}$$

where

$GPCP_t$ = gross trading return of the market portfolio of public pools (percentage of equity per month),

TABLE A3-1

Comparison of Public Commodity Pool Returns over July 1979–June 1985

Sample Period	Irwin, Krukemyer, and Zulauf				No. of Pools	Elton, Gruber, and Rentzler		
	No. of Pools	Average Return		Standard Deviation		Average Return		Standard Deviation
		MHP[a]	AHP[b]			MHP[a]	AHP[b]	
		Percent per month				Percent per month		
July 1979–June 1980	12	2.20	0.73	15.71	12	1.82	0.27	15.77
July 1980–June 1981	16	2.05	1.31	10.56	16	2.19	0.90	12.11
July 1981–June 1982	34	1.54	1.19	8.00	34	1.49	1.12	8.24
July 1982–June 1983	49	-1.94	-2.70	11.67	49	-1.91	-2.67	11.67
July 1983–June 1984	72	-0.17	-0.48	7.64	70	-0.20	-0.54	7.93
July 1984–June 1985	88	1.05	0.58	9.26	85	0.97	0.48	9.43
Average		0.79	0.10	10.48		0.73	-0.07	10.86

Note: The returns reported under the heading of Irwin, Krukemyer, and Zulauf are based on original calculations. The returns reported under the heading of Elton, Gruber, and Rentzler are drawn from Table I (p. 178) of their 1987 article.

[a]Monthly holding period.

[b]Annual holding period.

$NPCP_t$ = net return of the market portfolio of public pools (percentage of equity per month),

TB_t = Treasury bill return (percentage per month),

$CCPCP_t$ = public pool commission cost (percentage of equity per month),

$MMPCP_t$ = public pool management cost (percentage of equity per month),

$IPCP_t$ = public pool incentive cost (percentage of gross trading returns).

Commission, management, and incentive costs are calculated based on the rates reported in the first row of Table 3–6. The rates are assumed to be fixed. Monthly commission (0.775 percent per month) and management (0.417 percent per month) costs are calculated by dividing the annual rates reported in Table 3–6 by 12. The incentive cost (20 percent of gross trading return) is conditionally applied only when gross trading returns before incentive costs are greater than zero.

The second step is the calculation of net commodity pool returns based on the lower institutional costs. This return is calculated as follows:

$$NICP_t = GPCP_t - CCICP_t - MMICP_t + TB_t \text{ if } GPCP_t \leq 0 \quad (6a)$$

$$NICP_t = GPCP_t(1 - (IICP_t/100)) - CCICP_t - MMICP_t + TB_t \text{ if } GPCP_t > 0 \quad (6b)$$

where

$NICP_t$ = net return of the market portfolio of institutional pools (percentage of equity per month),

$GPCP_t$ = gross trading return of the market portfolio of public pools (percentage of equity per month),

TB_t = Treasury bill return (percentage per month),

$CCICP_t$ = institutional pool commission cost (percentage of equity per month),

$MMICP_t$ = institutional pool management (percentage of equity per month),

$IICP_t$ = institutional pool incentive cost (percentage of gross trading returns).

Again, fixed values for commission, management, and incentive costs are assumed (second row, Table 3–6). Monthly commission (0.167 percent per month) and management (0.208 percent per month) rates are calculated by dividing the annual rates by 12. The incentive cost (25 percent of gross trading return) is conditionally applied only when gross trading returns exceed zero.

To illustrate the generation of the institutional commodity pool returns, assume a net public commodity pool return and Treasury bill return of 1.0 and 0.5 percent, respectively, for month t. Then, the gross trading return to public pools is calculated as

$$GPCP_t = (1.000 - 0.500 + 0.775 + 0.417)/(1 - (20/100)$$
$$= 2.115\%$$

and the net institutional commodity pool return is

$$NICP_t = 2.115(1 - (25/100)) - 0.167 - 0.208 + 0.5$$
$$= 1.711\%$$

Finally, note that the calculation of incentive costs is a simplification of the actual calculation used by public commodity pools. Incentive fees for a given month actually are paid only on net new profits. The following example illustrates this calculation. First, assume the following sequence of net asset values for a pool: 100 at the end of January, 75 at the end of February, and 125 at the end of March. In this case, the trading advisor will be paid an incentive fee in March based only on the $25 gain above the previous high net asset value of $100.

Pro forma returns also are calculated assuming incentive fees are paid only on net new profits. Average returns change only slightly and portfolio break-even results are unaffected. Hence, the results of the simpler procedure are presented in the article. Results of the alternative simulation are available from the authors upon request.

BIBLIOGRAPHY

Angrist, W.W. "The Big Money Gives Futures a Whirl," *The Wall Street Journal,* May 11, 1992, p. C1.

Basso, T.F. "A Review of Public and Private Futures Funds—1988," Working Paper, Trendstat Capital Management, St. Louis, 1989.

Brorsen, B.W., and Irwin, S.H. "Examination of Commodity Fund Performance," *Review of Research in Futures Markets,* no. 4, 1985, pp. 84–94.

Brorsen, B.W., and Irwin, S.H. (1987): "Futures Funds and Price Volatility," *Review of Futures Markets,* no. 6, 1987, pp. 119–135.

Chowdhury, A.D. "Futures Market Efficiency: Evidence from Cointegration Tests," *The Journal of Futures Markets,* no. 11, 1991, pp. 577–590.

Commodity Futures Trading Commission, Division of Economic Analysis. "Survey of Pool Operators in Futures Markets with an Analysis of Interday Position Changes," Washington, DC, 1991.

Cornew, R.W. "Commodity Pool Operators and Their Pools: Expenses and Profitability," *The Journal of Futures Markets,* no. 5, 1988, pp. 617–637.

Edwards, F.R., and Ma, C. (1988): "Commodity Pool Performance: Is the Information Contained in Pool Prospectuses Useful?" *The Journal of Futures Markets,* no. 8, 1988, pp. 589–616.

Elton, E.J.; Gruber, M.J.; and Rentzler, J.C. "Professionally Managed, Publicly Traded Commodity Funds," *Journal of Business,* no. 60, 1987, pp. 175–199.

Elton, E.J.; Gruber, M.J.; and Rentzler, J.C. "The Performance of Publicly Offered Commodity Funds," *Financial Analysts Journal,* no. 46, 1990, pp. 23–30.

Fama, E.F. "Efficient Capital Markets: A Review of Theory and Empirical Work," *Journal of Finance,* no. 25, 1970, pp. 383–417.

Grossman, S.J. "A Note on Elton, Gruber, and Rentzler's: "Professionally Managed, Publicly Traded Commodity Funds," Working Paper, Department of Economics, Princeton University, 1987.

Grossman, S.J., and Stiglitz, J.E. "On the Impossibility of Informationally Efficient Markets," *American Economic Review,* no. 60, 1980, pp. 393–408.

CHAPTER 4

MANAGEMENT SUMMARY

Title: "Managed Futures and Hedge Fund Investment for Downside Equity Risk Management" (1996)

Publication: *Derivatives Quarterly* 3, no. 1 (1996), pp. 62–72.

Authors: Thomas Schneeweis, University of Massachusetts
              Richard Spurgin, Clark University
              Mark Potter, University of Massachusetts

Data: Monthly return data for individual CTAs, the S&P 500, the Fidelity Magellan mutual fund, the Morgan Stanley Capital International equity index, and the Hedge Fund Research short-sellers index from 1985-1995.

Synopsis: The study showed that, for the period studied, a portfolio of equal investment in a managed futures index and the S&P 500 outperformed a protective put strategy consisting of the S&P 500 index plus a simulated at-the-money put. These results indicate that managed futures may offer some of the hedging properties of a put option at a lower cost.

              Similar tests were conducted for managed futures and hedge funds that specialize in equity futures and/or short selling. Results indicate similar downside risk protection—however, at the cost of upside returns.

Managed Futures and Hedge Fund Investment for Downside Equity Risk Management

Thomas Schneeweis
Professor of Finance, CISDM, University of Massachusetts

Richard Spurgin
Assistant Professor of Finance, Clark University

Mark Potter
Ph.D Student, SOM, University of Massachusetts

INTRODUCTION

During the past decades, the investment management industry has undergone numerous changes. New forms of investment products have come into existence to meet the needs of changing financial regulation, information technology, and investor demands. Today, most investors concentrate on traditional investment vehicles such as stocks, bonds, and currencies. However, an increasing number of investors use managed futures[1] investment vehicles such as direct investment with commodity trading advisors (CTAs), or purchase of commodity funds and pools[2] and hedge funds. Commodity trading advisors use global futures and options markets as their investment universe. Hedge funds trade in these markets as well as the underlying security and physical commodity markets.

Although academic and practitioner literature has shown that investment in managed futures/hedge funds offers investment benefits (e.g., increased Sharpe ratio), both as stand-alone investments and as additions to existing traditional assets or asset portfolios, managed futures and hedge funds investment may also offer unique risk and return opportunities in "downside" risk control.[3] Specifically, in contrast to passive equity index investment, the differing managed futures/hedge fund investment styles enable investors to create managed futures/hedge fund and equity portfolios that offer positive returns in upside equity market cycles while offering positive returns or limiting losses in downside equity markets. Results presented in this chapter indicate that, while managed futures returns are uncorrelated with the equity market on an overall basis, they are negatively correlated when the stock market posts their largest declines and positively correlated when equities have their largest gains. Since this pattern is similar to the payoff of many equity risk management strategies, the return of a mixed equity and managed futures portfolio is compared to a traditional protective put equity strategy. Results show that, for the period studied, an equity/CTA portfolio outperforms an equity/at-the-money put portfolio, such that a CTA investment may offer downside equity protection at lower cost than a protective put.[4]

ECONOMIC BASIS FOR MANAGED FUTURES RETURNS

Although futures and options markets provide economic benefits to the underlying users of their markets, traders in futures and options markets are often viewed as operating in a zero sum game; that is, where investor losses equal investor gains on any given day and the long-term return to a managed futures position is simply the risk-free return on invested capital. However, the existence of a zero sum game does not restrict commodity trading advisors from obtaining superior risk and return trade-offs relative to the assets underlying the traded futures and options markets. First, cost of carry and put/call parity models ensure that CTAs can create futures and options positions similar if not identical to investment positions in the deliverable cash instruments. Given the lower transaction costs of trading in futures and options markets, these 'synthetic' cash position returns may be superior to the returns of underlying cash markets for comparable long (short) positions. Secondly, institutional characteristics and differential carry costs among investors may permit CTAs to take advantage of short-term pricing differences between theoretically identical futures, options, and cash market positions. Thus, for CTAs, in contrast to a large number of traditional security traders, opportunities exist for arbitrage profits to be made under varying market conditions.

Arbitrage profits and risk/return positions that replicate the underlying cash markets, however, are not the only potential benefits of managed futures. Market participants using futures and options to hedge underlying equity positions may create excess demand for long or short derivatives positions. This hedging demand may create investment situations where hedgers are required to offer speculators a "risk" premium for holding open long(short) positions even in a world of arbitrage traders. This positive return to holding open futures positions that are opposite those of the desired hedgers may produce positive rates of return in the underlying futures and options markets. This return to traders for offering liquidity to hedgers desiring to limit losses may exist not only in futures markets but in a wide range of derivative products. Lastly, evidence exists in academic literature [Chan et al. (1995); Jagadeesh (1990)] that due to institutional factors (e.g., end-of-month window dressing, portfolio rebalancing, specialist risk positions, government actions), markets may trend for varying time periods in various markets. Low transaction costs combined with the ability to go short may permit the use of technical trading rules by managed futures to obtain positive returns in markets which, for short time periods, may be overvalued. In fact, these market cycles, embedded in cash market trading styles, have been used to explain some portion of the return to a technically based commodity futures trading system (BARRA/MLM reports).

PATTERN OF MANAGED FUTURES RETURNS

Academic and practitioner literature [Schneeweis (1996)] has shown that investment in managed futures may offer investment benefits both as stand-alone investments and as additions to existing traditional assets or asset portfolios. Traditional analysis of managed futures performance, however, is concentrated in comparing managed futures in terms of return and standard deviation,[5] and measuring the risk/return contribution of managed futures indexes to a portfolio of traditional assets. Table 4–1 shows the relative performance of Managed Accounts Reports dollar-weighted CTA index, the S&P 500, the Morgan Stanley Capital International equity index (MSCI), and the Fidelity Magellan fund for the period 1985–1995. Managed futures, represented by a dollar-weighted portfolio of commodity trading advisors compiled by Managed Accounts Reports (MAR$CTA index), has a stand-alone performance similar to that of traditional equity investment vehicles (S&P 500, MSCI, and the Fidelity Magellan fund) while having less negative minimum and higher maximum returns. For the period 1985–1995 MAR$CTA had an annualized Sharpe ratio of 1.08 while the Sharpe ratios for the S&P 500, MSCI, and Magellan fund were 1.00, 1.00, and 1.04, respectively. The minimum (maximum) monthly return for the MAR$CTA was –6.37 percent (17.83

TABLE 4-1

Performance Measures for Managed Futures and Other
U.S. Assets, January 1985 to December 1995

1/85 to 12/95	MAR$CTA	S&P 500	MSCI	Fidelity Magellan
Average annual return	15.81	15.11	14.86	17.96
Annual standard deviation	14.58	15.06	14.85	17.20
Sharpe ratio	1.08	1.00	1.00	1.04
Minimum monthly return	−6.37	−24.31	−18.59	−29.85
Maximum monthly return	17.83	12.66	11.13	12.22
Correlation with MAR	1.00	0.12	0.08	0.10
Excess annual break-even	0.00	8.79	9.14	8.75

percent) while the minimum (maximum) returns were more negative and less positive for the S&P 500 (−24.31 percent and 12.66 percent), the MSCI (−18.59 percent and 11.13 percent), and Magellan fund (−29.85 percent and 12.22 percent).

In addition, using traditional excess break-even analysis, results in Table 4–1 also show that the MAR$CTA increases the Sharpe ratio of comparison stand-alone investments when considered as an addition to existing equity portfolios.[6] In all cases, the excess annualized break-even rate was greater than 8 percent. This is greater than the cost generally charged by portfolio managers for creating a multiadvisor CTA portfolio (i.e., 1-2 percent). As mentioned previously, a reason for the diversification benefits of managed futures is the low correlation of managed futures products with many traditional asset vehicles. This is also supported in Table 4–1, where the correlation of MAR$CTA with the comparison assets is approximately zero (S&P 500 (.12), MSCI (.08), and Magellan fund (.10)). This low correlation is due in part to the diversity of markets that managed futures can trade as well as the variety of trades available (e.g., both long and short futures, calls and puts). The wide variety of markets and styles is indicated by the number of indexes compiled by Managed Accounts Reports (MAR). MAR classifies CTAs into a number of different subclasses. These groups are currency, energy, financial, diversified, stock, and trend-following. For hedge funds, firms such as Managed Accounts Reports and Hedge Fund Advisors also produce performance indexes for hedge funds specializing in financial, diversified, discretionary, and short-selling investments or trading styles.[7]

COMMODITY TRADING ADVISORS AS DOWNSIDE RISK PROTECTION

Although the correlation between managed account performance and traditional asset classes is low when measured over entire periods, the greatest investor benefit to managed account investment may be their ability in unique investment periods to offer positive returns when the underlying cash markets experience negative returns. In Table 4–2, for instance, results for the period 1985-1995 show that the MAR$CTA index outperformed the S&P 500 index in each of the 12 worst S&P 500 return months.[8] Moreover, the negative correlation (-.12) in Group 1, which contains the 12 lowest equity return months, indicates that lower returns in this group for the S&P 500 are offset by higher returns for the MAR$CTA index. In contrast, the positive correlation (.46) in Group 11, the highest 12 return months, means the higher the S&P 500 return in the group, the higher the MAR$CTA index return. This result, which covers the period 1985-1995, indicates that a diversified portfolio of managed futures traders who trade over a large range of alternative styles and products may provide potential for downside risk protection for equity products such as the S&P 500 while offering upside potential in months with high S&P 500 returns.[9] Results in Table 4–2 also indicate that managed futures provide returns similar to those obtained through traditional downside risk protection strategies such as purchasing put options. Specifically, the performance of a combination S&P 500 (50 percent) and MAR$CTA (50 percent) portfolio is similar to that of an S&P 500 at-the-money protective put strategy. For the protective put strategy, an at-the-money put value was derived with a rolling 35-day maturity using implied volatility estimates from Salomon Brothers. The pricing model used is the Black-Scholes dividend-adjusted option pricing model.[10]

Results in Table 4–2 show the number and percentage of months in each group that the MAR$CTA (MAR), the S&P 500 plus MAR$CTA portfolio (SP/MAR), and the protective put strategy (SP/Put) outperform the S&P 500 index. As expected, the SP/Put portfolio strictly dominates the S&P 500 in the lowest return group while it fails to outperform in any months in the high return group. Similarly, the SP/MAR portfolio dominates the S&P 500 in the lowest S&P 500 return group and, in contrast to the SP/Put portfolio, also provides higher returns than the S&P 500 in some of the months when S&P 500 posts its highest returns. Thus the SP/MAR portfolio may provide both downside protection as well as upside return potential during periods in which the S&P 500 performs well. Of special note is that the SP/MAR portfolio strictly dominates the

TABLE 4-2

Performance of Managed Futures Relative to Protective Put Strategy

	Portfolio Performance by Group				Relative Portfolio Performance by Group							
					MAR> S&P 500		SP/MAR>SP Put		SP/Put>SP		SP/MAR>SP50	
Group	S&P 500	MAR	SP/MAR	SP/Put	Months	%	Months	%	Months	%	Months	%
1	-7.46	2.57	-2.45	-2.23	12	100%	8	67%	12	100%	12	100%
2	-2.57	-0.40	-1.49	-1.62	8	67	7	58	11	92	8	67
3	-1.20	0.70	-0.25	-1.71	9	75	10	83	4	33	9	75
4	-0.10	1.04	0.47	-1.64	7	58	11	92	0	0	7	58
5	0.91	1.31	1.11	-1.23	7	58	12	100	0	0	7	58
6	1.58	0.01	0.79	-0.25	4	33	9	75	0	0	4	33
7	2.37	0.66	1.52	0.52	3	25	9	75	0	0	3	25
8	3.16	0.31	1.74	1.38	1	8	6	50	0	0	1	8
9	4.04	1.33	2.69	1.85	3	25	8	67	0	0	3	25
10	5.00	2.39	3.69	2.78	3	25	7	58	0	0	3	25
11	8.11	4.58	6.34	5.64	1	8	9	75	0	0	1	8

Correlation between S&P 500 and MAR

Group 1   -0.12
Group 11   0.46

Group: Group of 12 months ranked by S&P 500 Return. Group 1 contains lowest returns, Group 11 the highest
S&P 500: Standard and Poor's 500 Total Return Index
MAR: MAR Dollar-Weighted CTA Index
SP/Put: S&P 500 Index combined with 1-month at-the money put option on index.
SP/MAR: Portfolio with equal weights in S&P 500 and MAR

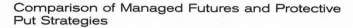

FIGURE 4–1

Comparison of Managed Futures and Protective Put Strategies

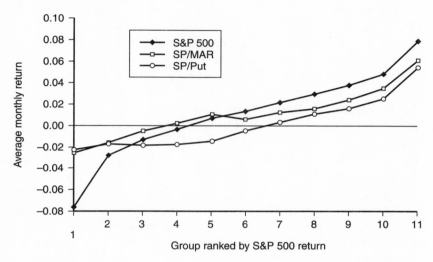

SP/Put portfolio in group 5 for which the return for the S&P 500 reflects its average monthly return. If, as reported in Table 4–1, the mean return of the S&P 500 is similar to the mean return of the MAR$CTA index, then a portfolio composed of the S&P 500 and the MAR$CTA will have a similar return to an all-equity portfolio. Moreover, this portfolio will always dominate a SP/Put portfolio, whose expected return is about half the expected return of the S&P 500 (because the put delta of –½ means the instantaneous rate of return of the portfolio is ½ the return of the underlying security). For the entire period, the Sharpe ratio of the SP/MAR strategy was the highest (1.39) of any of the comparison benchmarks (S&P 500, 1.00; MAR$CTA, 1.08; SP/Put, .47).[11]

The pattern of relative return dominance is shown in Figure 4–1. After ranking on S&P 500 returns in ascending order and separating the data into eleven 12-month periods, average returns in each group for the S&P 500, the MAR$CTA, the SP/Put and the SP/MAR portfolio are illustrated. For the period 1985-1995, the SP/MAR portfolio dominates the returns the SP/Put strategy except marginally for the lowest return group. It is, of course, important to point out that the performances of the equity/protective put position and the equity/managed futures position are not strictly comparable since the performance of the managed futures position is stochastic. That is, the return from holding the SP/Put strategy is known for a given S&P 500 return level (the put is either exercised if it is in the money, or not). However, basis risk exists for the equity/managed futures position to the extent that there is a positive variance around its return level. The individual investor must determine whether the potential relative return compensates for the expected risk.

The recent performance for the period 1994-1995 is also consistent with performance over the longer 1985-1995 period. For the period 1994-1995, tests similar to those presented in Table 4–2 are conducted for MAR$CTA. In Table 4–3, S&P 500 returns are ranked from low to high and divided into four 6-month subperiods.

The number of months in which the MAR$CTA provides returns superior to the comparative asset or portfolio is given. As in Table 4–2, in the low S&P 500 return group the CTA and hedge fund vehicles outperformed the S&P 500 at least 50 percent of the time. In contrast to Table 4–2, however, for the high return groups, the MAR$CTA had negative average returns and rarely outperformed the S&P 500. One reason for this differential performance is that over the 1994-1995 period the S&P 500 performed exceptionally well. For instance, in 1995 the annual return of the S&P 500 was 37.11 percent in contrast to its average annualized return from 1985 through 1995 of only 15 percent. In contrast the 1995 annual return for the MAR$CTA was 16 percent, which is in line with its annual average since 1985 (15.5 percent).

EQUITY-BASED COMMODITY TRADING ADVISORS/HEDGE FUNDS AS DOWNSIDE RISK PROTECTION

The MAR$CTA index reflects the returns of numerous CTAs whose trading area (e.g., metals, commodities) does not correspond directly to the comparison equity benchmarks. For the period 1994-1995, tests similar to those presented in Table 4–3 for the MAR$CTA index are conducted for the MAR stock index trading advisors (MARSTK) index and the Hedge Fund Research Short-Sellers index (HFRSTK). In Table 4–3, S&P 500 returns are ranked from low to high and divided into four 6-month subperiods. The number of months in which the MARSTK (Table 4–3B) and HFRSTK (Table 4–3C) provide returns superior to the comparative index or portfolio is given.

TABLE 4-3A

Performance of Managed Futures Relative to Protective Put Strategy, 1994-1995

Portfolio Performance by Group

Group	S&P 500	MAR	SP/MAR	SP/Put
1	-2.72	1.25	-0.73	-1.23
2	1.45	0.95	1.20	-0.26
3	2.92	0.34	1.63	1.37
4	3.88	-0.35	1.76	2.46

Relative Portfolio Performance by Group

	MAR> S&P 500 Months	%	SP/MAR>SP Put Months	%	SP/Put>SP Months	%	SP/MAR>SP50 Months	%
1	6	100%	5	83%	5	83%	6	100%
2	3	52	6	100	0	0	3	50
3	1	14	2	33	0	0	1	17
4	1	17	2	33	0	0	1	17

Correlation between SP500 and MAR

Group 1   -0.14
Group 4   -0.08

TABLE 4–3B

Performance of MAR Stock Subindex Relative to Protective Put Strategy, 1994-1995

Portfolio Performance by Group

Group	S&P 500	MSTK	SP/MSK	SP/Put
1	-2.72	4.19	0.73	-1.23
2	1.45	1.32	1.39	-0.26
3	2.92	-2.81	0.06	1.37
4	3.88	-3.62	0.13	2.46

Correlation between S&P 500 and MSTK

Group 1	-0.68
Group 4	-0.05

Relative Portfolio Performance by Group

	MSTK> S&P 500 Months	%	SP/MSK<SP Put Months	%	SP/Put>SP Months	%	SP/MSK>SP50 Months	%
	6	100%	6	100%	5	83%	6	100%
	4	67	6	100	0	0	4	67
	0	0	1	17	0	0	0	0
	0	0	1	17	0	0	0	0

TABLE 4-3C

Performance of HFR Short Sellers Index and Protective Put Strategy, 1994-1995

Portfolio Performance by Group

Group	S&P 500	HDG	SP/MHDG	SP/Put
1	-2.72	6.58	1.93	-1.23
2	1.45	1.67	1.56	-0.26
3	2.92	-5.66	-1.37	1.37
4	3.88	-4.43	-0.27	2.46

Correlation between S&P 500 and HDG

Group 1	-0.40
Group 4	0.19

Relative Portfolio Performance by Group

	HDG> S&P 500		SP/HDG>SP Put		SP/Put>SP		SP/HDG>SP50	
	Months	%	Months	%	Months	%	Months	%
	5	83%	5	83%	5	83%	5	83%
	4	67	5	83	0	0	4	67
	1	17	1	17	0	0	1	17
	0	0	0	0	0	0	0	0

Group: Group of 6 mos. ranked by S&P 500 Return. Group 1 contains lowest return, Group 4 the highest

S&P 500: Standard and Poor's 500 Total Return

MAR: MAR Dollar-Weighted CTA Index

STK: MAR Hedge Fund Short-Sellers Index

HDG: Hedge Fund Research (HFR) Short-Sellers Index

SP/Put: S&P 500 Index combined with 1-month at-the money put option on the index

SP/(MAR/STK/HDG): Portfolio with equal weights in S&P 500 and comparison index

Consistent with the MAR$CTA index in Table 4–3, both the MARSTK and HFRSTK have negative Pearson correlations with the S&P 500 in the low return groups (MAR$CTA, –.14; MARSTK, –.68; HFRSTK, –.40). In the S&P 500 high return months there is little evidence of correlation with the S&P 500 for any of the comparison CTA or hedge fund indexes (MAR$CTA, –.08; MARSTK, –.05; HFRSTK, .19). However, the two largest negative correlations (MARSTK and HFRSTK) are observed in the CTA and hedge fund indexes with investment styles that are expected to provide returns based on equity performance. This is expected, since the MARSTK and HFRSTK represent traders who specialize in taking positions in corresponding equity markets while the MAR$CTA index is a broad index of all CTAs. Table 4–3 also provides a comparison of equity CTA and hedge funds with the MAR$CTA as alternatives to a protective equity put strategy. The relative performance of a 50 percent investment in the S&P 500 and 50 percent investment in each of MAR$CTA, MARSTK, and HFRSTK is contrasted with the return to an at-the-money protective put strategy. Average returns to the SP/MAR portfolio exceed the SP/Put portfolio in three of the four periods, while the SP/MARSTK and SP/HFRSTK outperform this portfolio in only the two worst groups.

In Figures 4–2A—2C, the performance of the S&P 500, SP/Put, and combined SP/(managed futures or hedge fund) indexes is plotted. Total return is not calculated sequentially, but in order of lowest to highest S&P 500 return. As returns for the S&P 500 grow increasingly positive, the returns on MARSTK and HFRSTK grow increasingly negative. In contrast, as the returns for the S&P 500 grow increasingly positive, the returns on the MAR$CTA also experience positive returns such that when S&P 500 has its highest return, the final return of SP/MAR exceeds that of the SP/Put.

MANAGER SELECTION

Empirical results for the 11-year period studied support the use of managed futures, as represented by the MAR$CTA, as a means of controlling downside equity risk while offering reasonable return potential in equity markets experiencing positive returns. Results for the most recent 2-year period indicate that while various CTA and hedge fund products offered protection against equity losses, they often failed to offer comparable returns during stock market rallies. The fact that S&P 500 performance was abnormally high during this period clearly contributed to the poor

FIGURE 4-2A

Total Return of SP/MAR Portfolio and Protective Put
Strategies, 1994–1995

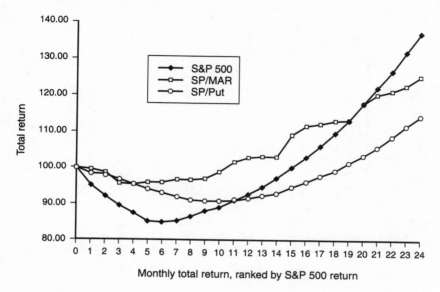

Monthly total return, ranked by S&P 500 return

FIGURE 4-2B

Total Return of MAR Stock Subindex and Protective Put
Strategies, 1994–1995

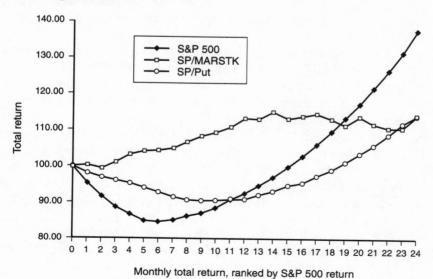

Monthly total return, ranked by S&P 500 return

FIGURE 4–2C

Total Return of HFR Short-Sellers Index and Protective Put
Strategies, 1994–1995

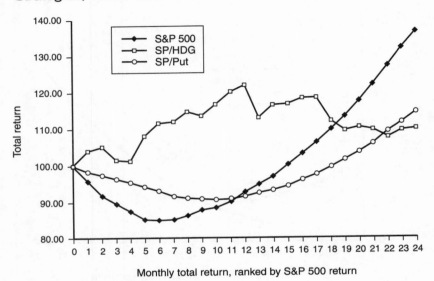

Monthly total return, ranked by S&P 500 return

performance of CTAs and hedge funds that specialize in equity short sales
(MARSTK and HFRSKT). However, not all of these funds performed
poorly. For instance, many managers of short-selling hedge funds posted
positive or small negative returns despite the performance of the equity
market in the past two years.

Table 4–4 reports the performance of MAR hedge fund short-sellers
divided into the high quartile (HFHQ), median (HFMED), and bottom
quartile (HFBQ) index performance for the 20 months beginning June
1994 and ending December 1995. Results indicate that during the 10 worst
months for the S&P 500 months there is a negative correlation between
hedge fund returns and S&P 500 returns (HFHQ, -.60; HFMED, -.46;
HFBQ, -.47) and there is a positive correlation for the 10 best months
(HFHQ, .12; HFMED, .04; HFBQ, .11).

In contrast to the HFRSTK results in Table 4–3, as shown in Table
4–4, the returns to high quartile hedge funds dominate the S&P 500 index
in both high and low return months. However, the HFMED outperforms
the S&P 500 only for the 10 months with the lowest S&P 500 returns. The
HFBQ underperforms the S&P 500 in both up and down markets. Thus as

TABLE 4-4

Performance of High Quartile, Median, Bottom Quartile Short-Selling Hedge Funds, June 1994–December 1995

Portfolio Performance by Group

Group	S&P 500	HQ	Med	BQ
1	0.08	7.40	0.34	-6.03
2	3.57	7.77	0.01	-0.196

S&P 500 Correlation	HQ	Med	BQ
Group 1	-0.60	-0.46	-0.47
Group 2	0.12	0.04	0.11

Relative Portfolio Performance by Group

HQ> S&P 500 Months	%	Med>S&P 500 Months	%	BQ> S&P 500 Months	%
9	90%	5	50%	1	10%
6	60	0	0	0	0

Group: Group of 10 mos. ranked by S&P 500 Return. Group 1 contains lowest returns, Group 2 the highest

S&P 500: Standard and Poor's 500 Total Return Index.

HQ: Average of top quartile of short-selling hedge funds reported by MAR

Med: Performance of the median short-selling hedge fund reported by MAR

BQ: Average of bottom quartile of short-selling hedge funds reported by MAR for many other alternative investment choices such as mutual funds, the ability to obtain superior risk/return trade-offs over all investment scenarios may be manager dependent.

CONCLUSIONS

Correlation tests comparing managed futures indices with traditional assets reveal an interesting property of the relationship between managed account returns and returns to traditional asset classes such as the S&P 500. Overall, the correlation between managed asset returns and the S&P 500 is approximately zero. However, when the data are segmented according to whether the stock market rose or fell, results indicate that managed futures and hedge funds were negatively correlated when the S&P 500 posted significant negative returns and were positively correlated when the S&P 500 reported significant positive returns. Thus managed futures may offer unique asset allocation properties.

Results also show that managed futures offer risk/return benefits when compared to a partially hedged position in the stock market. For instance, it is shown that an equal-weighted investment in the MAR$CTA index and the S&P 500 outperformed investment in the S&P 500 plus a simulated at-the-money put under most market conditions. These results indicate that managed futures may offer some of the hedging properties of a put option at a lower cost. However, analysis of recent data on short-selling hedge funds indicates that, for that asset category, earning positive returns in upmarkets requires the ability to select superior managers, and that the typical manager produces zero returns in this environment.

ENDNOTES

1. The term "managed futures" generally refers to investment vehicles based on returns due to direct investment in commodity trading advisors and/or commodity funds/pools. However, hedge funds are also often included under the term.
2. On a relative basis, the performance of lower-cost direct investment in CTA products generally outperform the higher cost retail managed futures products such as commodity pools and funds. For studies analyzing the benefits of these products, see Chance (1994) and Schneeweis (1996).
3. Books that include information on the history of managed futures and hedge funds include Chandler (1994), Lederman and Klein (1995), and Fox-Andrews and Meaden (1995). Books that include discussions on the

history of futures and options markets and the economic benefits of derivative products include Peck (1985, Vols. 1-5).

4. It is of course important to point out that the performances of the equity/protective put position and the equity/managed futures position are not strictly comparable since the performance of the managed futures position is stochastic. The individual investor must determine whether the potential relative return compensates for the expected risk.

5. The use of the Sharpe ratio as a measure of relative performance may be suboptimal to other measures of relative performance, such as semivariance, for investment strategies that are designed to truncate returns below a specified threshold level. Although this study does not test for performance using alternative 'semivariance' performance measures, it should be noted that using mean-variance analysis to evaluate investment portfolios with skewed return distributions can lead to suboptimal portfolios [Bookstaber and Clarke (1985); Marmer and Ng (1993)].

6. As in previous analyses [Elton, Gruber, and Rentzler (1987, 1990), Irwin, Krukemyer, and Zulauf (1992), Schneeweis, Savanayana, and McCarthy (1992)], excess break-even analysis is used to test for the contribution of CTAs to the risk/return profile of stocks, bonds, and other asset classes such as real estate. As in earlier studies, the excess break-even rate of return necessary for a security to enter a portfolio is computed as follows: $EBV=$

   $R_c - \left[\dfrac{R_p - R_f}{\sigma_p} \rho_{cp} \sigma_c + R_f \right]$, where R_c = Return for CTA; R_f = Riskless rate of

   return; R_p = Rate of return on index p; ρ_{cp} = Correlation coefficient between CTA c and index p; σ_c = Standard deviation of CTA c; σ_c = Standard deviation of index p.

7. For a complete discussion of Managed Accounts Reports CTA and Hedge Fund indexes, call MAR on the World Wide Web. For instance, the MAR Hedge Fund short-sellers indexes track hedge fund managers who take positions that stock prices will go down. A hedge fund borrows stock and sells it, hoping to buy it back at a lower price. A hedge is for long-only portfolios and those who feel market is approaching a bearish trend. Similarly, the Hedge Fund Research indexes for short-sellers simply defines the index and managers who go short securities.

8. Other studies analyzing the downside risk potential of managed futures include Peters (1992) and Schneeweis (1996). Peters (1992) argues that portfolio diversification with managed futures provides partial stochastic dominance in the lower return ranges and produces long-term effects similar to insurance; that is, reduction to upside performance (cost) with protection in down markets. As the use of alternative risk measures capturing semivariance gain popularity, these benefits of managed futures may become more apparent.

9. Similar tests were conducted for world, regional, and country-specific equity and bond markets, as well as various portfolios of these assets, including
   and excluding commodities. Results are similar to those presented here
   [See Schneeweis (1996)].
10. For individual managers, results may differ from indexes used. For a study
    on the stability of CTA equity managers, see Potter and Schneeweis
    (1996).
11. For a parallel discussion on the benefits of managed futures as portfolio
    insurance, see Peters (1992). Preliminary results indicate that a greater pos-
    itive correlation exists between the performance of the CTA equity traders
    and a straddle position than between CTA equity traders and the S&P 500.
    This is consistent with CTA equity traders who take short positions in down
    markets and long positions in up markets [Schneeweis and Spurgin (1995)]

REFERENCES

Bookstaber, R. and R. Clarke. "Problems in Evaluating the Performance of
Portfolios with Options." *Financial Analyst Journal*, January/February 1985, pp.
48–62.

Chan, A.; N. Jagadeesh; and J. Lakonishok. "Momentum Strategies," *NBER
Working Paper #5375,* 1995.

Chance, Don. *Managed Futures and Their Role in Investment Portfolios.*
Charlottesville: AIMR, 1994.

Chandler, B. *Managed Futures: An Investor's Guide.* New York: John Wiley &
Sons, 1994.

Elton, Edwin J.; Martin J. Gruber; and Joel C. Rentzler. "The Performance of
Publicly Offered Commodity Funds," *Financial Analysts Journal*, July-August
1990, pp. 23–30.

"———. Professionally Managed, Publicly Traded Commodity Funds," *Journal
of Business* 60, no. 2, 1987, pp. 175–200.

Fox-Andrews, M. and Nicola Meaden. *Derivative Markets and Investment
Management.* Hertfordshire, G.B.: Prentice Hall, 1995.

Irwin, Scott H.; Terry Krukemyer; and Carl R. Zulauf. "The Investment
Performance of Public Commodity Pools over 1979-1989," *Journal of Futures
Markets*, October 1993, pp. 799–820.

Irwin, Scott H. and Diego Landa. "Real Estate, Futures, and Gold as Portfolio
Assets," *Journal of Portfolio Management*, Fall 1987, pp. 29–34.

Jagadeesh, N. "Evidence of Predictable Behavior of Security Returns," *Journal
of Finance*, 1990(3), 881–98.

Lederman J. and Robert Klein, eds. *Hedge Funds.* N.Y.: Irwin, 1995.

Lewis, A. "Semivariance and the Performance of Portfolios with Options," *Financial Analyst Journal*, July-August 1990, pp. 67–76.

Marmer, H.S. and F.K. Ng, "Mean-Semivariance Analysis of Option-Based Strategies: A Total Mix Perspective," *Financial Analyst Journal*, May-June 1993, pp. 47–54.

Peck, A.E., ed., *Selected Writings on Futures Markets*. Vol. 1-5, Chicago Board of Trade., 1985.

Peters, C.C., ed. *Managed Futures: Performance Evaluation and Analysis of Commodity Funds, Pools and Accounts*. Chicago: Probus Publishing, 1992.

Potter, M., and T. Schneeweis. "Equity CTAs as Asset Allocators." *Working paper,* Center for International Securities and Derivative Markets, University of Massachusetts, June 1996.

Schneeweis, T., "The Benefits of Managed Futures," *Technical Report of the European Managed Futures Association* (forthcoming).

Schneeweis, T.; U. Savanayana; and D. McCarthy. "Alternative Commodity Trading Vehicles: A Performance Analysis." *Journal of Futures Markets,* August 1991, pp. 475–90.

Schneeweis, T.; U. Savanayana; and D. McCarthy. "Multi-Manager Commodity Portfolios: A Risk/Return Analysis;" In C. Epstein, ed., *Managed Futures*. New York: Wiley, 1992, pp. 81–102.

Schneeweis, T. and R. Spurgin. "Comparisons of Benchmark Indices in Futures Markets." *Working paper, Center for International Securities and Derivative Markets, University of Massachusetts,* July 1995.

CHAPTER 5

MANAGEMENT SUMMARY

Title: "The Potential Role of Managed Commodity-Financial Futures Accounts (and/or Funds) in Portfolios of Stocks and Bonds"

Presentation: Annual Conference of the Financial Analysts Federation, May 1983.

Author: John Lintner, Harvard University

Data: Monthly prices and returns from 42 months, from July 1979 through December 1982, for 15 futures-account managers' composite performance, eight publicly offered commodity funds, averages of all stocks listed on the NYSE and American Stock Exchanges, the Salomon Brothers high-grade corporate bond index, U.S. Treasury bills, and the Consumer Price Index.

Synopsis: Managed futures returns from trading advisors and public funds were analyzed in comparison to stocks, bonds, and bills, both on an actual and real (adjusted for inflation) basis. Lintner found the ratio of return to risk (standard deviation) to be higher for a substantial fraction of trading advisors and public funds than for stock and bond portfolios. A portfolio of equally weighted managed accounts and equally weighted futures funds similarly outperformed stock and bond portfolios on a return/risk basis. Even stronger results were obtained by allocating funds selectively among different managers (or among different funds).

Lintner also found that portfolios of stocks and/or bonds combined with managed futures showed substantially less risk at every possible level of expected return than portfolios of stocks and/or bonds alone. These results are true for both inflation-adjusted and real rates of return.

The Potential Role of Managed Commodity-Financial Futures Accounts (and/or Funds) in Portfolios of Stocks and Bonds*

John Lintner

Diversification can substantially reduce the risks involved in portfolio returns and provide superior returns relative to the risks incurred. This basic insight was well understood by prudent and successful investment managers long before the advent of Markowitz and Modern Portfolio Theory. Investors, trust officers, and institutional portfolio managers for many decades have diversified their holdings of stocks across different companies and industry groups—and they have limited their maximum investment in any one company—in order to avoid having all their eggs in one basket, subject to all the risks of that one basket. They realized the very real possibility that unanticipated adverse developments could seriously reduce the returns on any one security below the return they anticipated. But they also recognized from experience that such adverse outcomes (relative to their expectations) on any particular stock would

*Paper presented at the Annual Conference of the Financial Analysts Federation, Royal York Hotel, Toronto, Canada, May 16, 1983. Shortly after this paper was presented Dr. Lintner died. When an author delivers a paper at a conference he normally reserves the right to revise the work after hearing the comments of his colleagues. His work is reproduced herein with the understanding that it may not have been Dr. Lintner's final word on the subject.

This paper has benefited from helpful discussions with Andre Perold and the use of his efficient programs for computing minimum variance portfolios. Patrick O'Connor and Ram Willner provided fine programming assistance.

probably have a much smaller (and possibly even no) effect on the returns on others. They also recognized that unanticipated adverse developments affecting some securities were likely to be offset by equally unanticipated good fortune and favorable surprises (relative to their expectations) on others. They allowed for the sea-tides that would raise or lower the returns on almost all their stocks in forming their judgments of the expected returns on the individual stocks in their portfolios. They then held diversified portfolios of stocks in order to use the law of averages and very substantially reduce the *net* impact on their *portfolio* returns of the unanticipated developments that would cause the returns actually realized on individual stocks to deviate (favorably or unfavorably) from their expectations.

On such intuitive and rather general grounds as these, most investment managers[1] have traditionally broadened the diversification of their portfolios by also including a substantial fraction of bonds, along with their stocks, in their overall investment position. While both bond and stock returns respond to changes in interest rates, they do so in different degrees, and stocks also respond to unanticipated changes in earnings and dividends that affect bond returns much less directly. Over the last decade or so, many major institutional investors have broadened the diversification of their portfolios still further by investing modest fractions of their assets in the direct ownership of real estate, and even in such other nontraditional outlets as diversified holdings of oil-well exploration pools and venture capital companies.

The managers of these large institutional investment portfolios must have diversified within their stock portfolios (and diversified further by adding bonds and some other types of investments) because they believed that the resulting broader portfolios would give them (on the basis of their own assessments and judgments) a *combination* of expected returns and overall risks that they preferred to any of the risk-return combinations available from any less diversified portfolios. Since these managers are all, as we say, risk-averse—they are always seeking higher returns, but avoid taking risks unless they think they are going to be adequately compensated for doing so—they must have believed that the resulting broader and more diversified portfolios would *either reduce* the overall risks involved in getting any given expected portfolio return, *or increase* the expected portfolio return attainable from bearing any given level of risk on their overall portfolio.[2] From either perspective, the diversification was undertaken in order to improve the trade-offs of the expected returns and the overall risks of their combined portfolios of risk assets. In modern terminology, the diversification was believed to shift the efficient frontier of portfolio returns and portfolio risks upward and/or to the left when returns are plotted vertically and risks horizontally.

Over the years, most investment managers have undoubtedly made all or most of their decisions on the appropriate allocation of the funds in their portfolios—and their decisions on whether to add a new security or a new class of investments to their portfolios—largely on the basis of their information and assessments of the prospects and risks of the particular securities or groups of assets, and their usually rather intuitive judgments regarding the benefits of more or less diversification (or different patterns of diversification) in their portfolios. The great contribution of Modern Portfolio Theory, based on Markowitz's pioneering work in the 1950s,[3] is not to displace the judgment and responsibility of the investment manager, but rather to provide a rigorous framework for determining what the best allocation of funds invested in individually risky assets will be *if* the responsible manager decides that he wants to allocate his funds on the basis of a *given* set of judgments and assessments.[4] It has provided valuable insights into what assessments need to be made, how they interact with each other, and the relative importance of the different characteristics of a security being considered for a portfolio. In particular, it has rigorously established that *every* risk-averse investor—regardless of the degree of his risk-aversion—should add at least some investment in a new security (or group of new securities) to whatever portfolio he already holds *if* doing so will improve the return-risk trade-off of that portfolio in the precise sense stated in the preceding paragraph.

This condition *will* be satisfied *if* (but *only if*[5]) a simple regression of the returns on the candidate security (or securities) against the returns on the existing portfolio shows a positive intercept or constant term—i.e., *if* it provides a higher risk-adjusted return than that provided by the existing portfolio. But while this condition is exact, it is not very informative regarding the particular characteristics of the candidate securities that will enable them to meet the test in any particular situation. A strictly equivalent but much more intuitively informative test is the following:[6]

> The risk and return characteristics of any given candidate security (or group of securities) will improve the risk-return trade-off provided by *any* existing portfolio *if* and *only* if the *ratio* of the expected rate of return of the candidate(s) divided by the standard deviation of their returns is larger than the *product* of (a) the corresponding ratio assessed for the existing portfolio with (b) the correlation between the returns on the candidate(s) and the returns on the existing portfolio.

Moreover, this test is still valid when the nominal returns or securities and portfolios are redefined as excess returns (over the short-term rates available each period) or as real returns (over inflation rates each period).

PURPOSE AND ORGANIZATION OF CHAPTER

The purpose of the present chapter is to explore whether investments in managed accounts of trading advisors in the commodity and financial futures markets, and/or publicly traded futures funds, have shown risk and return characteristics that would make them a desirable means of further diversification for portfolios of stock and bond investments. As previously explained, they will be desirable supplements to more conventional stock and bond portfolios *provided* they improve the reward-risk trade-offs for the overall portfolios by shifting the efficient frontier of portfolio returns and portfolio risks upward and/or to the left when returns are plotted vertically and risks horizontally. The body of the paper uses the rigorous but intuitively informative "reward/risk ratio" and "degree of intercorrelation" test described earlier. Since some investment managers are primarily concerned with nominal holding period returns as such—while others are more concerned with excess returns over short-term investment alternatives, and still others with real returns after allowing for inflation—all three measures of returns and risks will be examined.

To build up our analysis in an orderly progression from the raw data to our final conclusions, Section I will review the returns and the risk characteristics of the pooled accounts of leading trading advisors and of publicly offered funds, each manager or public fund considered separately. As a benchmark for our comparisons, the returns and risks of a well-diversified portfolio of common stocks and of a diversified portfolio of corporate bonds will be noted. Since many investors hold a basic portfolio invested roughly 60 percent in stocks and 40 percent in bonds, the returns and risks of a 60:40 stock-bond portfolio are also included. Section II analyzes the potential improvements in reward/risk ratios that have been available from holding diversified futures portfolios using a group of account managers or investing in several public funds. Section III then goes on to examine whether the addition of such a diversified sub-portfolio of investments with futures-account managers, or investments in futures funds, would have improved the risk/return performance of stock portfolios or the performance of combined stock and bond portfolios, using the tests previously described.

PREVIEW AND SUMMARY OF OUR FINDINGS AND CONCLUSIONS

As would have been expected, the managed futures accounts and futures funds are shown to be investments with high risks but also high expected returns. It turns out that the return/risk ratios of a substantial fraction of the futures-managers and funds are higher than those on diversified stock (or stock and bond) portfolios. Moreover, a considerably larger fraction have shown higher ratios when the comparison is made with excess returns or real returns.[7]

The return/risk ratio of a separate portfolio with equal dollar investments in the hands of each of the 15 futures-account managers in our sample (or equal dollars invested in each of the eight futures funds) would also have been substantially larger than that shown by a well-diversified portfolio of common stocks—and the ratio for portfolios of corporate stocks is in turn substantially larger than that for portfolios of corporate bonds.

Since several of these futures managers (or funds) have shown considerably higher return/risk ratios than this evenly spread composite of managers (or futures funds)—*and* since the intercorrelations between the return experience of these various "high ratio" managers or funds turn out to have been rather moderate—there are very large *additional* benefits obtainable by spreading the funds to be dedicated to futures investments selectively ("efficiently") among different managers (or diversifying selectively across different funds). This is shown by the impressive improvements in the return/risk ratios produced by this kind of optimizing and selective diversification. Equivalently, it is shown by the large reductions in the risks required to obtain any given expected rate of return on the funds invested in managed commodity-financial futures or in publicly offered funds.

Indeed, the improvements from holding efficiently selected portfolios of managed accounts or funds are so large—*and* the correlations between the returns on the futures-portfolios and those on the stock and bond portfolios are so surprisingly low (sometimes even negative)—that the return/risk trade-offs provided by *augmented portfolios,* consisting partly of funds invested with appropriate groups of futures managers (or funds) combined with funds invested in portfolios stocks alone (or in mixed portfolios of stocks and bonds), clearly dominate the trade-offs available from portfolios of stocks alone (or from portfolios of stocks and bonds). Moreover, they do so by very considerable margins.

The combined portfolios of stocks (or stocks and bonds) *after* including judicious investments in appropriately selected subportfolios of investments in managed futures accounts (or funds) show substantially less risk at every possible level of expected return than portfolios of stocks (or stocks and bonds) alone. This is the essence of the "potential role" of managed futures accounts (or funds) as a supplement to stock and bond portfolios suggested in the title of this chapter.

Finally, *all* the above conclusions continue to hold when returns are measured in real as well as in nominal terms, and *also* when returns are adjusted for the risk-free rate on Treasury bills.

THE DATA USED

Our statistical analysis is based on two sets of data. The *first* is a file of the monthly returns shown in the available composite account performance reports filed by 15 futures-accounts managers with the CFTC, and the S.E.C., covering the 42 months beginning with July 1979 and ending with December 1982. We had access to these reports as filed by 32 of the largest account managers, but several had only been in business for a short period of time and several of the others provided only quarterly data over all or substantial parts of their record. Because of the substantial volatility in these accounts and markets, we believed we should have access to at least 40 "data points" in order to get reasonably good measures of the stochastic characteristics of any manager's performance. We also believed it would be desirable to use the most recent period of sufficient length available, in part because of the difficult times many of the managers experienced in late 1979 and again in 1982. The 15 series used include all those for which we had data that meet these two conditions.

The monthly rate of return reported to the CFTC is the percentage of beginning equity represented by the sum of all profits or losses taken on all positions closed within the month, plus the net profit or loss on all positions open at the end of the month, and plus interest earned on all T-bills held in lieu of margin deposits and other income on short investments of investors' equity not actively committed to futures positions, *less* all brokerage commissions, operating expenses, and management fees and bonuses. This official calculation of the rate of return based on beginning equity will obviously overstate the true rate of profit (or loss) when net new funds have been added to the accounts during the month—and correspondingly understate the rate of profit (or loss) when funds on balance have been withdrawn from the accounts during the month. One of the managers in our sample only entered additions or withdrawals on the last day of each month, so no adjustment was required. The monthly rate of return for the other 14 managers was adjusted on the assumption that the net additions or withdrawals reported during the month were evenly spread over 22 trading days in the month.[8] Even though this adjusted figure is still only an approximation for individual months for particular managers,[9] this adjustment should provide quite accurate estimates of the means, standard deviations, and intercorrelations over the 42 monthly returns as a whole (which are the critical statistics in our analysis). All our work and tables reported below are based on these adjusted returns. [We did, however, recalculate the risk/reward ratios and correlations using the "raw" (unadjusted) monthly rate of return on the CFTC basis; all of our substantive conclusions are robust with or without this adjustment.]

The data for each of the 15 futures-account managers represent the *composite* performance on all their accounts as given in their performance reports required by the CFTC. There is scattered evidence that the performance of smaller accounts on average tends to be somewhat less favorable than that on larger accounts,[10] and readers can bear this in mind in interpreting the implications of our results for their individual situation.

The *second set of data* on managed futures accounts used in this study is a file of the monthly changes in the net asset value of eight publicly offered commodity funds over the same 42 months, July 1979 through December 1982. The data were compiled from public reports by Jay Klopfenstein of Norwood Securities in Chicago and Frank S. Pusatri in New York and reported in Managed Account Reports, Columbia, MD. The number of these publicly offered funds has been increasing rapidly over the last two or three years, but for reasons explained above, we confined our analysis to the eight funds having an adequately long record of performance for our purposes.

We will analyze these two sets of data separately and in parallel. Each is of interest in its own right. A further reason for not merging the two records is that some of the performance records of managers in the first set include the assets of the publicly offered funds under their management along with their other individual accounts.

Our data on the returns available over the same period on a well-diversified portfolio of *common stocks* are the weighted averages of the monthly holding period returns (including dividends) on all stocks with returns available listed on the NYSE and the AMEX, as reported on the tapes of the Chicago Center for Research in Security Prices. For the performance of corporate *bond portfolios,* we used the monthly total returns (including coupons) on Salomon Brothers' high grade corporate bond index. The monthly rates of return on Treasury bills were computed from the *Federal Reserve Bulletin,* and the monthly inflation rate was based on the Consumers Price Index.

I. OVERALL RETURNS AND RISK PERFORMANCE OF MANAGED COMMODITY-FINANCIAL ACCOUNTS AND PUBLICLY OFFERED FUNDS

There is no question that even professionally managed futures accounts and funds involve substantial risks—as all prospectuses assert, often in italics or capital letters. The data in the first part of Table 5–1M(a) show that the standard deviations of the monthly holding period returns on the corporate accounts under the management of 15 leading futures-account management companies ranged from 4.65 percent to 21.71 percent. The pooled accounts under each management has a maximum loss (in some one of the 42 months from July 1979 to the end of 1982) that ranged from a mere 9.5 percent to as much as 38 percent. The *average* of the maximum loss in any month over the 15 managers was 23 percent, and the average of the standard deviations of monthly returns was 12.36 percent.

Correspondingly, from Table 5–1F(a) the standard deviations of the monthly returns on the shares of the eight publicly offered funds ranged from 6.5 percent to over 13 percent per month. Over this 42-month period, the greatest loss in any one month ranged from 11.0 percent for holders of one of the funds to over 44 percent for holders of another fund. The *average* of the maximum loss in any month over the eight funds was more than 18 percent, and the average standard deviation of the monthly returns over these funds was 9.58 percent.

For perspective, these risks of loss in managed futures accounts or funds should be compared with those on the well-diversified portfolios of common stocks and corporate bonds shown in Section C of the same Tables. The monthly standard deviations of the monthly returns on 15 managed accounts ranged from one to over four times the 5.0 percent monthly standard deviation on stocks and the 4.3 percent S.D. on a 60:40 stock-bond portfolio; the S.D. for the eight futures funds ranged from 1.2 times to about 3 times as large as those on traditional stock and bond portfolios. The *average* of the maximum loss (for any one month) for the 15 managers (20.6 percent), and for the eight funds (18 percent), were, respectively, 1.91 and 1.69 times the 10.77 percent maximum loss on stocks in any month—and 2.67 and 2.36 times the 7.71 percent maximum loss on a 60:40 combined portfolio of stocks and bonds.

For the reader's convenience, all these comparisons of the risk and loss experience of managers and futures funds are brought together in

Section A of Summary Table 5–4. To this point, we have been discussing the risks and losses incurred by investors in the managed accounts or funds, without any adjustment for inflation or the returns on alternative "safe" investments. The other two sections of this Summary Table show that both the absolute and the comparative risk experience of futures managers and funds is very much the same when returns are measured after deducting the "opportunity cost" of the foregone returns on "safe" investments in T-bills—and also when they are measured in "real" terms after subtracting the current (CPI) monthly inflation rate.

But while investments in managed futures accounts and publicly offered futures funds generally involve very high risks, the evidence is equally strong that many of the managers and funds have provided very high average returns. The data in Table 5–1.M(a) show that 13 of the 15 managers over the period July 1979 through the end of 1982 provided *average* monthly rates of return (in spite of their loss-months) that were larger than the average monthly return on diversified portfolios of either stocks or bonds (or mixtures of the two). Correspondingly, Table 5–1.F(a) shows that six of the eight funds provided larger average monthly returns than diversified portfolios of stocks, and seven of the eight showed higher average returns than corporate bond portfolios over these 42 months. One of the managers produced pooled returns for his clients over six times that produced by average stock portfolios over the same period, and one of the public funds had returns over *three* times that of average stock portfolios (and over six times that of portfolios restricted to corporate bonds). Similarly, favorable comparisons are shown in Tables 5–1.M(b) and (c), and 5–1.F(b) and (c), when returns are measured net of T-bill yields or inflation rates.

These high returns provided by many of the managers and funds raise the question of whether they have been high enough to justify the risks incurred, which we have already seen also to be high. The first step in the analysis of this issue is to consider the reward/risk ratios provided by each manager or fund, and compare them with those that have been available on stocks and bonds. The data in Summary Table 5–2 show that these reward/risk ratios for different managers and funds covered a rather wide range. In terms of "raw" returns (Part A), the average ratio over the 15 managers of 0.21 was about 80 percent of that for stocks alone (or mixed portfolios of stocks and bonds), but over half-again as high as for portfolios of bonds alone. In Parts B and C, adjustments are made for foregone earnings on T-bills and for inflation. Here the comparisons are much more favorable. The average manager (or fund) provided an "Excess return/risk" ratio about *four* times as large as that provided by a 60:40 mixed portfolio of bonds and stocks—and provided a "real return/risk" ratio roughly twice that of the stock-bond portfolio. It is also worth noting that while the "raw return/risk" ratios of only six of 15 managers (and only three of eight funds) were larger than that for the mixed stock-bond portfolio, *13* managers (and six of the eight funds) had larger "excess return/risk" ratios—and *12* of the 15 managers (and five of the eight funds) provided larger "real return/risk" ratios than mixed stock-bond portfolios.

II. POTENTIAL IMPROVEMENTS IN RISK/REWARD RATIOS FROM DIVERSIFYING INVESTMENTS AMONG FUTURES MANAGERS (OR FUTURES FUNDS)

As indicated in the introduction, when returns are imperfectly correlated with each other, diversification can substantially reduce the risks involved in producing any given expected rate of portfolio return, and thereby substantially improve the reward/risk ratio available. This general principle is well illustrated (as are others) by the data included in the "B" Sections of the six larger Tables at the end of the chapter. Consider Table 5–1.M(a) covering the experience of 15 managers, using returns with no adjustment for inflation on T-bills. The first line shows the results of an *undiscriminating* ("broadside") *diversification* that assumes that equal fractions of the total funds to be invested in managed futures accounts are placed in bonds of each of the 15 managers. This pooled investment would have shown an average monthly *return* of 2.72 percent, which is just the unweighted average of the returns of the separate managers. But note that the *maximum loss* in any one of the 42 months would have been –9.77 percent—which is *substantially less than half the average* (–20.59 percent) of the maximum losses of the 15 managers. In part, this reflects the fact that the different managers had their big loss months at different times. More fundamentally, this reflects the fact that the average correlation between the monthly returns of each manager with those of every other manager was only 0.285.[11] The fact that this average correlation among the monthly returns of different managers is so relatively low also explains the fact that the *standard deviation* of the returns on this evenly spread futures investment is only 7.35 percent—very substantially less than the average (12.36 percent) of the σs of the 15 managers considered separately.[12] This reduction in the standard deviation of the returns on this evenly spread "Portfolio of Managers" in turn means that its reward/risk ratio (0.372) is correspondingly higher than the *average* (0.210) of the μ/σ ratios of the 15 managers considered separately.

So far, these results simply illustrate the well-known general principle stated in our introductory paragraph that when different investment returns have low intercorrelations with each other, the law of averages comes into play and substantial reductions in the portfolio risks—and substantial improvements in expected returns relative to the risk incurred—can be obtained by even a rather naive "broadside" diversification over different investments. In the present instance, the improvements have come simply from spreading funds evenly over the accounts of different managers.

But not all these 15 managers have equally attractive performance records. Several have shown reward/risk ratios[13] substantially larger than the average of the group (0.210), and two have shown ratios actually higher than the pooled accounts of the 15 managers (0.372). Taken together with the fact that the intercorrelations between the returns of different managers are relatively low or moderate, this suggests that *a selectively diversified portfolio, efficiently allocating funds among fewer* (but still several) *managers,* could *match* the expected monthly *returns* (2.72 percent) of the "broadside" equally allocated portfolio *while substantially reducing the portfolio risk.* The second line of section B in Table 5–1.M(a) shows that this is indeed possible. The computer was programmed to find the allocation of funds over any subset of managers that would reproduce the 2.723 percent expected return but that would *minimize the standard deviation* associated with this return. The result is a portfolio that optimally allocates the funds targeted for futures investments over only 7 of the 15 managers.[14] The expected return is the same (2.723 percent) as that provided by the broadside diversification, but the standard deviation of the returns on this efficiently diversified portfolio have been reduced to 4.987 percent—about two-thirds the risk involved in the undiscriminating diversification over all 15 managers. Correspondingly, with the same expected returns, the efficiently allocated portfolio over 7 managers has a reward/risk ratio of 0.546, which is 47 percent *greater* than that (0.372) of the indiscriminating 15-manager portfolio.

This part of our work is brought together in Section A.a of the Summary Table 5–3. It will be observed that the efficient portfolio of selected managers just described produces a reward/risk ratio that is about *double* that on a well-diversified portfolio of common stocks, and more than twice that on a 60:40 portfolio of stocks and corporate bonds.

Section A.b of the Summary Table shows that very much the same benefits are realized when investors diversify however discriminately over the eight publicly offered futures funds—and that the *additional benefits* from diversifying among fewer funds on a selective and efficient basis are also similar in magnitude.[15] Sections B and C then show that the benefits of diversification *per se*—and the *additional* benefits of optimal selective diversification—are equally dramatic when the returns (and risks) in question are measured by "excess returns" (over T-bills) or in "real" terms after adjusting for inflation.

The third line in Section B of Table 5–1.M(a) shows that if investors were wanting to allocate their funds among managers to incur the smallest possible risks on their subportfolio of futures investments, the standard deviation on their monthly returns could be reduced to 3.574 percent. *No* other allocation of funds among managers could produce a lower risk level. But the "risk-minimization" strategy would involve accepting expected monthly returns on managed futures investments of "only" 0.947 percent. (Even this is not much below the 1.076 percent expected return on a 60:40 mixed portfolio of stocks and bonds). But the second and third lines in Section B are both risk-minimizing ("efficient") portfolios to attain the indicated expected rates of return. Together, they tell us that *if* investors want to reduce their risks on funds put in the hands of futures-account managers from a standard deviation of 4.99 percent to 3.57 percent (the minimum attainable), they *must* at the same time be willing to accept a reduction in their expected returns from 2.72 percent to 0.95 percent. These two combinations of expected return and (minimized) risk define two points on the "efficient frontier" for investments with future-account managers.

These are, of course, intermediate (as well as still higher) combinations of expected return and the minimum risk consistent with each return. The other four lines in Section B identify four such additional points on the efficient frontier for these investments. As an illustration, suppose an investor wanted and expected a return of 2.00 percent. Section A shows that he *could* get this expected return by putting all his futures accounts under the management of M7—but the standard deviation around this return would be a lofty 14.25 percent per month. The line for M7 in Section B shows that *if* he optimally allocated his accounts over a group of managers, he could have the *same expected return* with standard deviation of only 4.12 percent—less than *three-tenths* as large. Other entries in the lower part of Section B in all the tables tell the same story, varying only in degree of gain in risk reduction.

A good picture is said to be worth a thousand words. The expected returns along with the standard deviations of the returns provided by the 15 individual managers are plotted as heavy dots in Figure 5–1 on page 134. The heavy dots along the *solid line* show the risks involved in the *optimally allocated* portfolio of futures accounts with managers, which would have *minimized the risk* of producing the *same return* that each manager produced. The horizontal distance from each heavy dot to the *solid* line on the left show the risk-reducing potential of efficient diversification among futures-account managers. With the single exception of M11 at the extreme upper right of the graph,[16] the risk-reductions (at *every* level of return) available from using the "efficiently selected and allocated portfolio-of-managers" approach are very impressive. The solid line itself defines the *efficient frontier* of the minimal sacrifices in expected returns that must be accepted if given reductions in risks are desired on the investment monies to be invested in futures-accounts managed by appropriate subsets of these 15 managers. (We come to the *dashed* line further to the left in a moment). Every investor and every manager will have his own preference and his own feelings about how much more (minimized) risk he is willing to bear in order to get a little more expected (but uncertain) yield. The efficient frontier merely defines the best attainable set of choices he has among different combinations of the returns and risks he faces, so far as money to be invested with futures-account managers. *Where* he chooses to sit along the best attainable frontier is purely a question of his own choice, given the trade-offs he faces.

These principles and these qualitative conclusions are *completely general.* They are illustrated again in Figure 5–2, which shows the efficient frontiers available to (presumably individual) investors choosing how to allocate some "futures money" among the eight publicly offered futures funds for which we have as much as 42 months' data. Again, we see the large horizontal gains in risk reduction from using a selected portfolio of funds to gain a given expected return. Indeed, in one respect, Figure 5–2 (and the associated underlying data in the tables) is even more dramatic than Figure 5–1: four of the eight funds had a *lower* average return (and *very* much greater risks) than the minimum variance portfolio of funds![17]

III. THE EFFECTS ON RISKS AND RETURNS OF ADDING DIVERSIFIED SUBPORTFOLIOS OF INVESTMENTS WITH FUTURES-ACCOUNT MANAGERS (OR PUBLICLY OFFERED FUTURES FUNDS) TO PORTFOLIOS OF COMMON STOCKS AND/OR BONDS

To this point, we have considered only the improved trade-offs between risks and returns that are available from the optimal diversification (over different managers or different publicly offered futures funds) of the investment monies targeted for investment in the futures markets. But a glance at Figure 5–1 shows that the efficient frontier of futures investments with account-managers would provide the same average return as our very comprehensive portfolio of common stocks (or a 60:40 mixture of stocks and corporate bonds) with considerably less risk. Similarly, Figure 5–2 shows that even the minimum variance (and hence minimum return) portfolio of public future funds had a substantially higher expected return *and* somewhat less risk than either our diversified portfolio of stocks *or* our high-grade corporate bond portfolio.

These observations strongly imply that using at least moderate investments in such optimized subportfolios of futures investments *as a supplement* to the traditional common stock (or stock and bond) portfolios would produce *augmented portfolios* with much more favorable reward/risk trade-offs than those provided by stock portfolios alone (or mixed stock and bond portfolios). In other words, the combined portfolios including futures investments will provide a higher return for *any* given acceptable level of risk—or equivalently, a lower level of risk associated with *any* given targeted expected rate of return—than can be provided by a portfolio of stocks alone (or by any mixed portfolio restricted to stocks and bonds). Risk-averse investors *always* prefer the portfolio combination that will give more return for the same risk, or the one that will reduce the risks involved in getting any given return—and this is accomplished by adding funds in diversified combinations of futures-account managers (or publicly traded funds) to the traditional stock and bond portfolios.

The improvements in the return/risk trade-offs made available by combining properly selected combinations of futures investments with traditional stock and bond portfolios are dramatically shown by the (*dashed-line*) efficient frontiers shown in Figures 5–1 and 5–2. The efficient frontier of the *augmented portfolios* of futures and stocks and bonds lie substantially to the left (lower risk) and/or above (higher return for same risk) the attainable frontier with futures alone (the solid line), or those attainable from different combinations of stocks and bonds alone. (In order not to complicate the graph, the latter was not drawn in. The reader can find the x's denoting the STK, the BD, and the mixed 60:40 SB portfolio. The efficient frontier for various mixtures of stocks and bonds in a portfolio is essentially the curve (bending left) through these three points.[18]

The essential reason why the efficient frontier for the augmented portfolios of stocks and bonds and futures lies to the left (and above) that for portfolios of futures alone or portfolios of stocks and bonds alone is brought out by the elements of the *test* of whether a given candidate group of investments will improve the reward/risk performance of any existing portfolio, which was stated in the introduction, *the* candidate investment will always improve the performance of the existing portfolio whenever its (μ/σ) ratio is *larger than the product* of (a) the correlation of its returns with those of the existing portfolios with (b) the (μ/σ) ratio of the existing portfolio. The needed data are brought together in Summary Table 5–4. The most striking aspect of this exhibit is the remarkably *low correlations* between an optimized portfolio of futures-account managers and portfolios of *either* stocks or bonds (or both). Although somewhat higher, the correlations of portfolios of public futures funds with stocks and bonds are still relatively low.

As a result of these low correlations, the portfolio of Ms passes the test as a desirable investment to be added to an existing bond portfolio and/or to a mixed stock and bond portfolio. Moreover, this is true whether the investment manager is concerned with rates of return *per se,* or with "excess" returns over bills, or with real returns after inflation. (To illustrate with the least favorable case, the M's (μ/σ) ratio of excess returns (on its minimum risk portfolio)[19] is only 0.009, but this is still nearly double the test statistics for stock portfolios of $0.059 \times 0.082 = 0.0048$—and it is nearly three times the test statistic of mixed S&B portfolios of $0.104 \times 0.032 = 0.0033$.) The results of the test are equally favorable to adding a selected portfolio of public futures funds to existing stock and/or bond portfolios, as may readily be confirmed.

CONCLUSIONS

The overall conclusions of our analysis were summarized—in ordinary language, but without filling in numbers—in the preview and summary section and need not be repeated here (except by reference). The numerical analysis supporting these conclusions is supplied in the ensuing text, tables, and charts. It should be apparent that certain very basic general principles and relationships have been at work throughout. But while all the general principles and all the *qualitative* conclusions we have stated have universal applicability and validity, the particular numerical results we have given depend on the particular data we have used. We have been conservative in restricting ourselves to futures funds or futures management companies that had at least 42 months of recent data to work with. But the period from July 1979 through the end of 1982 may not be a fully adequate basis for forming numerical assessments of the future levels of returns and risks. Responsible portfolio managers will want to (and should) use all their other information and judgments in forming their assessments of these matters for the relevant future periods with which they are concerned. But although the specific numbers may change, it is much less likely that the basic general interrelations will be greatly (or rapidly) altered—in particular the critical finding of the *low* intercorrelations between portfolios of futures accounts and stocks and bonds are very likely to persist strongly into the future. And, in that event, all the general conclusions of this study will prove to be solid and robust.

TABLE 5-1M(a)

Average Monthly Returns and Risks (Overall Performance of 15 Account Managers)

	Average Monthly Return (μ)	Standard Deviation of Return (σ)	Return-Risk Ratio (μ/σ)	Avg. Correl. with the 14 Other Mgrs.	Largest Loss in Any Month	Highest Return in Any Month	Months of Gain/ Loss
A. Data for Individual Managers:							
M1	2.734%	11.693%	0.234	0.206	-15.61%	40.58%	26/16
M2	1.434	12.350	0.116	0.369	-20.62	47.44	21/21
M3	1.424	5.945	0.240	0.282	-13.14	18.15	20/22
M4	2.107	15.751	0.134	0.266	-34.33	53.67	20/22
M5	1.458	9.178	0.159	0.355	-16.79	27.71	24/18
M6	3.586	9.905	0.362	0.156	-13.06	26.49	24/18
M7	1.999	14.247	0.140	0.279	-22.01	58.13	23/19
M8	3.589	14.213	0.253	0.380	-12.61	69.93	24/18
M9	2.311	11.647	0.198	0.331	-18.10	33.39	22/20
M10	3.813	13.293	0.287	0.313	-20.52	48.00	26/16
M11	8.420	21.709	0.388	0.242	-30.26	87.04	27/15
M12	2.940	8.881	0.331	0.370	-15.71	24.70	27/15
M13	0.940	16.820	0.015	0.203	-37.96	54.14	19/23
M14	4.981	15.097	0.330	0.421	-28.67	42.64	27/15
M15	-0.206	4.651	-0.044	0.064	-9.52	10.05	19/23
Avg. of Columns:	2.723%	12.359%	0.210	0.285	-20.59%	42.80%	23.2/18.7

TABLE 5–1M(a) *(continued)*

Average Monthly Returns and Risks (Overall Performance of 15 Account Managers)

	Average Monthly Return (μ)	Standard Deviation of Return (σ)	Return-Risk Ratio (μ/σ)	Avg. Correl. with the 14 Other Mgrs.	Largest Loss in Any Month	Highest Return in Any Month	Months of Gain/ Loss
B. Data for Portfolios of Managers:							
a. Amts. M1–15	2.723%	7.315%	0.372		−9.77%	23.38%	25/17
.PTF (same μ):	2.723	4.987	0.546		−5.84	13.28	28/14
b. Risk PTF:	0.947	3.574	0.265		−6.09	9.84	22/20
.PTF for μ of M3:	1.424	3.683	0.387		−5.13	9.78	27/15
.PTF for μ of M7:	1.424	4.116	0.486		−4.64	11.20	27/15
.PTF for μ of M12:	2.940	5.297	0.555		−6.24	13.90	29/13
.PTF for μ of M14:	4.981	9.214	0.541		−9.53	25.14	29/13
C. Portfolios of Stocks, Bonds, or Bills:							
STK	1.351%	4.999%	0.270		−10.77%	12.57%	25/17
BD	0.665	5.207	0.128		−8.90	14.19	22/29
S&B	1.076	4.306	0.249		−7.71	10.69	25/17
BILL	0.935	0.193	4.845		−0.57	1.27	42/0

TABLE 5-1M(b)

Average Monthly Excess[1] Returns and Risks (Overall Performance of 15 Account Managers)

	Average Monthly Excess Return (μ)	Standard Deviation of Excess Return (σ)	Excess Return-Risk Ratio (μ/σ)	Largest Loss in Any Month	Highest Return in Any Month	Months of Gain/ Loss
A. Data for Individual Managers:						
M1	1.799%	11.661%	0.154	−16.65%	39.63%	26/16
M2	0.499	12.304	0.041	−21.69	46.25	20/22
M3	0.489	6.007	0.081	−14.06	17.36	18/24
M4	1.172	15.752	0.063	−35.03	52.72	17/25
M5	0.523	9.178	0.057	−17.71	26.76	22/20
M6	2.651	9.862	0.269	−14.06	25.31	23/19
M7	1.064	14.218	0.075	−22.58	56.92	22/20
M8	2.654	14.194	0.187	−13.25	68.98	26/16
M9	1.376	11.696	0.118	−19.00	32.75	26/16
M10	2.878	13.259	0.217	−21.14	47.19	26/16
M11	7.485	21.688	0.345	−30.88	86.08	26/16
M12	2.005	8.851	0.227	−16.68	23.54	25/17
M13	−0.688	16.816	−0.041	−39.04	53.50	16/26
M14	4.046	15.106	0.268	−29.73	41.69	27/15
M15	−1.141	4.638	−0.246	−10.26	9.19	17/25
Avg. of columns:	1.787%	12.348%	0.121	−21.45%	41.86%	21.8/20

See Note

TABLE 5-1M(b) (continued)

Average Monthly Excess[1] Returns and Risks (Overall Performance of 15 Account Managers)

	Average Monthly Excess Return (μ)	Standard Deviation of Excess Return (σ)	Excess Return-Risk Ratio (μ/σ)	Largest Loss in Any Month	Highest Return in Any Month	Months of Gain/ Loss
B. Data for Portfolios of Managers:						
Equal Amts. M1-15	1.787%	7.294%	0.245	-10.67%	22.43%	23/19
Eff. PTF (same m)	1.787	4.954	0.361	-6.53	12.22	28/14
Min. Risk PTF:	0.032	3.570	0.009	-6.72	8.97	19/23
Eff. PTF for ~ of M3:	0.489	3.671	0.133	-6.04	8.93	23/19
Eff. PTF for ~ of M7:	1.064	4.090	0.260	-5.76	10.12	27/15
Eff. PTF for ~ of M12:	2.005	5.271	0.380	-6.97	12.81	27/15
Eff. PTF for ~ of M14:	4.046	9.181	0.441	-10.18	24.35	29/13
C. Portfolios of Stocks and Bonds:						
STK	0.416%	5.099%	0.082	-11.96%	11.87%	23/19
BD	-0.270	5.243	-0.052	-9.83	13.15	18/23
S&B	9.141	4.393	0.032	-8.63	9.99	20/22

[1] Monthly returns less bills, and standard deviations of the excess returns.

NOTE: The average correlations of the returns of each manager with those of the others are the same as those given in Table 5-1.M(a).

TABLE 5-1M(c)

Average Monthly Real[1] Returns and Risks (Overall Performance of 15 Account Managers)

	Average Monthly Real Return (μ)	Standard Deviation of Real Return (σ)	Real Return-Risk Ratio (μ/σ)	Largest Real Loss in Any Month	Highest Real Return in Any Month	Months of Gain/ Loss
A. Data for Individual Managers:						
M1	2.016%	11.558%	0.174	−16.73%	39.15%	26/16
M2	0.716	12.217	0.059	−20.84	46.01	20/22
M3	0.606	5.931	0.119	−14.03	17.06	20/22
M4	1.389	15.695	0.088	−34.54	52.23	18/24
M5	0.740	9.075	0.082	−17.60	26.28	22/20
M6	2.900	9.837	0.295	−12.96	25.06	23/19
M7	1.284	14.265	0.090	−23.11	57.27	22/20
M8	2.872	14.096	0.204	−12.52	68.50	24/18
M9	1.593	11.700	0.136	−18.65	33.31	20/22
M10	3.095	13.151	0.235	−20.80	46.96	26/16
M11	7.702	21.645	0.356	−30.53	85.98	27/15
M12	2.222	8.880	0.250	−16.06	23.84	25/17
M13	−0.471	16.960	−0.028	−38.87	54.06	17/25
M14	4.265	14.960	0.285	−28.88	41.20	26/16
M15	−0.924	4.777	−0.193	−10.58	9.77	17/25
Avg. of columns	2.005%	12.311%	0.143	−21.12%	41.78%	22.2/19.8

See Note

TABLE 5–1M(c) (continued)

Average Monthly Real[1] Returns and Risks (Overall Performance of 15 Account Managers)

	Average Monthly Real Return (μ)	Standard Deviation of Real Return (σ)	Real Return-Risk Ratio (μ/σ)	Largest Real Loss in Any Month	Highest Real Return in Any Month	Months of Gain/ Loss
B. Data for Portfolios of Managers:						
Equal Amts. of M1-15:	2.005%	7.223%	0.278%	-10.32%	21.94%	24/18
Eff. PTF (same μ):	2.005	4.851	0.413	-6.51	12.21	28/14
Min Risk PTF:	0.337	3.578	0.094	-6.79	9.54	21/21
Eff. PTF for μ of M3	0.706	3.669	0.192	-6.11	9.56	25/17
Eff. PTF for μ of M7	1.284	4.050	0.317	-5.50	10.09	26/16
Eff. PTF for μ of M12	2.222	5.157	0.431	-6.92	12.80	28/14
Eff. PTF for μ of M14	4.265	9.055	0.471	-9.79	24.10	29/13
C. Portfolio of Stocks, Bonds, or Bills:						
STK	0.633%	5.188%	0.124	-12.21%	12.36%	24/18
BD	-0.0534	5.352	-0.010	-9.80	13.07	20/22
S&D	0.358	4.458	0.080	-8.60	10.48	19/23
BILL	0.217	0.409	0.531	-0.53	1.11	42/0

[1] Monthly "raw" or nominal returns less the monthly percentage change in the CPI.

TABLE 5-1F(a)

Average Monthly Returns and Risks (Eight Publicly Offered Futures Funds)

	Average Monthly Return (μ)	Standard Deviation of Return (σ)	Return-Risk Ratio (μ/σ)	Avg. Correl. with the 14 Other Mgrs.	Largest Loss in Any Month	Highest Return in Any Month	Months of Gain/ Loss
A. Data for Individual Funds:							
F1	2.695%	9.632%	0.278	0.484	−14.205	25.20%	15/27
F2	1.360	11.775	0.115	0.478	−18.00	36.40	12/30
F3	0.907	11.986	0.076	0.484	−18.10	37.30	10/32
F4	1.998	13.366	0.149	−0.133	−44.10	30.80	15/27
F5	3.393	6.539	0.519	0.505	−11.00	22.30	18/24
F6	1.421	7.275	0.195	0.550	−13.60	17.20	15/27
F7	0.245	8.182	0.030	0.360	−15.10	20.40	18/24
F8	4.188	7.892	0.531	0.400	−11.20	28.60	15/27
Avg. of columns:	2.026%	9.581%	0.237	0.390	−18.16%	27.28%	14.0/28

TABLE 5–1F(a) *(continued)*

Average Monthly Returns and Risks (Eight Publicly Offered Futures Funds)

	Average Monthly Return (μ)	Standard Deviation of Return (σ)	Return-Risk Ratio (μ/σ)	Avg. Correl. with the 14 Other Mgrs.	Largest Loss in Any Month	Highest Return in Any Month	Months of Gain/ Loss
B. Data for Portfolio of Funds:							
Equals Amts. F1-8:	2.026%	6.252%	0.324		-7.70%	21.40%	25/17
Eff. PTF (same μ):	2.026	5.026	0.403		-6.13	19.74	29/13
Min. Risk PTF:	2.009	5.017	0.401		-6.15	19.72	29/13
Eff. PTF for μ of F1:	2.695	5.177	0.521		-5.84	20.55	30/12
Eff PTF for μ of F5:	3.393	5.696	0.596		-7.05	21.04	28/14
C. Performance of Stocks, Bonds or Bills:							
STK	1.351%	4.999%	0.270		-10.77%	12.57%	25/17
BD	0.665	5.207	0.128		-8.90	14.19	22/20
S&B	1.076	4.306	0.250		-7.71	10.69	25/17
BILLS	0.935	0.193	4.845		-0.57	1.27	42/0

TABLE 5–1F(b)

Average Monthly Excess[1] Returns and Risks (Eight Publicly Offered Futures Funds)

	Average Monthly Excess Return (μ)	Standard Deviation of Excess Return (σ)	Excess Return-Risk Ratio (μ/σ)	Largest Loss in Any Month	Highest Return in Any Month	Months of Gain/ Loss
A. Data for Individual Funds:						
F1	1.760%	9.610%	0.183	−15.06%	24.34%	15/27
F2	0.424	11.817	0.036	−19.17	35.75	10/32
F3	−0.028	12.041	−0.002	−19.27	36.65	9/33
F4	1.063	13.434	0.079	−45.31	29.87	10/32
F5	2.458	6.502	0.378	−11.90	21.35	15/27
F6	0.486	7.252	0.067	−14.25	16.25	14/28
F7	−0.690	8.174	−0.084	−16.03	19.45	12/30
F8	3.253	7.857	0.414	−12.06	27.65	15/27
Avg. of columns:	1.091%	9.586%	0.134	19.13%	26.41%	12.5/29.5

See Note

TABLE 5–1F(b) (continued)

Average Monthly Excess[1] Returns and Risks (Eight Publicly Offered Futures Funds)

	Average Monthly Excess Return (μ)	Standard Deviation of Excess Return (σ)	Excess Return-Risk Ratio (μ/σ)	Largest Loss in Any Month	Highest Return in Any Month	Months of Gain/Loss
B. Data for Portfolios of Funds:						
Equal Amts. of F1-8*	1.091%	6.274%	0.174	–8.60%	20.45%	25/17
Min. Risk PTF:	1.097	5.038	0.218	–7.03	18.79	24/18
Eff. PTF for μ of F1:	1.760	5.181	0.340	–6.82	19.59	26/16
Eff. PTF for $\mu\sim$ of F5:	2.458	5.695	0.432	–8.06	20.12	27/15
C. Performance of Stock and Bond Portfolios:						
STK	0.416%	5.099%	0.082	–11.96%	11.87%	23/19
BD	–0.270	5.243	–0.052	–9.83	13.15	18/24
S&B	0.141	4.393	0.032	–8.63	9.99	20/22

[1] Monthly returns less bills, and standard deviation of the excess returns.

*Since the minimum risk PTF has a *larger* return than the "Equal Amts. of F1-8," there is no interest in the Efficient portfolio with the *same* (lower) return.

NOTE: The average correlations of the returns of each manager with those of the others are the same as those given in Table 5–1.F(a).

TABLE 5–1F(c)

Average Monthly Real[1] Returns and Risks (Overall Performance of Eight Publicly Offered funds)

	Average Monthly Real Return (μ)	Standard Deviation of Monthly Real Return (σ)	Real Return-Risk Ratio (μ/σ)	Largest Real Loss in Any Month	Highest Real Return in Any Month	Months of Gain/ Loss
A. Data for Individual Funds:						
F1	1.977%	9.639%	0.205	−14.49%	24.91%	15/27
F2	0.642	11.771	0.055	−18.81	36.32	11/31
F3	0.189	11.987	0.016	−18.91	37.22	10/32
F4	1.280	13.356	0.096	−44.96	29.87	13/29
F5	2.675	6.442	0.415	−11.55	20.87	15/27
F6	0.703	7.250	0.097	−13.43	16.52	14/28
F7	−0.473	8.122	−0.058	−16.03	18.97	12/30
F8	3.470	7.769	0.447	−11.49	27.55	15/27
Avg. of columns:	1.308%	9.542%	0.159	−18.71%	26.53%	13.1/28.9

See Note

T A B L E 5–1F(c) (continued)

Average Monthly Real[1] Returns and Risks (Overall Performance of Eight Publicly Offered funds)

	Average Monthly Real Return (μ)	Standard Deviation of Monthly Real Return (σ)	Real Return-Risk Ratio (μ/σ)	Largest Real Loss in Any Month	Highest Real Return in Any Month	Months of Gain/ Loss
B. Data for Portfolio of Funds:						
Equal Amts. F1{8*	1.308%	6.205%	0.211	–8.25%	19.97%	24/18
Min. Risk PTF:	1.330	4.930	0.270	–6.45	18.35	26/16
Eff. PTF for μ of F1:	1.977	5.060	0.391	–6.37	19.13	27/15
Eff. PTF for μ of F5:	2.675	5.587	0.479	–7.60	19.61	27/15
C. Performance of Stocks, Bonds, or Bills:						
STK	0.633%	5.118%	0.124	–12.21%	12.36%	24/18
BD	–0.0534	5.352	–0.010	–9.80	13.07	20/22
S&B	0.358	4.458	0.080	–8.60	10.48	19/23
BILL	0.217	0.409	0.531	–0.53	1.11	42/0

[1] Monthly "raw" or nominal returns less the monthly percentage change in the CPI.

*Since the minimum risk PIF has a *larger* return than the "Equal Amts. of F1–8," there is no interest in the Efficient portfolio with the *same* (lower) return.

NOTE: The average correlations of the returns of each managers with those of the others are the same as those given in Table 5–1.F(a).

SUMMARY TABLE 5-1

Relative Risk and Loss Experience, 7/79-12/82 Managed Futures Accounts and Public Futures Funds and Stock and Bonds*

A. Using Actual Monthly Returns

	Range	Average	Ratio Avg. to Stocks	Ratio Avg. to 60:40 S&B
15 Managers				
S.D. of monthly returns	4.65%–21.71%	12.36%	2.47	2.87
Max. loss any one month	9.52%–37.96	20.59	1.91	2.67
Eight Public Funds				
S.D. of monthly returns	6.54%–13.37%	9.58%	1.92	2.22
Max. loss any one month	11.00%-44.10	18.16	1.69	2.36

Portfolios of Stocks or Bonds or a 60:40 Mixed Portfolio of S&B:

	Stocks	Bonds	Mixed Pft S&B
S.D. of monthly returns	5.00%	5.21%	4.31%
Max. loss any one month	10.77	8.80	7.71

B. Using "Excess" Returns (Subtracting T-bill yields):

	Range	Average	Ratio Avg. to Stocks	Ratio Avg. to 60:40 S&B
15 Managers				
S.D. of monthly returns	4.64%–21.69%	12.35%	2.42	2.81
Max. loss any one month	10.26%–39.04	21.45	1.79	2.49

	Range	Average	Ratio Avg. to Stocks	Ratio Avg. to 60:40 S&B
Eight Public Funds				
S.D. of monthly return	6.50%–13.43%	9.59%	1.88	2.18
Max loss any one month	11.90%–45.31	19.13	1.60	2.22

Portfolio of Stocks or Bonds or a 60:40 Mixed Portfolio of S&B:

	Stocks	Bonds	Mixed Pft S&B
S.D. of monthly returns	5.10%	5.24%	4.39%
Max. loss any one month	11.96	9.83	8.63

*Data from Tables 5–1M(a)–(c) and 5–1F(a)–(c) at end of chapter.

S U M M A R Y   T A B L E   5–1 *(continued)*

Relative Risk and Loss Experience, 7/79-12/82 Managed Futures Accounts and Public Futures Funds and Stock and Bonds*

C. Using "Real" Returns (Subtracting CPI):

	Range	Average	Ratio Avg. to Stocks	Ratio Avg. to 60:40 S&B
15 Managers				
S.D. of monthly returns	4.78%–21.65%	12.31%	2.40	2.76
Max. loss any one month	10.58%–38.87	21.12	1.73	2.46
Eight Public Funds				
S.D. of monthly returns	6.44%–13.36%	9.54%	1.86	2.14
Max. loss any one month	11.49%–44.96	18.71	1.53	2.18

Portfolios of Stocks or Bonds or a 60:40 Mixed Portfolio of S&B:

	Stocks	Bonds	Mixed Pft S&B
S.D. of monthly returns	5.12%	5.35%	4.46%
Max. loss any one month	12.21	9.80	8.60

*Data from Tables 5–1M(a)–(c) and 5–1F(a)–(c) at end of chapter.

SUMMARY TABLE 5–2

Relative Reward/Risk Ratios*
Managed Futures Account and Public Futures Funds and Stock and Bonds

A. Using Actual Monthly Returns:

	Range	Avg.	Ratio Avg. to Stocks	Ratio Avg. to Bonds	Ratio Avg. to S&B
15 Managers	−0.04–0.39	0.210	0.78	1.64	0.84
Eight Futures Funds:	0.03–0.53	0.237	0.88	1.85	0.95
Diversified Stock Ptf.:		0.270			
Diversified Bond Ptf.:		0.128			
60:40 Stock and Bonds		0.250			

B. Using "Excess" Returns (Over T-bills):

	Range	Avg.	Ratio Avg. to Stocks	Ratio Avg. to Bonds	Ratio Avg. to S&B
15 Managers	−0.25–0.345	0.121	1.48	**	3.78
Eight Futures Funds:	−0/08–0.378	0.134	1.63	**	4.19
Diversified Stock Ptf.:		0.082			
Diversified Bond Ptf.:		−0.052			
60:40 Stock and Bonds		0.032			

C. Using "Real" Returns (After CPI Inflation):

	Range	Avg.	Ratio Avg. to Stocks	Ratio Avg. to Bonds	Ratio Avg. to S&B
15 Managers	−0.193–0.476	0.143	1.153	**	1.788
Eight Futures Funds:	−0.058–0.415	0.159	1.282	**	1.988
Diversified Stock Ptf.:		0.124			
Diversified Bond Ptf.:		−0.010			
60:40 Stock and Bonds		0.080			

*Data from Tables 5–1M(a)–(c) and 5–1F(a)–(c) at end of chapter
**Not Applicable

SUMMARY TABLE 5-3

Relative Reward/Risk Ratios (μ/σ) Available with Diversification over Futures Managers or Funds*

A. Using Actual Monthly Returns:	This (μ/σ):	Ratio to Stocks (μ/σ):	Ratio to Bonds (μ/σ):	Ratio to S&B (μ/σ):
a. 15 Managers:				
***MEMO: Ave. of 15 (μ/σ) ratios:	0.210	0.78	1.64	0.84
Pft. of Equal Amts. in M1–M5:	0.372	1.38	2.91	1.49
Eff. Ptf. (with same expected return):	0.546	2.02	4.26	2.19
Min. Risk Ptf:	0.265	0.98	2.07	1.06
b. Eight Future Funds:				
***MEMO: Ave. of 8 (μ/σ) ratios:	0.237	0.88	1.85	0.95
Pft. of Equal Amts. in F1–8:	0.324	1.20	2.53	1.30
Eff Ptf. (with same expected return):	0.403	1.49	3.15	1.61
Min. Risk Ptf.:	0.401	1.49	3.13	1.60
B. Using "Excess" Returns (over T-bills):				
a. 15 Managers:				
***MEMO: Ave. of 15 (μ/σ) ratios:	0.121	1.48	**	3.78
Pft. of Equal Amts. in M1–15:	0.245	2.99	**	7.66
Eff. Ptf. (with same expected return):	0.361	4.40	**	11.28
Min. Risk Ptf:	0.009	0.11	**	0.28
b. Eight Futures Fund:				
***MEMO: Ave. of 8 (μ/σ) ratios:	0.134	1.63	**	4.19
Pft. of Equal Amts. in F1–8:	0.174	2.12	**	5.44
Min. Risk Ptf.:	0.218	2.66	**	6.81
C. Using "Real" Returns (after CPI inflation):				
a. 15 Managers:				
***MEMO: Ave. of 15 (μ/σ) ratios:	0.143	1.15	**	1.79
Pft. of Equal Amts. in M1–15:	0.278	2.24	**	3.48
Eff. Ptf. (with same expected return):	0.413	3.33	**	5.16
Min. Risk Ptf:	0.094	0.76	**	1.18
b. Eight Futures Bonds:				
***MEMO: Ave. of 8 (μ/σ) ratios:	0.159	1.28	**	1.99
Pft. of Equal Amts. in F1–8:	0.211	1.70	**	2.64
Min. Risk Ptf.:	0.270	2.18	**	3.38

*Data from Tables 5–1M(a)–(c) and 5–1F(a)–(c) at end of chapter.

**Not applicable

***Data from Summary Table 5–2

SUMMARY TABLE 5-4

Reward/Risk Rations (μ/σ) and Intercorrelations
Five Alternate Subportfolios of Managed Futures, Stocks, and Bonds

A. Using Actual Monthly Returns:

	(μ/σ)	M	F	Stocks	Bonds	S&B
				Intercorrelations		
Min. Risk Ptf. of Ms	0.265	1.000				
Min. Risk Ptf. of Fs	0.401	0.637	1.000			
All NYSE & AMEX Stocks	0.270	-0.065	0.234	1.000		
Salomon Hi-grade Corporates	0.128	0.148	0.151	0.417	1.000	
60:40 Mixture, Stocks & Bonds	0.249	0.116	-0.024	0.898	0.774	1.000

B. Using "Excess Returns" (Over T-Bills):

	(μ/σ)	M	F	Stocks	Bonds	S&B
Min. Risk Ptf. of Ms	0.009	1.000				
Min. Risk Ptf. of Fs	0.218	0.652	1.000			
All NYSE & AMEX Stocks	0.082	0.059	0.250	1.000		
Salomon Hi-grade Corporates	-0.052	0.130	-0.017	0.408	1.000	
60:40 Mixture, Stocks & Bonds	0.032	0.104	0.167	0.899	0.767	1.000

C. Using "Real Returns" (After CPI Inflation):

	(μ/σ)	M	F	Stocks	Bonds	S&B
Min. Risk Ptf. of Ms	0.094	1.000				
Min. Risk Ptf. of Fs	0.270	0.770	1.000			
All NYSE & AMEX Stocks	0.124	0.012	0.233	1.000		
Salomon Hi-grade Corporates	-0.010	-0.134	-0.017	0.446	1.000	
60:40 Mixture, Stocks & Bonds	0.080	-0.056	0.153	0.903	0.787	1.000

FIGURE 5-1

Overall Performance—15 Futures-Accounts Managers and Stocks, Bonds, and Bills
(7/79–12/82) (Percent per Month)

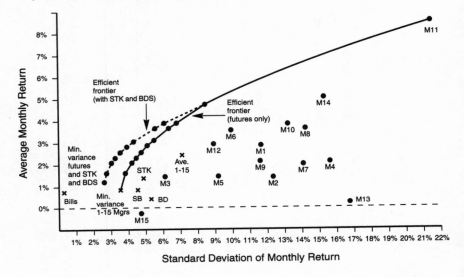

FIGURE 5-2

Overall Performance—Eight Publicly Offered Future Funds (and Stocks, Bonds, and Bills)
(7/79–12/82) (Percent per Month)

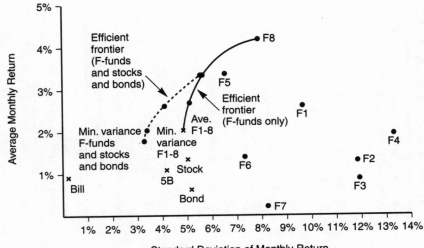

ENDNOTES

1. Except, of course, managers of specialized mutual funds.

2. Either of these seemingly alternative possibilities clearly implies the other. If the broader portfolio satisfies one of the conditions, it necessarily satisfies the other along the relevant upper portion of the efficient frontier when portfolio returns are plotted on the vertical axis and portfolio risks horizontally.

3. Harry M. Markowitz, "Portfolio Selection," *Journal of Finance,* March 1952, pp. 77–91, and *Portfolio Selection: Efficient Diversification of Investments* (New York: John Wiley & Sons, 1959).

4. Correspondingly, it provides him a rigorous basis for determining how much different his best allocation would be if, instead, he were to believe (and act upon) a different set of assessments.

5. This statement is rigorously true whenever the investment manager is willing to rely on the statistical relationships shown by past data in forming his assessments of the relevant future relationships between the risks and returns over the set of securities in question. As a theoretical proposition, it is equally true with respect to whatever set of modified or adjusted set of assessments the manager wishes to use on the basis of his own best judgment, relying on his experience and any other information he may have that indicates that the future relationships between securities will differ in some particular ways from the historical patterns. It is recognized, however, that the interrelationships among the security risks and returns underlying this "regression test" are quite complex and it is difficult to apply this test when managers want to make their decisions on the basis of judgmental assessments that differ very much from historical patterns. In the latter case, the alternative (but mathematically equivalent) formulation given in the immediately following text will probably be more intuitively appealing and reliable.

6. For readers who like symbols, the condition stated in the text for a favorable shift in the efficient frontier due to the addition of some at least modest investment in the candidate security (or securities) is simply

$$\theta_i > \rho_{ip}\,\theta_p$$

where $\theta_i = \bar{r}_i/\sigma_i$ and $\theta_p = \bar{r}_p/\sigma_p$

and ρ_{ip} is the simple correlation between $\tilde{r}_i$ and $\tilde{r}_p$, while $\bar{r}_i$ and $\bar{r}_p$ are the expected rates of return on the candidate(s) for the portfolio and on the existing portfolio, respectively, and σ_i and σ_p are their corresponding standard deviations of return.

7. The fractions having higher return/risk ratios are also considerably larger in each case when the comparison is made with the ratios provided by a portfolio of corporate bonds.

Excess returns are computed as the actual return less the return on T-bills, and real returns are measured by actual returns less the inflation rate shown by the CPI in the given month

8. Let E be the beginning equity and P the net monthly profit defined by the CFTC. The monthly rate of return on the CFTC basis is R = P/E. Let A be the net additions and withdrawals during the month, and R* be the adjusted monthly rate of return allowing for additions and withdrawals. We assume (a) the A is spread evenly over the 22 trading days of the month, and (b) that simple interest is an adequate approximation within the month—i.e., that the funds added on the X/th day will earn at a rate of R*/22 per day for the (22-X) days it was in the account. We then have:

$$P = R* \left[E = \frac{A}{22} \left(\frac{21}{22} + \frac{20}{22} + \ldots + \frac{1}{22} \right) \right]$$

$$= R* \left[E + \frac{A}{22} \left(\frac{1}{22} \right) \left(\frac{22*21}{2} \right) \right]$$

$$= R* \ E \left[1 + \frac{A}{E} \left(\frac{21}{44} \right) \right]$$

$$R* = \frac{P}{E \left(1 + .477 \ A/E \right)}$$

which is the formula used.

9. This adjustment was the best we could make in the absence of more detailed information on the actual amount added or withdrawn each day of each month for each of the 14 managers.

10. There was not enough data to pursue this line of analysis in the present study.

11. The average correlation of the returns of any 1 manager with the returns of each of the 14 others ranged from a low of .064 to a high of .421.

12. The latter are given in the second column of the A section of the total just above.

13. See the third column at the top of Table 5–1M(a).

14. Three of the managers (M3, M6, M15) would each be handling over 20 percent of the funds, M1 would have 13.5 percent, M11 8 percent with small amounts (3.6 percent and 2.3 percent) to M12 and M4.

    We might observe that the only intercorrelations that count in these allocations are those with the other funds in the efficient portfolio—the intercorrelations, risks, and returns of the others rule them out of the final optimal portfolio.

15. They also come about for exactly the same reasons. Section A of Table 5–1.F(a) shows that three of the eight public funds have a higher (μ/σ) ratio than the average (0.237), and two are higher than that of the "equal amounts" portfolio (0.324). The average inter-fund correlation is 0.391

(higher than that for managers but still moderate). The optimal portfolio for the second line of section B uses 5 of the 8 funds—23.8 percent in F4, 28.6 percent in F5, 12.5 percent in F6, 27.1 percent in F7 but only 8.0 percent in F8. The allocation to F8 is surprisingly low in spite of its high and (μ/σ) ratio because of intercorrelations, and the surprisingly high allocation to F4 arises from its negative average intercorrelation with the returns on the other funds.

16. Since all other managers show lower expected returns, any investor wanting as high an expected monthly return as the 8.42 percent provided by M11 must accept the 21.71 percent monthly standard deviation involved. But it should be noted that because of the low correlations of the M11 return with those of other managers (knowing the full set of returns on the other managers would explain only 5.9 percent of the variance of the M11 return), combined with its high average returns, M11 forms an important part of the optimal portfolios of managers all along the efficient frontier.

17. F4 vividly illustrates the importance of correlations in determining optional portfolios. The average return on F4 was slightly less than that on the minimum variance portfolio of funds, and its standard deviation (13.37 percent) was 2.7 times as large as that on the minimum variance portfolio of funds. But since its average correlation with the seven other funds was negative (−0.133), it represents 23.8 percent of that minimal variance portfolio of funds.

18. In fact the minimum variance (most leftward) point on this curve would be a 46–54 percent mixture using the stock-bond performance of the 42 months 7/79 through 12/82.

19. Note that the M's (μ/σ) ratio is larger on all other efficient portfolios.

CHAPTER 6

MANAGEMENT SUMMARY

Title: "Commodity Futures as a Hedge against Inflation"
Publication: *The Journal of Portfolio Management,* Spring 1983.
Author: Zvi Bodie, Boston University
Data: Annual prices for 29 years, 1953-1981, for commodity futures, 30-day U.S. Treasury bills, 20-year U.S. Treasury bonds, and the S&P 500.
Synopsis: The study acknowledges the conservative approach of using a strict buy-and-hold strategy for futures. However, it was observed that the only possibility for long-term, positive return is through unanticipated increases in commodities spot prices (inflation). In doing his portfolio analysis, Bodie made the very conservative assumption that long-term, real rates of return from futures would be between 0 percent and 2 percent. His study showed the real returns to be 5.69 percent for the period studied. A favorable shift to the efficient frontier occurred from the use of futures.

Commodity Futures as a Hedge against Inflation*

Zvi Bodie

The purpose of this chapter is to explore how investors can use commodity futures contracts as a supplement to more conventional investments to improve the risk-return trade-off in an inflationary environment. Admittedly, the economic raison d'etre of existing commodity futures markets is to provide a way of hedging risks of unanticipated changes in the prices of basic agricultural and industrial commodities, while investors are typically concerned with the real value of their income and wealth measured in terms of final consumption goods and services. Nevertheless, commodity futures markets can offer substantial hedging opportunities to the general investor as well as to the commodity specialist.

The chapter is organized as follows. I will first discuss why real or inflation-adjusted rates of return and their uncertainty ought to be the main concern of investors. I will present an analytical framework for formulating investment strategy, will examine the historical record of real rates of return on four asset categories: stocks, bonds, bills, and commodity futures, and will then demonstrate how the use of commodity futures can improve the risk-return trade-off.

I wish to thank my colleague, Alex Kane, and my research assistant, Michael Rouse, for their valuable help in preparing this chapter.
*The Journal of Portfolio Management, Spring 1983. Reprinted with permission.

WHY REAL INVESTMENT RETURNS AND THEIR UNCERTAINTY MATTER

With respect to the individual investor, i.e., the household, there can be little doubt that the dollar value of its investment portfolio is not what counts, but, rather, its real value in terms of purchasing power. Consequently, households will be concerned about the real or inflation-adjusted rate of return rather than the nominal rate of return on their investments.

If the future rate of inflation were known with certainty, it would make no difference whether investors were making their investment decisions on the basis of real or nominal rates of return, because the expected real rate of return on any asset would just be the nominal rate less the known inflation rate, and its real risk would be the same as its nominal risk. When inflation is unpredictable, however, a guaranteed nominal rate of return may be a highly uncertain one in real terms. As inflation becomes more uncertain, conventional private pension plans and contractual savings schemes offering a money-fixed stream of benefits, and conventional bonds and mortgages offering a fixed nominal rate of return become riskier and less attractive to investors.

What about institutional investors? The survival and success of institutional investors depend upon providing households with the kind of financial assets that households want to hold. As households become more and more interested in real rates of return, institutional investors must respond by offering new products and adjusting their investment policies accordingly. For example, if a life insurance company is offering a money-fixed savings plan to a household, then it can hedge simply by investing the funds it receives from households in long-term bonds and other assets that offer a guaranteed nominal rate of return. On the other hand, as households begin to demand innovative products that offer some kind of purchasing power guarantee, life insurance companies and other institutional investors must change their hedging strategies to compensate for the changed nature of their liabilities. Ultimately, if households are concerned about real rates of return, then financial institutions will be too.

THE ANALYTICAL FRAMEWORK

The analytical framework underlying the investment strategies I will present in this chapter is known as mean-variance analysis, and it goes back 30 years to the pioneering work by Harry Markowitz.[1] The basic premise underlying this approach is that the investor is risk averse: Given a choice between two investments offering the same mean (or average) rate of return, the investor would always choose the one that has less risk. Risk in the context of this analysis is identified with the unpredictability or uncertainty of achieving a given expected rate of return and is measured by its variance or standard deviation.

The investor's decision process falls into two stages. The first stage involves the computation of the risk-return opportunities; the second involves the choice of the most appropriate risk-return combination. In stage one, the investor starts by finding the minimum-risk strategy, determines the mean rate of return associated with it, and then seeks to derive other portfolios that offer higher and higher means with the least possible risk. The result of this part of the process is a trade-off curve showing the terms-of-trade between risk and expected return.[2]

The inputs needed to generate the trade-off curve are the means and standard deviations of the real rates of return on the assets being considered for inclusion in the portfolio and the correlations among them. In the following section, we examine what these parameters have been over the past 28 years and discuss our assumptions about their current values.

INFLATION AND INVESTMENT RETURNS: THE HISTORICAL RECORD

Table 6–1 contains the historical record of real pretax rates of return on bills, bonds, stocks, and commodity futures for the period 1953 through 1981. The measure of the price level that was used in adjusting these rates of return was the Bureau of Labor Statistics' Consumer Price Index.

The first column in Table 6–1 is the real rate of return on a policy of "rolling over" 30-day Treasury bills and is representative of the rate of return on money-market instruments. This is by far the least volatile series, with a standard deviation of only 1.68 percent, because short-term interest rates have tended to follow closely movements in the rate of inflation over this period.

Of course, this is not a coincidence. All market-determined interest rates contain an "inflation premium," which reflects expectations about the declining purchasing power of the money borrowed over the life of the loan. As the rate of inflation has increased in recent years, so too has the inflation premium built into interest rates. Although long-term as well as short-term interest rates contain such a premium, conventional long-term bonds lock the investor into the current interest rate for the life of the

TABLE 6-1

Annual Real Rates of Return 1953-1981 (Percent per Year)

Year	(1) Bills	(2) Bonds	(3) Stocks	(4) Commodity Futures	Rate of Inflation (5) CPI
1953	1.19	2.99	−1.60	−3.48	0.62
1954	1.37	7.73	53.39	13.23	−0.50
1955	1.20	−1.66	31.08	−7.63	.37
1956	−0.39	−8.22	3.60	12.38	2.86
1957	0.12	4.30	−13.40	−5.04	3.02
1958	0.22	−7.72	40.88	−3.47	1.76
1959	1.43	−3.70	10.30	−2.84	1.50
1960	1.16	12.12	−1.00	−3.93	1.48
1961	1.45	0.30	26.05	.022	0.67
1962	1.50	5.60	−9.83	−2.40	1.22
1963	1.45	−0.43	20.81	16.32	1.65
1964	2.32	2.29	15.11	4.54	1.19
1965	1.97	−1.18	10.33	5.13	1.92
1966	1.36	−0.29	−12.98	9.70	3.35
1967	1.34	−11.87	20.32	−.064	3.04
1968	0.47	−4.76	6.05	−3.18	4.72
1969	0.44	−10.55	−13.77	12.20	6.11
1970	0.99	6.27	−1.40	−1.62	5.49
1971	1.00	9.55	10.59	−1.65	3.36
1972	0.42	2.20	15.06	29.35	3.41
1973	−1.72	−9.11	−21.56	72.69	8.80
1974	−3.74	−7.0	−34.47	17.97	12.20
1975	−1.13	2.04	28.21	−10.03	7.01
1976	0.26	11.39	18.16	5.30	4.81
1977	−1.55	−6.92	−13.07	4.90	6.77
1978	−1.83	−7.34	−2.42	18.60	9.03
1979	−2.59	−12.82	4.53	15.91	13.31
1980	−1.79	−15.80	17.44	5.25	12.41
1981	4.35	−8.47	−12.68	−33.08	8.90
Mean	0.37	−1.65	6.68	5.69	4.50
Standard Deviation	1.68	7.43	19.48	17.36	3.86

TABLE 6–1 *(continued)*

Annual Real Rates of Return 1953-1981 (Percent Per Year)

Correlation Coefficients:

	Bonds	Stocks	Commodity Futures	Inflation (CPI)
Bill	.430	.252	−.312	−.673
Bonds		.187	−.230	−.579
Stocks			−.210	−.467
Commodity Futures				.247

Note: The real returns were calculated according to the formula:

$$\text{Real rate of return} = 100 \times \left(\frac{1 + \text{nominal rate of return}}{1 + \text{rate of inflation}} - 1 \right)$$

using the CPI inflation rate.

Sources: The data on 1-month bills, 20-year bonds, and stocks are from Ibbotson and Sinquefield, *Stocks, Bonds, Bills and Inflation,* Financial Analysts Research Foundation.

The Commodity futures series was derived from price data in *The Wall Street Journal* using a method explained in the text. The data on the CPI are from the U.S. Department of Labor.

bond. If long-term interest rates on new bonds subsequently rise as a result of unexpected inflation, the funds already locked in can be released only by selling the bonds on the secondary market at a price well below their face value. If, however, an investor buys only short-term bonds with an average maturity of about 30 days, then the interest rate earned will lag behind changes in the inflation rate by at most 1 month.

The problem with money-market instruments is their low rate of return. Over the last 29 years, the average pretax, inflation-adjusted rate of return on money-market instruments has been close to zero. In the most recent 6-year period, that return has actually been negative. Perhaps the most likely scenario for the future is that inflation-adjusted returns will hover around zero, i.e., the interest rate will be about equal to the rate of inflation.

Column 2 presents the real rate of return an investor would have earned by investing in U.S. Treasury bonds with a 20-year maturity. The assumption underlying this series is that the investor bought a 20-year bond at the beginning of each year and sold it at the end. The return therefore includes both coupon interest and capital gains or losses. As the relatively low mean and high standard deviation indicate, the past 28 years was a bad period for the investor in long-term bonds. Capital losses caused by unanticipated increases in interest rates tended to more than cancel the coupon yield over this period.

It would probably be a mistake to assume that the mean real rate of return on long-term government bonds in the future is going to be the −1.65% per year that it was over the 1953-1981 period. A more reasonable approach to estimating the *ex ante* mean real rate would be to take the yield to maturity on long-term government bonds and subtract an estimate of the mean rate of inflation expected to prevail over the next 20 years. When we do this, we find a mean real rate of return on U.S. Treasury bonds of 3 percent per year.

Column 3 in Table 6–1 presents the real rate of return on the Standard and Poor's Composite Index of common stocks, which is a value-weighted stock portfolio of 500 large corporations in the United States. The return includes dividends and capital gains. The mean real rate over our sample period was 6.68 percent per year, which we will round off to 7.0 percent per year in our computations of the trade-off curve.

Finally, let us focus our attention on column 4 in Table 6–1, which presents the annual rate of return one would have earned on a well-diversified portfolio of commodity futures contracts over the 1953-1981 period. The rate of return on a futures contract reflects the proportional change in the futures price over the holding period. The series was generated by assuming a "buy-and-hold" strategy whereby contracts were entered into at quarterly intervals, held for 3 months, and then liquidated. The number of commodities included varies over the period and depends primarily on the availability of reliable price data. Table 6–2 presents a full list of commodities and the year in which each was first added to the portfolio. The number was initially 13 in 1953; it increased to 22 in 1970, but subsequently declined to 18 by 1981. The portfolio was assumed to consist of equal dollar amounts invested in each commodity contract.

The rates of return for commodity futures listed in column 4 of Table 6–1 require an interpretation that is different from the real rates in columns 1 through 3. When investors take a long position in a futures contract, they do not buy it in the sense that they would buy a stock or bond or the physical commodity itself; rather, they agree to purchase the commodity for a specified price at a certain point in the future. The commodities exchange, which acts as an intermediary, requires all parties to a futures contract to post bond called "margin" to guarantee performance.[3] Investors are permitted to post Treasury bills, on which they continue to earn the interest,

TABLE 6-2

List of Commodity Futures Contracts Included in the Portfolio

Commodity	Year in Which It First Entered the Portfolio
Wheat	1953
Corn	1953
Oats	1953
Soybeans	1953
Soybean Oil	1953
Soybean Meal	1953
Potatoes	1953
Wool	1953
Cotton	1953
Eggs	1953
Cocoa	1953
Copper	1953
Sugar	1953
Silver	1963
Cattle	1964
Platinum	1964
Pork Bellies	1964
Hogs	1966
Orange Juice	1966
Broilers	1968
Lumber	1969
Plywood	1970

so the funds used as margin are therefore not strictly speaking an investment in commodity futures. The rates of return reported in column 4
should, therefore, be interpreted as the addition to the total investment
portfolio rate of return the investor would have earned in each year on a
position in commodity futures with a face value equal to the total investment in other assets.

In order for a buy-and-hold strategy in the futures market to be profitable, it is not enough for spot prices to be rising; they must rise by more
than was anticipated in the futures price at the time the contract was entered
into. On average, one might expect the spot price forecasts implicit in

futures prices to be right and would therefore expect the mean rate of return on futures contracts to be zero.[4] More important for our purposes, however, futures contracts will yield a positive rate of return when there are *unanticipated* increases in spot prices, and it is this feature that makes them valuable as an inflation hedge.

A comparison of columns 4 and 5 in Table 6–1 shows that our buy-and-hold investment strategy in commodity futures tended to do well precisely in those years when the rate of inflation was high. We are probably safe in assuming that much of the increase in the CPI in those years was unanticipated. The mean rate of return on our well-diversified commodity futures portfolio during the entire 1953-1981 period was 5.69 percent per year, a strikingly large number, indicating that the period as a whole was probably one of unanticipated inflation.

The glaring exception is the year 1981, in which one would have lost 33 percent on our buy-and-hold strategy in commodity futures. In one sense, 1981 is not an exception: The 8.9 percent rate of inflation during the year, although still relatively high by historical standards, was considerably lower than the forecasts of most experts at the beginning of the year. It would probably be correct to say, therefore, that 1981 was a year of unanticipated deceleration in the rate of inflation. Just as we expect unanticipated acceleration in the rate of inflation to be associated with positive rates of return on a buy-and-hold strategy in commodity futures, so we should expect unanticipated deceleration in inflation to be associated with negative rates of return on futures. Of course, investors who had foreseen the deceleration in inflation ahead of time could have made a large positive rate of return by going short in commodity futures, but doing so would have had to be classified as speculating on one's own forecast of inflation, rather than hedging against inflation.

It is not at all clear what mean value we should assume for the rate of return on commodity futures in computing the trade-off curve for the future. For this reason, we will assume two alternative values for this parameter, zero and 2 percent per year, and we will trace the consequences of each.

The other parameters that play a crucial role in determining the shape of the trade-off curve are the correlation coefficients presented at the bottom of Table 6–1. Perhaps the most significant thing to notice is that the real rates of return on bills, bonds, and stocks are all negatively correlated with inflation and all positively correlated with one another. Commodity futures, on the other hand, are positively correlated with the rate of inflation and negatively correlated with the real rates of return on the other major asset categories. Therefore, they can serve to reduce the risk associated with any portfolio containing them.

Before proceeding to our presentation of the risk-return trade-off curves, let us summarize the assumptions that we are making about the key parameters relating to the real rates of return on bills, bonds, stocks, and commodity futures and the interrelationships among them. With regard to the means, we assume zero on bills, 3 percent on bonds, 7 percent on stocks, and two alternative values on commodity futures: zero and 2 percent. With regard to the standard deviations and correlations, we assume the ones reported in Table 6–1.

THE RISK-RETURN TRADE-OFF

The purpose of this section of the chapter is to show how commodity futures can improve the risk-return trade-off faced by a tax-exempt investor. We will first consider what the trade-off curve looks like when the set of asset choices is restricted to stocks, bonds, and bills and will then compare that to the trade-off curve with commodity futures included.

Table 6–3 and Figure 6–1 contain all of the information relevant to the first of these two curves. Each row of the table corresponds to a point on the curve, starting from the minimum-risk point (A) with a mean real rate of return of zero and a standard deviation of 1.68 percent to the maximum return point (H) with a mean of 7 percent and a standard deviation of 19.48 percent. The last three columns of the table show the portfolio proportions corresponding to each point on the curve. These are the portfolio proportions that will produce the given mean real rate of return with minimum risk, and we find them by using an optimization procedure originally developed by Markowitz.[5] In our analysis, we have ruled out short sales or the purchase of securities on margin.

In order to provide a clearer picture of the meaning of a movement along the risk-return trade-off curve, I have graphed in Figure 6–2 three probability distributions, corresponding to the first three points on the trade-off curve in Figure 6–1. I based them on the assumption that the distribution of the real rates of return on the portfolios is normal, i.e., a "bell-shaped" curve. The first corresponds to the portfolio consisting of bills only, which has a mean of zero and a standard deviation of 1.68 percent. The second corresponds to the portfolio that has 74 percent invested in bills, 20 percent in bonds and 6 percent in stocks, with a mean real rate of return of 1 percent per year and a standard deviation of 2.81 percent. The third corresponds to a portfolio that has 48 percent invested in bills, 40

TABLE 6-3

Risk-Return Trade-off Curve: Stocks, Bills, and Bonds

Point	Mean	Standard Deviation	Slope	Portfolio Proportions Stocks	Bonds	Bills
A	0%	1.68%		0	0	1.00
			.88			
B	1	2.81		.06	.20	.74
			.60			
C	2	4.47		.12	.40	.48
			.56			
D	3	6.24		.17	.60	.23
			.55			
E	4	8.06		.25	.75	0
			.33			
F	5	11.06		.50	.50	0
			.25			
G	6	15.07		.75	.25	0
			.23			
H	7	19.48		1.00	0	0

Assumptions about real rates of return:

	Bills	Bonds	Stocks
Mean	0%	3%	7%
Standard Deviation	1.68%	7.43%	19.48%
Correlations:			
Bonds	.430		
Stocks	.252	.187	

percent in bonds, and 12 percent in stocks, with a mean of 2 percent per year and a standard deviation of 4.47 percent. As the mean goes up, the bell-shaped curve shifts to the right and becomes more flat or stretched out, indicating greater upside potential but also greater downside risk.

Now we are ready to introduce commodity futures contracts into the portfolio. Remember that we are not actually using up any of our funds when we take a position in commodity futures; the funds are invested in stocks, bonds, and bills. We are simply taking a position that has a face value equal to some specified proportion of the total amount invested in these other assets. The only restriction on the portfolio imposed by the futures contracts is that we must have an amount invested in bills equal to at least 10 percent of the position in commodity futures, to serve as margin.

The results with commodity futures included appear in Table 6–4 and Figure 6–3. Note that the minimum-risk strategy is still to invest 100 percent

FIGURE 6–1

Risk-Return Trade-off Curve: Stocks, Bonds, Bills

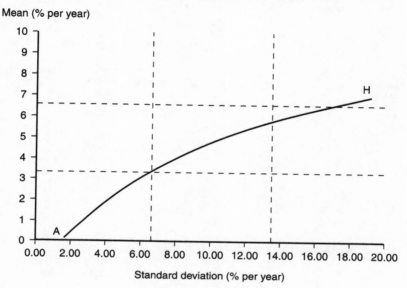

FIGURE 6–2

Probability Distributions of Portfolio Rates of Return

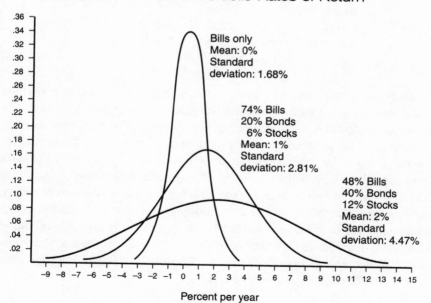

TABLE 6–4

Risk-Return Trade-off: Stocks, Bonds, Bills, and
Commodity Futures

| Mean | Standard Deviation | Slope | Portfolio Proportions | | | |
			Stocks	Bonds	Bills	Commodity Futures
0%	1.44%		0	0	1.00	.05
		.91				
1	2.54		.06	.19	.75	.07
		.61				
2	4.18		.12	.39	.49	.09
		.57				
3	5.93		.18	.58	.24	.11
		.55				
4	7.74		.26	.73	.01	.13
		.33				
5	10.79		.51	.48	.01	.14
		.25				
6	14.86		.76	.23	.01	.15
		.22				
7	19.48		1.00	0	0	

Assumptions about real rates of return:

	Bills	Bonds	Stocks	Commodity Futures
Mean	0%	3.0%	7.0%	0%
Standard Deviation	1.68%	7.43%	19.48%	17.36%
Correlations:				
Bonds	.430			
Stocks	.252	.187		
Commodity Futures	−.312	−.230	−.210	

of our funds in bills, but it is now optimal to hedge that investment with a small position in the well-diversified commodity futures portfolio by taking a long position with a face value equal to 5 percent of the investment in bills. Under our assumption that the mean rate of return on commodity futures is zero, the mean real rate of return on the portfolio will remain unaffected, but there will be a reduction in standard deviation. Comparing curves 1 and 2 in Figure 6–3, we see that, for any mean real rate of return, introducing the right amount of commodity futures contracts into the portfolio enables us to reduce the standard deviation. It shifts the trade-off curve to the left. The reduction in standard deviation is .24 percent at the minimum-risk end of the curve, increases to .32 percent in the middle, and then declines to .21 percent at the other end.

FIGURE 6–3

Risk-Return Trade-off Curves

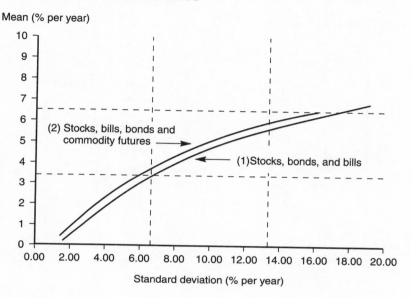

Mean (% per year)

(2) Stocks, bills, bonds and
commodity futures

(1)Stocks, bonds, and bills

Standard deviation (% per year)

   If we look at the last four columns in Table 6–4 and compare them with the last three columns of Table 6–3, we see that the addition of commodity futures contracts does not change the portfolio proportions of stocks, bonds, and bills by much. The major effect is that bills do not disappear entirely from the portfolio when we move to high mean real rates of return, because we need bills to serve as margin on the commodity futures contracts. We also see that, as we move to higher mean real rates of return and the investment in stocks goes up, the size of the relative position in commodity futures increases steadily, although it never exceeds 15 percent of the total value of the investment portfolio.

   What is the effect on the trade-off curve of assuming a positive mean rate of return on commodity futures? Table 6–5 and Figure 6–4 present the results of assuming a 2 percent per year mean rate. Perhaps the best way to describe the effect is as an upward shift of the entire curve. At any level of risk, we can achieve a higher mean real rate of return, with the gain being larger the higher the level of risk. Even the minimum-risk portfolio now has a positive mean rate of return of .1 percent per year. It now becomes possible to attain a 7 percent mean real rate of return with a standard deviation of only 16.05 percent instead of 19.48 percent, by holding

Risk-Return Trade-off Curves

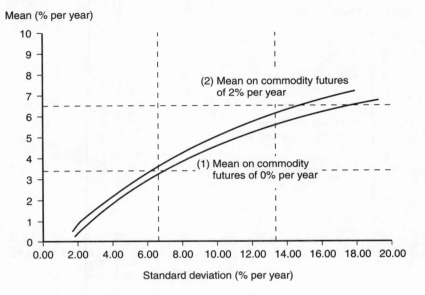

Mean (% per year)

(2) Mean on commodity futures of 2% per year

(1) Mean on commodity futures of 0% per year

Standard deviation (% per year)

Effect of Increased Mean Rate of Return on Commodity Futures to 2 Percent Per Year

Mean	Standard Deviation	Portfolio Proportions			
		Stocks	Bonds	Bills	Commodity Futures
0.1%	1.44%	0	0	1.00	.05
1.0	2.31	.05	.15	.80	.09
2	3.81	.11	.33	.56	.13
3	5.45	.16	.52	.32	.16
4	7.12	.21	.70	.09	.20
5	9.23	.37	.70	.03	.30
6	12.40	.57	.39	.04	.43
7	16.05	.77	.18	.05	.55

a portfolio consisting of 77 percent stocks, 18 percent bonds, 5 percent bills, and a position in commodity futures equal to 55 percent of the portfolio's value.

SUMMARY AND CONCLUSION

The objective of this paper has been to explore how a tax-exempt investor can use a passive buy-and-hold investment strategy in a diverse basket of commodity futures contracts as a supplement to common stocks, bonds, and bills to improve the risk-return trade-off in an inflationary environment. We made the argument that such a broad-based position in commodity futures would tend to do well when there is unanticipated inflation, because commodity prices and consumer prices tend to move together. The evidence of the period from 1953 through 1981 seems to support this hypothesis. The evidence also suggests that the returns on stocks, bonds, and bills were negatively affected by inflation.

Using the historical correlations between the returns on these four categories of investments and making plausible assumptions about their mean rates of return, we then derived the pretax, real risk-return trade-off curve facing an investor. By comparing the curve derived with commodity futures to the one without, we demonstrated that there was a substantial gain from including commodities.

ENDNOTES

1. See H. Markowitz, "Portfolio Selection," *Journal of Finance,* Volume 7 Number 1, March 1952.
2. For a discussion of how to choose the optimal point on the trade-off curve, see Z. Bodie, "Hedging Against Inflation," *Sloan Management Review,* Fall 1979.
3. Margins on commodity futures contracts are typically low, ranging from 7 percent to 10 percent of the face value of the contract. For more detail about the commodity futures series, see Z. Bodie and V. Rosansky, "Risk and Return in Commodity Futures," *Financial Analysts Journal,* May/June 1980.
4. There is a good deal of controversy in the economics literature on this point. For further discussion and references, see Bodie and Rosansky, op. cit.
5. The optimization procedure is described in Markowitz, op. cit.

PART TWO

Managed Futures Product Development

CHAPTER 7

MANAGEMENT SUMMARY

Title: "Institutional Managed Futures Overlay: Innovation in Portfolio
Theory, Risk Reduction, and Alpha Generation"

Author: Patrick F. Hart III and Richard E. Bornhoft
Hart-Bornhoft Group, Denver, CO

Synopsis: Many institutional investors have redefined their approach to
managed futures, and are redesigning or implementing programs around the overlay strategy application. The structure
offers the same benefits of traditional managed futures programs
without the necessary capital funding requirements. Some of the
advantages of overlay programs include additional performance
enhancement, noncorrelative alpha, and a minimal required cash
commitment.

Institutional Managed Futures Overlay: Innovation in Portfolio Theory, Risk Reduction, and Alpha Generation

Patrick F. Hart III

Richard E. Bornhoft*
Hart-Bornhoft Group

The objective of this chapter is to explore the significant investment opportunities afforded institutional investors through a managed futures overlay strategy. We begin with an overview of managed futures in general.

To effectively respond to a constantly changing investment environment, institutional portfolio managers and investors must continually redefine and expand their investment strategies and policies. Prudence and logic dictate incorporating complementary, noncorrelated strategies that simultaneously manage the volatility and risk of a portfolio, enhancing its overall risk-adjusted performance.

Obtaining a diversified portfolio mix is critical in minimizing risk. The proliferation of innovative financial instruments and sophisticated investment strategies over the past 15 years has greatly expanded the portfolio and risk-management alternatives available to institutional investors—in particular, exchange-listed futures and options, and over-the-counter (nonexchange-traded) derivative instruments. It is interesting to note that the futures markets predated the equity markets by almost 200 years, yet it was not until the 1970s that the use of futures and derivative strategies to manage risk in stock, bond, and currency portfolios, and later the application of managed futures as a diversifying strategy within an institutional portfolio, began to emerge.

---

*Hart-Bornhoft Group, Inc., is a Registered Investment Advisor specializing in managed futures. The firm structures multi-advisor portfolios for U.S. and internationally based private and institutional investors.

MANAGED FUTURES DEFINED

The term *managed futures* describes a strategically designed investment vehicle structured to participate in global futures, options, and foreign-exchange markets through a professionally managed program. Such programs are commonly organized and actively managed by independent experts who perform the role of a "Futures Portfolio Manager," and systematically allocate investment capital among a diversified composite of professional commodity trading advisors. Commodity-trading-advisor firms provide the trading expertise and money management directives on behalf of the managed futures program. Trading activity involves systematic and/or discretionary participation in the futures and cash markets. Historically, the role of the independent futures portfolio manager has been performed by Registered Investment Advisors or Consulting Firms specializing in managed futures.

MANAGED FUTURES–EVOLUTION OF THE MARKET

The managed futures sector of the futures industry has evolved rapidly. Industry sources estimate that assets under management grew from $500,000 in 1980, to over $24 billion by the beginning of 1996. High-net-worth investors, attracted to the unique benefits that this alternative investment medium provides when included in a diversified investment portfolio, were among the first to discover managed futures.

More recently, interest and participation from institutional investors such as foundations, endowments, corporations, financial institutions, and public pension plans has appeared in greater frequency. For institutional participants, managed futures represents a dynamic and flexible investment tool providing features and advantages not obtainable from traditional investments. When strategically integrated into a diversified portfolio mix, a managed futures program can contribute value-added benefits to the entire portfolio.

OVERALL PORTFOLIO DIVERSIFICATION

Managed futures programs provide institutional participants access to, and diversification among, a wide breadth of United States and international futures market sectors; to a variety of proven money management strategies and disciplines; and to professional management of capital at both the futures portfolio manager and commodity trading advisor levels.

Enhanced Returns with Less Risk

Over a 10-year period, a model institutional portfolio comprised of 60 percent U.S. equities and 40 percent U.S. fixed-income securities would have generated a 13.34 percent net average annual compounded return (Table 7–1). However, had 10 percent of that portfolio been allocated to a diversified, actively managed futures program (reducing both equity and debt exposure by 5 percent), the net average annual return would have risen to 13.76 percent. Increase the managed futures allocation to 20 percent (again decreasing the original asset allocation proportionately), and the portfolio's overall net return increases to 14.15 percent, or an 81-basis-point gain over the original 60 percent equity and 40 percent fixed-income allocation. Equally important, the risk and volatility of the portfolio would have actually decreased with each increase in the managed futures allocation.

The Benefit of Noncorrelation

Managed futures programs can offer attractive returns, as well as the ability to diminish overall portfolio risk through diversification, which is the primary reason for the aforementioned industry growth. A landmark study published in 1983 by Harvard Business School professor John Lintner found that including managed futures in an investment portfolio of equity and fixed-income securities "reduces volatility while enhancing returns." Furthermore, the Lintner study concluded that such portfolios "have substantially less risk at every possible level of return than portfolios of stocks, or stocks and bonds." Lintner's theory was subsequently confirmed through practical application.

Lintner's research broadened and further supported what has become known as "Modern Portfolio Theory"—the foundation for which was the "Portfolio Selection - Efficient Diversification of Investments" study published by Yale University Professor Harry Markowitz in 1952. The findings of these studies, together with results from an increasing number of institutional managed futures applications, strongly suggests that the selection of optimal combinations of assets in an investment portfolio is essential to produce the least possible risk for a given level of return. The key is incorporating assets that are "noncorrelated," or whose values tend not to move simultaneously in the same direction. Historical returns of managed futures programs show little correlation to the value movements of equity and fixed-income securities, which loosely mirror each other. At certain times, managed futures have in fact exhibited negative correlation,

TABLE 7–1

Portfolio Asset Allocation Comparison
January 1986 – December 1995

Portfolio Allocation %	Net Average Annual Return	Largest Consecutive Decline	Standard Deviation (Annualized)
60% Stocks 40% Bonds 0% Managed Futures	+13.34%	(17.38%)	9.98%
55% Stocks 35% Bonds 10% Managed Futures	+13.76%	(15.26%)	9.44%
50% Stocks 30% Bonds 20% Managed Futures	+14.15%	(13.12%)	9.17%

Stocks: S&P 500 Total Return Index (Dividends Reinvested)

Bonds: Lehman Government/Corporate Bond Index (Interest Reinvested)

Managed Futures: Managed Account Reports Qualified CTA Universe (Interest Reinvested) - This is a managed futures benchmark that compiles a "peer group" of commodity trading advisors.

Please note: The performance figures for managed futures would improve, if we used a longer time period.

or value movement in the opposite direction of equity and debt markets. Historically, this relationship is most pronounced when traditional investments experience prolonged corrections.

Additional Advantages

In addition to the potential for enhanced portfolio returns with less overall risk, managed futures programs offer the following investment advantages:

- ***Global Market Diversification and Access to International Investment Opportunities.***
  Futures exchanges extend from the United States to London, Paris, Tokyo, Singapore, and Australia, providing institutional users the opportunity to capitalize on entirely new categories of international profit opportunities, and to benefit from changes in global interest-rate and equity markets, currency-rate shifts, and changes in worldwide supply and demand for traditional commodities.

- ■ *Market and Contract Diversification.*
  Managed futures market and contract diversification encompasses all of the world's major market groups, which include but are not limited to (specific examples shown parenthetically):

  - ■ Interest rates (U.S. Treasuries, Eurodollars, German bund, French notional bond).
  - ■ Stock indexes (S&P 500, London FT-SE 100, French CAC-40, Nikkei 225).
  - ■ Foreign currencies (U.S. dollar, Japanese yen, German deutschemark, Swiss franc, Canadian dollar).
  - ■ Precious and base metals (gold, silver, copper).
  - ■ Energy (crude oil, heating oil, natural gas, unleaded gasoline).
  - ■ Agricultural commodities (corn, wheat, soybeans).
  - ■ Softs (cotton, coffee, cocoa, orange juice, sugar).

- ■ *Bi-Directional Profit Opportunities and Low Transaction Costs.*
  Futures market participants can establish short positions with the same ease as long positions (unlike equity markets, there are no cumbersome restrictions). Thus, commodity trading advisors have the ability to capitalize on both rising and declining markets, in addition to favorable and unfavorable economic conditions and political developments. This important characteristic provides an investment alternative to traditional investments that historically have been vulnerable to directional bias. Moreover, transaction costs are a fraction of dollar-equivalent stock and bond transactions (for example, a $1 million currency trade can be executed for as little as $200).

- ■ *Hedge the Portfolio against Inflation and Deflation.*
  Managed futures programs can also profit in inflationary and deflationary periods, when prices of interest-rate sensitive financial instruments and physical commodities (e.g., equity and debt instruments, precious metals, and energy products) react to these forces.

■ *Liquidity.*
Futures market trading volume has expanded more than 2000 percent since the late 1960s, and the annual dollar value of all futures contracts traded in the United States alone surpassed $10 trillion in the early 1990s. Furthermore, an estimated $1 trillion of trades are executed in the Interbank Foreign-Exchange market during each 24-hour period. Such liquidity, coupled with the aforementioned low transaction costs, enables commodity trading advisors to quickly initiate or liquidate positions, and to capitalize on price movements when they occur.

■ *Interest Income.*
Because capital deposits utilized for margin requirements are typically pledged as "good faith" in the form of interest-bearing cash market instruments, most, if not all of a managed futures program's equity balance generates interest income to the benefit of the investor.

■ *Regulatory Control/Oversight.*
Futures market participants benefit from government (Commodity Futures Trading Commission) and self-regulatory body (National Futures Association) regulation, as well as oversight by most non-U.S. futures exchanges. These rules and regulations promote accountability and provide additional oversight of trading activities and disclosure requirements.

INSTITUTIONAL APPLICATIONS

Institutional managed futures programs are highly customized to the investor's precise investment objectives and policies. Investor-specific programs can be employed in a number of effective strategies, providing flexible solutions to enhance a portfolio's risk and return characteristics. Institutional applications for managed futures generally fall within three primary categories (Table 7–2):

1. Direct allocation
2. Structured product
3. Overlay strategy

TABLE 7-2

Institutional Managed Futures Applications

Institutional Considerations	Direct Allocation	Structured Product	Overlay Strategy
Investment Objective	Absolute Return/ Portfolio Diversification	Absolute Return/ Portfolio Diversification	Portable Alpha Generation/ Portfolio Diversification
Attributable Returns	Manager Skill	Manager Skill	Manager Skill
Time Horizon	Long-Term	Long-Term	Long-Term
Required Funding	Yes	Yes	No
Customization	Yes	Yes	Yes
Diversification	Global/Specialized	Global/Specialized	Global/Specialized
Liquidity	Complete	Complete/Limited	Complete
Transparency	Complete	Standard	Complete

Direct Allocation

Institutions have traditionally adopted the direct allocation approach when investing in managed futures. This involves a direct cash allocation *(part of the asset allocation policy)* to a futures portfolio manager who designs, structures, implements, and manages a managed futures portfolio comprised of a diversified composite of professional commodity trading advisors. The long-term objective is to generate absolute returns that will in turn enhance the institution's overall investment portfolio.

Structured Product

Structured products typically offer a guaranteed principal feature and an underlying managed futures portfolio component, all within the structure of a conventional security (e.g., note, bond, certificate of deposit, fund-to-fund). Such products provide an institutional user with a familiar investment vehicle that provides the positive diversification aspects of managed futures, the potential to deliver enhanced performance, and the benefit of limited liability.

Overlay Strategy

A managed futures overlay strategy is an enhancement program that can be applied to any or all other asset classes within an institution's portfolio, with the objective of providing manager skill and overall portfolio "alpha." However, unlike a direct allocation or a structured product, implementing managed futures as an overlay strategy requires minimal, if not zero, funding by an institution.

INSTITUTIONAL MANAGED FUTURES OVERLAY

Many institutional investors have redefined their approach to managed futures, and are re-designing or implementing programs around the overlay strategy application. In essence, the structure offers the same benefits of traditional managed futures programs without the necessary capital funding requirements. In addition, managed futures overlay strategies have several important advantages not available with traditional equity and fixed income overlays.

Advantages of Managed Futures as an Overlay

Additional Performance Enhancement

As previously established, including managed futures in an investment portfolio of equity and fixed-income securities reduces volatility while enhancing returns. Accordingly, managed futures applied as an overlay strategy further enhances these existing attributes.

It is apparent from Table 7–3 that the absolute return of the portfolio with a 10 percent managed futures overlay strategy exceeds the absolute return of the portfolio consisting entirely of stocks and bonds. Furthermore, the inclusion of managed futures improved the risk-adjusted return at every point along the efficient frontier for the portfolio of stocks and bonds.

Portable Alpha

Institutions are embracing the concept of "portable alpha," which allows the transfer of value from one market to another. Managed futures employed as an overlay strategy is an exceptional candidate for portable alpha because it does not require capital, and the alpha generated is not dependent upon an inherent capital market return from the underlying futures markets. These advantages allow managed futures to be transported to a specific sector or the entire portfolio mix.

TABLE 7–3

Portfolio Asset Allocation Comparison
January 1986 - December 1995

Portfolio Allocation %	Net Average Annual Return	Largest Consecutive Decline	Standard Deviation (Annualized)
60% Stocks 40% Bonds 0% Managed Futures Overlay	+13.34%	(17.38%)	9.98%
60% Stocks 40% Bonds 10% Managed Futures Overlay	+15.08%	(16.61%)	10.32%

See footnotes on Table 7–1.

Noncorrelative Alpha

The majority of the return from managed futures is attributable to the trading skill of the selected commodity trading advisors, together with that of the futures portfolio manager. Managed futures diversification encompasses all traditional asset classes and "hard assets" (e.g., stock indexes, interest rates, currencies, metals, energies). As such, the presence of noncorrelative alpha allows an institution to overlay a specific asset class or the entire portfolio.

Minimal Cash Commitment Required

Managed futures applied as an overlay strategy allows an institution to enhance the overall investment allocation of its portfolio without the actual transfer of cash from other asset classes. A managed futures overlay requires minimal, if not zero, cash commitment, and an institution is able to utilize existing securities in its portfolio as margin collateral.

OVERLAY STRATEGY DESIGN, STRUCTURE, AND IMPLEMENTATION PROCESS

Due to the intricacies of a managed futures investment, in particular an overlay strategy, many institutions choose to outsource the responsibilities of portfolio and risk management to an independent professional such as a futures portfolio manager. Such firms specialize in the area of managed futures and provide an additional layer of research, management, and oversight, which in effect is an extension of an institutional participant's staff. Futures portfolio managers play a crucial role in assisting an institution in designing, structuring, and implementing a managed futures overlay strategy (Figure 7–1). This process consists of several distinct stages:

1. Development of an investment policy and objective.
2. Commodity trading advisor identification and selection.
3. Composite portfolio design and structure.
4. Portfolio implementation.
5. Risk management, monitoring, and review.
6. Cash management.
7. Accounting and reporting.

Development of an Investment Policy and Objective

The first stage of the investment process is to develop an investment strategy that is consistent with the objectives, procedures, and mandates of the institution. Working in tandem, the futures portfolio manager and the institution must determine a number of factors including, but not limited to:

■ The projected return (targeted alpha) of a specific asset class or the overall portfolio that in turn will determine the allocation commitment to the overlay strategy.
■ Risk-tolerance and volatility parameters.
■ Market and trading-strategy diversification.
■ Determination of an appropriate benchmark(s).
■ Additional parameters and constraints unique to the institution.

Commodity Trading Advisor Identification and Selection

Once the investment objectives have been established, the futures portfolio manager will design a diversified portfolio of commodity trading advisors that complies with the institution's specific investment policy requirements, seeks consistent, long-term performance, and focuses on capital preservation. Most futures portfolio managers have established research

FIGURE 7–1

Futures Portfolio Manager Investment Approach Summary

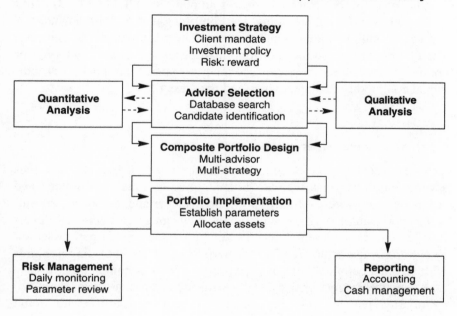

facilities with proprietary analytical tools, as well as extensive commodity trading advisor databases that are used in the identification and selection process. An exhaustive quantitative and qualitative review process is performed. Quantitative factors that should be analyzed include statistical measures that quantify risk, correlation, and performance cycles. Qualitative analysis, which is equally important, should include performance record verification, on-site due diligence, personal and professional reference checks, and a complete review of the commodity trading advisors trading program and operational infrastructure. Following this review, commodity trading advisors possessing the ability to contribute toward achieving the overlay program's investment objectives are identified as potential portfolio candidates.

Composite Portfolio Design and Structure

A multi-advisor portfolio is then structured specifically for the overlay program, diversified among a strategically designed composite of commodity trading advisors employing differing investment methodologies and money management strategies. In designing the portfolio, research and analysis should focus on the interrelationships among the individual commodity trading advisor trading programs. The contribution of each trading advisor is assessed and incorporated into the composite portfolio selection process. The objective of the futures portfolio manager is to create a multi-advisor composite that offers more consistent performance than that of any individual commodity trading advisor, and with less risk.

Portfolio Implementation

The next stage is the portfolio implementation process. This involves several important steps, such as: (a) incorporating investment policies and risk parameters with the futures portfolio manager and the outside consultant (if applicable); (b) the completion of legal agreements between all parties; (c) performing a search and deciding upon the counter-party relationships (brokerage firm(s), and FX dealer(s)); (d) opening trading accounts with selected commodity trading advisors, as well as completing the cash management arrangements (usually with the custodian/trustee); and (e) negotiating fee and commission schedules. There may be additional responsibilities, depending upon the managed futures application.

Risk Management, Monitoring, and Review

Risk management is an integral part of a managed futures overlay strategy. The investment objective of the overlay strategy is coordinated with the specific mandates and investment parameters outlined in the institution's investment policy. Prior to implementation, each individual commodity trading advisor component, as well as the composite portfolio, is assigned preestablished investment parameters. These include:

- Margin: Equity limits
- Volatility ranges
- Market restrictions

- Maximum loss
- Contract exposure
- Market exposure

Daily trade and cash management information flows from the brokerage firm/cash dealer and the custodian/trustee to the futures portfolio manager providing total transparency and allowing staff members to assess the risk exposure of each commodity trading advisor and the entire composite portfolio on an intraday basis. Portfolio monitoring and review allows the futures portfolio manager to refine the portfolio mix, responding to new commodity trading advisor opportunities and to re-allocate assets among existing advisors and/or eliminate a selected advisor. This process is outlined in Figure 7–2.

Cash Management

Unlike participation through a direct managed futures allocation or structured product, the margin requirements of an overlay strategy can be met by pledging a minimum amount of collateral in the form of cash and/or securities already owned by the institution (U.S. Treasury notes and bonds are acceptable as collateral by most brokerage firms). Furthermore, if existing securities are utilized as collateral, it should be noted that the yield from the committed securities will continue to accrue to the institution.

FIGURE 7–2

Portfolio Risk Management

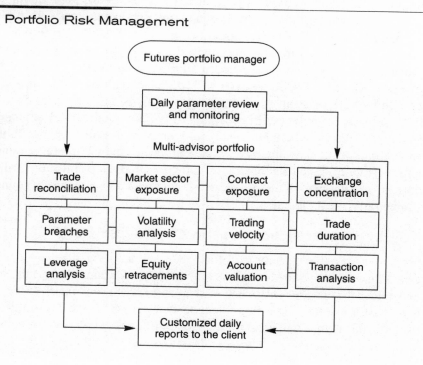

Accounting and Reporting

Once the managed futures overlay program is implemented, the futures port-folio manager provides a reporting schedule tailored to the institution's spe-cific requirements. This is comprised of daily reports that disclose the current status of the portfolio, as well as monthly, quarterly, and annual performance reviews. Specific information includes, but is not limited to:

- Market overview.
- Summarized daily trading activity.
- Review of risk parameters (volatility, leverage, profits/losses, etc.).
- Realized and unrealized positions.
- Exchange concentration.
- Commodity trading advisor valuation.
- Composite portfolio valuation.

ADDITIONAL CONSIDERATIONS

Expense Structure

Institutional managed futures programs have historically maintained an expense structure higher than their equity and debt counterparts. If imple-mented as a direct allocation or structured product, the ability to earn inter-est income on the entire allocation will offset a majority of the expense. Furthermore, if managed futures are applied as an overlay strategy, the expense structure is competitive with alpha or value-added strategies offered by traditional investment managers. This is attributable to the fact that the majority of the return generated from traditional overlay strategies is achieved through the inherent capital market return (or "beta"). Only a small fraction of the return represents alpha. Conversely, performance returns from managed futures are essentially "all alpha." Thus, the cost of obtaining alpha from a traditional overlay approach or a managed futures strategy is virtually identical.

Benchmark Selection for the Overlay Strategy

Traditional investments have performance benchmarks that allow an institu-tional investor to passively replicate the asset class using a long-only, buy and hold methodology. The selection of an appropriate benchmark for deriv-atives, such as managed futures, is dependent on whether the institutional user's belief is that managed futures are entirely skilled-based, or should be categorized as an investment class that has an inherent return, or

FIGURE 7–3

Key Components of a Managed Futures Strategy

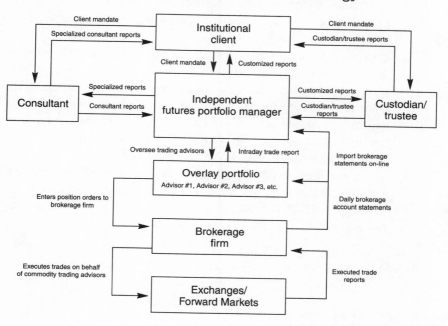

possibly a combination thereof. If the determination is that managed futures is entirely skilled-based, whereby the performance is a result of manager skill, then a benchmark that replicates a passive approach is not practical and an absolute return performance objective is more appropriate. Conversely, if an institution believes that managed futures do possess an inherent return that can be passively replicated, the benchmark selection process may point to several alternative quasi-passive indexes that presently exist in the futures industry (i.e., Goldman Sachs Commodity Index, MLM Index). When managed futures are being applied as an overlay strategy, an institution should consider one or several of the following benchmark alternatives:

- ■ *A targeted rate of return.* This approach determines an expected absolute return, which is measured over a complete market cycle of at least 3 to 5 years. In addition to a "targeted rate of return," specific risk parameters can be defined to measure volatility.

- *Peer group comparison.* This benchmark compares performance to that of commodity trading advisors employing similar trading strategies. This measurement should reflect like diversification, fee structures, and interest income as represented in the actual overlay strategy.

- *Comparison to other alpha strategies.* This alternative would include all other alpha strategies, such as alpha received from traditional active management, as well as strategies from investment alternatives. The benchmark would require adjustment so that the overlay parameters were consistent across the alpha strategies being compared (e.g., equivalent risk tolerance levels, similar portfolio overlay allocations).

- *A "zero-return" approach.* A "zero-return" benchmark assumes that the entire performance from managed futures is "alpha-based," and therefore any positive return is recognized as value-added.

In actual practice, most institutions use a combination of benchmarks to provide several comparisons from varying points of view.

IN SUMMARY

Managed futures is a strategically designed investment vehicle designed to participate in global futures, options, and foreign-exchange markets through a professionally managed program. Such programs are highly flexible and can be customized to accomplish a variety of investor objectives, and include multiple levels of portfolio monitoring and risk control.

Specifically:

- Managed futures returns are largely noncorrelated to the price movement of traditional equity and fixed-income securities over the long term.

- A landmark study published by Harvard Business School professor John Lintner found that including managed futures in an investment portfolio of equity and fixed-income securities reduces volatility while enhancing returns. The study concluded that such portfolios have substantially less risk at every possible level of return than portfolios of stocks or stocks and bonds.

- In addition to providing noncorrelative returns that can enhance the overall return of a portfolio while reducing its risk, managed futures programs offer global market diversification and access to international investment opportunities, extreme liquidity, and low transaction costs.

■ Institutional applications for managed futures generally fall within three categories:

  ■ **Direct allocation,** in which capital is allocated directly to a futures portfolio manager who structures a well-diversified portfolio.

  ■ **Structured products,** which offer both a guaranteed principal feature and underlying managed futures portfolio component within the framework of a conventional security.

  ■ **Overlay strategy,** which can be applied to any or all asset classes within a portfolio and requires a minimal capital commitment, if any funding at all (existing securities in the portfolio can be used as collateral).

■ Most institutions would be well advised to consider outsourcing the overlay strategy design, structure, and implementation responsibilities to an independent futures portfolio manager, who structures and manages the program according to the institution's specific risk parameters and return objectives.

■ Virtually all of the return derived from an overlay strategy is considered "alpha"—that is, attributable to the trading expertise and money management directives of professional commodity trading advisors in addition to the program's allocation and management skill of an independent futures portfolio manager.

■ A combination of appropriate benchmarks may be determined to measure the effectiveness of the strategy. These include:

  ■ **Targeted rate of return**
  ■ **Peer group comparison**
  ■ **Comparison to other alpha strategies**
  ■ **Zero-return approach**

CHAPTER 8

MANAGEMENT SUMMARY

Title: "The Role and the Value of the Trading Manager

Author: David M. Love, CFA, President
            Kenmar Institutional Investment Management LLC.

Synopsis: This chapter discusses the role of the Trading Manager in the
            implementation of a managed futures investment program. The
            responsibilities include designing the program to the specific
            risk/reward parameters of the client, trader research and selec-
            tion, ongoing management of the portfolio composition and risk,
            and reporting.

The Role and the Value of the Trading Manager

David Love

The diversification attributes of managed futures are well documented; when included in portfolios of conventional investments, managed futures tend to raise returns and reduce risk. This dual effect is true whether managed futures are implemented as a separate allocation or, more efficiently, as an overlay. Likewise, the existence of a "manager skill premium," or *alpha*, is a widely accepted characteristic of an active managed futures program. The role and value of the trading manager are to find, structure, and manage alpha.

The trading manager makes no direct trading decisions. Rather, he or she identifies and manages the traders who in turn are responsible for making all the trading decisions relating to the client's managed futures account. There is a direct parallel to the equity manager who researches, structures, and manages the risk in portfolios of stocks with the trading manager who researches, structures, and manages the risk in portfolios of managed futures traders.

Creating a managed futures investment is a several-stage program encompassing an array of considerations for the trading manager. The initial phase, which involves the design of the program, centers on the following:

- Client objectives and program parameters.
- Trader selection.
- Portfolio design and structure.

Once the program has been implemented, the process of program management incorporates the following activities:

- Trader and trading performance evaluation.
- Reallocations and portfolio rebalancing.
- Reporting.

Each of these disciplines is critical to the ongoing success of the program. While designing the portfolio is certainly an essential element in eventual success, it is only the first step in the ongoing active management of the program and its mix of traders.

CLIENT OBJECTIVES AND PROGRAM PARAMETERS

The trading manager begins each investment program with a thorough and carefully considered discussion of each client's specific objectives and risk tolerances. This interchange sets the guidelines and parameters of the program structure within which the traders and trading manager will operate.

In the case of a managed futures overlay program, the trading manager must discuss and preestablish with the client the following key elements of the program:

- Return objectives, benchmarks, and time frames for performance evaluation.
- Acceptable levels of volatility.
- Allowable exposure to market sectors.
- Maximum collateral available.
- Maximum loss limit.
- Commission levels.
- Trader and trading manager management and incentive fees.

Once these elements of the program are decided, the trading manager can then proceed with the development of the trader composite.

TRADER EVALUATION

Research on traders begins with quantification—and the absolute starting point is the database. Although there are numerous nonproprietary trader databases available, the larger, more-established trading managers generally have proprietary data banks encompassing hundreds of different traders and trading systems.

The quantitative process decodes the statistical data offered by traders into meaningful insights about their performance characteristics, trading methodologies, and management styles. The trading manager looks at performance from several different perspectives, including statistical measures of risk versus return to identify traders who, on a long-term basis, are capable of generating consistent premiums over the risk-free rate. Proprietary computerized models are used to enhance the quantitative analysis. These models analyze individual trades over several years of data, allowing the trading manager to investigate the characteristics of individual trades and of trading performance in each market group. By digging deep into the details of a trader's actual trading activity, the trading manager is able to analyze each trader's losing periods, recovery periods, and overall performance patterns. After all statistical measures are completed, traders are categorized by trading methodology and ranked against other traders within their own category.

Quantitative performance data alone, however, are insufficient in making decisions about trader suitability—because past performance, by itself, really is no indication of future results. To obtain a more rounded viewpoint of a trading program, the trading manager conducts detailed interviews with his or her trading candidates. Using both the qualitative information supplied by direct interviews and the statistical data provided through quantitative analysis, the trading manager then conducts an in-depth evaluation of trading activity, characteristics of individual trades, and—most important— an analysis of how and when a trading program profits.

As an example of how this research process actually works, recently there was a well-established trader that had compiled an exceptional record using what he described as a pure arbitrage strategy. As a result of his record and his unique approach, the trader had attracted a large inflow of assets under management. The trading manager's trade-by-trade analysis, however, suggested that the trader was supplementing his arbitrage positions with directional trades. This research then provided the foundation for a series of questions during the interview stage. When these concerns were not satisfactorily addressed, the trading manager elected not to place any assets with the trader. Subsequently, the directional trades that were, in fact, being implemented went against the trader, generating substantial losses. Absent the in-depth due diligence, there would have been no way to ascertain that the trader was following a system that was different from what was advertised.

Examinations of trading methodology serve two additional important purposes. First, they give the trading manager a thorough understanding of the trader's ability to trade profitably in varying market climates. Second, they help identify a trader's strengths and weaknesses. This is important in determining how a trader might complement different trader groupings in a portfolio structure.

Although a trading manager will employ the services of many well-known and well-established traders, his or her future lies in part in his or her ability to identify, support, and develop new trading talent. (In fact, many of the "well-known, well-established" traders were at one time part of various trading managers' development programs and experienced their first substantial success in a trading manager's investment portfolio.) New traders, passing stringent due diligence, may be allocated proprietary capital on a test basis. During this time, the trading manager discusses the activities and results of the investment with the trader in order to gain an added dimension of understanding of that particular trader's specific characteristics. An important test of the confidence of a trading manager in his or her trader selection process is whether or not he or she has proprietary capital with every trader to which he or she has allocated client capital.

PORTFOLIO DESIGN—DETERMINING TRADER MIXES

The second stage of the trading manager's investment process focuses on controlling risk by combining traders with varying approaches and performance characteristics. Here, the objective is to construct a team of traders whose combined performance will best suit the program's risk /return objectives.

The process is complex, but pivotal to success. To perform this function well, the trading manager must consider whether the differing strategies and markets traded provide sufficient diversification. Weightings must then be evaluated on a constant basis and shifted to optimize opportunity in response to changes in the global climate. An example of the trader diversification across styles, analytical tools employed, and markets traded is shown in Figure 8–1.

Once the trading manager has identified the appropriate traders, he or she must determine the leverage to apply to each. By modifying leverage when appropriate, the trading manager is better able to take advantage of each trader's strengths within the context of both the current market environment and the client's specific performance goals. This step in the process can only be achieved as a result of extensive analytical work, affording the trading manager the opportunity to select a trader that is at the bottom of its performance cycle, rather than chasing the "hot" trader.

FIGURE 8-1

Representative Portfolio Structure
Trader Diversification

Traders:

Style	A	B	C	D	E	F	G	H	I	J	K
Discretionary	✓				✓	✓		✓			✓
Computerized			✓	✓							
Systematized		✓					✓		✓		
Discretionary overlay		✓					✓				
Analytical tools											
Technical	✓	✓	✓		✓	✓	✓	✓	✓	✓	✓
Fundamental	✓				✓	✓		✓			
Markets traded											
Diversified	✓	✓	✓				✓			✓	
Specialized				✓	✓	✓		✓	✓		✓
U.S. markets	✓	✓	✓	✓	✓		✓		✓		
Non-U.S. markets	✓	✓	✓		✓	✓		✓		✓	✓

Additionally, the analytical data are useful in determining points at which to reduce the commitment to a trader, which often occurs following a significant surge in performance.

Although there is no guarantee a group of traders will perform with less volatility than one single trader, common sense and statistical analysis both indicate that trader teams will generally produce lower volatility than a single trader. This means lower risk and a smoother return curve over the life of the program.

MONITORING AND ONGOING MANAGEMENT

The selection of traders is not a one-time decision, although trading managers will vary in the degree of hands-on management applied to the trader portfolios. For a trading manager that believes that market conditions must dictate the selection of a portfolio of traders and the reallocation of assets among the traders, the function must be a continuous, dynamic process, requiring daily monitoring and time-sensitive changes.

Key to this process is the regular examination and evaluation of the traders, including extensive and exhaustive return attribution analysis.

These procedures form the basis for reallocations, new trader selections, and the termination, if required, of existing traders.

The trading manager must monitor each portfolio on a real-time basis. At the conclusion of each day's trading, activity and position statements detail every trade. The portfolios are examined from three perspectives daily:

- By each trade
- By trader
- By market

Flags and violation thresholds are preestablished so, if they occur, they will be automatically triggered through the reporting process. Trades are cross-checked each evening between reports received from the brokerage houses and from the traders. These trades are input into computer systems for ongoing analysis through the research process. Figure 8–2 is a schematic representation of this process. Should action be required, the trading manager will immediately consult with the trader, reallocate capital, or, in some instances, remove or replace the trader.

To illustrate the importance of the monitoring function, it is useful to reflect on a situation that unfolded a number of years ago. A trader who was widely respected as one of the most successful developers of sophisticated trading systems had been managing funds for a trading manager for some years. Through the monitoring process, it became clear to the trading manager's research staff that the trader was trading in a pattern different from the signal recognition system that had served it so well in the past. When confronted with this evidence, the trader confirmed that he, in fact, was making a discretionary override of his system based on his independent perceptions of developments in the market. The trading manager wished the trader well with this new strategy—and asked for the immediate return of his money. It did not matter to the trading manager whether or not the discretionary override worked; what was critical was that the trader had departed from his system. As it turned out, the new strategy did not work at all and the trader imploded. Had the trading manager not implemented his disciplined monitoring and ongoing management process, he and his clients would have suffered alongside the rest of the trader's customers.

Clearly, the trading manager function is a continuous process, involving daily monitoring of performance, trading activity, and market conditions. Experience has shown that even the best traders are not equally successful in all market environments, requiring the mix of traders to be

FIGURE 8–2

Trader Accountability

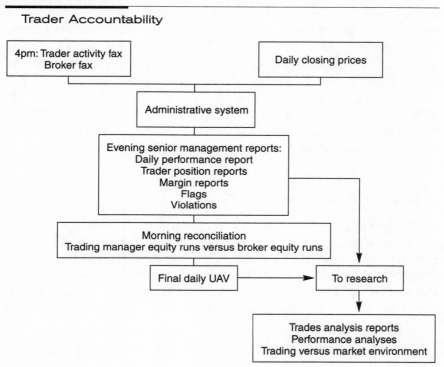

adapted to new conditions or trends by the trading manager. The result is a client-specific investment management program that is responsive initially and on an ongoing basis to the individual preferences of the client while providing the diversification and return characteristics that drive managed futures investment programs.

IS A TRADING MANAGER NECESSARY?

An institution could implement a managed futures allocation or overlay through a passive strategy that would obviate the need for traders or a trading manager. However, this approach obviates the opportunity to access the manager skill premium that is endemic to managed futures. To obtain the managed futures alpha, the institution is relegated to employing active trading talent.

An investor *could* place funds with one or more traders based on historical performance data and do just fine. However, without the internal research structure and ongoing monitoring and risk management systems, the institution is placed in a vulnerable position as a fiduciary should one or more of the traders go off track. Because this is a specialized function, only the largest institutions could economically justify building the internal staff to support this activity. This also assumes that it could find people with sufficient skill and experience to perform this function effectively. Generally, it will be much more efficient to bear the relatively modest additional cost of employing a trading manager to fulfill this responsibility.

CONCLUSION AND SUMMARY

Manager skill premium or alpha is an integral component of the return enhancement and risk reduction attributes of managed futures. Whether as a separate allocation or as a portfolio overlay, the most effective way for an investor to access this premium is through an active trader composite. The trading manager makes no trading decisions directly, but rather identifies and manages the traders in the portfolio. His or her responsibilities encompass a spectrum, including:

- Helping design the program to the specific risk/reward parameters of the client.
- Trader research and selection.
- Ongoing management of the portfolio composition and risk.
- Performance evaluation.
- Reporting.

As a result, in most cases, the employment of a trading manager is the most effective way for an investor to implement and obtain the maximum diversification benefits of a managed futures program and, at the same time, fulfill its fiduciary obligation.

CHAPTER 9

MANAGEMENT SUMMARY

Title: "The Logic of Currency Overlay"
Author: Barbara Rockefeller, President
           Rockefeller Treasury Services
Synopsis: This chapter discusses how risk management is a rational
           approach to the problem of currency volatility and translation.
           As opposed to hedging, currency overlay programs have the
           potential to add value to the investment process.

The Logic of Currency Overlay

Barbara Rockefeller

The central issue of currency overlay management is whether foreign portfolios should be hedged against falling currency values that result in unfavorable translation of returns in dollar terms. It seems obvious that there's no point in taking sovereign and other risks by investing in foreign countries, only to see gains be apparently washed away by currency depreciation vis-a-vis the home currency (here assumed to be the U.S. dollar).

A portfolio manager may excel as a stock-picker or yield-curve player when judged solely in local currency terms; it's unfair to judge him on an overall dollar basis if he gains 20 percent in his chosen market and gives much of it back on the currency translation.

Every major newspaper publishes the performance of foreign stock markets in local currency and U.S. dollar terms. The contrast can be shocking.

Barbara Rockefeller, President of Rockefeller Treasury Services and Rockefeller Asset Management, is an economist and technician specializing in the foreign exchange market. Rockefeller Treasury Services publishes daily and monthly reports on the major currencies and cross-rates that provide buy/sell signals and commentary. The report's 5-year track record is 10.5 percent p.a. on average per currency. Clients include multinational corporations and fund managers. Rockefeller Asset Management manages client funds. B.A., Reed College and M.A., Columbia University.

World Stock Market Performance
Year-to-Date, April 26, 1996

Country	Return, Local currency (%)	Return, U.S. dollars (%)
United Kingdom	4.9%	2.0%
Germany	16.5	10.5
Switzerland	11.5	3.8
Japan	7.8	5.2

Source: *The New York Times*, April 28, 1996.

A portfolio manager in *these* markets in *this* timeframe would have excelled in local currency terms and underperformed in U.S. dollar terms solely because of the translation effect. The opposite situation can happen, too: poor local currency market performance brightened by translation, as shown in the next chart.

World Stock Market Performance
Year-to-Date, April 26, 1996

Country	Return, Local currency (%)	Return, U.S. dollars (%)
Australia	4.5%	11.0%
Italy	12.2	13.8
Mexico	18.3	23.3
New Zealand	−1.1	3.5

Source: *The New York Times*, April 28, 1996.

To hedge everything at all times is to miss the return-enhancement opportunity represented by the local currency performance shown in the first table. To hedge nothing is to pass up protection of the home-currency value of returns shown in the second table. This is the classic cash versus opportunity problem: you never know in advance whether investments fall into the appreciating or depreciating currency class.

What's worse is that there is no perfect hedge. Even if you could forecast future exchange rates precisely, you would still need to know the expected holding period of the underlying asset, and no investment manager will provide such information. Moreover, the currency market offers only two hedging techniques, and neither is satisfactory. The forward market is deep and liquid, but forward rates are determined by interest rate differentials. They are not forecasts, and can worsen (or improve) results arbitrarily. The option market is said to be "pure" insurance, but the buyer of a foreign currency put is getting an at-the-money strike price of... the outright forward rate. **If the central issue is *whether* to hedge, hard on its heels is *how* to hedge cost effectively once the hedging decision has been made.**

Many studies, several of which are offered in this book, describe the correlations among currencies and markets and try to estimate the validity and efficiency of hedging. Very few go to the heart of the matter, which we call the simple logic of overlay. To the extent that currency hedging is a form of insurance, currency overlay lies in the continuum of "portfolio insurance" analysis. It's easy, however, to become distracted by statistics (the trees) and lose sight of the core business goal (the forest).

WHY INVEST IN FOREIGN MARKETS IN THE FIRST PLACE?

Understanding the purpose of foreign investment is the key to understanding currency overlay. We start with a textbook assumption:

The only reason to make a foreign investment is to get a real return in the home currency (after-tax) higher than the real return available in the home currency.

The home-currency real return is one of the Treasury yields in the fixed-income market, or one of the stock indexes in equities. At this writing, the yield on the 30-year U.S. Treasury bond is 6.79 percent. You can buy these bonds, hold them to maturity, and be sure of getting 6.79 percent plus the original capital (assuming no U.S. government default). In equities, the S & P returned 16.33 percent on average over the past three years (calendar 1993-95) with dividends reinvested. The range is wide—37.6 percent in 1995 compared with a mere 1.3 percent in 1994—but typically investments are made for some unspecified "long-term."

The goal of foreign investment is to outperform these benchmarks because of the extra risks taken. We may also want to mention that diversification reduces risk, and optimal portfolio allocation among markets is a fine and clever thing—but diversification is not the true goal. Making more money than can be made at home is the true goal.

The risks of foreign investment are substantial and the only reason to take them is the expectation of offsetting them with returns higher than the returns at home. Foremost is the **price risk** of the underlying asset. Next is **sovereign risk**, which encompasses the inability or unwillingness to repay debt, outright expropriation of assets, the blocking of funds, new tariffs and other taxes, and other unpleasant and unprofitable events.

Credit risk includes misunderstood foreign accounting conventions as well as deliberate fraud arising from lax supervision. **Liquidity risk** is a function of much smaller markets elsewhere, sometimes dominated by very few participants. **Legal risk** includes the use of different principles altogether along with lack of clarity on shareholder rights. **Operations risk** covers issues like registration and custody. **Currency risk** is but one of these.

These risks are not rare and unusual, but very, very common. Stories abound. In the 1980s, Mexico and a host of others defaulted on sovereign issues and the Philippines blocked repatriation of "offshore" dollar deposits. In 1992 when the European Rate Mechanism came unglued, there was no market for Greek drachmas—literally. T. Boone Pickens discovered in the early 1990s that Japanese practice and regulations would not allow him to get on the board of directors at a company in which he was the single largest shareholder. "Big Bang" in London revealed massive amounts of lost and missing stock certificates. Just in the past 3 years we have had rogue traders in Japanese equity futures (Barings), in U.S. bonds, twice (Salomon and Daiwa), and copper (Sumitomo).

Many foreign portfolio managers argue that they do, indeed, expect to get a higher return overseas than at home and one basis for the expectation of higher returns is currency risk. Aside from the few places like Bermuda, Panama, and Hong Kong, which effectively use the U.S. dollar, all foreign investments are by definition denominated in foreign currencies. It's the only risk that can benefit the foreign investor as well as damage returns; it is unique in that it cuts both ways. Currency risk can contribute to the extra return sought to offset the other, mostly negative risks, or it can reduce or destroy returns made on the underlying assets.

WHY HEDGE? IT'S ONLY TRANSLATION

Many portfolio managers argue that the taking of currency risk, along with all the other risks associated with foreign investments, is part of what they are paid to do. Exchange rate risk can work in their favor as well as against it, and to hedge currency risk away is to unjustly deprive them of some of that extraordinary return they are seeking. As it happens, for most long time periods since the dollar was floated, they are right. The dollar has consistently, if irregularly, devalued against all the major tradable foreign currencies.

Besides, it can be argued, these are permanent investments; the sum allocated to, say, Germany may shift around within a European portfolio, but it has been decided that some amount will always be invested in Germany, out into the foreseeable future. Always to hedge the currency component of that investment is actually to *add* risk, since some hedges will be losers and since currency trends don't fit neatly into accounting periods. After all, the money is not actually going to be sent back into dollars as a transaction.

Accounting for foreign investments by translating them into dollar terms according to arbitrary accounting schedules is just accounting, not economic reality. Over the long holding period envisioned for the investment, the ultimate investor should accept currency risk as a natural aspect of the overall foreign investment decision and hope that the diversification works out favorably on the now-unforeseen day when the investment really is liquidated and sent home in dollar form.

Further, as multinational corporations hedging their exposures have learned to their sorrow, foreign exchange hedging is fraught with problems. Most hedges are inefficient, and some currencies can't be hedged at all. The forward rate is not an unbiased predictor of the future rate. Options are expensive. Currencies are highly trended, and trends can be identified reasonably well—but not in advance. Forecasting has a terrible track record. Then there is the issue of correlation between a currency and its stock or bond market. If you hedge all of a currency exposure, are you not also unwittingly hedging the underlying asset, too? If the hedge goes against you, you've got a double whammy.

This is why currency overlay "benchmarks" range from 100 percent (hedge all the risk away at all times) to zero (keep all the currency risk), with many overlay participants opting for 50 percent (hedge half). It *seems* to be a logically insoluble problem, and only well-conducted empirical studies will give us an answer as to the most cost-effective and profitable approach as globalization of markets proceeds.

CASH IS KING

To cut through this tangle, we have to go back to our simple definition:

The only reason to make a foreign investment is to get a real return in the home currency (after-tax) higher than the real return available in the home currency.

"Real return" means not only "after-inflation" but "real" in the sense that it's money that can be spent, i.e., cash. Money is the way we keep score, and the only money that matters is the stuff we can spend. Tell a retired Detroit production line worker that the German stocks in his pension fund are doing well in Deutschemarks, and he will rightly give you the raspberry. Dollars are all that matter to him, the ultimate investor, and accordingly, dollars are all that should matter to the plan sponsor or fund manager, too. In other words, it's simply false that "it's only translation"— the money *is* actually going to be sent back into dollars. To say that it isn't going to happen today (or in the near future) is to miss the point.

To say that this is a mere translation issue has a lot of appeal—but it's only partly correct. It may well be true that investing in foreign assets offers optimum diversification and reduction of risk, and that those investments are "permanent" in some sense, but it is also true that we keep score in our home currencies for the simple and practical reason that investments, and the seeking of extraordinary returns elsewhere, are made ultimately to get a home currency return. Otherwise we would not make any investments at all, let alone foreign ones, but bury gold coins in the backyard instead.

The desire to ensure that a foreign investment can be realized (cashed in) in the home currency is not simple-minded. Countries have been known to impose exchange controls with no advance notice. Markets can crash, and can crash in domino fashion. It's only common sense to want to secure the ability to get your money back, and not at some "temporarily" reduced level, either.

The purpose of overlay management is to try to neutralize any fall in the dollar value of foreign currency-denominated investments in order to obey this principle and to keep cash king. What is lost in German stocks, say, is gained on a forward foreign exchange contract or option. The "loss" in the translation of the German stock is not realized—it is not cash—but the gain in the forward contract is cash, and it's dollar investible cash. For the accounting period at hand, one offsets the other and the foreign position could be liquidated *if necessary* with no net gain or loss. The investment goal is to keep the foreign account returns always ahead of the home-currency benchmarks, and currency overlay is a necessary part of that process.

This implies that a valid currency overlay management program takes no action when the foreign currency is rising against the dollar. To hedge all exposures automatically would indeed be to deprive the manager (and owners) of the underlying assets of a key source of the expected "extraordinary" return. Therefore, if the goal of currency overlay managers is to protect the home-currency value of foreign investments at all times, sometimes this means "doing nothing."

Logically, then, currency overlay managers must engage in a dynamic process of continuous evaluation of the market; they must be opportunistic because what they are attempting is to capture opportunity (a rising foreign currency) while at the same time to protect capital (a falling foreign currency). "Dynamic" is semantically a more acceptable word, but we shouldn't shrink from the real word: opportunistic. So-called "passive" hedge-everything or hedge-nothing overlay doesn't match our underlying business goal of seeking an extraordinary return from participation in foreign markets.

Protecting against a falling foreign currency is analogous to pulling out of a country newly hostile to foreign investment, or reducing exposure if banks and brokers start to fail. Just as a portfolio manager should not ignore fresh sovereign, or credit, or liquidity, or legal risk, he should not ignore currency risk either. In a country whose currency is not hedgible, emerging currency risk may impel an exit from the country allocation altogether; in countries where the currency is hedgible, the portfolio manager has the luxury of letting the overlay manager hedge that one particular risk away. The hedge may be imperfect, but that's no reason not to use it once an authentic danger has been identified.

PHILOSOPHY AND STATISTICS

We need to know, therefore, when to do something and when to do nothing. **Timing** of hedging decisions is a controversial subject in its own right, but we assert that it is possible to get most of the timing right, most of the time in the foreign exchange market. It is a highly trended market and trend turning points can be identified reasonably well. Technical analysis is the timer's chief tool, and it can be demonstrated that robust yet simple systems (including techniques such as moving averages) outperform human judgment over long periods of time.

A major problem is time-frame. Most systems are short-term trader's systems that trade currencies as a stand-alone asset class. This is the realm of the speculator and should be avoided in the overlay context, if only because such systems tend to trade a lot, and that is not our purpose. What's needed is a big, powerful trend-identifying system that reliably signals the *primary* trends.

There are plenty of technical analysis systems in the marketplace today, many with real-time performance track records. Our own system gained about 3.5% p.a. on average over each of 5 years, and was "out of the market" (i.e., currencies rising) slightly over 70 percent of the time. Whatever system is selected, it's critical to accept that overlay hedging will have losses. Nobody has a crystal ball. The point is to have a system in the first place, and to have one which earns money to offset translation losses when needed and stays out of the market otherwise.

VOLATILITY AND OTHER BUZZWORDS

The last point is worth repeating: the purpose of putting on a hedge, in forward contract or option form, is to make a cash gain that will offset the translation loss on the underlying assets. **The purpose of the hedge is not to reduce volatility of returns, but rather to protect the return itself.** If the purpose of the hedge is to reduce volatility of returns, we would always hedge at least some portion of a foreign portfolio all the time. But hedging *all the time* is inherently inefficient because currencies go up as well as down, and hedging all the time eliminates one of the very factors expected to enhance yield. Further, the only hedges available are priced at the forward rate, which is a function of interest rate differentials and not a forecast or even necessarily a desirable target. (Obviously putting on options at desirable targets can get very expensive.)

This logic is not accepted by purveyors of "replicated options" and other structured transactions whose goal is to add to the menu of portfolio insurance. This camp *can* measure volatility and risk in a dozen ways now, and so they do. It is true that the proverbial Detroit auto worker does not want to see a 40 percent gain one year and a 40 percent loss the next, and it is the fiduciary responsibility of the manager to keep that variability at an acceptable level. To do so with continuously rolling "hedges" in the currency market is to violate our "first principle"—the only reason to make a foreign investment is to get a higher real cash return in your home currency. A rising foreign currency enhances that return, and to hedge it away in the name of reducing volatility is arbitrary and capricious. Variability of returns should be controlled by the asset allocation and country allocation process, and not laid at the feet of the only hedgible component.

Hedging the foreign exchange component of a foreign investment should be viewed as an action of last resort. The portfolio manager who is successful in local currency terms should be protected against the translation effect, but only when really needed. The use of technical analysis in hedging reduces the odds of being wrong, but doesn't eliminate it, and over-hedging can actually increase risk rather than reduce it because of the built-in inefficiency of the forward rate.

SUMMARY AND CONCLUSIONS

■ Foreign investments are made in order to obtain a return higher than the one available in the home market. Diversification for its own sake is not a valid reason to make a foreign investment, given the extra risks.

■ Translation of the investment into dollars should not show inordinate variability of return *due to translation alone*.

■ Currency risk can enhance or diminish overall home currency returns, forcing optimal currency overlay management to be dynamic (opportunistic) by definition.

■ The purpose of hedging is not to reduce volatility of returns, but rather to earn cash to offset falling home-currency translation of returns.

■ All currency hedges are imperfect as "insurance" but technical analysis can improve the timing of hedges, which should be put on only as a last resort.

CHAPTER 10

MANAGEMENT SUMMARY

Title: "Mean/Variance Analysis of Currency Overlays"
Publication: *Financial Analyst's Journal,* May-June 1994, pp. 48–56.
Author: Philippe Jorion, University of California at Irvine.
Synopsis: The study found that the current methods of currency overlay
              implementation—optimizing on total portfolio risk and return,
              and optimizing separately on currencies—produces subopti-
              mal performance. However, there is some evidence that
              returns on currencies are predictable. If so, the value added by
              overlay managers could outweigh the inherent inefficiencies
              of the set-up.

Mean/Variance Analysis of Currency Overlays

Philippe Jorion

Global investors are now paying more attention to the management of the currency risks of their portfolios. Some have started to delegate currency management to "overlay" managers. These managers use currency futures and forwards to minimize the risks or maximize the returns of the underlying asset portfolios.

With the accelerating trend toward international investing, U.S. investors are paying more attention to the impact of currency risk on their portfolio returns. Believing that many international equity managers do not have sufficient expertise in exchange rates, some institutional investors have turned to specialized "overlay" managers. They delegate selection of the "core" portfolio to a primary equity manager, either active or passive, but hire an expert to manage the currency risk of the portfolio separately. Out of a total of about $200 billion of U.S. pension funds invested abroad, about $50 billion are now actively managed as overlay portfolios.[1]

These developments raise several questions. Should currencies play a role in global portfolios? Is the delegation of currency management seriously suboptimal? Is

Philippe Jorion is Associate Professor of Finance at the Graduate School of Management of the University of California at Irvine.

there convincing evidence of predictability that would support the use of tactical currency allocation? This article reviews the theoretical and empirical arguments and analyzes conditions under which separate management of two asset classes, such as equities and currencies, is desirable.[2]

The overlay structure is inherently suboptimal because it ignores interactions between the assets in the underlying portfolio and exchange rates. Based on historical data, the efficiency loss appears to be on the order of 40 basis points for equity portfolios. This loss, of course, must be balanced against any excess returns that may be generated by specialized overlay managers.

Three approaches to currency management are considered in a mean/variance framework—(1) a *joint*, full-blown optimization over the underlying assets (stocks or bonds) and currencies, (2) a *partial* optimization over the currencies, given a predetermined position in the core portfolio, and (3) a *separate* optimization over currencies. We compare the portfolio allocations derived from these approaches and analyze conditions under which the second and third approaches are globally optimal.

Approach 1 assumes the manager has expertise in many asset classes and can structure a portfolio to account for correlations between assets and currencies. The performance of the portfolio optimized over both currencies and underlying assets can be compared with the performance of an optimal portfolio comprised of the underlying assets only. The difference measures the benefit (or cost) of managing currency risk within the global portfolio.

Approaches 2 and 3 assume currency management via an overlay program. Investors may turn to an overlay manager if they feel the core manager lacks expertise in currencies. For instance, equity managers may neglect exchange rates because currencies are less volatile than equities, hence likely to contribute less to value added. Also, many equity managers may be regional specialists, or may focus on micro rather than on macro factors in the stock-picking process. In partial optimization, Approach 2, currencies are managed separately from the core portfolio, but the manager still controls *total* portfolio risk. In separate optimization, Approach 3, currencies are managed completely independently of the rest of the portfolio, and their performance is measured against a separate benchmark—cash, for instance.

As we show, the mean/variance approach provides a unified framework for evaluating different approaches to currency management. It also includes, as special cases, "unitary" and "universal" currency hedging. Unitary ("full") currency hedging has attracted considerable attention because it has been advocated as a "free lunch," offering reduced risk with no commensurate reduction in returns.[3] Proponents of full currency hedging argue that international portfolio performance should be measured against a benchmark that is always fully hedged against currency risks.[4] In contrast, "universal" currency hedging implies that foreign asset positions should be only partially hedged, with the optimal hedge ratio being common to all assets and investors.[5]

More generally, this article discusses conditions under which currency hedging adds value to global portfolios, using historical data on major stock, bond, and currency markets over the 1978-91 period. Currency positions are kept constant throughout the sample period. This may understate the benefits from currency management if active managers systematically outperform their benchmarks. To account for this possibility, the chapter presents an active management strategy, using a foreign exchange anomaly in the context of a disciplined investment management program.

OPTIMIZING GLOBAL PORTFOLIOS

The portfolio decision problem for global investments involves a joint choice over the underlying assets and currencies. In situations where there are no restrictions whatsoever on positions, closed-form solutions can be derived for the optimal portfolio. The appendix gives these solutions. We discuss here the intuition behind the results.

In a mean/variance framework, investors choose investment weights, w, so as to maximize an objective function that is positively related to the portfolio mean, μ_p, and negatively related to the portfolio variance, σ^2_p. This trade-off between return and risk is reflected in the function $U(\mu_p, \sigma^2_p)$. In what follows:

p = the total portfolio
x = the underlying assets (stocks and bonds) and
f = the currency forward contracts.

We can now summarize the three implementations of currency management. In *a joint optimization*, Approach 1, positions in assets and currencies are determined simultaneously so as to optimize the trade-off between risk and return for the portfolio as a whole. In this case, the problem is stated:

$$Max_{w_x, w_f} \, U(\mu_p, \sigma^2_p). \tag{1}$$

The optimal positions are w^*_x (x, f) and w^*_f (x, f) where the optimal hedge positions, w^*_f (x, f), generally depend on the optimal asset positions, w^*_x (x, f), which themselves are affected by the presence of currencies in the portfolio. Also, the hedge positions contain both a speculative return component, driven by expected excess returns on currency forwards, and a variance-reduction component.

A *partial optimization*, Approach 2, is conditioned on the predetermined underlying asset positions. The asset weights, w_x, are first determined optimally without regard to the hedges. The currency weights are then optimally determined, given w_x. This two-step approach is described by:

$$\left(\begin{array}{c} Max_{w_x} \, U(\mu_x, \sigma^2_x) \\ Max_{w_f} \, U(\mu_p, \sigma^2_p | w_x) \end{array} \right). \tag{2}$$

The positions can be written as $w^*_x(x)$ and $w^*_f(f/x)$. As before, the optimal hedge positions depend on the positions in the core portfolio.

In a *separate optimization*, Approach 3, asset and hedge positions are determined independently. The weights are found by independently solving two optimization problems:

$$\left(\begin{array}{c} Max_{w_x} \, U(\mu_x, \sigma^2_x) \\ Max_{w_f} \, U(\mu_f, \sigma^2_f) \end{array} \right). \tag{3}$$

The optimal asset and hedge positions are $w^*_x(x)$ and $w_f^*(f)$. Neither the core position nor the currency position depends on the other asset class.

Currency Overlays are Suboptimal

Clearly, going from Approach 1 to Approach 3 is successively less optimal. Figure 10–1 illustrates the loss of efficiency. It displays the performances of portfolios built using these three approaches. The portfolios consist of five bonds and four forward contracts (data presented below) and assume no restrictions on the positions.

The curve on the left represents the efficient portfolios obtained under the joint optimization scenario. It can be obtained from maximizing the investor's utility function over nine parameters (the investment weights for the five bonds and four forward contracts) for different levels of risk aversion. By definition, this line dominates all other approaches.

The curves in the middle and on the right correspond to the partial and separate optimizations, respectively. In both approaches, the optimal bond portfolio, represented by the square, is first determined by maximizing the Sharpe ratio of the bond portfolio. With a partial optimization, the overlay manager then chooses the portfolio of currencies that provides the best portfolio risk/return combination. Because the bond position has already been determined the manager cannot fully exploit interactions between bonds and currencies. The curve representing the second efficient set must therefore be inside the first efficient set, reflecting the suboptimality of the partial optimization approach.

The curve on the right representing the separate optimization case, is also suboptimal. Here also bond positions are predetermined, and the optimization focuses on the risk and return of the currency portfolio. Extremely risk-averse managers will choose to have no position in currencies; their overall portfolios will coincide with their bond portfolios. Of course, this choice will not minimize total portfolio risk. This illustrates the basic inconsistency between focusing on currencies as a stand-alone portfolio and incorporating them as part of the overall portfolio.

Simulated results over the 1978-91 period indicate that overlay management can add value to global equity and bond portfolios. It cannot enhance performance by as much as an integrated approach to currency management, however.

In fact, optimizing separately is equivalent to managing in terms of *relative*, rather than absolute, returns. Roll shows that a manager who tries to minimize the variance of total tracking error, relative to a benchmark, will not produce an overall mean/variance efficient portfolio.[6] Implementing a separate optimization is the least efficient method of managing currencies and should be ruled out in favor of partial optimization.

International Bond Portfolios with Different Optimization
Methods, 1978-91

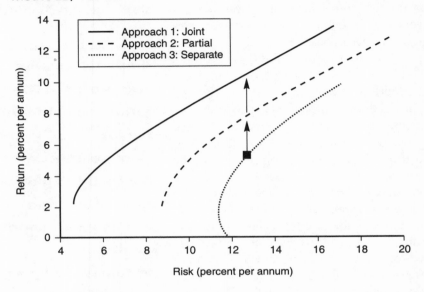

The remaining question is whether partial optimization can provide a close substitute for the more general model. The appendix shows that positions that solve Objectives 1 and 2 will be identical if returns on underlying assets, measured in dollars, are uncorrelated with exchange rates. In this case, the currency positions are equal and there is no loss of efficiency from optimizing assets and currencies separately. Furthermore, if expected returns on currencies are zero, the currency positions are zero, and there is no reason to invest in currencies.

Currency returns in our context are payoffs from positions in forward contracts. For them to equal zero, the forward rate must be an unbiased forecast of future spot rates; that is, "uncovered interest rate parity" holds. Whether this assumption is true is subject to active debate, to which the following section is devoted.

The first assumption—that dollar returns on underlying assets are uncorrelated with exchange rates—is unlikely to be met in practice. If the underlying assets are foreign stocks or bonds, then their *dollar* returns are likely to be correlated with dollar exchange rates. A less unrealistic assumption is that local-market returns are uncorrelated with exchange rates. In this case, unitary hedging is optimal, or:

$$w_f^*(x, f) = -w_x^*(x, f),$$

and each foreign market should be fully hedged against currency risk.

Unitary hedging is therefore optimal if local-currency returns are unrelated to exchange rates and if currency returns are expected to be zero. Under these stringent assumptions, fully currency hedging provides less risk at no cost. Note, however, that the partial-optimization approach is still inefficient unless core positions are determined on the basis of currency-hedged returns.

The Zero Risk Premium

It is important to emphasize that the assumption of zero risk premium drives the "free lunch" argument first advanced by Pérold and Schulman.[7] One argument posits that there should be no long-term payoff from buying a forward contract on another currency, because any gains must be offset by losses to the counterparty. Because of this symmetry, and because forward contracts are in zero net supply, currencies should offer no risk premium.

This argument is incorrect, as an analogy with stock index futures shows. Stock index futures are also in zero net supply, but they are linked to the underlying stocks through a cost-of-carry relationship: When held to maturity, a long position in futures is equivalent to a long position in the underlying cash instruments. But it is generally accepted that stocks generate long-term excess returns of about 5 percent to 10 percent annually. This risk premium must also be embedded in long positions in stock index futures. The fact that a contract is in zero net supply thus does not necessarily imply a zero risk premium.

International asset pricing models, such as the IAPM developed by Solnik, actually show that, in equilibrium, risk premiums depend on investors' risk aversion and on whether countries are net investors or net borrowers.[8] To simplify, assume a world with two investors only—U.S. and British. If British investors as a whole are net investors in the U.S., they will generally seek to reduce risk by hedging to some extent against exchange rate changes. They will thus sell dollars even if it involves a slight loss or if the forward price of the dollar is lower than the expected future spot price. In this world, U.S. investors must be net borrowers.

Therefore, U.S. investors will seek to hedge by buying the pound forward, even if the forward price of the pound is above the expected future spot price. Thus, in equilibrium, there will be a nonzero expected return to forward contracts, despite the fact that for every Briton selling dollars, an American will be buying the currency. Currencies can very well, in equilibrium, be characterized by nonzero expected returns.

Black's "universal" hedge ratio has both speculative and risk-minimization motives and implicitly assumes nonzero risk premiums.[9] Black's results, as in the IAPM, derive from the aggregation of individual optimal portfolios across countries, but also from the assumptions that all investors have the same risk tolerance and that each national wealth is exactly equal to the value of each stock market. Under these assumptions, the hedge ratio reduces to the "universal" value $h = (1 - \lambda)$.

Admittedly, the risk premium on forward contracts can be positive or negative, unlike the risk premium on stocks, and may be difficult to identify. It can even change sign if asset supplies change over time. Furthermore, the empirical evidence on expected returns on forward contracts seems to indicate that, on average, returns are close to zero. Table 10–1 reports average returns on forward contracts, measured over 1978-91; because these positions involve no net investment, these are excess returns. Over this period, returns ranged from –0.16 percent (deutschemarks) to 3.01 percent (pounds sterling) per annum.

None of the returns is statistically different from zero. This, however, may have more to do with the power of the tests than with a truly zero risk premium. From an economic perspective, the numbers are significant because they are of the same magnitude as the value added we would expect from active management. An added value of a few percentage points per annum is more than satisfactory. Yet conventional hypothesis tests with 14 years of data are not powerful enough to detect statistical significance: Assuming a 12 percent annual volatility for the pound, a t-test yields $3.01/(12/\sqrt{14}) = 0.9$.[10] To attain a t-statistic above 2, which would correspond to the conventional 5 percent significance level, one would need 64 years of data. Over this period, however, a dollar invested at the excess return of 3 percent would have grown to $6.6! Clearly, waiting for statistical significance entails a very significant opportunity cost.

Properly interpreted, the statistics tests indicate that the evidence on average returns is inconclusive, not that currency forwards have zero expected returns. In addition, realized returns on currencies appear to vary over time, from positive to negative values; measuring average returns might very well hide predictable temporal variations in return.

EMPIRICAL EVIDENCE

Instead of assuming a zero risk premium and a simplified covariance matrix structure, we use actual estimates of return and risk measured over the 1978-91 period. Five stock and bond markets are considered—the U.S., Japan, Germany, Britain and France. Tables 10–1 through 10–3 present estimates of average excess returns, risks, and correlations for currencies, stocks, and bonds, respectively. Correlations between currencies and both unhedged and hedged returns are reported. All returns are translated into U.S. dollars and measured in excess of the U.S. risk-free rate (taken as the one-month Treasury bill rate).

Unhedged stock returns appear to be positively correlated with exchange rates, with average correlation coefficients ranging from 0.3 to 0.6. Therefore, optimizing currencies and underlying unhedged assets separately cannot be optimal. In contrast, hedged stock returns appear uncorrelated with currencies. Full currency hedging may be an acceptable strategy for stocks.

For bonds, we observe high correlations for both unhedged and hedged returns. The positive correlations for hedged bond suggest that bond yields are negatively associated with the dollar value of foreign currencies. This implies that currency forwards can to some extent cross-hedge changes in foreign yields. Partial optimization and full hedging must be suboptimal for international bonds.

The question of interest, however, is how much efficiency is lost by separately optimizing the core portfolio and currencies in a realistic framework. A loss of a few basis points would cause no concern and possibly be more than offset by the value added from specialized currency managers. A loss of a few percentage points, however, would raise serious doubts about the currency overlay approach.

We consider the following three situations:

- A full optimization over N + 1 assets (stocks or bonds, including U.S. assets) plus N currencies, compared with a full optimization over N + 1 assets only.
- A partial optimization over N currencies, given an optimal position of N + 1 assets.
- A separate optimization over N currencies, given an optimal position in underlying assets.

Tables 10–4 and 10–5 present the optimal positions under each of these three approaches. To be realistic, we allow no short selling for the

TABLE 10-1

Annualized Excess Returns, Risks, and Correlations of
Forward Contracts, 1978-91

	Yen	Mark	Pound	Franc
Return	1.76%	−0.16%	3.01%	2.03%
Risk	13.40	13.07	12.67	12.47
Correlations				
JY	1.00			
DM	0.65	1.00		
BP	0.58	0.72	1.00	
FF	0.67	0.96	0.72	1.00

TABLE 10-2

Excess Annualized Returns and Risks of Stocks, 1978-91

	$	Yen	Mark	Pound	Franc
Return	7.63%	12.38%	8.02%	11.52%	13.47%
Risk	16.18	24.19	23.39	22.36	25.10
Correlations					
$	1.00				
Yen	0.24	1.00			
Mark	0.35	0.39	1.00		
Pound	0.57	0.41	0.48	1.00	
Franc	0.40	0.37	0.55	0.46	1.00
Unhedged					
Yen	−0.03	0.64	0.32	0.27	0.35
Mark	−0.03	0.32	0.53	0.29	0.44
Pound	−0.01	0.32	0.37	0.53	0.30
Franc	0.00	0.34	0.50	0.32	0.49
Hedged					
Yen	−0.03	0.12	−0.04	−0.07	0.02
Mark	−0.03	−0.05	−0.03	−0.13	−0.04
Pound	−0.01	−0.01	−0.04	−0.04	−0.07
Franc	0.00	−0.04	−0.04	−0.10	−0.01

TABLE 10-3

Excess Annualized Returns and Risks of Bonds, 1978-91

	$	Yen	Mark	Pound	Franc
Return	2.38%	3.18%	1.96%	1.46%	0.97%
Risk	10.51	6.63	5.84	10.13	6.05
Correlations					
$	1.00				
Yen	0.42	1.00			
Mark	0.52	0.58	1.00		
Pound	0.40	0.43	0.40	1.00	
Franc	0.34	0.40	0.51	0.32	1.00
Unhedged					
Yen	0.19	0.94	0.61	0.49	0.65
Mark	0.22	0.61	0.94	0.55	0.88
Pound	0.18	0.55	0.67	0.84	0.64
Franc	0.22	0.64	0.90	0.52	0.91
Hedged					
Yen	0.19	0.40	0.23	0.16	0.15
Mark	0.22	0.28	0.34	0.08	0.10
Pound	0.18	0.25	0.24	0.26	0.04
Franc	0.22	0.29	0.33	0.04	0.09

underlying assets and allow positions in the dollar, yen, and European currencies to vary only between zero and the total portfolio value. These constraints are typical of restrictions placed on overlay managers, who are generally allowed to cross-hedge European currencies.

The tables report portfolio excess return, volatility, and Sharpe ratio. For stocks, adding currencies to an optimized portfolio of stocks and reoptimizing increases the Sharpe ratio by 0.116 (= 0.805 - 0.689). At a typical 15 percent volatility level, this translates into added value of 173 basis points. Adding currencies and performing a separate optimization, given fixed positions in stocks, increases performance by 92 (= 0.781 − 0.689), which translates into 139 basis points of value added. Optimizing separately on currencies leads to an increase of only 72 basis points.

TABLE 10–4

Optimal Positions with Stocks and Currencies, 1978–91

| | | With Currency | | |
	No Currency	Joint	Partial	Separate
Return	11.1%	12.9%	11.8%	12.2%
Risk	16.1	16.1	15.1	16.6
Sharpe ratio	0.689	0.805	0.781	0.735
Value added (at 15% risk)		1.73	1.38	0.72
Positions (%)				
Stocks:				
U.S.	29*	3*	29	29
Japan	29*	39*	29	29
Germany	0*	4*	0	0
U.K.	16*	18*	16	16
France	26*	36*	26	26
Currency:				
Yen	–	–39*	–29*	0*
Mark	–	–58*	–42*	–42*
Pound	–	30*	28*	8*
Franc	–	15*	13*	40*
Net Foreign exchange exposure	71%	45%	41%	77%

*Denotes an optimized position.

The 173 basis points, however, should be interpreted with caution. Because the same period is used for the optimization and the performance measurement, adding assets must by definition improve portfolio performance. The number is biased upward because, at worst, the optimizer could take no position in currencies.[11]

The estimation error inherent in these numbers can be recognized explicitly by test statistics of performance improvement.[12] By comparing the observed value of the test statistic with a distribution obtained under the null hypothesis that currencies do not improve performance, one can

TABLE 10-5

Optimal Positions with Bonds and Currencies, 1978–91

		With Currency		
	No Currency	**Joint**	**Partial**	**Separate**
Return	3.7%	3.6%	3.6%	4.2%
Risk	11.3	5.9	8.2	11.7
Sharpe ratio	0.331	0.604	0.432	0.366
Value added (at 10% risk)		2.73	1.02	.037
Positions (%)				
Bonds:				
U.S.	44*	0*	44	44
Japan	39*	48*	39	39
Germany	0*	0*	0	0
U.K.	17*	3*	17	17
France	0*	49*	0	0
Currency:				
Yen	–	–48*	–39*	0*
Mark	–	–42*	–17*	–17*
Pound	–	18*	12*	7*
Franc	–	–9*	7*	16*
Net Foreign exchange exposure	56%	9%	19%	62%

*Denotes an optimized position.

gauge the extent to which the observed number may be due to sampling variability in the date. In this case, the statistic was exceeded in 23 percent of the samples, leading us to conclude that the performance-improvement numbers are in line with what could be expected because of chance alone. There is no statistical evidence that currencies add value to global equity portfolios.

The 173 basis points should thus be considered an upper bound on the value added from static management of currencies in equity portfolios. Because the same data and degrees of freedom are used in the partial and separate optimizations, one can conclude that partial optimization decreases returns by about 35 basis points, and that separate optimization decreases returns by a further 66 basis points. These are nonnegligible costs.

Including currencies in a fully optimized bond portfolio adds 273 basis points, given the 10 percent volatility typical of bond indexes. Currencies add 102 and 37 basis points, respectively, when managed using partial and separate optimizations. Because 273 is much higher than the 173 basis points reported above, it appears that fixed-income portfolios benefit much more than equity portfolios from the management of currencies. The reason for this can be traced to the high correlations between bond returns and currencies, which lead to substantial portfolio adjustments when currencies are included.

In Table 10–5, for instance, the optimal bond portfolio is drastically altered when currencies are added. The initial composition of 44 percent U.S. bonds, 39 percent Japanese, and 17 percent British becomes 48 percent Japanese, 3 percent British, and 49 percent French, with positions in Japanese bonds fully hedged; a cross-hedge is also implemented, short the mark and long other European currencies.

These reallocations, much larger than for equity portfolios, translate into a higher value added, 273 versus 173 basis points. Furthermore, the 273 points are too large to be attributed to chance. The same test methodology as used above indicates that adding currencies to bond portfolios significantly improves performance.

Finally, the large drop from 273 to 102 basis points when the bond portfolio is predetermined demonstrates that it makes little sense to use currency overlays for bond portfolios. Given the high correlation between bonds and currencies, these two asset classes must be managed together. This is why, in practice, currency overlays are only applied to equity portfolios.

The last lines in Tables 10–4 and 10–5 report the net foreign currency positions. For instance, the net foreign exchange exposure of fully optimized stock portfolios is 71 percent (29 percent yen, 16 percent pound sterling, 26 percent franc). When adding currencies, the foreign exchange exposure of the portfolio decreases from 71 percent to 45 percent for the joint optimization.[13] Because hedging entailed an opportunity cost over this period, there was never full hedging into dollars. Hedging also appears to be far from universal. For instance, currency positions in the yen and mark are generally negative, while positions in the pound and franc are generally positive. This suggests that unitary hedging and universal hedging are both suboptimal.

Active Hedging

These results may be of little relevance to actual investment decision rules, as the optimal positions are derived from "ex post" data. The results suggest that, over this period, it would have been possible to enhance portfolio performance by using forward contracts; unfortunately, the optimal weights are revealed only after the fact. The problem is compounded by the apparent instability of the currency hedges. For instance, in the early 80s it would have been generally advantageous to hedge foreign currency exposures back into dollars, since the dollar appreciated, but the reverse was true later, when the dollar depreciated sharply.

Does the performance improvement survive an "ex ante" rule, where all investment decisions are based on prior information? Furthermore, is it possible to identify changes in expected returns and incorporate these changes into active management of currency allocations?

Previous research on the efficiency of the foreign exchange market has shown that the forward premium can help in predicting expected returns on forward contracts.[14] Because, by interest rate parity, the forward premium is also the interest rate differential, the evidence generally implies that investors should go long high-interest-rate currencies and short low-interest-rate currencies. The following discussion shows how to exploit this anomaly using a mean/variance optimizer.

The strategy is implemented as follows. Consider a passive benchmark actively hedged with four forward contracts. This suboptimal but easy to implement, as bid-ask spreads in the foreign exchange market are very low, while stock and bond positions, more costly to alter, are fixed. The decision variable are the amounts to buy or sell in the four forward contracts.

Each month, expected returns and risk measures are estimated from a 4-year moving window. Returns are forecast from the estimated coefficients of a regression of past returns on the forward premium, combined with the most recent forward premium. The variance/covariance matrix is also estimated over the same time period. These parameters are fed into a portfolio optimizer that determines the forward positions of the portfolio with the highest excess return-to-risk ratio. The performance of the optimal portfolio is recorded for the following month, after which the process is repeated. The strategy is realistic in that investment decisions are based only on prior information, which is kept current, and only feasible positions are implemented.

Table 10–6 reports the results from this active hedging rule, as implemented over the 1978–91 period. The performance of the world stock

TABLE 10-6

Active Currency Hedging

	World Stock Index		
	Unhedged	Fully Hedged	Actively Hedged
1978–1991			
Average Annual Return	8.11%	6.81%	12.14%
Annual Volatility	15.21	14.11	17.54
Sharpe Ratio	0.533	0.483	0.692
1978–1984			
Average Annual Return	3.50	6.31	6.20
Annual Volatility	13.25	11.70	15.46
Sharpe Ratio	0.264	0.539	0.401
1985–1991			
Average Annual Return	12.77	7.59	18.22
Annual Volatility	16.72	16.08	19.11
Sharpe Ratio	0.764	0.472	0.953

index with actively managed currency exposure is compared with the performances of the unhedged and fully hedged passive indexes. Clearly, the currency rule adds substantial value. Assuming 15 percent volatility, excess returns are increased by 2.3 percent annually relative to the unhedged index and by 3.1 percent relative to the fully hedged index. The enhanced performance of active hedging more than offsets the transaction costs incurred by using forward contracts, which are very modest.[15] In addition, the results seem constant across the two subperiods of dollar strength (1978–84) and dollar weakness (1985–91).

A caveat, however, is in order. For exchange rates measured against the dollar, risk can be reasonably well assessed from the volatility of historical series. Realignment risk in fixed-exchange-rate systems, however, may not be adequately represented by historical data. Because it underestimates devaluation risk, the forward-premium strategy applied to European cross-hedges tends to take large long positions in high-yield currencies offset by short positions in low-yield currencies, which can unravel with currency realignments. Over 1978-91, the strategy excess returns indicate that realignments have been more than offset by forward-premium gains; forward-premium gains, however, accumulate slowly over time, whereas realignment losses are large and occur suddenly. To address this asymmetry, the strategy should be augmented by realignment probabilities, and perhaps diversified with technical rules.[16] Nevertheless, one would hope that this simple model provides a lower bound on the value added by overlay managers.

CONCLUSIONS

Currency overlays are generally suboptimal. Overlays are implemented in two ways—either by optimizing on total portfolio return and risk, or by optimizing separately on currencies. In the former case, the performance of the overlay is measured in conjunction with that of the core portfolio. In the latter, the only objective of the overlay manager is to add value, measured in absolute returns. In both cases, returns suffer vis-á-vis a policy of managing underlying assets and currencies in an integrated fashion. Furthermore, underperformance increases, the higher the correlation between currencies and the underlying assets.

Whether the underperformance is significant must be judged against the benefits from using specialized overlay managers. There is some evidence that returns on currencies are predictable. If so, the value added by overlay managers could outweigh the inherent inefficiency of the set-up.

At the very least, performance should be measured in the context of the total portfolio. This means that the core portfolio manager must regularly communicate positions to the overlay manager, who would then evaluate risk and return for the combined portfolio. In this context, the partial-optimization approach may be an acceptable, albeit second-best, solution to the management of currencies in global portfolios. But the onus is on overlay specialists to prove their worth as active managers.[17]

APPENDIX

The portfolio decision problem for global investment involves a joint choice over the underlying assets and currencies. Assume for simplicity that investors maximize the following objective function, reflecting the trade-off between expected portfolio return (in excess of the risk-free rate) $\mu_p = w'\mu$ and risk $\sigma_p^2 = w'\Sigma w$:

$$\mu_p - (1/2\lambda)\sigma_p^2, \tag{A1}$$

where w represents positions, μ represents expected excess returns on all assets (with covariance matrix Σ) and λ is the investor's risk tolerance. Returns on all assets are measured in U.S. dollars in excess of the risk-free rate.

The optimal positions are given by $w^* = \lambda\Sigma^{-1}\mu$, with the remainder of the portfolio invested in the riskless asset. Further insights can be obtained by decomposing w^* into a core portfolio and currency portfolio. Partition μ and Σ into components that correspond to underlying assets, represented by x, and currently forwards, represented by f:

$$\mu = \begin{pmatrix} \mu_x \\ \mu_f \end{pmatrix}, \Sigma = \begin{pmatrix} \Sigma_{xx} & \Sigma_{xf} \\ \Sigma_{fx} & \Sigma_{ff} \end{pmatrix}. \tag{A2}$$

Then define

$$\beta = \Sigma_{ff}^{-1}\Sigma_{fx}$$

as the regression coefficients of the assets on the hedges and

$$\Sigma_{x \cdot f} = \Sigma_{xx} - \beta'\Sigma_{ff}\beta$$

as the covariance matrix of underlying asset returns conditional on the hedges. The optimal portfolio is then derived from the partitioned inverse of the matrix Σ, which can be written as:

$$\Sigma^{-1} = \begin{pmatrix} \Sigma_{x \cdot f}^{-1} & -\Sigma_{x \cdot f}^{-1}\beta' \\ -\beta\Sigma_{x \cdot f}^{-1}\Sigma_{ff}^{-1} & +\beta\Sigma_{x \cdot f}^{-1}\beta'. \end{pmatrix} \tag{A3}$$

We can now detail the optimal positions in currencies and underlying assets for three separate implementations of currency management. In *a joint optimization*, where w_x and w_f are determined simultaneously:

$$\begin{pmatrix} w_x^*(x,f) = \lambda(\Sigma_{x \cdot f}^{-1}\mu_x - \Sigma_{x \cdot f}^{-1}\beta'\mu_f) \\ w_f^*(x,f) = \lambda(\Sigma_{ff}^{-1}\mu_f) - \beta w_x^* \end{pmatrix}. \tag{A4}$$

Note that the optimal hedge positions w_f^* depend on the optimal asset positions w_x^*, which themselves are affected by the presence of currencies in the portfolio. Also, the hedge positions have a speculative component, driven by nonzero expected returns in currencies, as well as variance-reduction component related to β.

A *partial optimization* is conditioned on predetermined underlying asset positions. When these are determined optimally without regard for the hedges, the weights are:

$$\left(\begin{array}{c} w_x^*(x) = \lambda(\Sigma_{xx}^{-1}\mu_x) \\ w_f^*(f|x) = \lambda(\Sigma_{ff}^{-1}\mu_f) - \beta w_x \end{array} \right). \qquad (A5)$$

Note that, as before, the optimal hedge positions (symbol) depend on the positions in the core portfolio. Because the core positions do not account for hedges, neither core nor currency positions are globally optimal.

Partial optimization is efficient under the following conditions. Positions A4 and A5 will be identical if returns on underlying assets, measured in dollars, are uncorrelated with exchange rates ($\Sigma_{fx} = 0$, $\beta = 0$, $\Sigma_{xf} = \Sigma_{xx}$). In this situation, the globally optimal weights simplify to

$$w_x^*(x,f) = \lambda(\Sigma_{xx}^{-1}\mu_x)$$

and

$$w_f^*(x,f) = \lambda(\Sigma_{ff}^{-1}\mu_f).$$

In *a separate optimization*, asset and hedge positions are determined independently. The weights are:

$$\left(\begin{array}{c} w_x^*(x) = \lambda(\Sigma_{xx}^{-1}\mu_x) \\ w_f^*(f) = \lambda(\Sigma_{ff}^{-1}\mu_f) \end{array} \right). \qquad (A6)$$

Here, neither the core nor the currency position depends on the other asset class.

ENDNOTES

1. As reported by *Pensions & Investment Age*, May 17, 1993.
2. See, for instance, A. F. Lee, "International Asset and Currency Allocation," *Journal of Portfolio Management*, Fall 1987.
3. A. Perold and E. Schulman, "The Free Lunch in Currency Hedging: Implications for Investment Policy and Performance Standards," *Financial Analysts Journal*, May/June 1988.
4. Indeed currency-hedged benchmarks have recently appeared in response to market demands. For instance, Morgan Stanley Capital International started to report currency-hedged international stock indexes in June 1989; Salomon Brothers has constructed currency-hedged bond indexes since March 1988.

5. See F. Black, "Equilibrium Exchange Rate Hedging," *Journal of Finance*, 1990, and also Adler and Prasad, "On universal currency hedges," *Journal of Financial and Quantitative Analysis*, 1992.

6. R. Roll, "A Mean-Variance Analysis of Tracking Error," *Journal of Portfolio Management*, 1992.

7. Pérold and Schulman, "The Free Lunch," *op. cit.*

8. See B. Solnik, "An Equilibrium Model of the International Capital Market," *Journal of Economic Theory*, 1974.

9. Black, "Equilibrium Hedging," *op. cit.*

10. Changing the observation interval in order to increase the number of observations would have no effect on these tests. The numbers reported in the table are annualized from monthly data, with returns multiplied by 12 and standard deviations multiplied by the square root of 12, assuming independence over time. Going back to monthly data, the t-test expressed in month terms is $(3.01/12)/((12/\sqrt{12})/\sqrt{14\times12})$, which is the same as before.

11. The bias resulting from the optimization has been noted by R. Michaud, "The Markowitz Optimization Enigma: Is Optimized Optimal?" *Financial Analysts Journal*, January/February 1989.

12. The statistic that represents the increase in performance is

$$F = (T - N_2)/(N_2 - N_1)(\theta_2^2 - \theta_1^2/(1 + \theta_1^2),$$

where T is the number of observations, N_1 the restricted number of assets, N_2 the enlarged number of assets, and 0_1 and 0_2 are the maximum Sharpe ratios with N_1 and N_2 assets, respectively. The methodology employed here is explained in P. Jorion, "Portfolio Optimization in Practice," *Financial Analysts Journal,* January/February 1992. Formal statistical tests are presented in J. Glen and P. Jorion, "Currency Hedging for International Portfolios," *Journal of Finance* 48 (1993), 1865-86.

13. The latter number is obtained from the algebraic sum of positions in four foreign stock markets plus four currencies.

14. This was first shown by J. F. O. Bilson, "The 'Speculative Efficiency' Hypothesis," *Journal of Business* 54 (1981), 435–52. Recent attempts to explain these results in terms of a rational risk premium mare reviewed in Hodrick, *The Empirical Evidence on the Efficiency of Forward and Futures Foreign Exchange Markets* (Harwood Academic Publishing, 1987).

15. For instance, a typical two-way spread on the pound is 5 points, or about 0.03% in relative terms. So, rolling over 12 monthly swaps involves an annual transaction cost of 12(0.03%/2) = 0.18%.

16. See, for instance, R. J. Sweeney, "Beating the Foreign Exchange Market," *Journal of Finance* 41 (1986), 163-82.

17. I thank Michael Alder for his useful comments.

CHAPTER 11

MANAGEMENT SUMMARY

Title: "Managed Futures Structured Notes"
Author: Jan Holland and Fred Hirshfeld
           Nesbitt Burns Managed Futures Corporation
Synopsis: This chapter introduces the concept of structured notes as an easy
           first step into a managed futures investment. Areas of customiza-
           tion and the benefits and risks to the investor are also discussed.

Managed Futures Structured Notes

Jan Holland

Fred Hirshfeld

Structured notes are fixed-income instruments whose yields are determined from some other underlying investment. They can be issued by corporations, banks, financial institutions, municipals, government agencies, sovereigns, and supranationals. An example of a bank structured note is included in Figure 11–1.

Structured notes can take the form of any of the following: debentures, commercial paper, bank certificate of deposit, bank note, medium-term note (MTN), corporate bond, and private placements. Structured notes can be either senior or subordinated, and are very seldom secured by an underlying asset, relying instead on the underlying ratings of the issuer for its credit rating.

Managed futures is an ideal investment to be delivered via a structured note. On average, the commodity trading advisors (CTAs) use 5 percent to 20 percent of the capital under management for initial margins and variation margin. The 80 percent that is not used for margin is available to be invested in liquid investments, such as short-term money market investments, commercial paper, bonds, or general banking purposes.

MANAGED FUTURES CERTIFICATE OF DEPOSIT

A managed futures certificate of deposit (CD) offers the investor access to ALL the attributes and returns of a managed futures program while providing for the full return of principal at maturity. The CD often does not pay any coupon and has a yield linked to the appreciation in the managed futures program. The summary terms of the Bank of Montreal managed futures certificate of deposit are included as an example of a structured note (Figure 11–1).

Each investor makes a deposit with the issuer for his committed amount to acquire the certificates of deposit. Approximately 70 percent of the proceeds of the offering stay on deposit (Strip) with the Treasury of the issuer at a fixed rate of interest. The Strip grows to assure the investor the full return of his invested capital at maturity. Approximately 30 percent of the proceeds of the offering are used to capitalize and operate a managed futures program. The capital and earnings of the managed futures program accrue to the benefit of the investor.

Even though only 30 percent of the proceeds of the offering are available for margin, the investment advisors will trade the program as though 100 percent were available.

A pension executive from a large corporate pension plan that recently made an investment in a managed futures certificate of deposit was quoted in the July 1996 issue of *Managed Account Reports* (an industry trade journal), "Despite the diversification, noncorrelation and potential return benefits of managed futures, the main reason the fund's investment committee approved the certificate of deposit was the bank's guarantee of its principal. It's never easy to sell these things (editor note - new ideas - managed futures) to the investment committee."

In addition to the portfolio benefits of managed futures, structured notes provide investors with the following seven items:

1. Limited liability and Return of Principal

Pension regulations in Canada prohibit pension funds from pledging, mortgaging, or hypothecating the assets of the pension fund. Short selling and the use of leverage on a direct account may contravene this provision. By wrapping managed futures into a structured note the investor has limited liability and can never receive a margin call. The investor who holds the structured notes to maturity is assured the return of his principal. The risk to the investor is the credit risk of the issuer.

2. Leverage

Managed futures programs may involve holding positions of up to 2 to 2 ½ times the face value of the investors commitment. By doing this as a

FIGURE 11–1

Bank of Montreal
Managed Futures Certificate of Deposit

June 30, 1995

Issuer:	Bank of Montreal
Issue:	Bank of Montreal Managed Futures Certificates of Deposit with principal protection (CDs).
Issue Size:	Up to Maximum: Cdn. $150,000,000.
Maturity:	February 2, 2001
Price:	100% (par). No placement agency fee.
Coupon:	0%
Yield:	Linked to the performance of an actively managed multi-advisor managed futures program. Contracts traded as part of the program will be exchange listed commodity and financial futures and options and interbank foreign exchange contracts.
Eligibility:	"Legal for life" for pension plans governed by "prudent person" legislation. Not foreign property.
Settlement:	February 2, 1996
Agent:	Nesbitt Burns Inc. (a subsidiary of the Issuer).
Rating:	DBRS: AA CBRS: A+ (high).
Ranking:	CDs will rank *pari passu* with all other Bank of Montreal deposit liabilities.
Denomination:	Minimum Cdn. $5,000,000 per investor. Issue in registered form in multiples of Cdn. $500,000.

The information that appears above is selective only and is qualified in its entirety by reference to the term sheet relating to these investments, a copy of which is available upon request.

direct account again the institutional investor may be in conflict with the regulation of not pledging, mortgaging, or hypothecating the assets of the pension fund.

3. Valuation - Economic Value

The investor has a line item in his custodial statement that includes the number of units owned, the current unit value, and the total current value. The client's custodian values the CD investment using the economic value (see example of client reporting, Table 11–1). The value of the structured

TABLE 11-1

Example of Client Reporting

		Prior Quarter End		Current Month	
	Issue Date	Straight Line	Economic Value	Straight Line	Economic Value
Strip	73.6298	75.5059	73.5303	75.8995	74.2810
Trading	26.3702	22.8854	22.8854	21.4843	21.4843
	100.00	98.3913	96.4157	97.3838	95.7653

note is determined by the issuer aggregating the net futures positions for the program and marking them to market at the close of each business day. The market value of the futures contracts is added to the market value of the strip portion. The strip portion is valued by comparing the stated coupon on the imbedded strip and the term to maturity versus current market yields of a similar maturity and credit quality. The imbedded strip exposes the investor to an interest rate risk on a mark to market basis.

Valuation - Straight Line

The straight line valuation marks to market the aggregated futures positions and adds the principal of the strip and the interest earned on the strip. Although this valuation is provided to the institutional investors it only serves to isolate the changes in valuation as a result of the trading activity versus the changes in current interest rates. If the CD is held to maturity the investor receives the accumulated interest on the strip plus the accretion from the trading. This valuation allows the investor to understand the returns and the variability of the returns that a managed futures investment can provide while assuring them the safety of their principal.

Valuation - Benchmark

Managed futures are categorized as either a separate asset class or bundled into the alternative investment category of a pension portfolio. However, the custodial statements set up to hold these investments are often compared against the returns of short-term money market investments. Hence, managed futures seem to be valued on an absolute return basis.

4. Risk Control and Administration

The issuer of the structured note is responsible for aggregating all the futures positions, daily valuation, risk control, capital usage, reporting, contracting with the managers, manager selection, manager reviews, setting the mandate, setting the policies, and monitoring the program for conformance.

The issuer is responsible for monitoring the program for conformance to the established mandate and includes having the appropriate procedures and reports to review markets traded, leverage, capital usage, margin to equity ratios, trading styles, and market exposure.

The structured note simplifies the investment process for the pension fund and allows them to gain an understanding of managed futures while assuring the safety of principal.

5. Risk Allocation and Diversification

Pension funds and their consultants recommend that these institutions initially allocate 1 percent to 5 percent of their portfolio. Since this initial allocation is usually quite small the pension funds like the investment to be simple. That is, they do not want a 100-page prospectus and they don't want a special purpose investment vehicle. These institutional investors have invested in special purpose investment vehicles for venture capital transactions. These venture capital transactions often required an enormous amount of time and resources to resolve legal disputes and bankruptcies for an investment that often represented less than 5 percent of the assets of their portfolios.

6. Accessibility

A structured note provides access to managed futures through a traditional investment medium; a fixed-income instrument. A typical institutional investor has a pension executive who is responsible for screening potential investments. A managed futures salesman may spend 2 years educating and discussing managed futures with this pension executive. The pension executive may bounce the idea off one or two colleagues internally. If the concept is not vetoed during this phase a manager will be invited to make a presentation to the board of trustees. The presentation will be allotted approximately 45 minutes to 1 hour. At the end of the presentation the manager is thanked and the committee discusses what they have heard and makes a decision to proceed or to defer.

Derivatives have received negative press of late and a member of the board of trustees who arrives uninitiated often relies on hearsay to make his investment decisions. By embedding managed futures in a structured note the salesman and the board of trustees can rely on the reputation, relationship, risk control, and credit rating of the issuer to make an investment in an area that is not well understood.

A structured note has the additional benefit of not requiring prospectus disclosure and can be bought from the issuance of a term sheet. This avoids a lot of detail legal work for the pension plan and simplifies the investment process.

7. Customization

A managed futures structured note can be customized as follows:

A. Term to maturity
B. Seniority
C. Zero coupon or minimal coupon
D. Single advisor or multiadvisor
E. Market exposure, i.e., financials only
F. Minimum investment
G. Currency of investment

A. Term to Maturity

The maturity of structured notes range from as short as 3 months to as long as (or longer than) 10 years. The length of term is determined by matching the duration objective of the investor with the regulatory capital requirements of the issuer. For a bank the length of term of capital and the seniority of the structured note determine the amount of regulatory capital the bank must keep on hand to support the obligation.

A structured note provides for lots of flexibility. An investor who wants a 5-year investment can be matched with an issuer who wants to issue 10-year paper by customizing the note with step-up call provisions after year 5.

B. Seniority

The seniority of the structured note can vary from very senior bank certificate of deposit (see Figure 11–1) to unsecured debentures. Certificates of deposit rank ahead of all other liabilities of a bank. An unsecured debenture, depending on the specific provisions of the debenture, may rank with the general creditors of the bank or corporation.

C. Zero Coupon or Minimal Coupon

In Figure 11–1, the Bank of Montreal Managed Futures Certificate of Deposit offers a stated coupon of zero with a yield linked to an actively managed multiadvisor managed futures program. Other structured notes provide for a low fixed-rate coupon in addition to the variable return that is embedded in the note.

The coupon and/or the yield on these structured notes may be paid on a frequent periodic basis such as semiannual or they may be structured to only pay the coupon and/or yield at maturity. These periods of payment are trade-offs between investor cash flow requirements and the ability to let the capital work and compound uninterrupted in the managed futures program.

D. Single Advisor or Multi-advisor

A managed futures structured note can be offered with one commodity trading advisor (CTA) or with one trading manager (TM) and one CTA or any combination of single or multiple TMs and single or multiple CTAs. The permutation and combination is dependent on the philosophy, objectives, and risk controls of both the investor and the issuer.

E. Market Exposure

Managed futures structured notes can be built to provide access to a single market such as a financials only program. This program limits the market exposure to bond futures, stock indexes, and currency contracts, which may or may not include interbank currency trading. Often futures on metals are included as eligible contracts to be traded. This program may be designed to include the above contracts traded on any futures exchange around the world or it may be limited to contracts traded on United States exchanges.

The market exposure offered by the structured note is tailored to meet the investor's particular investment objective. The objective may be to augment a long only, stock and bond portfolio with a long, short, neutral managed futures financials program.

F. Minimum Investment

The minimum size of the investment per investor can be established at any level. If the structured note is intended to be offered to multiple investors, then the minimum investment per investor can be reduced. The minimum investment per investor is dependent on the intended target market.

Structured notes are offered for both institutional and retail investors. The managed futures structured note has to raise sufficient capital to be economic and practical for both the investor and the issuer.

SUMMARY

A managed futures structured note is an easier first step towards making managed futures an accepted investment alternative. By committing a small initial allocation to a managed futures structured note, an investor is able to learn about managed futures through a safe vehicle. It offers the investor access to ALL the attributes and returns of a managed futures program while providing for the full return of principal at maturity.

Once an investor has had a real-time experience with a managed futures structured note, he can confidently increase the allocation to the investment through other limited liability vehicles and eventually to an overlay product.

CHAPTER 12

MANAGEMENT SUMMARY

Title: "Institutional Product Packaging for the Managed Futures Industry"

Authors: Sarah E. Street, Funds Team Executive in Global Commodity Finance, Client Management
The Chase Manhattan Bank

Synopsis: In an effort to escape the label of "alternative investments," managed futures have been actively repackaged to become more palatable to institutional investors. Managed futures programs are embedded in many different forms of capital market instruments—including structured notes, bond issues, certificates of deposit, and warrant transactions. It is hoped that over time, there will be a "blurring" of the current distinction between managed futures and other mainstream investment strategies. For institutional clients, this would create an acceptable alternative to owning traditional equity and fixed-income products.

Institutional Product Packaging for the Managed Futures Industry

Sarah E. Street
Funds Team Executive in Global Commodity Finance,
Client Management
The Chase Manhattan Bank, New York

INTRODUCTION

Over the past 5 years, the managed futures industry has witnessed a dramatic evolution in the way its returns can be "packaged" into instruments that have appeal to a broad range of investors. In the early nineties, most managed futures programs were only available in two primary forms—either direct managed account allocations to commodity trading advisors or through investments in either limited partnership units or nonvoting shares in limited liability entities. Today, managed futures programs are embedded in or linked to many different forms of capital market instruments—including structured notes, bond issues, certificates of deposits, warrant transactions, and, in the industry's most recent development, asset swaps—to offer investors cashflows dependent upon the performance of an underlying managed futures program. The managed futures industry continues to push forward in this direction and will gather momentum through successful offerings.

In addition, as investment professionals operate within the global capital markets under mandates to originate new structures to raise capital for corporates and/or offer investment alternatives for their institutional clientele, further new product initiatives will emerge and further innovation will take place. The managed futures industry will also be a direct beneficiary of such continued product development.

To put this evolution in context, it is important to recognize that these product enhancements within the managed futures arena have been driven by efforts of many of the leading industry participants to expand the investor base of managed futures beyond its historical reach, which, in the main, has been high-net-worth individuals, funds of funds, and domestic retail markets. Much of the impetus has come from their desire to tap into the institutional investor base, whose investible assets are enormous, and who have already been responsible for funding the growth of many traditional and alternative asset classes. Many of these firms have hired individuals with experience in marketing traditional fixed income and equity portfolio strategies to the institutional marketplace who are now applying their expertise to designing product structures that appeal to mainstream users. These new target clients include small and medium-size pension funds, foundations, endowments, and insurance companies.

The initial marketing strategies revolved around selling managed futures solely as an independent asset class. Although pockets of success can be identified, on a broad-based evaluation (as measured by the stagnant $25 billion size of the managed futures industry's asset pool), this approach received, at best, a "luke-warm" reception from institutional audiences around the world. However, many institutional investors *do* recognize the value of a managed futures investment strategy as a way of improving the overall performance of any traditional equity and/or fixed income portfolio. This willingness to contemplate allocating capital to managed futures springs principally from the strong negative correlation of managed futures to stocks and bonds. The high degree of "alpha" inherent in returns on managed futures investing, when coupled with the absolute returns that such programs generate, creates the opportunity for more balanced and more profitable investing with less overall volatility. The positive impact of adding managed futures to the portfolio mix can be particularly noticeable when the traditional markets are producing low to negative returns.

Recognizing these circumstances, certain industry practitioners started to focus on reasons for the industry's failure to attract significant institutional capital in their industry. They quickly identified two principal challenges that needed to be faced for their product to be attractive in the institutional marketplace. First, to escape the label of "alternative investments" within an institutional portfolio, managed futures investments need to be repackaged to fit within the predefined investment parameters of the more traditional portfolio segments managed by these conservative, risk-averse investors—that is, to no longer be "different" from other investment products. Second, in order to establish and retain credibility with this new investor base, fund managers and CTAs have recognized that they must create products that offer a high probability to deliver on promised returns. Considerable progress has been made in addressing the first challenge through innovative product packaging, which the remainder of this chapter describes. However, only recently has the issue of high probability of achieving expected "total" rates of return come on the radar screen of many in the managed futures industry as an issue of critical importance. Until more disciplined programmatic efforts to reduce leverage, dampen volatility and manage risk are more widely accepted and implemented by the managed futures industry, interest amongst institutional clients will be limited. These investors will continue to seek investments that have some reliability of meeting the projected returns discussed in prospectus and marketing materials.

PRODUCT PACKAGING

Since the institutional money management arena seeks products that can be clearly explained in language that managers can understand (and subsequently reexplain), products must be slotted into traditional investment "buckets." The focus has become the development of instruments that fall within the fixed-income category, in particular, with offerings in the form of either notes or bonds, which incorporate the key structural and return components that are critical to institutional investors. Although these may vary among the different investor niches (e.g., pension funds versus insurance companies) and across geography, the following broad criteria can be consistently identified:

■ **Formal investment-grade ratings from established rating agencies on the instruments.** In certain markets, such as Europe, this rating needs to be at least AA, whilst in others, such as the U.S. insurance market, who are traditional buyers of corporate private debt placements, A-rated paper is acceptable. This rating requirement can be achieved in numerous ways, the most common being through the existence of a bankruptcy remote issuer with some form of credit enhancement that carries an investment-grade rating. The credit enhancement can range from the existence of investment-grade securities, pledged to support the issuer's obligation under the debt issue to the investors to an "insurance" policy—in the form of a letter of credit or guarantee from an investment-grade rated financial institution—that ensures the performance of the issuer under its debt obligations. Recent institutional product launches have successfully incorporated the credit enhancement into the traditional principal protection mechanisms. This approach, in which the investors are not exposed to any loss of principal if they hold the investment to maturity, effectively limits the investment's downside to the opportunity cost of the capital allocated, significantly reducing the "career risk" to an institutional investor of making this asset allocation. The form can range from simple "money-back" guarantees at the end of the investment to a guaranteed floor, for example, of anywhere between 90 percent and 115 percent of the original investment. Some products give the ability to lock in trading gains with "ratchet-up" clauses.

■ **Instruments with minimum-yield components through prede-termined minimum or fixed coupons, which carry some form of credit enhancement (in the same rating category as the capital support above) to ensure the issuer's ability to perform.** Many of the original structured note issues did not incorporate any minimum yields. This cre-ated reluctance amongst some institutional clients who needed "current" income. As significant to the structure, certain rating agencies were unable to assign an overall rating to the issue, as they are required to evaluate an issuer's ability to service all of its debt obligations—including both princi-pal and interest payments. Without comparable credit enhancement to any fixed or minimum coupon, the agencies have been unable to assign the same rating to the interest component. This would lead to split ratings (where the interest component is not rated and lower rated), no doubt rais-ing many questions in the minds of potential investors.

■ **Listing on recognized exchanges and compliance with all regu-latory criteria.** There are various exchanges around the world that have been used by many investment management firms to distribute and trade their products in the more traditional marketplaces. Indeed, it has become commonplace to have a listing on all instruments. The most frequently used exchanges by the managed futures industry to date have been Luxembourg and Dublin, although in 1995 a new issue was listed on the Zurich Stock Exchange at its launch. Each exchange has its own minimum requirements, such as structure and reporting standards, that must be met and maintained for the listing to be approved. The existence of listings gives investors com-fort of independent oversight and secondary market liquidity.

■ **Liquidity provisions through embedded "put" options or inde-pendent market makers that have the financial wherewithal to per-form their obligations throughout the life of the issue.** This component is critical to most institutional clients, as is the transparency of the "exit" price. In 1994, when the financial world experienced dramatic roller coaster markets, the liquidity of many structured note issues in the more tradit-ional asset classes (CMOs, asset-backed paper, and tailored derivative transactions) disappeared, leaving institutions unable to unload their investments or forcing them to execute on extremely wide bid-offer spreads. This has made them very wary of instruments that are not actively traded on exchanges.

■ **Return "dynamics" that can be compared with other investments in the fixed-income market and can be objectively evaluated against other instruments available to them.** The best way to demonstrate this point is by example: a portfolio manager within an insurance company who is focused on the corporate private placement market is generally pricing his or her investments on a Treasury bond basis. Typically, the portfolio manager compares the rates of return offered on proposed investments by focusing on the spreads above the relevant Treasury rate for the proposed tenor and the premium required to compensate the portfolio for assuming the issuer credit risk. Where potential returns are not fixed—due to the existence of some form of equity participation (as is the case in certain mezzanine deals)—the portfolio manager must evaluate the potential incremental yield that this piece of paper could create and assess the real probability of the underlying investment generating that additional equity yield. Having established these parameters, they must focus on the "cost" of assuming the probability of incremental upside of the equity returns. The cost is generally reflected in fixed coupons that are below the coupon level on similarly rated paper without any equity participation. This approach allows them to make objective investment decisions, as they have parameters around which to judge their downside.

It is the existence of such features—many of which were not attached to the original notes launched—that allows the bonds to be categorized appropriately in an institutional portfolio.

Using the individual features of structured products as financial "building blocks," issuers can create tailored instruments to meet specific investor objectives. The great advantage of the institutional marketplace is the potential size of any individual allocation; given the amounts in question, fund managers can easily justify launching "private label" products for each institution or group of institutions in the same investment niche. While one group of investors may require a registered note or bond that carries credit ratings from established agencies, for example, another will want minimum fixed-income coupon payments or flexible redemption provisions—all variables that can be worked into the issuer's product to the marketplace. Even a level of principal protection can be calibrated to investors' risk appetite: one investor group may accept an 85 percent guaranteed return of principal, while another may want trading gains withdrawn from the trading advisors and rolled into the guaranteed component. Various currency denominations can also be incorporated into the product so as to meet the needs of a global investor base.

With each of these components of the instrument's structure, the fund manager should be striving to meet stated investor objectives for such things as minimum yields and volatility of returns, recognizing that the various structural components are interdependent. Once the fund manager has identified the features that are critical to the targeted investor base, a structured product with the appropriate principal protection feature can be engineered to raise new capital on terms attractive to all parties.

Once a good understanding of the investors' key needs have been reached, the challenge of the fund manager, and its financial advisors, is to develop a product package that exceeds those requirements whilst giving sufficient flexibility to the fund manager to execute the trading program to generate the expected level of returns. This is without doubt "an art rather than a science," as all of the individual building blocks are interrelated. Those practitioners who can adapt to the new philosophy and develop agility with the structuring components will be truly successful in attracting an institutional clientele. To demonstrate the type of approaches that can be used and the considerations that need to be addressed, included below are two examples of the types of packaging that have occurred. These two examples have many similar characteristics but some fundamental differences as well. The differences were driven by the particular requirements of the investor bases and by the trading strategies employed by the fund manager.

(a) Bond Issue with "AA" credit enhancement in the form of underlying zero coupon bonds. In this product variation, a new company, established as an offshore special-purpose vehicle and managed by an independently operated fund management company, issues medium-term bonds that have no fixed yield. Part of the proceeds are used to purchase AA-rated zero-coupon notes that match the face amount and tenor of the bond. These notes are the debt obligations that will determine the rating on the bonds. The remaining proceeds from the bond offering—along with an equal amount of bank debt—are used to purchase shares in an existing fund. These shares, which are pledged to the Bank as security for the loan, are the instruments that will generate the return on the bonds. The fund is also required to pledge a pool of liquid collateral to the Bank as additional protection against deterioration in the value of the shares.

FIGURE 12-1

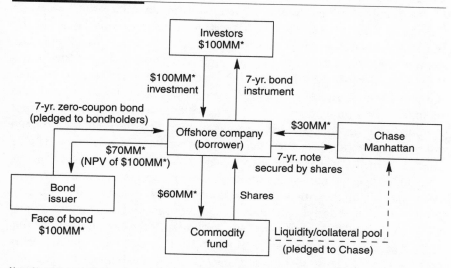

Note: Numbers are *indicative* only. Actual figures will depend upon prevailing interest rates at fund closing.

The bond structure is most appropriate for investors looking to make leveraged investments in a single commodity fund or hedge fund but also wanting a fixed-income instrument. For the investor, the bond offers principal protection and approximately 60 percent of the performance of the underlying. The bonds are typically rated by one or more of the rating agencies and can be listed, making the investment more attractive to institutions. The fund manager can undertake to make a market in the bond, thereby providing investors with liquidity without forcing early redemption. Extending or shortening the tenor of the bond will vary its yield and determine the level of embedded leverage in the underlying commodity fund investment. The bond can be structured with a fixed coupon or with a minimum cash payout per annum that increases if trading profits are accrued in the underlying commodity fund.

The fund manager will have to operate within some restrictions, which include the type of trading, the amount of leverage, and the markets traded. The bank's total credit appetite will be limited to an exposure appropriate to the strength of the fund.

(b) De-Leveraging Bond with Bank guarantee. In this bond issue, the issuer is an offshore special-purpose vehicle that arranges a private placement of senior noncallable AA-rated bonds to its investors. The terms of the bond offering include a guarantee or stand-by letter of credit ("SBLC"), which is issued by a AA financial institution on behalf of the issuer. The guarantor undertakes to guarantee that the issuer will repay the bond proceeds at maturity and, as such, the bond issue—if structured appropriately with regard to bankruptcy considerations—will be granted the credit rating equal to that of the guarantor. The guarantee can also include a minimum annual coupon payment, for example, 3 percent coupon to be paid annually. By varying the currency, the tenor, or the fixed coupon of the offering, the overall assets available for trading will be altered, something that will have a clear and measurable impact on the offering's expected returns. In addition, the bond terms can require that the issuer pay out an incremental annual coupon that is determined by the performance of an underlying managed futures program. This can require that all of the annual trading profits be distributed to the bondholders or that only a certain percentage be remitted, with the remaining profits being reinvested in a managed futures program. If all terms meet the requirements of a particular exchange, the bonds can be listed. The end result is that the investor purchases an "AA" list bond with a 3 percent annual coupon with an incremental yield potential tied to the underlying performance of the trading manager.

By guaranteeing the bond proceeds, the guarantor has exposed itself to trading losses in the fund, a risk that is dynamically managed by the guarantor. Importantly, trading must cease when the value of the fund reaches the present value of the guarantee.

The financial strength and track record of the fund manager become critical in any deleveraging arrangement, as the guarantor is relying upon the risk management and MIS capabilities and—ultimately—the capital resources of the manager to ensure investors' return of principal. Accordingly, the trading manager will have to operate within some restrictions vis-a-vis the types of trading done, the markets traded, and the amounts of leverage used.

The fund managers are willing to operate within tighter guidelines and provide more detailed information on trading performance for several reasons. First, eliminating the initial purchase of a zero-coupon bond for the principal protection component frees up considerable cash, an important consideration for managers not focused exclusively on the futures markets or where allocations to CTAs are being executed through investments in their pools. Second, some trading advisors are reluctant to accept "notional capital" allocations, which is the standard arrangement under the

FIGURE 12-2

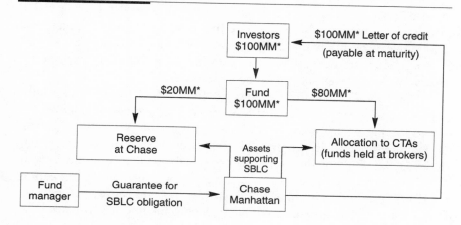

zero-coupon-backed structures. Under a deleveraging arrangement, trading advisors receive full capital allocations in cash. It is important to note that while this structure makes more cash available, it does not change the amount of losses that can accrue before the fund is closed out.

In both the products above, the form of the investment purchased is the same, but the expected results can differ depending upon whether the managed futures program embedded in the issue is the same. This is principally because the upfront cash available for trading and the policy of reinvesting trading profits are different, which will drive the overall total return on the investment at maturity. These examples should demonstrate some of the flexibility that can be used to develop packaging for product to institutional clients.

Another recent product packaging development has been the increased use of the swap structure as an overlay to a traditional fixed-income portfolio, where the end result for the investor is a net cashflow linked to the underlying performance of a managed futures investment strategy. This structure has the potential to bring significant amounts of capital from the institutional market into the leveraged funds industry. "Total Return Swaps" can be structured as overlay transactions, such that the investor does not need to disrupt its traditional portfolio; also, the swap structure permits considerable flexibility to alter the embedded leverage in the instrument to manage exposure to trading performance. The investment is made on a notional basis: no initial cash investment is necessary.

The investor does not need to fit the swap investment into one of its pre-defined "buckets." Instead, the swap works well as an overlay to a fixed-income investment, where the fixed-income instruments generate a LIBOR-based cashflow that will be passed on to the bank under the swap. In return, the investor receives a cashflow based on the net performance of the trading strategy employed in the investment.

The fundamental idea behind the total return swap is a periodic (e.g., quarterly) exchange of cashflows between the bank and an investor, where the net cashflow paid out is based upon the underlying performance of a fund. To accomplish this, the investor enters into a swap with the bank, whereby the investor agrees to pay the bank an amount equal to LIBOR-plus-credit-spread on a notional amount of investment capital ("LIBOR Notional Amount"). In return, the bank agrees to pay the investor a payment stream that is equivalent to the net performance of an underlying fund or managed futures portfolio on a synthetic investment ("Equity Notional Amount") of the same amount. Cashflows are calculated quarterly, with the net amount due to either the bank or the investor paid in arrears.

In order to hedge its swap payment obligation, the bank must enter into an offsetting transaction with a special-purpose vehicle ("SPV"), which enters into a back-to-back swap with the bank and arranges a loan with the bank to fund the investment. The SPV then purchases an investment in the fund or managed futures portfolio in an amount equal to the Equity Notional Amount—effectively "capitalizing" the swap.

This approach has broad appeal, as it provides great flexibility in adjusting the "equity" exposure of a portfolio without disrupting the allocations to fixed-income instruments. In fact, by generating the stream of cashflows that are exchanged in the swap, the fixed-income segment of the portfolio that remains in place is a natural hedge for the institutional investor.

SUMMARY

Many different forms of product packaging already exist. New product will continue to be developed in the future and will offer further opportunities for returns of managed futures programs to be embedded into such instruments. As this continues and (hopefully) gathers momentum, there will be a "blurring" of the current distinction between managed futures and other mainstream investment strategies. For institutional clients, this would create a very stable and very strong alternative to just owning equity and

FIGURE 12–3

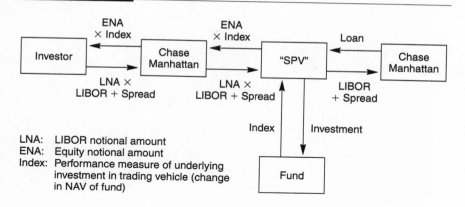

LNA: LIBOR notional amount
ENA: Equity notional amount
Index: Performance measure of underlying
        investment in trading vehicle (change
        in NAV of fund)

equity indexes. This will enable investors to focus on the exciting total absolute return results that this industry offers to the institutional investors. This will be a hard-earned and welcome development for the managed futures industry.

CHAPTER 13

MANAGEMENT SUMMARY

Title: "A Framework for Index-Linked Commodity Pools"

Author: Eric S. Goodbar, Executive Vice President, Fund Management and Research

New Century Investment Research and Management, Inc.

Synopsis: The design and performance of a commodity pool linked to the MAR Trading Advisor Dollar-Weighted Index is examined. There are several benefits to a pool of this design. The pool would give investors the average "real" extractable returns from the managed futures activity. Further, fees could be smaller than traditional pools because the product is only trying to track an index rather than outperforming it through active management. There are also advantages in performance evaluation and the long track record of the index.

A Framework for Index-Linked Commodity Pools

MAR Indexed Commodity Pool Research

Eric S. Goodbar*

INTRODUCTION

This chapter will be devoted to expanding the knowledge and understanding about the usefulness of managed futures in a total portfolio/return framework. The usefulness of managed futures in an institutional portfolio has been generally agreed upon by all the professionals in the managed futures industry and some, if not most, of the professionals in institutional money management. The closure needed for a more complete acceptance of the managed futures product in the institutional community will come from three general areas. First, the evidence must be clear, not just compelling, that there is an inherent return in the managed futures product. Second, institutional money managers and the managed futures industry must come to an agreement, albeit in broad terms, about fee structures that are fair and justified. Lastly, the performance measurement and attribution techniques concerning the managed futures product required by the users must allow for detailed comparison to existing asset class choices.

This research will address these concerns and issues with the desire to broaden the professional community's understanding about how a managed futures index product can more fully add value to traditional investment portfolios. Specifically, this discussion will present some recent research showing how a hypothetical commodity pool of trading advisors

*Eric S. Goodbar is Executive Vice President, Fund Management and Research with New Century Investment Research and Management, Inc., Hinsdale, Illinois.

could replicate a well-known managed futures industry benchmark: the MAR Trading Advisor Dollar-Weighted Index (now MARTAI).

A pool designed to track this index will benefit potential investors in ways that address the three specific issues previously mentioned. The MARTAI, although a combination of the qualified group of trading advisors that does not give trading advisor "skill-free" returns, it does portray an average talent that extracts the returns inherent in managed futures. Therefore, a pool linked to the index will give investors the average "real" extractable returns from the managed futures activity. Further, because the product is only trying to track an index rather than aggressively outperform it through active management—typically by a trading manager or commodity pool operator (CPO)—fees can be correspondingly less. This is analogous to the lower fees paid to the equity index mutual fund managers that track the well-known S&P 500. Performance evaluation for a pool tracking an index can then be made simpler. Tracking error becomes a predominant source of trading manager performance, rather than total returns. Additionally, the MARTAI has a history going back to 1980, making the institutional investors' asset allocation historical studies potentially more meaningful.

In our discussion I will present research that will eliminate some of the typical hindsight bias found in the managed futures industry. Advisors chosen for inclusion in the hypothetical pool have passed through filters for performance and correlation to the index for a significant period prior to the start of a "walk-forward" test. The results show that over a 4-year period from 1992 to 1995 a hypothetical commodity pool of 17 trading advisors benchmarked to the MARTAI would have matched returns fairly consistently with some degree of additional volatility and a tracking error on the order of approximately 8.1 percent per year. Although results measured by tracking error are not completely comparable to the tracking errors found in the best equity index funds, the results I show do hold some promise for commodity pools designed to capture the benefits of the managed futures industry with efficiency and added definition.

BACKGROUND FOR THE RESEARCH

The Managed Futures Value Added

There has been a continuous stream of research and discussion surrounding the managed futures industry from practitioners, academics, and professionals in institutional money management addressing the fundamental question confronting the self-called asset class; namely: do managed futures yield long-term sustainable returns that are in line with the risk taken measured by standard deviation and other means? Figure 13–1 depicts the index of returns for the MARTAI and the S&P 500 Index with dividends reinvested. Whether skill or implicit returns are driving the MARTAI, it is clear that from January 1990 to March 1996, aggregate managed futures investors were receiving somewhat comparable returns from this form of aggregate alternative investment vehicle relative to the benchmark for equity fund management.

This brings up an important question: How much skill is involved with the act of being a commodity trading advisor (CTA)? Perhaps a more interesting question is, If skill levels double within the industry with no advisors entering or leaving the business, will the returns of the MARTAI go up significantly? Traders entering the marketplace certainly have computers that can ascribe to some recent "lifting of all boats by the tide." But what is the skill that these traders are honing or—we hope—self-generating? Price trends are easily spotted with hindsight when looking at a graph of prices. Although computers are difficult to persuade to form intelligent generalized statements about something as amorphous as a price trend, it is not that difficult to teach them to follow rules designed to swath out major portions of trending price behavior.

It is well known in the academic community that managed futures return streams suffer or benefit from leptokertosis or "fat tailed" distribution of returns. Leptokertosis means that returns over longer periods of time exhibit the tendency to either "stay put" or run in one direction or another. What is often ignored with this explanation of trend following evidence is the opposite side of the trend, namely, mean reversion behavior. Mean reverting price action—the tall middle of a leptokurtic distribution—is also pronounced in managed futures. When there is not a clear trend there is a tendency not to random walk, rather, to mean revert to an equilibrium price. Trading advisors populate themselves on both sides of this fence. Portfolios, indexes, and commodity pools all benefit from the blending of trend followers and mean reversion traders.

The risk warehousing function that the managed futures industry performs has been studied for several years by Alan Kaufmann and Charles A. Baker, both currently with Trilogy Capital Management, L.L.C. in Princeton, New Jersey. According to Alan Kaufmann, "The commodity speculator does not create price risk. He merely assumes such risk in much the same manner as the owner of a stock assumes the risk of a particular business."[1] It is this risk-taking process that should command a risk

FIGURE 13–1

MARTAI versus S&P 500 (div reinv.)

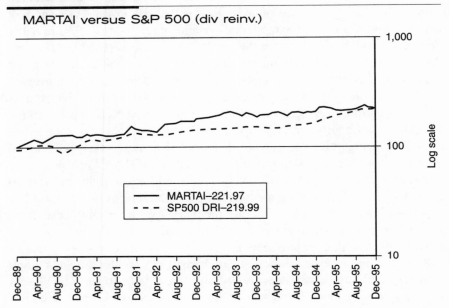

premium, according to John Maynard Keynes (1930). Charles A. Baker, in a January 1995 article in *Pensions & Investments*, suggests, "Investors become 'owners' of price volatility."[2] He goes on to mention that the managed futures industry is providing a "function akin to an insurance company providing 'price insurance' to hedgers in the futures market and earning a commensurate return."

Skill-Removed Managed Futures Returns

J.C. Louis, in a recent *Derivatives Strategy* article, suggests that the inherent return streams derived from the managed futures industry can be replicated through a simple long "at-the-money" straddle on the basket of commodities and noncommodities that comprise an index. This approach attempts to capture the volatility of the market and the trendiness at the same time.[3] Louis suggests that: "This options strategy (long straddles) capitalizes on intriguing evidence that CTAs and managed futures advisors' apparently directional style are actually variations of a widely accepted institutional portfolio tactic: volatility based trading."

Another way to approach extraction of the inherent returns from the market is to follow the MLM Index. MLM stands for Mount Lucas Management. The MLM Index was introduced in 1988 as a benchmark for the returns of managed futures.[4] The index is really a package of returns of a basket of different futures contracts that can come from either an assumed long position established from the current price being over a moving average or the reverse, a short position coming from the current price being below the same moving average. The MLM index, which picks some of the effects of trend followers, has shown a remarkable ability to perform well over long periods of time. The MLM time series gives clear evidence that managed futures can have substantial inherent returns.

So if it is possible to synthetically replicate the aggregate trading advisor returns or the inherent return component, is it desirable to do so? It requires endurable effort to wrench returns, however inherent they may be, from the markets every month. The real extractable return streams, although we may academically define them otherwise, are those generated by the managed futures professionals. The trading advisors deal with illiquid markets, bad fills, and an ever-changing market backdrop, yet they are still able to give value to the investor.

MAR Trading Advisor Index ($ Weighted)—MARTAI

The index suggested for use in this discussion is published by Managed Account Reports (MAR) on a monthly basis with the following criteria established for the advisors desiring inclusion in the MARTAI.

> "To become 'qualified' for inclusion in the trading advisor index, an advisor must EITHER:
>
> - Have $500,000 under management and 12 months trading client assets. These are the current requirements for inclusion of an advisor's performance record in MAR's Performance and Evaluation Directory (QPR Rule), or
>
> - Manage funds for a public fund listed in MAR (MAR Rule). This rule acknowledges the strict audit and regulatory demands that face public funds, and the demands that public fund operators place on advisors."[5]

As of July 1996 there were 399 advisors that qualified for inclusion in the MARTAI, representing approximately $15.7 billion in equity under management.[6] MAR estimates the size of the global managed futures industry in 1994 to be approximately $19 billion.[7] Assuming somewhat flat growth over 1995 and 1996, the MARTAI reflects approximately 82 percent of the entire industry as defined by MAR.[8]

Adding Value to Traditional Investment Methods

Risk reduction and return enhancement are typical goals for managed futures portfolio allocations. It is the goal of this discussion to put forth a managed futures product that can perform these goals in a new context. Specifically, a MARTAI indexed commodity pool provides the investor with an index that can be used in asset allocation back testing going back to January 1980. The lack of track record, typical in most commodity pools, is mostly solved with an index product. This leaves the investor with the analysis of the consistency—read "tracking error"—of the trading manager relative to the index. It is important to note that the model presented in this paper can be fitted to most of the indexes that the managed futures industry uses with an expected deterioration in tracking error occurring for any index where a relatively smaller number of trading advisors are available for inclusion in the indexed commodity pool.

HYPOTHETICAL NEW CENTURY INDEX FUND

Construction

The construction of a hypothetical commodity pool has several advantages and disadvantages. The advantages include the insights gained from research about driving parameters used in an optimization system, persistence of individual trading advisors over a walk-forward back test and appropriate correlation filtration. Disadvantages include the assumption that the discrete allocations can actually be achieved throughout the life of the back test (which has implications regarding the right size for a commodity pool structured in this manner) and hindsight bias; although most of this problem has been addressed. This research presented throughout this discussion is meant to provide a framework for promoting the thinking about indexed linked commodity pools rather than formally positing a model that has been rigorously tested in all market conditions.

The walk-forward back test of the hypothetical pool called the New Century Index Fund (NCIF) assumed that reallocations to 17 chosen trading advisors would have occurred on a quarterly basis without regard to any stated minimums or unit sizes any trading advisor may require. No additional fees would have been paid to a trading manager other than those that could have been negotiated on a split basis with the trading advisors, similar to current institutional based fee arrangements.[9] The process of developing hypothetical return series an a MARTAI linked "walk-forward" back test for a commodity pool followed these steps:

- Establish a broad universe of trading advisor returns and related statistics that match time frame criteria.

- Filter those advisors based on "lower-is-better" monthly standard deviation of their published fully funded returns *prior* to the walk-forward test.

- Filter those advisors based on "higher-is-better" monthly correlation to the MARTAI of their published fully funded returns *prior* to the walk-forward test.

- Calculate quarterly covariance matrixes used in a single-factor beta model.

- Establish appropriate allocation cap for all trading advisors of 8 percent.

- Optimize each quarter during the walk-forward back test so that the mix of chosen trading advisors will best track the MARTAI.

The universe of 17 trading advisors chosen for this research were all reporting monthly returns prior to June 1989 and continued reporting through December 1995. The advisor group was a result of a screening process for correlation to the MARTAI for the period June 1989–December 1991. The filter was set to include advisors with approximately +0.60 correlation or higher to the MARTAI. This filter is in addition to the other filters that are used by the New Century System ("NCS") for other related managed futures research.

Table 13–1 shows the trading advisor summary information. The trading advisor correlation to the MARTAI is displayed along with the categories of market sectors that each advisor trades. It is clear that the group is currently diversified across most markets.

Table 13–2 shows that the group is mainly a technical, systematic group with occasional discretionary overrides. Overall, the 17 trading advisors display similar characteristics: diversified, systematic trend following trading techniques. As a group, the advisors have not changed much since January 1992, except for one of the advisors (number 15), which went through a change in management in 1995. All of the trading advisor programs are still currently open, except for advisor 15, which formally changed the program structure as the management change occurred.

The Beta (β) Approach

Using a β in the context of an indexed linked equity fund is not new; it is, however, rather unique in the context of managed futures. The typical

TABLE 13–1

Advisor	Correlation to MARTAI Jun 89-Dec 91	Agricultural	Energy	Financial	Metal
1	0.91	Yes	Yes	Yes	Yes
2	0.88	Yes	Yes	Yes	Yes
3	0.87		Yes	Yes	Yes
4	0.86	Yes	Yes	Yes	Yes
5	0.86	Yes	Yes	Yes	Yes
6	0.85	Yes	Yes	Yes	Yes
7	0.85	Yes	Yes	Yes	Yes
8	0.85	Yes	Yes	Yes	Yes
9	0.84	Yes	Yes	Yes	Yes
10	0.80	Yes	Yes	Yes	Yes
11	0.75	Yes	Yes	Yes	Yes
12	0.72			Yes	Yes
13	0.63	Yes	Yes	Yes	Yes
14	0.62	Yes	Yes	Yes	Yes
15	0.56			Yes	
16	0.56		Yes	Yes	Yes
17	0.53	Yes	Yes	Yes	
Count		**13**	**15**	**17**	**15**

calculation of β that is often used in practice is to think about the covariance of a trading advisor's returns as some ratio to the variance of the overall market, or in this case a unique index, MARTAI. The formula then is:

$$\beta = \frac{Cov_{ta,MARTAI}}{VAR_{MARTAI}}$$

Where $Cov_{ta,MARTAI}$ is the covariance over a price return series of an individual trading advisor (*ta*) to the MARTAI. Var_{MARTAI} is the variance of the price return series of the MARTAI over the same time period. β is then estimated for each of the trading advisors as each quarter is about to be optimized. The optimization process then attempts to find the best mix of the 17 advisors that matches the β of 1.0 for an upcoming quarter. In order to keep the optimization process from concentrating an allocation to any one advisor, a percentage allocation cap of 8.0 percent was used. This

TABLE 13–2

Advisor	Technical	Fundamental	Systematic	Discretion-ary	Arbitrage
1	Yes		Yes		
2	Yes		Yes	Yes	
3	Yes		Yes		
4	Yes		Yes		
5	Yes		Yes		
6	Yes		Yes		
7	Yes				
8	Yes		Yes	Yes	
9	Yes		Yes		
10	Yes		Yes		
11	Yes		Yes	Yes	
12	Yes		Yes		
13	Yes		Yes		
14	Yes		Yes	Yes	
15	Yes		Yes		
16	Yes		Yes		
17	Yes			Yes	
Count	**17**	0	**15**	**5**	0

means that in any one quarter's re-allocation calculation, no one advisor received more than 8.0 percent of the entire hypothetical capital.

The Results of the Research

The initial results of the walk-forward back test are favorable. Figure 13–2 shows that on a log scale the hypothetical commodity pool NCIF closely captures the value being generated by the MARTAI.

The ending index of returns for the period of January 1992 –December 1995 was 152.46 for the NCIF and 150.59 for the MARTAI. Upon examination, Figure 13–2 portrays the NCIF returns as somewhat more volatile than the MARTAI. The main concern for potential users of this kind of methodology is the long-term wealth building of an indexed managed futures product as well as the relative performance within a larger traditional investment portfolio. Investors should be willing to

FIGURE 13-2

NCIF versus MARTAI

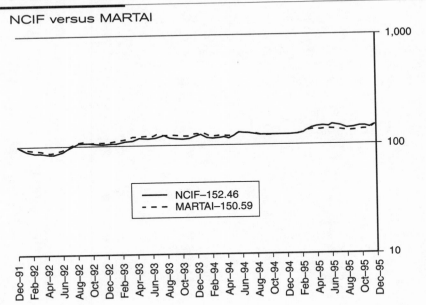

experience moderately higher volatility in order to achieve the long-term results of benchmarking an index.

Table 13–3 shows the return series for the NCIF and for the MARTAI. The summary statistics are displayed for each of the 4 years. For example, the monthly compounded average annual return for the NCIF for 1995 was 15.54 percent.

The return for the MARTAI for the same time period was 15.13 percent. The returns for the NCIF, when viewed through the summary statistics, indicate that the group of 17 advisors are keeping pace with the value building of the large number of trading advisors in the MARTAI. Remember, the 17 advisors were chosen based on data prior to the start of the walk-forward back test. In a real application of this methodology in a commodity pool, the trading manager would be constantly evaluating the universe of advisors looking for the incremental advantage of including the trading of an advisor in order to better match the performance of the MARTAI.

Figure 13–3 shows the NCIF and the MARTAI indexed over the 4 years on a normal scale. Performance during 1992 and 1993 (as indicated in Table 13–1) is lower for NCIF. However, in 1994 and 1995 the performance of NCIF is greater relative to the MARTAI. This over- and under

TABLE 13-3

NCIF Hypothetical Return Comparison to MARTAI

Month	1992 MARTAI	1992 NCIF	1993 MARTAI	1993 NCIF	1994 MARTAI	1994 NCIF	1995 MARTAI	1995 NCIF
January	(5.59)	(8.14)	0.79	(3.05)	(2.73)	(4.47)	(2.12)	(4.69)
February	(2.97)	(3.95)	7.17	8.03	(2.52)	(4.08)	4.21	5.50
March	(0.25)	(0.89)	(1.35)	0.67	2.87	5.73	8.19	10.37
April	(2.26)	(0.49)	3.24	4.75	(1.30)	(2.14)	1.69	2.83
May	0.44	(1.34)	1.13	1.35	2.94	8.96	0.90	2.39
June	5.79	7.40	2.63	(0.45)	3.64	3.35	(1.56)	0.46
July	8.24	11.40	4.63	6.95	(2.10)	(2.09)	(2.01)	(5.40)
August	3.99	5.52	(0.27)	(2.79)	(3.14)	(3.93)	1.30	(0.99)
September	0.57	(3.10)	(1.00)	(2.44)	1.56	3.12	(1.51)	(2.13)
October	2.31	(1.15)	(0.14)	(2.57)	0.01	(2.31)	0.36	(1.23)
November	1.26	3.11	(0.42)	1.07	1.60	4.88	1.59	0.72
December	(1.25)	(1.39)	2.19	7.18	(1.20)	(1.22)	3.62	7.92
Avg. Mo. Ret. per Yr.	**0.79**	**0.45**	**1.52**	**1.48**	**(0.06)**	**0.39**	**1.18**	**1.21**
Ann. Ret. per Yr.	**9.90**	**5.54**	**19.86**	**19.29**	**(0.70)**	**4.81**	**15.13**	**15.54**
Mo. Std. Dev. per Yr.	**3.85**	**5.38**	**2.54**	**4.17**	**2.46**	**4.50**	**3.03**	**4.79**
Avg. Mo. Ret./Std. Dev.	**0.21**	**0.08**	**0.60**	**0.36**	**(0.02)**	**0.09**	**0.39**	**0.25**

FIGURE 13-3

NCIF versus MARTAI

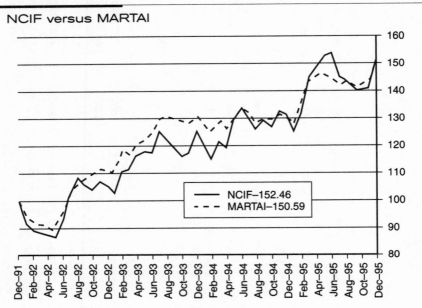

performance in any one year is to be expected. This is important to note. Underperformance in any one year does not mean the methodology is inappropriate. Multiyear time frames must be examined before a conclusion about trading manager performance can be finalized.

There are other statistics that can be used to monitor a trading manager's performance on a shorter time scale. Tracking error can be viewed as the standard deviation of differences in returns of, in this case, the NCIF and the MARTAI contemporaneous time series. The square root of the average squared differences in returns on a monthly basis will yield the monthly tracking error. Multiplying the monthly tracking error statistic by the square root of 12 (12 months in a year) will yield an annual tracking error. The annual tracking error statistic is a familiar term used in equity management, and equity fund managers should feel comfortable using this management tool.

Table 13-4 shows the return differences for the two return series with per year monthly tracking errors. A 4-year statistic of 2.35 percent summarizes the monthly tracking error and when multiplied by 3.464 it becomes approximately 8.1 percent. This annual tracking error value may seem high relative to typical tracking errors for indexed linked equity

TABLE 13—4

NCIF Hypothetical Return Differences to MARTAI

Month	1992 NCIF - MARTAI	1993 NCIF - MARTAI	1994 NCIF - MARTAI	1995 NCIF - MARTAI
January	(2.55)	(3.84)	(1.74)	(2.57)
February	(0.98)	0.86	(1.56)	1.29
March	(0.64)	2.02	2.86	2.18
April	1.77	1.51	(0.84)	1.14
May	(1.78)	0.22	6.02	1.49
June	1.61	(3.08)	(0.29)	2.02
July	3.16	2.32	0.01	(3.39)
August	1.53	(2.52)	(0.79)	(2.29)
September	(3.67)	(1.44)	1.56	(0.62)
October	(3.46)	(2.43)	(2.32)	(1.59)
November	1.85	1.49	3.28	(0.87)
December	(0.14)	4.99	(0.02)	4.30
Sqrd. Errors per Yr.	2.20	2.55	2.41	2.23
Tot. Sqrd. Errors	2.35			

funds, but the betas for equities are, as a group, closer to 1.0 and more stable through time. Tracking errors for indexed linked futures products should be judged on a peer-to-peer basis rather than outright comparison of tracking errors to equity fund management.

The monthly tracking errors that are displayed per year (Sqrd. Errors per Yr.) in Table 13–4 show some consistency across all 4 years. The range of 2.20 to 2.55 relates to annual tracking error estimates of the approximate range of 7.6 percent to 8.8 percent. This is encouraging, because stability of the tracking error is an important selling point for the methodology. An investor should be willing to endure longer periods of underperformance, or enjoy longer periods of overperformance, knowing that the index linked managed futures product is fluctuating in normal bounds defined by the normal distribution of differences in returns around the benchmark.

Table 13–5 shows the summary statistics for the back test. Specifically, the average monthly return for the NCIF is quite close, with

TABLE 13-5

Research Summary Statistics

Statistic	MARTAI	NCIF
Avg. Mo Ret 1992-1995	0.86	0.88
Avg. Ann. Ret. 1992-1995	10.78	11.12
Mo. S.D. 1992-1995	2.98	4.60
Ann. S.D. 1992-1995	10.33	15.94
Avg. Mo. Ret./S.D.	**0.29**	**0.19**
Avg Ann. Ret./Ann. S.D.	**1.04**	**0.70**

0.88 percent per month for the NCIF and 0.86 percent per month for the MARTAI. The average annual rate of return with monthly compounding was 11.12 percent for the NCIF and 10.78 percent for the MARTAI. These returns have to be adjusted for volatility, and monthly reward-to-risk ratios are displayed along with the annual reward to risk ratios. The annual standard deviation (Ann. S.D.) is calculated by taking the monthly standard deviation and multiplying the value by the 3.464 (square root of 12). The NCIF had more volatility, and this is to be expected because the methodology is attempting to mimic the return streams of a large number of advisors with 17 advisors. Overall, the hypothetical performance of the NCIF is reasonable and appears to have satisfied the challenge of benchmarking the MARTAI within acceptable ranges of absolute volatility and tracking error.

SUMMARY

The goal of this research was to introduce a method for benchmarking the MARTAI with a hypothetical commodity pool, with the focus on a low and stable tracking error. This discussion began by establishing three issues that an index linked commodity pool might help resolve. First, the issue of inherent returns was addressed by introducing some references to current research in this area as well the mentioning of techniques that can simulate the activity of extracting the inherent returns typically captured by trading advisors. The return series of the MARTAI, when compared to traditional asset classes, compares well; this lends evidence to the potential investor about the inherent returns of managed futures. If an investor can justify the inclusion of the MARTAI as an asset class suitable for an allocation in a traditional portfolio, then the methodology presented in this discussion should be appealing. Secondly, fee structures can be managed more effectively with an index linked managed futures product because of the potential large size of a commodity pool organized to have a larger number of advisors included and because of the focus on tracking the index rather than outperforming it. Again it is important to note that the size of a commodity pool must be larger to cover the costs associated with the trading manager. Lastly, the justification of using a benchmarked commodity pool is made easier when the track record of the index is as lengthy as the MARTAI. The return series for the MARTAI goes back to January 1980. This series covers several business cycles—the period of high inflation in the early eighties as well as the change in the political backdrop in the U.S. that has occurred in the early nineties.

The methods for benchmarking the index involved a simple application of a well-known capital market modeling technique using a beta statistic to relate individual trading advisor returns to the benchmark throughout a walk-forward back test. Filtering techniques involving monthly correlation to the benchmark and standard deviation of monthly returns were used to boil the universe of trading advisors down to 17 qualified candidates.

The future of the managed futures industry rests on its ability to serve the needs of the investment community in ways that no other asset class can. Addressing the concerns of inherent returns, fees, and comparability should be goals all managed futures professionals attempt to achieve.

ENDNOTES

1. Alan Kaufmann gives an excellent introduction into the reasons for inherent returns in managed futures in his article, "The source of futures investment returns," *Global Investor* (March 1993): 29-33.
2. Charles A. Baker, "Taking a hedge on much derivatives research," *Pensions & Investments* (January 23, 1995).
3. J.C. Louis, "6 Power Trades for 1996, Straddles that Mimic Commodity Trading Advisor Returns." *Derivatives Strategy*, (December/January 1996).
4. Reference again to Alan Kaufmann's article, "The source of futures investment returns," *Global Investor* (March 1993): 29-33.
5. This definition was obtained from Web page http//www.marhedge.com, FAQ MAR Trading Advisor Qualified Universe Indices.
6. Ibid.

7. These statistics can be found on the internet at the following Web page: http://www.marhedge.com/mar/faq_grth.htm.

8. It is important to note that the MARTAI has a significant amount of survivor bias. This means that since the inception of the index in 1980 to the present, some trading advisors have ceased trading leaving their returns in the index series. There is also a lesser effect that I will call reverse survivor bias. This relates to the traders that have ceased trading because of their success. It is not uncommon for an advisor that has achieved an amount of success measured by assets under management to withdraw from the reporting duties in order to minimize the effort of raising new funds. Both of these survivor biases net to some degree with the typical survivor bias predominating. These biases, in the author's opinion, do not inhibit the research presented in this discussion.

9. It is not uncommon for institutional clients to accept a fee arrangement that is a 2 percent management fee and a 20 percent incentive fee for an entire commodity pool or program with the understanding that the trading advisors and trading manager will somehow split the 2/20 arrangement. Although this is not quite a "wrap fee," it does provide a cleaner fee arrangement for the investor.

CHAPTER 14

MANAGEMENT SUMMARY

Title: "The Use of Managed Futures in Emerging Markets"

Author: Anthony V. Czapla, Senior Vice President
            LIT Asset Management, Inc.

Synopsis: The benefits of introducing speculative activity to emerging
            futures markets is examined. The use of managed futures in these
            markets adds liquidity, increases market efficiency, and allows
            for more effective hedging. Less developed markets also repre-
            sent excellent opportunities for commodity trading advisors
            (CTAs) to diversify. Unfortunately, government regulation is
            impeding the development process in many emerging markets.

The Use of Managed Futures in Emerging Markets

Anthony V. Czapla
and
William G. Cooley, Jr.

One can't help but find it ironic that the United States of America, a country barely more than 200 years old, today sets the global standard in defining emerging markets. For instance, the unified Chinese states have engaged in measurable commerce since 2852 B.C., yet China is still considered an emerging market under the definition offered by Frank Russell & Co.'s Elayne Sheridan. Sheridan writes that an emerging market is defined by "rapid economic growth, an immature equities market, government policies that promote growth through the private equity sector and a trend toward stable financial and political institutions." Currently, the International Finance Corporation recognizes 19 emerging markets worldwide. Beyond Sheridan's definition, one must also consider the significance of the establishment of futures exchanges, as they often earmark the transition of emerging economies.

Table 14–1 includes a partial list of futures exchanges open in emerging markets, including the futures and options contracts traded on these exchanges. As of this writing, the financial press has suggested that the birth of futures exchanges in Egypt, India, Poland, and the Ukraine is inevitable. This genesis is logical, representing the evolutionary pathway for countries that seek economic growth, mature equity markets, and stable

Anthony V. Czapla is Senior Vice President and Managing Director of LIT Asset Management, Inc., a trading manager that specializes in the development of managed futures programs for institutional investors. William G. Cooley, Jr., is a summer intern pursuing a B.S. degree in finance at Western Michigan University.

financial and political institutions. It is important to note that Table 14–1 features futures exchanges in emerging markets and *not* emerging futures exchanges. The latter list would include futures exchange activities in such countries as Portugal, South Korea, and Taiwan, countries whose equity markets are well established and ranked among the world's largest in U.S. dollar terms.

After all, the entire reason for futures trading is a very basic economic tenet. In a free and open market, true price will be discovered because of the competition between multiple buyers and sellers. In simple terms, buyers try to obtain the largest amount of a given commodity for the cheapest price. Sellers do exactly the opposite, striving for the highest price for the least amount of a given commodity. As a result of this pool of buyers and sellers, the equilibrium price for a commodity is reached throughout each trading day. In other words, the futures market will find the level of where the price of a commodity should be, given the supply and demand as well as other economic factors. If there is excess supply or surplus, the price will be driven lower until sellers either will not or cannot sell the product. In contrast, where there is a shortage of supply, price will continue to rise to a level that buyers think is the highest price that should be paid for a particular commodity before considering less expensive substitutes.

Futures can be used in two ways, hedging and speculation. Hedgers use the markets to protect themselves against price volatility, while speculators use the markets to achieve superior rates of return commensurate to the risk of loss. Both sides are necessary to efficient price discovery. Without hedgers, there would be no party to take delivery, or deliver the commodity traded. Without speculators, the market would be stagnant with no party willing to accept the risk of price volatility. Ultimately, the futures markets help to establish a continuous standard by which consumers and producers can effect transactions and nations can enjoy the benefits of commerce.

Another potential benefit to emerging economies from futures trading is the revenues to be derived from taxation. This is not a new concept, as nearly every U.S. president in modern times has proposed a futures transaction tax. In fact, as recently as 1995, President Clinton proposed a 10-cent ($.10) tax on futures and options trading that would have resulted in nearly $60 million for U.S. government coffers. Naturally, this tax was withdrawn from the final budget proposal, in no small part due to the powerful lobby of the U.S. futures and options exchanges. But in a new market such a tax may be more readily accepted as an inherent cost of doing

TABLE 14-1

Emerging Market Exchanges

Country	Exchange Name	Futures Traded	Options Traded
Argentina	Bolsa de Comercio de Buenos Aries	Interest Rate Index	Equities
		Merval Index	Public Bonds
		Cattle Index	Cattle Index
	MERFOX		
Brazil	Bolsa Brasileira se Futuros	Live Cattle (U.S.$, Pesos, DM)	Live Cattle (U.S.$, Pesos, DM)
		Avg. Interest Rate on Interbank Deposits	Avg. Interest Rate on Interbank Deposits
		Arabica Coffee	Arabica Coffee
		U.S. Dollar Exchange Rate	U.S. Dollar Exchange Rate
		Deutsche Mark Exchange Rate	Deutsche Mark Exchange Rate
		Japanese Yen Exchange Rate	Japanese Yen Exchange Rate
		Swiss Franc Future Exchange Rate	Swiss Franc Future Exchange Rate
		Long-Term Interest Rate	
		Stock-Price Future Return Index	
	Bolsa de Mercadorias & Futuros	Bovespa Stock Index	Bovespa Stock Index
		Gold	Gold
		Foreign Currency	Foreign Currency
		Interbank Deposits, 1 day	Interbank Deposits, 1 day
		Interbank Deposits, 30 day	Live Cattle
		Live Cattle	Arabica Coffee
		Feeder Cattle	
		Arabica Coffee	
		Robusta Coffee	
		Cotton	

TABLE 14-1 *(continued)*

Emerging Market Exchanges

Country	Exchange Name	Futures Traded	Options Traded
Brazil		Feeder Cattle	
		Soybeans	
		Crystal Sugar	
	Rio de Janeiro Stock Exchange	ISENN Stock Index	ISENN Stock Index
			Individual stocks
	Sao Paulo Stock Exchange	Equity Options	None
China	Shanghai Metal Exchange	Copper	None
		Aluminum	
		Lead	
		Zinc	
		Tin	
		Nickel	
	Shen Zhen Metal Exchange	Copper	None
		Aluminum	
		Tin	
		Zinc	
		Nickel	
		Antimony	
		Magnesium	
Hong Kong	Hong Kong Futures Exchange, Ltd.	Gold	Hang Seng Index
		Hang Seng Index	
		Rolling Forex (DM)	

TABLE 14-1 (continued)

Emerging Market Exchanges

Country	Exchange Name	Futures Traded	Options Traded
Hong Kong		Rolling Forex (Yen)	
		3-Month Hibor	
		Hang Seng Commerce & Industry Index	
		Hang Seng Properties Sub-Index	
		Hang Seng Finance Sub-Index	
		Hang Seng Utilities Sub-Index	
		Hong Kong Telecommunications Ltd.	
		HSBC Holdings PLC	
		Cheung Kong (Holdings) Ltd.	
Hungary	Budapest Commodity Exchange	Corn	None
		Milling Wheat	
		Feed Wheat	
		Feed Barley	
		Black Seed	
		BL-55 Wheat Flour	
		Live Hog No. 1	
		Live Hog No. 2	
		German Mark	
		U.S. Dollar	
		Japanese Yen	
		Italian Lire	
		Interest Rate	

TABLE 14-1 (continued)

Emerging Market Exchanges

Country	Exchange Name	Futures Traded	Options Traded
Hungary	Budapest Stock Exchange	Budapest Stock Index	None
		DEM/HUF	
		USD/HUF	
		ECU/HUF	
		Hungarian 3-Month Treasury Bill	
Israel	Tel-Aviv Stock Exchange, Ltd.	MAOF-25 Index	MAOF-25 Index
			Shekel/Dollar
Malaysia	Kuala Lumpur Commodity Exchange	Crude Palm Oil	None
		Crude Palm Kernel Oil	
		Cocoa	
		Tin	
		Rubber (SMR 20)	
	Kuala Lumpur Options & Financial Futures Exchange	KL Stock Exchange Composite Index	
Phillippines	Manilla International Futures Exchange	Sugar	None
		Coffee	
		Copra	
		Soybeans	
		Dry cocoon	
		Interest Rate U.S. Dollar/Japanese Yen	
		Interest Rate U.S. Dollar/German Mark	
		Interest Rate U.S. Dollar/British Pound	

T A B L E 14–1 (concluded)

Emerging Market Exchanges

Country	Exchange Name	Futures Traded	Options Traded
Phillippines		Interest Rate U.S. Dollar/Swiss Franc	
		Interest Rate U.S. Dollar/Peso	
		Interest Rate	

Note: The world is a rapidly changing place.
Sources: Arthur Andersen, Directory and Review, 1996.
Futures Industry Institute, *Futures and Options Fact Book*, 1996.

business, provided that this cost of doing business is not artificially high so as to breed unwelcome competition. For example, most professional traders prefer to trade the 10-year Japanese Government Bond (JGB) futures contract listed on the Singapore International Monetary Exchange (SIMEX), rather than the JGB listed on the Tokyo Stock Exchange (TSE) because the commission cost is significantly lower than the TSE's fixed commission (even after taking into account the TSE contract's larger size).

The aforementioned fixed commission instituted by the Japanese government is a classic example of how policies intended to preserve market share and protect franchise profitability often are recipes for failure. By attempting to guarantee the success of Japanese clearing firms through fixed commissions and transaction costs, the Japanese government created an opportunity for their "natural" contract to trade more successfully off-shore. Similar mistakes have been made elsewhere—in Germany, where traders of the German Bund futures contract found it easier to trade the same product in London; even in that bastion of futures trading—Chicago, which allowed New York to secure the precious metals market. Unfortunately, these miscues continue. Witness the Korean government's recent decision to limit foreign participation in the newly launched KOSPI 200 stock index futures contract to 500 contracts or less. It has been unofficially suggested that this policy was enacted to prevent foreign traders from manipulating the upstart market and causing price distortions. Though seemingly well intended, this decision to protect profit opportunities for Korean traders may ultimately cripple what could have easily been a burgeoning futures contract by limiting the KOSPI 200's natural growth rate and encouraging competition from non-Korean markets.

Often attempts are made to correct these mistakes; however, past experience suggests that once a futures contract has obtained sufficient trading volume or critical mass it becomes nearly impossible to unseat the competition. Remember, futures markets and their users are swift to seek equilibrium conditions.

In recent years, managed futures, a speculative investment strategy that uses professional trading advisors to trade a diversified portfolio of futures contracts, has received considerable attention from institutional and individual investors seeking enhanced performance results through broader portfolio diversification. This growing interest is attributed by futures industry observers to be the result of several socio-economic changes and events. Chief among these are: (a) investors' increased awareness and perception of stock market volatility heightened by the periodic global declines witnessed in 1987, 1989, and 1990; (b) continued academic endeavors into modern portfolio theory and the use of asset allocation models; and (c) the general positive performance and maturation of the managed futures industry over the past 2 decades.

In its most basic form the association between emerging markets and managed futures can be almost symbiotic in nature. Futures exchanges are created in emerging markets because of the need of "local" producers to hedge or transfer their respective business risks. Managed futures evolved because of the speculative nature of traders, their willingness to accept risk, and their successful pursuit of profit opportunity. Clearly, the use of managed futures in emerging markets can result in a mutually beneficial relationship for both parties.

One example of this relationship can be developed by examining the advent of futures trading in South Korea. Admittedly, South Korea is a somewhat imperfect example because it is futures trading and not the country that is emerging. Fortunately, the timeliness of this example makes it particularly poignant. South Korea is one of the most rapidly industrializing nations in the world with a vibrant economy and a well-established equity market. The time had come for South Korea to take its rightful place in the global economy. The development of futures trading was a necessary and natural step to meet the needs of its domestic as well as foreign market participants. The cooperative marketing effort and dissemination of information between the government and the private sector proved to be a powerful enticement to professional traders seeking new markets to trade. Based upon careful research into the historical price action of the cash index, numerous traders believed the KOSPI 200 would exhibit highly tradeable characteristics. Further, it was felt that due to the pent-up demand of investors seeking to insure stock portfolio holdings, that the contract would have sufficient volume and liquidity. Nothing frightens a professional trader more than the prospect of being unable to liquidate a position quickly when things go awry. Assume for the sake of this example that the 500 contract foreign limit was not established by the Korean government.

Buoyed by their research effort and the notion of a new market to trade, professional traders would undoubtedly begin to follow the daily price action of the KOSPI 200. In an effort to accelerate the growth of the KOSPI 200, one strategy might be for a financial institution with a vested interest in the contract to allocate a modest portion of its proprietary assets to judiciously chosen foreign trading advisors with the stipulation that a portion of their trading be committed to the KOSPI 200 futures contract. By promoting the speculative support of the contract it becomes easier to facilitate the true price discovery need of hedgers through liquidity. This new liquidity in turn deepens the breadth of players and a new wave of speculators enters the market. And so the cycle continues with new hedgers and speculators bringing the contract to a level of critical mass and ensuring that the long-term objective of the hedger is fulfilled. This tactic is not unusual, as a version of it was often used by the Chicago Mercantile Exchange (CME) to introduce new futures contracts. For instance, the CME frequently requested that floor traders spend 15 to 30 minutes a day in the CME's S&P 500 pit. Although the CME may not have thought of the idea, few exchanges have used it more successfully.

Although this strategy may make sense to stimulate the growth of new futures contracts, what of the financial institution that so magnanimously allocated its capital in the first place? History is full of examples of trading advisors that have been well rewarded for being among the first to speculate in new markets like global currencies, European interest rates, and Japanese commodities. And what of the money given to the professional trader that was not allocated to the KOSPI 200 futures contract in our example? Managed Accounts Reports (MAR), an independent publication that monitors the performance of trading advisors, reports that from 1980 through 1995, the MAR Trading Advisor "Qualified" Universe Index enjoyed a net compounded annual rate of return of approximately 16.0 percent, which rivals nearly every major global stock market for the same time period. Past performance is not necessarily indicative of future results.

Another interesting twist to the aforementioned managed futures allocation strategy can be utilized in countries where the yield on government instruments is around 10 percent per annum. Given that a trading advisor typically only uses 10 to 15 percent of the investment for margin purposes, in a 10 percent interest rate environment it becomes theoretically possible to "guarantee " the return of principal in 5 years by using approximately one-half of the intended allocation to purchase government instruments with a 5-year maturity and to speculatively trade the remaining one-half in a managed futures program. Again this "guaranteed" concept is not new and has been available through various investment vehicles worldwide. However, in countries where interest rates are low, the performance of these products has been considered somewhat disappointing because such a large portion of the investment had to be committed to secure the "guarantee." In addition, as less money is available for trading purposes, the investment becomes more susceptible to trading losses.

In summary, the use of managed futures programs in emerging markets can offer several potential benefits. First, such investment programs can provide the additional speculative volume necessary to facilitate the true price discovery critical to effective hedging. Secondly, as markets grow bigger, their volume and liquidity help to attract even more users. This creates an economic environment with certain hidden advantages (potential tax revenues, increased bank balances, and employment opportunities) to the nation's economy. Finally, "local" institutional investors in managed futures may benefit from the additional diversification and counter-cyclical nature of returns often found in futures speculation coupled with the ability of professional trading advisors to capture the enhanced returns sometimes resident in new contract markets.

CHAPTER 15

Issues of Implementation

INTRODUCTION

The selection and monitoring of CTAs are critical to the success of a managed futures product. In this chapter, experienced professionals share their expertise in choosing traders for institutional and large retail commodity pools.

The first section gives an overview of the managed futures industry. Commodity trading advisors (CTAs) are categorized by methodology (trend-following and discretionary), by sector (diversified, financial, currency, and stock index traders), and by location (Europe and the U.S.). The performance and assets under management in each sector are also presented.

Section II discusses how the willingness of a CTA to disclose his methodology can affect the money-raising effort. Information on a trader's background, approach, and risk management is critical in the prediction of a CTA's continued success. However, many money managers are hesitant to reveal their approach to the markets, for fear of disclosing important proprietary information. In the long run, managers who are more open about their approach will not only find it easier to raise customer assets, but also increase their chances of retaining those assets in drawdown periods.

Section III lists the advantages of evaluating traders using qualitative criteria. The limitations of traditional quantitative benchmarks are also discussed. The author contends that "the only tenable way to measure skill is to compare actual performance with a system's potential exploitation—

in relative, not absolute terms—of the profit-making opportunities presented to it".

Finally, Section IV examines the responsibilities of a trading manager in the design and implementation of an alternative investment program. Some of the roles of a trading manager include conducting a research and selection process, providing adequate accounting and reporting to investors, and ongoing monitoring of the CTAs in the portfolio.

Profile of the Trading Advisor

Lois Peltz
Managing Editor
Managed Account Reports

I. OVERVIEW

There are currently 412 trading advisors in the Managed Account Reports (MAR) database, representing $14.1 billion.[1] The typical advisor is a trend-follower, trading a diversified program. Based in the U.S., he has less than a 5-year track record and about $31.1 million under management. The average minimum investment for his program is about $500,000, and he charges a 2 to 3 percent management fee and 20 percent incentive fee.

Performancewise, the typical trading advisor (as measured by the MAR Trading Advisor Qualified Universe Index with an inception date of January 1980) generated an annualized compound rate of return of 15.8 percent. Annual returns have been in double-digits for 9 of those years and down only in 1 year—1994, with a loss of 0.7 percent. The typical advisor experienced a maximum cumulative decline of 20.4 percent over a 10-month period in late 1982-83.

Not everyone fits this typical trading advisor generalization. Some highlighted variations include:

- 180 advisors trade only one program. Forty-eight trade two, while 25 trade three. Another 10 have four programs; only 4 have more than five.

- Fifty-eight advisors, 14.1 percent, have over a 10-year track record, while 32.0 percent have between 5 and 10 years. The bulk, 53.8 percent, have less than a 5-year track record.

---

[1]The total assets invested in managed futures is estimated at about $25 billion.

- Thirty advisors have over $100 million; of those, four have over $1 billion. Another 25 advisors have between $50 million and $99 million; 44 advisors have between $25 and $50 million; 59 are between $10 and $49.9 million. The remainder have less than $10 million.
- Eight of every 10 advisors are located in the U.S. with the bulk of the remainder from Europe. Australia has four trading advisors reporting numbers while Japan has one.

II. PROFILE BY METHODOLOGY

Trend-Followers

Two-thirds of the traders are trend-followers representing $6.4 billion. The typical trend-follower has $22.9 million under management. While slightly more than half the trend-followers have less than a 5-year track record, 40 can boast over 10 years. The minimum investment for trend-followers is relatively high at $863,700.

Because of their high numbers in the advisor population, a very high correlation exists with the general advisor universe. The typical trend-follower (as measured by the MAR trend-follower subindex, which began in January 1983), has generated an annualized compound rate of return of 15.1 percent through mid-1996. In 8 years, the annual return has been in the double-digits. In 4 years—1986, 1989, 1992 and 1994—the results have been negative. The maximum cumulative decline occurred over a 9-month period in 1986 and resulted in a decline of 28.4 percent, which is larger than the advisor community in general.

Discretionary

Discretionary traders represent only 27.4 percent of the advisors in the tracked universe but represent about the same amount of assets as the trend-followers at $6.3 billion, thus indicating that each has a much larger amount of assets under management. In fact, of the four trading advisors managing over $1 billion, three describe themselves as discretionary. The typical discretionary trader has $51.1 million under management—much higher than the general advisor community.

Unlike the other advisor categories, the bulk of the track records lengths are 5 to 10 years in duration. Eighteen discretionary traders have more than a 10-year track record.

The typical discretionary trader has no correlation to the general trading advisor universe. The discretionary advisor (as represented by the MAR discretionary subindex, which began in January 1987) has generated a significantly higher annualized compound rate of return of 25.5 percent than the trend-followers, the general advisor community, or any of the other sector subindexes. In 8 years, the annual return has been in the double-digits. In 1994 alone, the results were negative. The maximum cumulative decline was only 5.6 percent—significantly more controlled than that of the general community. It occurred over a 4-month period in 1994.

III. PROFILE BY SECTOR

Looking at the advisors on a sector-by-sector basis, we see the following:

Diversified

Over half the advisors (52.7 percent) trade a diversified program. The 217 diversified programs represent about $6.5 million. The typical diversified trader has about $25.3 million under management. Of those programs with a 10-year plus track record, 69 percent are diversified.

Due to their large representation in the advisor community, the diversified trader has a significantly high correlation to the overall trader universe. The typical diversified trader (as measured by the MAR diversified subindex, which began in January 1987) has generated an average annualized compound rate of return of 12.8 percent. In 6 of those years, the annual return has been in the double-digits. In 1989 and 1992, the results were negative. The maximum cumulative decline of 16.6 percent occurred over a 5-month period in early 1992.

Financial

Financial programs are the most numerous of the sector-specific programs, representing 19.4 percent of the programs traded, representing $3.9 billion of assets. The typical financial trader has about $45.5 million under management—significantly higher than the typical trading advisor.

The typical financial trader has a significant correlation to the general advisor universe but has generated a slightly higher than average annualized compound rate of 16.9 percent. In 7 years, the annual return has been in the double-digits. In 2 years—1992 and 1994—the results have been negative. The maximum cumulative decline occurred over a 5-month period in 1992 and resulted in a decline of 16.1 percent.

Currency

Currency programs represent the second largest sector-specific category. The 66 financial programs represent $3.2 billion, or 16 percent of the programs traded.

The typical currency trader has $47.1 million under management—significantly more than the typical advisor. The currency trader also has the highest minimum investment of all the categories at $1.3 million. Also unlike the other sectors, a better balance exists among the currency traders between those with less than a 5-year record and those that are between 5 and 10 years, although the tilt is still in favor of the newer advisors.

The correlation with the typical currency trader and the overall trader universe is high. The typical currency trader generated an annualized compound rate of return of 14.3 percent (measured by the MAR currency subindex, which began January 1990). In 4 of those years, the annual return has been in the double-digits. In 2 years, 1993 and 1994, the results have been negative. The maximum cumulative decline is larger than that of the other sectors and lasted for the longest number of months. The maximum cumulative decline occurred over an 18-month period in late 1993-early 1995, and resulted in a decline of 28.7 percent.

Stock Index

The smallest sector category are stock index futures traders. The 30 stock index programs represent $0.2 billion. The stock index track records tend to be quite short with 73 percent of them starting in the last 5 years. Their minimum investment is well below the norm for the industry as well at about $320,000.

The stock index futures trader has no correlation to the general advisor universe and is notorious among the advisor universe for being the only sector to have generated negative average annualized returns. Since the inception of the stock index subindex in January 1994, the annualized return has been down 3.6 percent. Annual returns have been negative in 1995 and so far in 1996. The maximum cumulative decline occurred over a 13-month period in 1995 and 1996, with a decline of 24.1 percent.

Miscellaneous

The energy subindex, which had begun in January 1990, stopped being reported by MAR in mid-1996 as the number of advisors with pure energy programs had dwindled considerably. In addition, agriculture and metals subindexes do not yet exist since the MAR policy is to establish such an index if and when at least 20 programs exist at the start of the year. At this point in time, 22 agriculture and two metals programs exist.

IV. PROFILE BY LOCATION

Europe

At this point in time, Europe is the only location besides the U.S. where enough advisors are tracked to comprise a subindex; the 73 advisors represent $1.9 billion of assets under management. The U.K. has the largest representation of advisors, followed by Switzerland, France, and Ireland. The average asset holdings of the typical European trader is $24.7 million, noticeably lower than that of the general advisor community.

The typical European trader also stands out in that the minimum investment requirement is significantly higher at about $1,025,500 than other advisors. The European advisor also tends to have noticeably higher fees—2.5 percent management fee and 21.4 percent incentive fees.

The typical European trader (as reflected by the MAR European trader subindex, which began in January 1993) has generated a 5.8 percent average annual compound rate of return, which is significantly lower than the general advisor community. However, the maximum cumulative decline is much more controlled with a loss of only 3.6 percent.

SUMMARY TABLE

	Methodol(2)			Sector(2)			
	All	Trend(1)	Dis(1)	Div	Fin	Cur	Stock Index
Average annual return (%)	15.8	15.1	25.5	12.8	16.9	14.3	−3.6
Max. cumulative decline (%)	−20.4	−28.4	−5.6	−16.6	−16.1	−28.7	−24.1
Correlation to MAR trading universe	1.0	0.94	0.24	0.88	0.61	0.59	0.03
Number in universe	412	268	113	217	80	66	30

SUMMARY TABLE (concluded)

	Methodol(2)			Sector(2)			
	All	Trend(1)	Dis(1)	Div	Fin	Cur	Stock Index
Assets in universe ($b)	14.1	6.4	6.3	6.5	3.9	3.2	0.2
Minimum investment ($)	512,500	863,701	630,720	602,661	857,410	1,294,436	321,621
Average assets ($M)	31.1	22.9	51.1	25.3	45.5	47.1	6.4
Fees (%)							
Mgt	2.7	2.8	2.9	2.8	2.5	2.4	2.3
Incentive	20.4	20.6	20.4	20.7	20.3	20.2	20.6
Length of record (%)							
10+ years	14.1	15.3	15.9	18.4	10.0	9.1	3.3
5-9.9 years	32.0	32.8	47.8	28.1	41.3	42.4	23.2
< 5 years	53.8	51.9	36.3	53.5	48.8	48.5	73.3

	Location
	Europe
Average annual return (%)	5.8
Max cumulative decline (%)	−3.6
Correlation to MAR trading universe	0.51
Number in universe	73
Assets in universe ($B)	1.9
Minimum investment ($)	1,025,519
Average assets ($M)	24.7
Fees (%)	
Mgt	2.5
Incentive	21.4
Length of record (%)	
10+ years	2.8
5-9.9 years	34.2
< 5 years	63.0

Footnotes:

(1) Although most advisors categorize themselves as trend-following or discretionary, a few do not. Rather they use terms such as quantitative, mechanical, or arbitrageur.

(2) MAR establishes a subindex if 20 programs exist for a specific sector, location, or methodology as of January 1 of the year. If the subindex number dwindles significantly over time, MAR will make the decision on whether to stop tracking the subindex or not.

The Role of a Trading Manager

Jerry W. Joyner, Jr.
Director of Research
6800 Capital Corporation

Trading Managers (TMs) can play an essential role in the construction and implementation of alternative investment portfolios for institutional and wealthy individual investors. The requirements for putting together a successful, multiadvisor portfolio are legion and are apt to tax the time, energy, and capabilities of the most astute investment officers. The purpose of this chapter is to explain how an experienced and competent TM can help an investor achieve the goals he has set for his alternative investment program despite the complexities of the task. Although it is not our intent to provide details on the specific proprietary techniques that a TM will use to achieve his objectives, what we will do is provide insights into the numerous services that a TM provides, and demonstrate why a competent TM is of invaluable assistance in the process of developing and implementing an alternative investment program.

DETERMINATION OF OBJECTIVES AND NEEDS

The first area where a proficient TM is of help is in the determination of the needs and ultimate objectives of the investor. Aside from the obvious desire to utilize trading advisors who have profitable historical track records, there are a myriad of other concerns that are not so apparent, but are of equal importance to the successful development of an alternative investment program. Successful portfolio construction depends on the investor being aware of these more subtle issues and their potential to become significant performance-hindering problems in the near future. An experienced TM will help to uncover these questions and will provide alternatives for their resolution.

The list of abstract and qualitative issues that are not readily recognized as being potential areas for problems could go on and on. However, perhaps the best way to provide the reader with a feel for the types of questions that should be asked and answered with the help of a TM is to give a few important examples. Thus, the following is a very brief list to stimulate your imagination:

- What are the various types of risk associated with these types of alternative portfolios?
- What is the investor's tolerance for equity volatility and potential loss of capital?
- What is the time horizon or holding period for this investment to provide a benefit and achieve its objectives?
- How should the investment's success be measured? By its added diversification or maybe strictly by its rate of return? Should performance be measured on an absolute or a relative basis? What benchmark(s) should be used for comparison?
- What are the appropriate vehicles for investment and which does the investor prefer? Futures, option, currencies, others, or a combination of all types?
- Which market sectors or assets classes should be included in the portfolio?
- What are the types of trading strategies that will be employed by the selected advisors? Which methodology would the investor be the most comfortable with? Which would be best for the particular purpose and needs of this investor? Should it be systematic, discretionary, technical, fundamental, short-term, long-term, etc.?
- What are the minimum requirements for including an advisor in the portfolio? Besides a variety of minimum performance standards, there are issues such as length of track record, assets under management, willingness to trade with certain brokers, availability of managed accounts, use of leverage—these few examples are critical considerations and the list could (and should) continue on in much greater length.
- Where does one look to find an advisor who can meet the needs and criteria that you have established?

As the reader can see, the list of not-so-obvious questions and issues can become quite long. The implications and ramifications from this list are far reaching. The role of the TM is to help the investor come to terms with these issues and many, many more.

Of course, we have not even begun to talk about the more obvious and concrete issues such as the expected rate of return or the appropriate dollar amount of the investment. However, by now the reader should begin to realize that there is a plethora of important questions that require good answers in order for an alternative investment program to have even a chance of success. An individual needs to have been through this entire process several times before he can become cognizant of all the various questions and issues that require answers.

These answers and solutions, or lack thereof, will ultimately determine the success or failure of an alternative investment program. A seasoned TM will have experienced this process many times and will be aware of the potential for hidden problem areas to hinder the success of an investment program. More importantly to an investor, the right TM will know how to help a client address these issues and find the necessary solutions. Given all of the above, it becomes apparent that one of the roles of a TM is to help his clients determine their true needs and objectives by working with them to raise a number of serious issues that require resolution.

ADVISOR SELECTION

Once the broad picture of the needs and objectives of the client have been painted, the second area where a TM becomes of vital importance is in the actual research and selection of advisors for the portfolio. It should be pointed out that unless the TM is promoting his own in-house trading advisors, this should be an unbiased research and selection process. This is an important factor to be aware of. Although many trading advisors operate more than one trading program, the fact of the matter is that if a multi-program trading advisor is selected to help in designing an alternative investment program, you are going to end up investing exclusively in his trading programs despite the fact there may be better alternatives available. Which leads to the question, how do you find quality advisors who will best satisfy all the requirements that an analysis of your needs and objectives has established as crucial criteria for consideration? A quality TM will have the capability to tackle this difficult, time-consuming, and critical task for you.

If you are inclined to go it alone, there are a few trading advisor database services available for purchase on the public market. However, they are not inexpensive, and depending on the amount of time you have to spend learning how to use their software, the interfaces are not necessarily user-friendly, either. An established TM will most likely already subscribe to one or more of these services and will be proficient in their application. Perhaps even more importantly, the TM will have information on excellent advisors who have chosen not to report their performance results to the public domain database services.

Once a source of potential advisors has been identified, the demanding process of advisor selection begins in earnest. Oftentimes quantitative performance screens will be used to reduce the list of potential advisors down to a workable number. If the TM has been around long enough to know which historical performance characteristics tend to be indicative of good traders and if the TM has a strong enough research staff, these quantitative screens will likely have been developed by in-house R&D efforts. If the selection of an advisor is based solely on his historical performance without regard to other factors, it is unlikely that the alternative investment program is going to achieve the desired results. Although this examination of an advisor's past performance is critical, similar to the determination of what an investor's needs and objectives are, the evaluation of an advisor must extend well beyond merely reviewing obvious factors such as an advisor's rate of return.

In addition to a thorough statistical analysis of an advisor's past performance, true due diligence requires that an investor know the advisors on a personal basis. An investor or his TM must fully understand how an advisor arrives at his trading decisions. Given the axiom that past performance does not guarantee future results, a qualitative determination must be made regarding the soundness of an advisor's trading strategy and methodology. Even if the advisor's trading method and skill are sound, inadequate business skills or the lack of competent staffing will ultimately be the downfall of many advisors who have had excellent historical performance. A longtime TM will have reviewed the trading strategies, performance records, and the business (as well as the personal) history of hundreds of potential advisors. As a result of this experience, a TM will have amassed the knowledge that is needed to make these subjective judgments regarding the soundness of an advisor's trading talent and ability to operate a successful trading business.

Finally, it is essential to understand the nature of an advisor's trading strategy to determine how it might be expected to perform under varying and diverse market conditions. Often, advisor track records do not encompass the broad range of market conditions experienced in the past and thus, their past performance may not be representative of what may be experienced in the future in different market conditions. Consequently, a thorough analysis of how an advisor has generated his returns is required and an analysis must be made to anticipate how the particular strategy might be expected to perform under different market conditions.

PORTFOLIO DESIGN

Assuming that you and your TM have now selected advisors who (1) participate in the markets that you prefer, (2) employ a trading style that you are comfortable with, (3) have the necessary skills and staff to operate a business, and (4) have exhibited the historical performance characteristic that you desire, you are now ready to combine the chosen advisors into a portfolio.

Similar to the determination of the client's needs and objectives and the selection of advisors, portfolio design requires far more insights than merely making an equal allocation of capital to each advisor. An accomplished TM will structure the portfolio to reflect the specific and individual needs and objectives of the investor. It may be that an equal allocation of cash assets to each advisor will result in the correct trading level allocation as well. However, there can be a substantial difference between the cash asset level and the ultimate trading level employed by an advisor through his use of leverage and through the possible use of notional funding (an industry term for capital committed to an advisor for trading purposes and yet not actually transferred to the trading account). A competent TM will structure the portfolio in a manner that best fits your objectives. This means that the portfolio will not always be structured in a form that provides for the highest potential absolute return on investment. An investor's needs might be served best if the portfolio was constructed with a premium placed on limiting the drawdown potential or possibly with an eye towards achieving lower but more consistent returns. Each of these portfolios could conceivably, and in fact probably would, require the selection of different advisors or at the very least some variation in the trading level ultimately allocated to each advisor.

Other major considerations, such as diversification across the markets that are traded, mixture of high versus low volatility advisors, diversity of trading styles that are used and in the trading time frames of the different advisors, are of vital importance in constructing a portfolio in a fashion that provides for the highest probability of future success. Keep in mind that success for a given portfolio will not always be defined as the portfolio with the highest gain per annum over a given holding period.

The art in portfolio construction comes from the ability to blend advisors into a portfolio that meets the client's objectives whether that means high returns, consistent performance, low volatility, low drawdowns, non-correlation with other investments, or however you measure success as it applies to your alternative investment program. This intuitive, "artistic" skill is something the TMs develop over time as their experience in portfolio construction increases. Using a hazard method for combining advisors into a portfolio does not bode well for the probability of future success. Just as in the individual advisor selection, a long-standing TM will have acquired the know-how to combine advisors in a style that has been indicative of previously successful portfolios that had similar priorities.

IMPLEMENTATION

Having selected advisors and designed a portfolio structure, the next step in the process is the implementation. In this stage, a TM's expertise will be of added value to an investor when the time comes to negotiate the maze of agreements that must be signed. For starters, there are trading advisory agreements that include the obvious issues such as the calculation of the advisor's management and incentive fees and the terms for payment of such. Along with the obvious, comes a mountain of not-so-apparent issues such as liability and confidentiality clauses, the allowance for the use of leverage, and other constraints on trading techniques, just to give a few illustrations. Another area that requires negotiations arises in the form of the brokerage and clearing arrangements and the negotiations of commission rates. Ultimately, it is possible that the final terms of these agreements will determine the success or failure of the investment program for the client.

A TM who has earned a respected reputation and as a result has a fair amount of assets under its management will likely have developed good relationships with a number of top advisors and with the major clearing firms along the way. In turn, this TM will be able to rely on these relationships to obtain favorable fee and commission structures for their clients. A TM can also be indispensable when it comes to filing the legal documentation that is sometimes necessary if the portfolio is to be implemented in a partnership structure. The formation of limited partnerships, general partnerships, commodity pools, etc., is an area that is not typically a part of most investment managers' daily routines, and thus reliance on an accomplished TM who has routinely been placed in this position can be a great source of security in assuring that all applicable rules and regulations are adhered to.

The use of a TM adds a significant layer of protection for investors as well. For instance, a CPO is required to register with both the CFTC and NFA. As such they are subject to inspections and audits at all times. They must be able to produce a wide variety of accounting records on the demand of either of these agencies at a moment's notice. If problems are found, the NFA or the CFTC will have the ultimate authority to resolve them. This additional scrutiny provided by the government agencies and the industry watchdogs provides further protection for investment officers who are governed by ERISA regulations. Added fiduciary protection can also be drawn from the TM's own daily monitoring of the advisors used within a portfolio.

ADVISOR AND PORTFOLIO MONITORING

Once the selection and implementation process has ended and the advisors have been authorized to begin trading on behalf of the portfolio, a TM's work has just begun. One of several value-added services provided by the TM is the ongoing monitoring and reporting of the performance of the individual advisors and of the portfolio as a whole.

As you are learning by now, this effort extends far beyond merely informing the investor as to whether the combined portfolio is showing a gain or a loss for the year. This service is one of the more important benefits provided by a TM. A truly competent TM will monitor not only the advisor's returns on a daily basis, but also the advisor's open trading positions. The TM will watch for tell-tale signs that something is changing either for the better or for the worse with an advisor. A few examples may be helpful—Do the positions held by an advisor indicate that the advisor is adhering to their previous trading strategy or have they made modifications to their methods? Given their historical method of trading, should they have been making money in a current market environment and yet their performance is actually down? Is the advisor's current performance in line with historical precedents? These simple examples are only a small part of the extensive and ongoing monitoring that a TM will undertake.

As a result of their previous experience in monitoring advisor performance, TMs are in a unique position to assume an active role in the management of the portfolio. This means that a capable TM may potentially enhance the profitability of a portfolio by making timely recommendations for adjustments to an advisor's allocated trading level on an opportunistic basis. Perhaps an advisor's recent performance has indicated to the TM that the time is right for the investor to either increase the trading level of a particular advisor or to cut back on their allocation. A knowledgeable TM might even have gone so far as to research and develop predetermined criteria that establish levels for adding capital to or removing capital from an advisor. Or maybe, through the passage of time and the accumulation of profits and losses, it is merely time to re-balance the portfolio's assets back to their original levels. Only someone who is constantly in touch with the advisors and with the portfolio as a whole would have the insights needed to make these types of recommendations.

One of the benefits that comes from having a TM who will hold the portfolio's advisors under the microscope is the added security and increased risk control that comes from this dissection. The TM will be on the watch for advisor positions that are becoming more concentrated than expected or for returns that have become more volatile than anticipated. Anything that would indicate that the risk parameters for the portfolio are in danger of being breached or that the assets allocated to the advisor are not being used properly. To the extent that questions may arise regarding the honesty of an advisor, the TM is often installed in a position of control and authority that allows them to verify the advisor's reported returns with actual account statements from the clearing firm and to force the liquidation of all positions on demand.

ADVISOR AND PORTFOLIO REPORTING

A by-product of this intensive monitoring effort is the generation of numerous reports. The usual accounting reports include, but are not limited to, everything from cash receipts and disbursements to end-of-month account statements that completely disclose all portfolio fees and expenses as well as the return on investment. Aside from the large numbers of routine accounting records that a TM is required to maintain for the various agencies that oversee them and for the convenience of their individual investors, an adequately staffed and knowledgeable TM will include other timely reports such as a written narration used to update investors on the recent market conditions and on the performance of their advisors and portfolio relative to industry benchmarks.

SUMMARY

The role of a trading manager is so broad as to be difficult to summarize fairly, but a general outline might appear as follows:

- Assist in the determination of the investors' objectives and needs.

- Research and select advisors based upon their ability to fulfill the established objectives of the client.

- Design and implement a diverse portfolio which, based upon historical results, will have a high probability of success.

- Continuously monitor the performance of the advisors and make active allocation recommendations.

- Provide adequate accounting and reporting to the investors.

Given the wide variety of tasks that have been discussed and the high level of expertise that is necessary to successfully fulfill their responsibilities, the selection of a competent TM is of vital importance to an investor seeking to form an alternative investment portfolio. Attempting to construct a sophisticated, multiadvisor portfolio without the help of an experienced TM is likely to lead to less than satisfactory results for the investor. The use of a high-quality TM does not guarantee a profitable portfolio; however, a good TM can and will make a significant and worthwhile contribution toward increasing the probability of a successful alternative investment program.

CTA Disclosure and Methodology Issues

Joanne Rosenthal

Jon Knudsen
The Chase Manhattan Bank, New York

INTRODUCTION

When an asset allocator is searching for an investment manager, the first details that are of concern are the general style of the manager, the markets traded by the manager, and the historical performance record of the manager. After conducting an in-depth statistical analysis of the manager's performance record, the allocator will decide whether or not to pursue the trader further. If the investment manager passes the initial quantitative tests, a sophisticated allocator will quickly move to the qualitative measures of assessment. There is nothing that an allocator distrusts more than hearing that the methodology employed by the manager is proprietary and cannot be disclosed or described in depth. Even worse is a manager who offers an ill-prepared discourse that proves more confusing than enlightening. This problem tends to be less severe with respect to discretionary or fundamental traders than systematic traders; however, it is still a prevalent issue in the managed futures industry as a whole. Thus any attempt to compare a commodity trading advisor (CTA) to other types of investment managers, especially in terms of methodological disclosure, can often be an extremely frustrating exercise.

This section will review the key issues of CTA disclosure and methodology, focusing primarily on content and presentation. We begin by discussing how the CTA can generate interest among asset allocators by giving a concise overview and then proceed to define what essential material should be disclosed. Full disclosure is paramount, since the potential allocator should be able to understand the CTA's business and methods thoroughly and hopefully avoid any future surprises. This is accomplished by explaining the CTA's background, trading approach, and portfolio and risk management.

PHILOSOPHY

A trader seeking allocations must master core presentation skills in order to quickly capture the attention of the investor. The first minutes of a presentation are crucial for this. Failure to generate interest among the audience may prove fatal to one's asset-raising efforts. The introduction, either a face-to-face meeting or marketing materials, should present a brief summary of what the trader is offering. The four key items to communicate immediately are: (1) the trader's objective, vision, or mission statement, (2) the main aspects that distinguish the trader from the competition, (3) a characterization of the trading style, practices and policies, and markets traded to achieve the stated objective, and (4) if a "Black Box" trading methodology is used, a definition of the major inputs and an explanation of how output is generated. Further elaboration of these points should be reserved for later in the presentation or during the due diligence process.

An investment manager's objective should clearly state their approach and target performance. As an example: "Technical trend follower, maintains a diverse portfolio, seeks to earn moderate returns with low volatility resulting in attractive risk adjusted returns." Statements such as "Achieve profits by active trading" lack definition and are of no benefit to the asset allocator.

In describing the approach, the trader must strive to create a distinction between his approach and others in the industry by explaining where value is added, the premise for the approach, and how profits are extracted. Examples of how value is added are quicker entries, lower volatility, quicker exits, broad diversification, and very short-term trades that capture mispricing. The premise might be entry and exits based on exhaustive pattern studies; diversification allowing for the casting of several small insignificant bets followed by the aggressive trading of markets based on trend confirmation; or physics background providing the foundation for signal and noise extraction and the premise behind trend confirmation. The trader should also explain how profits are extracted from the market. For instance, seeking to capture two to three big moves per year while taking several small losses along the way; extracting small two to three day moves in the market; or identifying significant fundamental mispricings and trying to ride out a multiyear move.

In characterizing the approach of the trader, allocators also like to conduct "peer group" comparison. Accordingly, if a trader wants to avoid an erroneous label, it would be best if the trader preclassifies themselves vis-à-vis the industry, both in terms of markets and sectors traded, and in terms of style. Markets focus may be sector specific, foreign exchange, or financials only, or broadly diversified. Styles may include trend-following, short-term, fundamental, discretionary, or contrarian. The trader should also address the issue of risk management, specifically explaining their approach with respect to the use of protective stop-loss orders and leverage considerations. Finally, the trader should elaborate on the portfolio and why certain markets are included while others are excluded. A trader may describe himself as a fully diversified trend follower that opts not to forecast individual markets, preferring instead to place small bets in any market with sufficient liquidity and to pursue winners as they emerge. The trader may alternately describe himself as a fundamentalist who selects markets that exhibit imbalances and pursues opportunities, not necessarily a diversified portfolio.

If a trader is using a "Black Box" approach to make trading decisions, it is important to describe the inputs: GDP, interest rates, rates of change, moving average slope, and correlations; the processing method: multivariate regression, neural nets, genetic algorithms; and the type of output information yielded. Understanding how the trader applies the output to the trading approach provided and how it is to be applied to the trading approach will offer a measure of comfort for the asset allocator. The allocator needs to know how signals are generated, acted upon, and managed day to day. Thus, the allocator can formulate expectations as to when trades will occur and how the trader under evaluation might prove complementary in an investment portfolio.

All of these key points can be summarized into one broad statement. The important concept is to be thorough, but concise, providing the asset allocator with the key elements in an executive summary format that will generate an appetite for more information.

BACKGROUND

There are no hard and fast rules that hold in selecting a trading advisor. In fact, manager selection is far more of an art than a science. On the surface, quantitative analysis appears to be an effective objective performance gauge; however, choosing a manager should not be purely a numbers game.

When assessing the qualitative aspects of a trader, a good place to start is their background. No matter what trading style or methodology is employed, understanding a trader's background offers key insight into the trader himself.

The anecdotal history of how a trader became interested in the markets, who influenced his earliest trading, what he initially traded, where he first worked, and when he started trading often go a long way in explaining today's style; the past helps to define the present and future. Once you identify and comprehend a trader's network of key decision-making influences, you can begin to feel that there is a stability or predictability in how a trader will act in almost any given situation.

In our experience, the most successful traders tend to be individuals who are not only highly disciplined and passionate about trading and the markets, but are extremely focused and intense in all pursuits. Again, one needs to dig deep into the trader's background in order to get to the root of the trader's motivation, but it is worthwhile, as it will help to determine whether this is a passion or simply a paycheck.

Finally, examining the past to identify the evolution of a manager's style is a key factor in assessing a trader. Determining why the methodology was modified is as important as how the methodology was modified. What were the prime factors leading up to the change and was the change well-researched, or merely curve-fitted? Was the change part of a necessary evolution, or was it a result of a personality or lifestyle crisis?

A manager that acknowledges where he came from and can articulate that background well is usually one who has also considered where he is going. Planning for the future is a key to any successful business enterprise.

APPROACH

When elaborating on the approach to the markets during the due diligence process, the trader must be prepared for full disclosure. First, explain how the approach was conceived: observed trends, built econometric models, cash market background with excellent information sources, or created a methodology to capitalize on observation. After explaining the genesis of the approach, the trader should support the premise by describing how the method was validated. If an allocator can answer the following qualitative questions following their due diligence, the trader has done their job well:

- Describe the ideal market situations for the approach and why they are ideal.
- Describe the nightmare scenario.
- Are some markets avoided and why?
- How will changes in trend, volatility, and liquidity affect performance?
- Are all markets profitable on a stand-alone basis or are they added for portfolio performance reasons?
- Do certain markets account for the majority of profits or are the positions derived from a broad range of markets, e.g., how much from the Japanese yen in recent years?
- Does the approach use one or several models? Why?
- If several models are used, are they distinctly separate methodologies or simply using different parameters or time frames?
- Are the models linear or nonlinear, static or adaptive?
- What are the inputs for each model, time horizon tracked, and trading frequency?
- How do the models interact?
- Are they capturing different time periods but still trend following or are there trend and nontrend models?
- Are the models correlated or noncorrelated?
- Are you simply tracking a market across various time segments to build a position as the trend establishes itself or did you create a diversified portfolio of independent trading approaches?
- How is capital allocated amongst the systems (fixed or variable) and markets (fixed or variable)?
- How are positions increased and decreased?
- If a new trader, were historical simulations conducted or was trading conducted in personal accounts?
- How was the robustness of the system measured?
- Was the system subjected to random data, various parameter sets, a multitude of different markets?
- What was fundamental or cash market background, what are informational sources?

To enhance the allocator's understanding of your product, examples are highly beneficial. Complete commodity-specific and portfolio cycles illustrations detailing (1) entry, exit, re-entry, exit and/or reversal; (2) initial position size and subsequent adjustment for a specific commodity; and (3) changing portfolio composition, allocations, and leverage adjustments over the complete cycle, can be very useful to the allocator. Throughout these examples, the allocator will be looking for consistency of approach. The allocator will seek to determine how the trader has applied the method versus how the method was explained. Any inconsistencies will generate a red flag. Another aspect on which allocators may focus is the liquidity of the markets being traded and any control feature the trader employs to avoid being trapped in a position during illiquid markets.

Finally, the trader should highlight any ongoing research into new models, markets, or portfolio construction techniques. This is a key indicator of the trader's commitment to the business. The allocator will also want to know if models/approach are left to perform on their own or if parameters are periodically adjusted or optimized. What motivates the change, how is overoptimization avoided, how to detect deterioration and determine if materially significant or simply a temporary pause? Do tune-ups focus on parameters of models, introducing new models and developing old ones, new markets, or new portfolios? How is burnout avoided amongst discretionary, fundamental, and short-term traders?

This disclosure will provide a high degree of comfort to the investor in terms of what he can expect from the trader regarding returns and the risk exposure necessary to achieve these returns. Any deviation from the disclosure process should be thoroughly explained, ideally prior to the deviation. It is critical to avoid surprising the allocator. The key to account retention is communication, which prepares the allocator for the peaks and valleys of the program.

RISK MANAGEMENT

Once all the aspects of a trader's background and approach are reviewed, an asset allocator would be remiss if risk management were not considered. Risk is one of the most difficult concepts to reconcile. Typically, allocators are less concerned with the upside risks of trading than the inherent downside risks. However, the relationship between risk and return indicates that one does not exist independently of the other and that is why it is important to get a good handle on the risk management policies employed by a trader.

Perhaps one of the most important issues regarding risk management is how risk management is addressed by the methodology. Was it an afterthought, thrown in as a result of a significant loss or drawdown, or was it incorporated from the beginning as part of the methodology? The allocator wants to ensure that specific targets for return and risk are articulated and that they are upheld. Finally, the allocator needs to understand and feel comfortable with how risk is measured and monitored.

When assessing the risk management approach used by a trader, an allocator is most concerned with the manner in which the approach was developed. Is the risk approach qualitatively sound? Is risk assessed by market, by trade, by sector, and/or by portfolio. What are the advantages and disadvantages of each approach, given the trader's trading style?

Any trader that is unable to articulate his methodology's expected results, or that avers unrealistic targets, or whose expected results are far different from his historical performance is a potential problem. A trader should be able to articulate achievable targets that can be attained using the methodology espoused.

Even if a trader has a prespecified risk methodology, it is key to assess the measurement and monitoring techniques employed by the trader to ensure compliance with the established practices. Is risk management an ongoing process or is it conducted within finite time frames; daily, monthly, annually?

Another defining principle of portfolio risk management is addressed within the optimal account size versus minimum account size question. Often, a trader's stated minimum account size is far below what is optimal for risk management purposes. However, since the risk management minimum may be unpalatable for an allocator, a trader may lowball the figure. As such, an allocator who might want to start out with a small account in order to minimize the risk exposure to a given trader, may actually be trading a riskier, more highly leveraged, and therefore less optimal portfolio.

Finally, it is important to ascertain how and when changes to the risk policies are made. What occurred in the markets, or beyond for that matter, to cause these changes? How were the changes implemented and were they discussed or disclosed with clients? Were the modifications well-researched, real improvements or superficial and ultimately ineffective? An abrupt switch in risk strategy should be a warning sign.

Asset allocators are risking capital and want to avoid surprises. If the trader takes the time to fully explain the risks to which an account is subject at the outset of the relationship, the allocator will know what to expect and will probably be a better client in the long run.

Of course, downside management is key to all methodologies, but it is important not to choke off upside. The proper return/risk balance is exceptionally difficult to achieve and maintain; however, if realistic objectives are set within the methodology, the opportunity for success is heightened.

SUMMARY

It is essential that investment managers disclose a sufficient amount of information to the asset allocator, in order for the allocator to make an informed allocation decision. The allocator must possess a firm grasp of the manager's approach and portfolio management to instill a comfort level on what to expect from future performance, before any investment is made. Understandably, traders are naturally protective of their methodology and are reluctant to provide specifics. However, in order for the allocator to have a solid knowledge base, the trader must disclose the following at the very least. The foundation of the approach, when to expect position entry and exits, and how risk control is employed. The trader can either discuss these concepts or demonstrate through examples, while still preserving their proprietary information. This process also provides the trader with the opportunity to define his style or edge and to distinguish himself from the competition.

Ultimately, asset allocators are looking for consistency and predictability of return streams from their investments. An allocator must be able to examine an investment's performance and understand what occurred, in order to remain comfortable with retaining the investment.

Investment managers are seeking long-term commitments of trading capital, not "hot money" that follows the flow of recent performance. Investment managers are running a business, which combines trading, research, and product development. In order to plan for future research projects and new product ideas, they need to be able to count on stable and predictable assets under management.

These two goals are not mutually exclusive. If the traders and allocators work together to understand one another's objectives, the relationship may even be highly productive. If the trader is willing to fully disclose all aspects of his methodology, allocators are less likely to be surprised and more likely to maintain their confidence in the manager. Thus both the trader and allocator can work together to grow their respective businesses.

Evaluation of Derivatives Traders: Qualitative Considerations

Morton S. Baratz
Executive Vice President and Chief Operating Officer
Allied Capital Asset Management, Inc.

$\mathbf{P}$ick up any publication—magazine, general newsletter, broker's sales brochure—that ranks or rates the performance of managed-derivatives' traders and you're almost certain to find that performance is defined by reference to (a) net rates of return over some specified period of hours, days, weeks, months, or years; (b) one yardstick or more for risk, such as largest percentage drawdown on equity, standard deviation, or semideviation of monthly returns, and the probability of loss of some prespecified percentage of original investment; or (c) some combination of these measurements, usually labeled risk-adjusted rate of return. Undeniably, measuring rods such as these serve useful purposes. For one thing, they are screens through which are sifted only those traders who meet prespecified quantitative criteria for selection, whether by trading managers or prospective investors. For another, they provide evidence about how well or poorly any particular trader has been performing, evidence that may be (and usually is) extrapolated into the future.

Quantitative evidence has, however, serious limitations for purposes of trader evaluation. First of all, data such as rates of return, drawdowns, and the like are the product of a number of variables, of which the trader's skill is but one—and often not even the most important one. The other relevant variables include inherent rates of return to trading of certain assets; the level of fees and commissions; market conditions generally; and luck, either good or bad. All these latter variables are largely or wholly beyond a trader's control, except to the extent that most trading approaches are

305

designed to perform best under certain kinds of market conditions. Consequently, it is wrong to argue that simply because A's rate of return or risk-adjusted rate of return in a given year or period of years is higher than B's or C's, A is the "best" trader of the three.

The second reason for criticizing the conventional performance measurements gets closer to the heart of the matter. Comparing traders by reference to some standardized set of yardsticks defies the reality that although there are many similarities among traders, traders are like humans' fingerprints: none is exactly like anyone else's. Each trader differs from all others in one or some or all of the following: trading objectives, trading policies and practices, trading portfolio, and money-management policies and techniques. These differences make it meaningless to compare, say, the risk-adjusted rate of return of a short-term discretionary trader of financials and currencies with that of a long-term trend-following trader of agricultural, precious-metals, and energy futures. Ditto for a comparison of the reward/risk ratio of a trader bent on generating 40 percent per annum, while suffering no drawdown greater than 25 percent, with that of another trader whose target rate of return and maximal drawdown are 15 percent and 5 percent, respectively. There are countless other examples that may be offered. To reiterate, because each trader is unique, its performance must be evaluated on its own terms, that is, by reference to its own ends and means. That suggests, in turn, that the focus of all evaluative techniques and evidence must be upon the trader's skills, and those alone.

Conventional track records, as we have noted already, do shed light on those skills. But, as we have also said, the light is diffused by the presence of the many other variables that impinge upon performance. The most one can safely say about the contribution of trading skill to the compilation of a statistical performance history of the usual kind is that, in skill's absence, a better-than-average performance over time is happenstance, purely and simply. That being so, where must we look to find unqualified or "pure" evidence of trading skill? The answer is clear: to responses, both quantitative and qualitative (i.e., nonquantifiable), to these kinds of questions:

1. Does the trader have a well-defined set of trading objectives, defined as desired outcomes? That is, is its trading approach informed and driven by a pre-specified set of return and risk targets or does it instead just "go with the flow," passively accepting whatever results—positive or negative—the "flow" generates?

2. Does the trader have a well-researched set of trading and money-management policies and practices for achieving its declared objectives and will it provide incontrovertible evidence of the effectiveness of those policies and practices to a skeptical observer? Or does it instead rely upon the equivalent of a "black box," the contents and workings of which it refuses to reveal to a responsible interrogator?

3. Are its trading policies and practices well-integrated with its money-management policies and practices, such that the two reinforce one another at all times? Or do they tend to operate in semi-isolation from one another, risking occasional or frequent glitches in trading operations?

4. Is the pattern of actual trading consistent with the one explained during the due-diligence process? If not, are departures from "script" occasional or frequent and, in either case, are they logically defensible or do they instead reflect virtual abandonment of trading discipline?

5. Over time, does the trader monitor with care (a) the markets it trades and (b) the limitations of its trading policies and practices in market conditions of differing kinds? Or does it simply insist that, because no system has yet been designed that will function well in all sorts of market conditions, losing spells must be waited out in full confidence that the day will return when positive rates of return will again be the order of the day?

6. As a corollary to No. 5 above, under what circumstances (if any) and how does the trader decide that substantive changes should be made in its trading approach or methods or both?

7. How well or badly does the trader exploit the profit-making opportunities that present themselves? Does the trading system or set of systems perform as designed or are there significant slippages between signals to enter or exit and actual entrance and exit? And how effectively does it sustain its own risk-management objectives and procedures?

8. Does the trader conduct its business within the context of a well-ordered business plan or is it an unadorned trading operation that lacks (a) a strong back-office operation; (b) back-ups for all its human and technical inputs, especially including the principal trader; and/or (c) a well-thought-out position with respect to the maximal amount of money it is capable of managing with its present trading approach and operating mode?

All these questions may be investigated through direct interview, careful study of daily equity runs, and interpolation of performance data. The answers to some of them are, or should be, self-evident. A few call for brief elaboration.

Question 2 is one case in point. There is nothing inherently "wrong" or invalid about a black-box trading system, but all too often systems of that sort are allowed literally to run themselves, i.e., operate without supervision and without integration into a money-management system.

With too few exceptions, black-box systems of this kind behave errati-
cally over time, swinging between short periods of positive returns and
longer periods of nil or negative returns. What is almost as bad, many
black-box traders themselves fail fully to understand why the system is
performing as it is. That is their privilege as traders, but trading managers
and investors are well-advised to steer clear of them.

Question 4 addresses a point so well-known to all but the uninitiated
that one hesitates even to make it. Yet it cannot be overemphasized. With
no known exceptions, all professional traders vouchsafe that they trade
with iron discipline at all times. Doubtlessly, all strive to do so. But this
observer has seen first-hand evidence of highly seasoned traders who, in
the face of a sequence of losing trades, began "cherry-picking," that is,
abandoning disciplined trading of a predetermined portfolio of markets in
favor of a few markets chosen ad hoc on the ground that the latter presented
the choicest targets of opportunity. I know of several instances where cherry-picking has been rewarded fully, but the instances where the opposite
has occurred are far more numerous. In any event, the history of managed-
derivatives trading leaves little room for doubt that the traders with
professional integrity are the ones who will long outlast those who "play it
by ear."

Question 6 also calls for commentary. Traders are under neither a
heavenly nor an earthly mandate to modify their trading approaches, practices, and policies, no matter what happens. Some very successful traders
insist that the most they are prepared to do upon infrequent occasion is to
adjust a single parameter or two, and then only modestly. Others, no less
successful, stoutly maintain that markets are changing (in one sense or
another) over time and traders such as they must retune their systems
accordingly. The point to be made here is not that change is "good" or
"bad," but that whatever stance on the issue is taken by the trader, it must
be able to justify its course of action in terms other than vague or general.
In plainer language, it must know what it is doing and why. More than
that, a trading manager or investor need not require.

As for Question 7, I have tried to address this issue at length in an
article published in *Futures and Options World,* in February 1995. Stated
summarily, my argument is that the only tenable way to measure trading
skill is to compare a trader's actual with its potential exploitation—in relative, not absolute terms—of the profit-making opportunities presented to
it. For instance, if a trader is a long-term trend-follower, a reliable indicator of its skill is the percentage of each long-term trend it seeks to and does
capture in each of the markets in which it trades. Similarly, its risk-control

performance may be measured by the degree to which it holds its largest percentage drawdowns within the maximal amount it has preestablished as the upper limit for its drawdowns. A principal merit of this approach is that it de-emphasizes external standards for performance, in favor of yardsticks that measure a trader's performance against its own standards.

Concerning Question 8, a well-run trading operation is one that (among other things) has professionals who are at least partially cross-trained in one another's functions, so that the firm has some protection during the temporary absence of one or more of its key operatives. It's hardly necessary to add, by the way, that the firm's operatives must be personally, as well as professionally, compatible, so that there is among them a genuine esprit de corps.

A final point is obvious only after it has been stated: No trader is worthy of selection or retention who lacks personal honesty and integrity.

CHAPTER 16

MANAGEMENT SUMMARY

Title: "A New Direction for Managed Futures"
Author: Brian Cornell, Senior Vice President
          Sakura Dellsher, Inc.
Synopsis: The article discusses new ways the managed futures industry can position itself for growth in the future. Ideas include eliminating the asset class argument in favor of an overlay strategy, and lowering fees for institutional clientele.

A New Direction for Managed Futures

Brian Cornell

The current state of mind of the Managed Futures industry reflects a brewing identity crisis. Perhaps this stems from the recent decline in assets managed by the industry as of 1995 after subpar performance the last few years. Recent evidence suggests that the profitability of industry product, in general, has been at a low ebb since 1992. Or, the crisis may be a realization that the progression toward institutional acceptance has met with limited success. A continuing stream of derivative related scandals, coupled with strong performance of mainstream investments, makes it difficult for the industry to market product effectively. The purpose of this paper is to draw conclusions from recent experiences in the industry in order to construct a new more marketable direction toward which we should strive.

INSTITUTIONALIZING MANAGED FUTURES

The institutionalization of any new market is subject to the chicken or the egg theory. Must you develop both retail and institutional acceptance and, if so, which one comes first? In many Asian countries that are currently developing futures markets, this question is wrestled with every day. A primary concern relating to retail investor involvement is the necessary regulatory framework that will protect the consumer on the one hand and provide a basis from which to promote the product on the other. At the other extreme, institutional involvement typically requires some retail participation to lay off risks on the margin in order to generate a reasonable profit. The question of which comes first is not easily answered.

Sponsorship is a key element in attracting the retail investor. Reputable institutions must supply product to the investing public in order to generate interest and demand. Without such sponsorship, the institutional market will lack the marginal participant from which a significant portion of the profit margin of the business may rely. If the regulatory environment does not support this element of the business, perhaps under the context of *protecting* the little guy, the sophisticated end of the market will struggle to develop. As in most industries, the producer sells raw goods to the wholesaler, who distributes refined goods to the middlemen, who repackage and sell to the retailer, who marks up the product for final sale to the public. Although the variations on this stream are endless, the participation of the end user is critical.

The regulatory bodies are not always cognizant of the relative importance of all the elements in this food chain. The sophistication of the large players is evident in their ability to grasp the advanced concepts of the usage of futures for hedging, speculation, and everything between. However, the lack of sophistication of the retail investor requires education and protection provided by the regulators, exchanges, and institutions. Consequently, there exists the mismatch of product understanding and regulatory oversight between the participants. In many cases, the failure to encourage and develop the retail sector undermines the successful development of new markets. Several Asian countries are currently grappling with this problem as they struggle to boost participation in their markets. The institutions alone will not support this development since they will ultimately require sufficient retail participation to which they can parcel out high margin product in order to absorb cyclical excesses in their inventory.

The institutional side of the chicken or egg analogy also requires sponsorship. Without sufficient revenue streams available for capture, the large players will not express interest in a new market. In many of the Asian countries, outside vendors have established limited distribution channels through private banking networks. As the product moves into the hands of the wealthy investors in these countries, the word seeps into corporate boardrooms and social cocktail parties that an alternative investment is available in the market. Once in the personal portfolios of the appropriate decision makers, the concept of domestic production develops. With the right institutional interest and support, regulators will open up the markets for wider acceptance and the large players will step in to sponsor product.

Japan offers an interesting case study in this development process. Night sessions at the Chicago Board of Trade encouraged Japanese institutional trading of Treasury bonds beginning in 1987. The Ministry of

Finance followed this interest and approved Japanese trading financial futures on foreign exchanges in 1988. The first retail fund was offered later that year through the distribution network of Mitsubishi. The primary retail market was limited to the very high end, however, with minimum investments designed to limit distribution to institutions and wealthy individuals. Today, the minimums are still high (although they have been reduced over the years) and the bulk of product has been developed in concert with non-Japanese entities. Nevertheless, the institutional market has been broadened and deepened over the last 10 years to the point where regulations continue to relax and Japanese institutions are developing product independent of foreign interests. The successful development of this new market required the participation of the retail sector, the regulators, and the sponsorship of the institutional players in order to grow to its current size.

The development of the managed futures industry in the United States followed a different path. The origination of the first documented trend-following system in this country by Commodity Research Bureau in 1937 and the formation of the first commodity fund by Richard Donchian in 1949 were two milestones in the early years of the business. It was not until the 1970s that several organized fund products were offered to the public. This agonizingly slow process of development rested with the nature of the limited audience the commodity markets attracted. Largely an agriculturally based endeavor, the commodity markets were dominated by producers hedging their crops. The speculators absorbing the risk included the retail investor. The size and fees associated with these funds were definitely retail oriented in keeping with the brokerage commissions of the day.

Volume on the U.S. exchanges grew slowly during this century, first exceeding 10 million contracts annually in the mid-1960s. The breadth of products covered was largely related to agricultural contracts. With limited participants—largely producers, wholesalers, and speculators mostly related to agricultural interests—institutional sponsorship and involvement was limited. The retail speculator typically paid in excess of $100 per round turn commission during this era. As limited competition spread at this level, the brokerage firms recognized that structured product could enable them to pool customer capital in order to capture additional revenue streams other than commissions. In addition, the structuring of product provided an efficient vehicle to tap into a broader pool of capital in an effort to expand the market.

The watershed year of 1973 catapulted the commodity markets onto center stage. The first Arab oil embargo facilitated the worst inflation encountered in this country in the post-war era. The bear market in equities took hold in response to inflationary fears, the burgeoning Watergate scandal, and the escalation of conflict in the Middle East. With the primary investment markets headed south—both stocks and bonds were tumbling—an opportunity to shine from a performance point of view was made available. As luck would have it, the environment helped the industry along. The Soviet wheat crop failed, a major drought in the United States occurred, and freezes in coffee- and cocoa-growing regions sent prices soaring on many commodity markets simultaneously.

Meanwhile, the Chicago Mercantile Exchange had listed futures in foreign exchange contracts after the Bretton Woods agreement was torpedoed by Nixon. This development was the beginning of the transformation from an agriculturally based system of markets to the plum of all markets—the financials. Congress stamped its approval of this sea change by transferring regulation of the industry from the Department of Agriculture to a newly created body now called the Commodity Futures Trading Commission. No longer a peripheral player, the commodity markets established a foothold in the minds of a more sophisticated clientele.

The last half of the 70s decade brought the development of new markets and new products. The financial markets exploded with the listing of Treasury bond and Treasury bill futures. Their rapid acceptance by institutions brought about the sponsorship necessary for the eventual institutionalization of the industry. In addition, the increasing size and variety of commodity funds documented the rise in acceptance of the retail participant. Of course, the seemingly ever-present scandal existed, too. When Bunker Hunt attempted to corner the silver market in 1979–80, the abuse of leverage, the need for regulation, and the profit potential available via futures trading hit the front pages of newspapers around the world.

The confluence of events that dramatically expanded the futures markets beyond their original agricultural base facilitated institutional interest and participation in the product. The good fortune to exhibit superior returns during an otherwise bleak investment period thrust the attention of a broad class of investors toward the futures markets. The rapid growth of retail participation fostered the institutional sponsorship necessary to seize the opportunity to further develop a promising new industry.

THE PROMISE OF MODERN PORTFOLIO THEORY

Harry Markowitz contributed the classical foundation for Modern Portfolio Theory (MPT) in his work published in the 1950s.[1] His work provided a structure in which one could determine, according to a specific set

of parameters, an optimal allocation of funds among competing investments in order to arrive at a desired level of reward versus risk. This work
formalized what investment managers have recognized for thousands of
years (to paraphrase King Solomon): divide your holdings into portions of
seven or eight lest one fails. Moreover, this body of work provided an
increased level of understanding on the interactions of portfolio components. The foundation was laid for the development of quantitative methods and tools to analyze the interrelated contribution of each element in an
investment portfolio.

The nascent managed commodities business of the 1970s was not
in a position to utilize MPT to its advantage. There existed, at the time,
no substantive academic research incorporating commodities in an MPT
framework. The commodities industry was a niche investment market
that served the producers of physical goods (primarily agriculturally
based) and some speculators with an organized exchange for price
discovery. The limited audience for this market failed to raise a blip on
the radar screens of academics and institutions alike. The inclusion of
commodities in research and analysis of portfolio investing would await
the development of the industry in its ability to attract a broader and
deeper audience.

With the advent of financial futures in the 1970s and the rapid
involvement of financial institution participation in the world of derivatives, academic research turned its attention to analyzing the inclusion of
futures in investment theory. For the managed futures industry, the landmark academic work was provided by John Lintner of Harvard
University.[2] In this study, Lintner included the performance of commodity
funds from 1979 to 1982 in portfolios of stocks and bonds. Incorporating
commodities in an MPT framework anointed this investment arena a new
elevated status.

The Lintner study focused on the classical advantages of Modern
Portfolio Theory in reducing the risk profile of a combination of investments. The low level of correlation among commodities, stocks, and
bonds provided the necessary context in which one could diversify his
portfolio into different markets and improve the consistency of his performance. Of course, the performance of commodities had to exhibit similar
returns to stocks to be considered worthy. In addition, the variance of
returns from period to period also had to show similar results. In this
study, both requirements were met (albeit loosely), which gave substance
to the conclusion that a diversification into commodities from a mainstream stock and bond portfolio may prove valuable.

Three fundamental points were raised by the Lintner study that have affected the managed futures industry ever since. First, the inclusion of commodities in a stock and bond portfolio spawned the asset class argument that raged for the next 10 years. Second, the relative returns of active management results and passive indexes raised the issue of an apples to apples comparison in the context of MPT. Finally, the fact that commodity fund and managed account performance was reasonably similar to equity performance measures masked the issue of fees during this era. These three issues have been the focus of proponents and opponents of managed futures ever since Lintner's paper was delivered in Toronto in 1983.

The promise of Modern Portfolio Theory, according to the proponents of managed futures, was the classical argument that including such an investment in a traditional portfolio provided the highly sought after benefit of risk reduction without impairment to performance. Without generations of sponsorship and experience of actual investors that the equity markets enjoyed, the promise of the academic work relied on an acceptance and understanding of a moderate-level argument of statistical theory. This argument is a lay-up for sophisticated investors who look beyond the statistics to challenge the assumptions underlying the study. The retail investor, though, may have more trouble dealing with statistical theory and consequently may rely more on absolute performance or perceptions relating to performance. The trouble for the latter group is that the pervasive perception of commodity and/or futures investing is that it is inherently risky. The sophisticated investor group may focus a great deal more on the fundamental issues associated with creating value from the commodity markets. The retail investor will ultimately rely on faith while the sophisticated investor will require proof that investing in managed futures can and will deliver the value suggested in the academic work.

THE OLD ASSET CLASS ARGUMENT

The acceptance of commodities and/or futures as a separate asset class for investment purposes has failed to solidify. Despite the value shown in Lintner's study and a host of others since, performance results alone do not constitute an asset class. If the asset class assumption is rejected, then the value of MPT is in jeopardy when making the case for managed futures investing for traditional portfolios.

Among sophisticated investors, the assumption that futures investing may be regarded as an asset class is not readily accepted. Holders of equities and bonds note that they hold a claim on future cash flows of a company and, that in the event of a failure, their claim may ultimately extend to the remaining cash, physical plant, and land held by the company. Similarly, ownership in venture capital investments, oil and gas partnerships, real estate, and timber deals all have the same characteristic of ownership claims on cash flows and hard assets. These investments may have vastly different risk profiles and their liquidity may not be readily accessed, yet they have a direct claim on assets. The opponents of managed futures question the validity of a direct link to cash flows and hard assets. Some say a futures contract is just a viable instrument of intent.[3] Thus, the ownership of a futures contract prior to conversion into a physical asset is one step removed from the direct link to ownership, claim on cash flow, and claim on hard assets.

Another asset class argument rests on the value created in the underlying market. This may just be a variation of the claims argument above, but it bears noting. The zero sum game of futures investing (forgetting transaction costs) suggests that no value is created in the futures markets. The proponents of managed futures investing are quick to point out the risk transfer analogy to insurance markets. Value is created in the risk premium that speculators demand from hedgers in the marketplace. This insurance premium (read risk premium) is a measurable value that allows speculators to profit from these markets consistently over time. The proponents go on to suggest that this premium is akin to cash flow. And, of course, cash flow is an asset. So, futures represent a separate asset class! The argument is weak and often rejected on the spot.

THE BENCHMARK PROBLEM

Among some other asset class arguments the issue of benchmarks is inevitably raised. The managed futures industry has failed to agree on an acceptable benchmark and, consequently, has failed to provide the prospective investor with a measure with which to compare investment returns. There are essentially two kinds of benchmarks available for use. The first is a passive measure of performance of the markets and the second is a measure of the active management skill managers exhibit investing in the markets.

The classic study of passive performance measurement of the commodity markets was delivered in 1980 by Bodie and Rosansky.[4] In this work, the authors study commodity futures from a buy-and-hold perspective much like passive benchmarks for stocks and bonds. The results are astounding compared to equity investing. Returns and standard deviations of both types of investments are fairly similar. In fact, the downside risk exhibited in the performance measurement of commodities during this period is substantially less than that of stocks. Perhaps the diversification of the commodity markets is broader and deeper than that of equities. That would explain the lower risk profile. Anyway, the study provided a sound theoretical basis for measuring returns from the commodity markets in a passive style. At the time, however, the perception of commodities was high risk as evidenced by the gold and silver debacles of 1979-80. The explosive run-up in prices, the attempt by Hunt to corner the silver market, and the subsequent collapse of these markets held the public's attention far more than a bland academic study. The first opportunity to capitalize on an acceptable benchmark for the industry slipped through our hands.

The folks at Mount Lucas Management sought to expand the non-leveraged theory a bit further through the creation of the Mount Lucas Index.[5] Rather than settling with a passive buy-and-hold approach to measuring commodity market performance, this firm sought to establish a simple mechanism that allowed performance measurement from either the buy side or the sell side. In its simple form, the idea was that speculative value (or risk premium capture) is equally available from the long side as the short side. Since a buy-and-hold approach would fail to recognize value from a short in the market, Mount Lucas developed a simple trading rule to determine which side of the market value would be measured upon. Based upon a 12-month moving average of closing prices of the nearby contact, the position held for the following month sided with whichever side the closing market price was relative to the moving average.[6] The index raised the interest of a few institutional investors, but the index has yet to be embraced by the industry as a viable benchmark.

On the active side of benchmark performance, the primary database vendors in the industry offer a variety of suggestions. Managed Account Reports, Barclay, TASS, Stark, Norwood, Hedge Fund Research, and a host of others compile indexes of active management measurement. Whether the index is dollar-weighted or equal-weighted, includes or excludes non-participants in the database, retains or expunges failed managers, or is created in a fashion that represents market weightings, these indexes all have one thing in common: they measure active management skill. Lintner used this kind of performance measurement in his 1983 study. Yet, this performance measure is not widely touted in traditional asset classes. Most equity managers compare their performance to a relevant benchmark, whether it is the S&P 500 or the Wilshire 5000. Most databases of performance measurement in the equity world offer universes of manager skill in the context of benchmark comparison. Few investors seek to construct an index of manager skill from which to base their analysis. If an acceptable benchmark of measurement is available, investors use it. Without such a benchmark, valid comparisons to other investment fall short.

Therein lies the link to acceptability for managed futures investing in the mind of the general public. The failure to agree upon and promote a viable benchmark of performance measurement has haunted the industry as it promulgates the asset class argument. Academic studies must rely on comparing active management skill to passive management indexes. The lack of a benchmark, the lack of a direct claim on cash flows or assets, and the question of value inherent in the futures markets all contribute to the failure of applying the asset class argument to the futures markets.

THE ISSUE OF FEES

One of the hidden gems in the Lintner study was the absolute performance of the managed accounts and commodity funds despite the preponderance of fees and commissions. The results of this study and a host of others in the eighties make the comparison between the returns and standard deviations of stocks and commodities appear to be relatively equal. In a classical MPT context, this provides the statistical argument for a healthy dose of commodities as a diversifier in any stock portfolio. Yet, when provided with this tool, the marketers of commodity funds usually downplay the statistical logic and suggest that just a small portion of your portfolio invested in commodities would be the prudent course of action. After all, why buy too much of such a valuable thing when just a little bit will help? The prospective investor senses something amiss in the argument and oftentimes passes on the entire pitch.

For those less suspicious, the investigation into fees and commissions uncovers some startling information. The Irwin and Brorsen study of the early era of commodity funds discovered that, on average, the hurdle rate for commodity funds was in excess of 19 percent per annum.[7] A subsequent study by Elton, Gruber, and Rentzler concluded that for commodity funds to become attractive investments, management fees and commissions must be reduced.[8] Despite these excessive fee structures, the products offered were modestly profitable, generally speaking. The era within which these early products were developed contributed to the structural hurdles. Discount commissions were not popularized, competition among funds was hardly developed, and the cost in setting up and distributing a fund to market was substantial. In order to overcome the high hurdle rate and still deliver marketable returns required considerable leverage (which may be translated to read risk) on the part of the investment manager. Yet, the net performance characteristics were good enough for the industry to blossom. Moreover, Irwin, Krukemyer, and Zulaf concluded that an institutional hurdle rate of 10 to 12 percent would have provided institutions an excellent portfolio diversifier.[9] Despite the fees and commissions associated with commodity investments, there existed substantial evidence of profitability.

Toward the end of the 80s, pressure to lower commissions and fees was felt across the financial markets. Futures investments were no exception under the circumstances. Commission rates fell from the $80 to $110 range toward $25, management fees fell from the 4 to 6 percent range toward an industry standard of 2 percent, and incentive fees migrated lower toward an established norm of 20 percent of profits. Competition also reduced the cost structure of creating funds, particularly from offshore tax havens. With hurdle rates declining in this era, the risks associated with high degrees of leverage were reduced by many managers through a reduction in trading exposure.

The late 80s and early 90s witnessed the first wave of institutionalizing managed futures. Enough academic work was proffered in support of the value of managed futures and the attractiveness of the pattern of results from this kind of investment that a radical shift in the target market began in earnest. As managers sought to reduce volatility in order to gain the attention of prospective institutional investors, an almost cult-like atmosphere pervaded the industry. The heyday of gunslinging for high returns was over. Now, the rage was to appear less volatile, less risky, and to adopt a sophisticated investment management aura. Numerous advisors reduced leverage in this environment. The overall return profile was hardly altered as the risk reduction was reasonably commensurate with the cost structure reduction. All was well in the industry.

LEVERAGE: BANE OR GAIN?

The unique feature of futures investing lies in the leverage available to the user. A simple primer on the necessity of the existence of leverage in the futures markets may be helpful at this point. The futures markets exist as a tool to lay off risk. Whether a producer of raw material uses the market for hedging or a pension plan wants to limit equity exposure at a critical juncture in liability management, the markets provide a mechanism for the efficient transfer of risk from one party to another. This tool would cease to exist if subjected to the margin requirements established for equities after the 1929 crash. To buy equities today one must put up at least half the purchase price of the stock, unlike the highly leveraged investors of the 1920s. Despite numerous price explosions and subsequent collapses, despite numerous trading scandals, and despite the perceived risk to naive investors, margin requirements for futures investing will never resemble the margin requirements of stocks. This will never happen because to revise margin requirements up to 50 percent of the underlying value of the investment would price the hedgers out of the market. To once again make the insurance analogy, imagine paying $500,000 for a million-dollar life insurance policy. There would be no market. If hedgers and users of futures markets were required to post 50 percent margin to hold a position, there would be no market either.

The permanent existence of a high degree of leverage in the futures markets is without question. The baggage that this situation contains is considerable. Greed is a natural human condition. For most, playing by the rules allows plenty of opportunity for profit and enjoyment. However, for a small minority the greed factor contributes to rule breaking and power grabbing. The futures markets will always attract the abusers of leverage due to the very nature that leverage must exist for the markets to exist. Regulators routinely weigh the risk of constraints designed to limit abuse versus the liberty designed to foster increased usage of futures in order to provide tools to transfer risk. The regulators have performed an exemplary duty in designing the necessary systems and firewalls to prevent systemic abuse. The markets themselves do not appear to be the problem. Most greed-based behavior that becomes scandalous tends to emanate from within organizations that have not implemented the proper safeguards in the handling of the tools available in the markets. Much like the weekend golfer who blames the equipment rather than himself for his lack of success, the ill-informed public tends to blame the markets rather than the true culprits—the abusers of the markets.

Not everything associated with leverage is a bad thing, however. The very existence of these tools that allow the transferal of risk may have contributed to the overall decrease in volatility that we have experienced the last few years in a variety of markets. The financial engineering available through the sophisticated usage of futures is virtually limitless. Pension funds, mutual funds, corporate treasurers, banks, insurance companies, and many other institutions now routinely hedge some portfolio risk through these markets. The small amount of capital required to establish these hedging positions allows the institutions to maintain the portfolio strategic vision without sacrificing performance objectives by remaining near fully invested. Without leverage, these tools in the hands of the financial engineer would hold relatively little value.

CREATIVE STRUCTURES

Treasury bonds were first stripped in 1982 creating zero coupon bonds. With the leverage available to futures managers through low margin requirements, an investment structure was created utilizing zero coupon bonds for principal guarantee at a prescribed future date and the remaining cash posted as margin for a managed futures investment. This principal-guaranteed structure offered the skittish investor a comfort factor directly tied to his worst fear. The perception of futures as a risky investment venture was overcome with a creative structure that provided a safety net for principal without eliminating the opportunity for gain. This rudimentary bit of financial engineering was a giant leap forward in the development of the futures industry. In its simplicity, the guaranteed fund structure solved a multitude of fears, both real and perceived. The industry growth, spawned from this simple investment tool, was enormous.

Still, only a limited audience could participate in futures investing. Institutionally speaking, more often than not, there were not rules prohibiting such an investment. Rather, there rarely existed guidelines that allowed such an investment. Most institutions are unwilling to test the gray area in regulations. Consequently, additional creative structures were necessary to eliminate further barriers to entry.

The next structure successfully applied to managed futures investments was the structured note. By providing a rating associated with a fixed-income instrument to the returns of a futures portfolio through a swap transaction, the futures investment is at once securitized and rated. These conditions meet the requirements of a broader class of investor. In fact, this structure qualifies some very conservative institutional investors that would ordinarily never consider managed futures investing.

Another form of securitization is the listing of fund company vehicles on recognized stock exchanges. A popular exchange for this type of listing exists in Dublin. The listing requirements are fairly liberal, which allows offshore commodity pool structures to appear as equities for investment purposes. Of course, certain jurisdictions clarify the gray area much like the insurance regulators in London did when they prohibited such an equity transaction by insurance companies when the primary purpose of the equity was deemed to be the speculation in futures. Nevertheless, creating a shell in the form of an equity or a note is a popular way to structure this kind of investment to fit the stringent criteria of the institutional investor.

LESSONS LEARNED

A review of the history of the managed futures industry may provide some interesting lessons. The futures markets were created to fill a void where risk transfer was demanded. The result was an efficient market for price discovery whereby hedgers could transfer risk to speculators. Despite the nature of the market being zero-sum sans transaction costs, value is created in the transfer of risk. The hedger views this as a cost of protecting his assets while the speculator views this process as an opportunity for profit. Value, however, does not necessarily constitute an asset class. Benchmarking could aid in this argument, but the industry has failed to embrace and promote a benchmark, perhaps with good reason. The industry is left with manager skill attempting to capture the value created by the transfer of risk from one party to another.

Fees remain a hurdle in institutional acceptability. Two percent management fees, 20 percent incentive fees, and annual commissions averaging 2 percent or more outpace comparable structures in competing investments by a wide margin. Wrapping this investment in an acceptable package for institutional investment only adds to the cost. Unless the returns far exceed equity investing with much less volatility, the cost structure is prohibitive for the benefit received.

Recently, repackaging in the context of an overlay has become popular. The concept began with currency overlays as a hedge against foreign investment exposure. In the case of San Diego County, the overlay concept is employed in a diversified futures investment program relative to the entire investment portfolio. The focus of the overlay is the *alpha* generated by the managers hired for the program. Although not widely accepted yet, the delivery of the package rests on the value created by the managers' skill rather than some inherent return embodied, but not measurable, in the markets themselves.

Derivative scandals continue to plague the industry mind set. Institutional investors are far more understanding of the reality of the scandals and do not blame the markets or the tools themselves. However, the media blitz surrounding each scandal fosters an increasingly large chip on the shoulder of many industry proponents. Recognizing the scandals for what they are and understanding the nature of each scandal should provide for interesting cocktail conversation rather than excuses in marketing presentations.

Recognition of the limited resources available to the target institutional investor would reshape the thinking of many industry proponents. Many institutional investors track benchmarks as a way of measuring the success or failure of the implementation of their investment plan. Selling these investors the benefits of futures via the MPT argument is wasted breath. If the investment strategy is designed with specific benchmarks in mind, even from an asset allocation point of view, the implementation of the strategy will focus on relative returns. Providing a portfolio diversifier in order to provide better absolute returns versus risk is in conflict with the investment manager's objectives. In addition, trying to get the institutional investor interested in allocating precious resources to understanding and tracking the pork belly market, the platinum market, or even the German Bund market is an exercise in futility. Most pension funds are managed with relatively modest staffs and resources. Getting them interested in a product that requires understanding new, unrelated markets will consume far more of their time and energy than the ancillary benefits can justify. Selling them the benchmark they seek to track is the perfect investment. Enhancing the benchmark is even better.

How does one learn from these lessons in order to develop a strategy for promoting managed futures as we head toward the 21st century? Eliminate the asset class argument, the search for a benchmark, and the high fee structured product. Focus on what the markets provide, what the manager can deliver, and what the investor demands. The successful product that will propel this industry in a growth mode once again is a product wrought with simplicity.

At first, the *alpha* generated from manager skill will be accessed only from markets the institutional investor is currently invested in. These include the equity, U.S. fixed income, and, to a lesser extent, foreign currency markets. This alleviates the institutional investor from developing the fiduciary tools necessary to monitor, evaluate, and manage an investment in markets they are not yet invested in. Additionally, the focus of the managed futures investment in this situation will be the diversification characteristics the manager provides compared to other more mainstream investment managers operating in the same market through traditional channels. By emphasizing the value created in the risk transfer process, the prospective investor will relate manager skill to a partial hedge. The term *participatory hedge* may describe the investment opportunity available to the futures manager. A participatory hedge ideally is an investment that participates to a reasonable degree on the upside movement in a market while providing hedging characteristics during downward moving markets.

Ideally, the *alpha* will be generated from the same market from which a benchmark is selected. For example, if an institutional investor employs an equity strategy that measures against the S&P 500 index, the *alpha* should be derived from S&P 500 index futures. This matched book example requires no additional resources allocated to study another market. The *alpha* creation should be coupled with a passive investment in the underlying benchmark, in this case the S&P 500 index futures. The result is an enhanced index product requiring no special resource allocation or market study. The fee issue is tackled by deleveraging the *alpha* component to the point where fees are comparable to other product in the market. For instance, if the futures manager charges 2 percent management fee and 20 percent incentive, deleveraging by a factor of 10 equates to a management fee of 20 basis points. Of course, the commission hurdle would decrease by a similar amount. The result is a modest enhancement to the desired benchmark with an attractive fee schedule.

Financial engineers should have a field day with this type of structure. For every benchmark that does not have a futures market fully developed, proxy investments will be engineered. For complex portfolios that have weighted benchmark targets, engineers will develop the appropriate portfolio of passive futures investments and matching manager skill to create complex portfolio enhancers.

Providing these matched book vehicles will enable proponents of MPT to sell their wares. The *alpha* delivered by the futures managers may be greater in weak markets than in bull markets for the benchmark. The natural noncorrelation properties of the active manager who is indifferent between long and short positions should shine appropriately during bear markets for the benchmark since the passive investment has no relief from downward price action. Of course, the emphasis on active management suggests that there is no assurance that bear markets will always be traded profitably by the futures manager.

In a study performed by the author on the viability of such a product, the results of applying a matched *alpha* overlay to a passive index confirms the value of such a structured approach. The period covered in the study extends from January 1990 through May 1996. Five managed futures strategies employing only S&P 500 index futures and options on futures were analyzed. Performance figures were obtained from Disclosure Documents provided by each investment manager. The benchmark for comparison was the S&P 500 index including dividends. In each sample, one manager was deleveraged by a factor of 10 and then overlaid on the passive index. The performance results include fees assessed as published in the respective Disclosure Document for each investment manager.

The results in Table 16–1 show a significant value added in either return enhancement or volatility reduction relative to the index alone. In fact, in all cases the Sharpe ratio improves. In the weakest example of return enhancement, the reduction in the standard deviation is material. The conclusion reached is that product can be structured to meet the goals of the institutional investor from a fee standpoint since this study suggests a management fee of 20 basis points. In each case, the investment is confined to the S&P 500 market exchange traded derivatives. Additionally, the most widely followed benchmark in investing is the target of the study. One could enhance the structure further by providing a principal guarantee via the zero coupon structure outlined earlier.

This kind of simple financial engineering is targeted toward meeting the needs of the prospective institutional investor. Packaging the value offered in a managed futures investment tied directly to, and including, a passive benchmark makes the product inherently simple and easy to understand. Deleveraging the product brings the fees in line with competing investments and eliminates the concerns associated with highly leveraged investing. There is no need to rely on academic studies or statistical arguments as a foundation for investing. Any latent concern about the principal being lost is ameliorated through the zero coupon attachment. Managed futures investments will prosper in this context because it satisfies so many concerns and places the usage of the tools in their proper context. By capturing the value created in the futures market through risk transfer, the industry can tap the institutional market through enhanced index products via financial engineering.

ENDNOTES

1. Harry Markowitz, "Portfolio Selection," *Journal of Finance*, March 1952, pp. 77–91, and *Portfolio Selection: Efficient Diversification of Investments* (New York: John Wiley & Sons, 1959).

2. John Lintner, *The Potential Role of Managed Commodity - Financial Futures Accounts (and/or Funds) in Portfolios of Stocks and Bonds,* a paper presented at the Annual Conference of the Financial Analysts Federation, Toronto, Canada, May 16, 1983.

3. Zvi Bodie and Victor Rosansky, "Risk and Return in Commodity Futures," *Financial Analysts Journal*, May-June 1980.

TABLE 16-1

Test Results of a 10 Percent Managed Futures Overlay on the S&P 500 Index

	S&P 500 Index	Manager A	Manager B	Manager C	Manager D	Manager E
Cumulative return	123.14	152.97	139.21	144.01	138.99	126.53
Standard deviation	3.32	3.41	3.34	3.48	3.47	3.00
Sharpe ratio	0.74	0.89	0.83	0.83	0.80	0.83
Annual return	14.25	16.58	15.51	15.95	15.56	14.38

The period covered in this study extends from January 1990 through May 1996.

4. Zvi Bodie and Victor Rosansky, ibid.

5. In cooperation with BARRA, this index became modestly popular as the BARRA-MLM Index. However, the lack of a strong marketing push to establish this index as the mainstay benchmark of the futures markets ultimately led to the dissolution of the partnership. Mount Lucas has retained full ownership and responsibility for the index, which no longer bears the reference to BARRA.

6. For more information, contact Mount Lucas Management in Princeton, New Jersey. The concept behind acceptable benchmarks requires ease of measurement, reproducibility, and passivity. The argument relative to passivity in this case is the value present from both the long and short side to futures investors and the need for a simple mechanism to distinguish between the two.

7. Scott Irwin and Wade Brorsen, "Public Futures Funds," *The Journal of Futures Markets* 5, no. 2, 1985.

8. Edwin Elton, Martin Gruber, and Joel Rentzler, "The Performance of Publicly Offered Commodity Funds," *Financial Analysts Journal*, July - August 1990, pp. 23–30.

9. Scott Irwin, Terry Krukemyer, and Carl Zulaf, "Are Public Commodity Pools a Good Investment?" *The Journal of Futures Markets*.

PART THREE

Evidence Regarding Market Inefficiencies

CHAPTER 17

MANAGEMENT SUMMARY

Title: "Inefficiencies and Long-Term Profitability"

Author: Ben Warwick, Director of Marketing
          Abacus Trading Corporation

Synopsis: This chapter examines the implications of market inefficiencies
          to the investor. A literature review of both semistrong and weak-
          form efficiency studies is presented. If investment managers can
          successfully identify and exploit such inefficiencies, and their
          returns are not correlated with the returns from stocks and bonds,
          such trading would represent a "value-added" strategy.

Inefficiencies and Long-Term Profitability

Ben Warwick
Director of Marketing
Abacus Trading Corporation

One of the most commonly accepted paradigms in the investment realm is the concept of market efficiency. But as the quality and quantity of computational power continues to increase, traders and academicians are discovering that all is not as it seems in the financial markets. The purpose of this chapter is to explore the implications that the existence of market inefficiencies may pose to market participants.

The Efficient Market Hypothesis (EMH) states that all relevant and ascertainable information is instantly reflected in security prices. In other words,

> A market is efficient with respect to information set α if it is impossible to make economic profits by trading on the basis of information set α.[1]

The term *economic profit* refers to profits minus applicable transaction costs (slippage and commission).

Several versions of the Efficient Market Hypothesis have been discussed and tested in the literature. The differences revolve primarily around the definition of the information set used in those tests. The two broad categories of hypothesis that have developed are as follows:

1. The weak form of the EMH, in which the information set α is taken to be solely the information contained in the past price history of the market.

2. The semistrong form of the EMH, in which α is taken to be all information that is publicly available at any given time.[2]

WEAK-FORM VIOLATIONS

Traders exploiting weak-form violations of the EMH believe that the examination of past price behavior yields clues to future price direction. There are several areas of weak-form study, including trend analysis, price patterns, and chaos theory.

I. Trend Inefficiencies

Trend analysis is one of the most popular ways to exploit weak form violations of the EMH. The belief that prices occasionally exhibit autocorrelated behavior—that is, an "up" day is statistically favored to be followed by another "up" day (and vice versa)—is the guiding force behind many successful commodity trading advisors. Although a large majority of academic research generally supports the EMH,[3] there are several noteworthy studies that have found evidence of trending behavior:

Researcher	Title	Comments
Brinegar (1954)	A Statistical Analysis of Speculative Price Behavior[4]	Systematic price dependencies were found in the wheat market
Cargill, Rausser (1975)	Temporal Price Behavior in Commodity Futures Markets[5]	Results strongly suggested nonrandom behavior in 12 markets
Taylor (1988)	The Behavior of Futures Prices over Time[6]	Price trends were evident in several futures markets
Lukac et at. (1988)	A Comparison of 12 Technical Trading Systems[7]	Trend following approach created profits during test period
Neftci (1991)	Naive Trading Rules in Financial Markets and Wiener-Kolmogrov Prediction Theory: A Study of Technical Analysis[8]	Moving averages were shown to have predictive value

In summary, most of the studies found some evidence of price dependencies but the evidence was mixed. The results seem to depend heavily on the statistical techniques and the sample periods used. This is consistent with Irwin, who found that periods of high price inflation are associated with increased price inefficiencies.[9]

Price trend inefficiencies are probably best exploited by systematic, trend-following commodity trading advisors. These CTAs typically employ long-term holding periods and trade a diversified portfolio of futures contracts. The Managed Account Reports Trend Following Sub-Index is a good way to monitor the performance of such traders. The index is dollar-weighted, and represents about 262 commodity trading advisors (CTAs) with combined assets of about $6 billion (Figure 17–1). About 90 percent of the traders in the index use a systematic methodology. The index has an average annual return of 15.1 percent since inception in 1983.

II. Price Pattern Inefficiencies

The second type of weak-form inefficiency assumes that the study of price and volume patterns are useful predictive tools for speculation. Until recently most traders used patterns subjectively. However, the advent of cheaper and more powerful computers has enabled analysts to determine the value of such patterns more objectively:

Researcher	Title	Comments
Leuthhold (1972)	An Analysis of the Futures-Cash Price Basis for Live Beef Cattle[10]	Filter rules can be used to find nonlinear dependencies
Brock & LeBaron, Lakonishok (1992)	Simple Technical Trading Rules and the Stochastic Properties of Stock Returns[11]	Support and resistance levels give good buy and sell signals
Taylor (1994)	Trading Futures Using a Channel Rule: A Study of the Predictive Power of Technical Analysis with Currency Examples[12]	A simple technical trading rule produced profits in currency markets over a multiyear period
Blume & Easley, O'Hara (1994)	Market Statistics & Technical Analysis: The Role of Volume[13]	Volume provides information on information quality that cannot be deduced from pure price data.

Of special interest is the work of Houthakker,[14] who examined various stop-loss rules for wheat and corn during 1921-39 and 1947-56. His

FIGURE 17–1

MAR Trend-Follower Index
1983–96

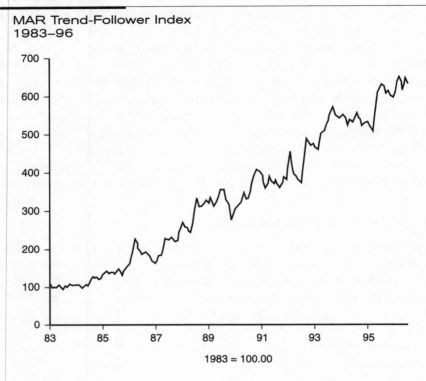

1983 = 100.00

approach was to compare profits (and losses) to a buy-and-hold (and/or sell-and-hold) strategy. An example of such a strategy would be to liquidate if the price falls below the entry level, or if prices fall to 95 percent of the entry level, etc. If price changes were random, such stop-loss rules would have no effect on long-term average returns. The results indicated definite evidence against randomness. In every futures contract, whether long or short, improvement was possible by using the stop-loss rules. The improvements were not always very large. The stop-loss rules seemed to be more effective in reducing losses than in increasing profits. And in no case did a stop policy turn an unprofitable buy-and-hold (or sell-and-hold) strategy into a profitable one. He finished his study by outlining a theory in support of certain types of price dependencies within the futures markets.

Stevenson and Bear[15] analyzed the use of both trading rules and statistical techniques on corn and soybean prices during 1957-68. They first applied statistical tests of frequency distributions, serial correlations, and analysis of runs, and found evidence of nonrandomness (negative correlation in the short term and positive correlation over the long term). Next, they applied three trading techniques to this same price series. One technique consisted of stop-loss rules similar to those of Houthakker's study. Another combined stop-loss rules with entry rules that allowed establishing positions after the market had moved a predefined percentage. Entry rules were tested that allowed establishing positions with the market, and then against market movements. The third technique involved buying (or selling) when the market moved a predefined percentage, and then selling (or buying) after the market had gone up or down a predetermined amount. After the position was closed the process was repeated. For all three trading strategies the amount of price movement allowed before stop losses, market entry, and profit (loss) points were triggered was varied in increments of 1.5 percent, 3 percent, and 5 percent of the price of each commodity. Commissions were included. The first technique (stop-loss only) was able to outperform a buy-and-hold strategy, to a small extent. The second technique (variable entry with stop-loss rules) produced interesting results. Entry with the market (i.e., going long after prices rise, or short after prices fall) using the larger filters, produced results superior to buy-and-hold. Entry against the market (i.e., establishing a short position after prices rise, or a long position after prices fall) produced better results for the smaller filters, but was poorer than the buy-and-hold. These results confirmed the tendency toward reversal in small price movements about a larger systematic trend. The final technique (variable entry and profit capture) was a poor performer. In summary, the profitability found over a buy-and-hold philosophy by playing long-term movements on both the long and short sides does cast considerable doubt on the applicability of the random walk hypothesis to the markets for commodity futures.

Many researchers have tested trading rules that have not worked, or found results that were not published. Academic journals have a natural bias toward publishing results that present new techniques. One can also assume that successful technical methodologies might not find their way to publication, as they could provide significant profit opportunities for the authors. The studies reported herein do show the possibility of earning profits through the use of nonlinear filters, and therefore make the point that the concept of efficient markets and a random walk model may not be entirely appropriate for the futures markets.

Many of the rules used by academics in their research, such as stop-loss rules and trend-following filters, are also part of the technical strategies used by commodity trading advisors. If academicians have found complex, nonlinear price dependencies within the futures markets using simple mechanical filters, then it is certainly possible that others, using more sophisticated techniques, have been even more successful. Research has shown that standard approaches using common mathematical and statistical analysis are inadequate for discovering market inefficiencies. Nonstandard, nonlinear approaches seem to be required.

III. Chaos Theory

The study of chaos theory is a relatively new innovation in the area of finance. Most chaos-related research involves finding repeatable patterns in price series that seem to be random. The majority of studies in this area have several things in common. First, they agree that nonlinear weak-form inefficiencies exist in capital markets. Second, using chaos as a forecasting tool is useful only in the very short term; long-term forecasting is impossible. Unfortunately, there have been very few studies published on successful application of the theory to the capital markets. I believe this to be forthcoming, as computing power continues to increase and the ability of researchers to solve complex differential equations becomes greater.

SEMISTRONG VIOLATIONS

Semistrong violations of the EMH imply that information is not instantaneously reflected in the price of a security. If there is a definable lag associated with the release of information, market participants could profit by trading immediately after the announcement to capture some of the excess return (Figure 17–2).

Like tests of weak-form inefficiencies, a great majority of studies have confirmed the semistrong version of the EMH. But there are studies that show a time lag associated with the releases of information in several markets:

Researcher	Market	Comments
Rendelman et. al. (1982)[16]	Equities	"Surprise" earnings announcements are not instantly reflected
Larson (1960)[17]	Corn Futures	Showed time lags associated with crop production reports
Schneeweis (1988)[18]	Debt Securities	Agency rating changes are not instantly reflected in prices

FIGURE 17-2

Efficient versus Inefficient Markets

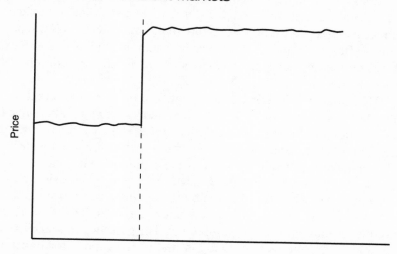

Time

Release of new information

(a) An efficient market responds quickly to releases of new information

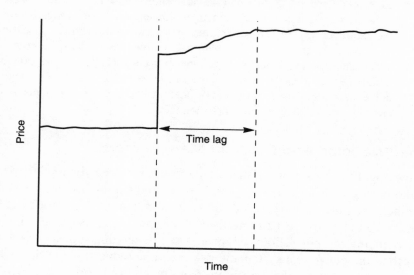

Time

Release of new information

(b) An inefficient market may exhibit a time lag. A prolonged time lag is called a market trend.

Source: From *Event Trading* by Ben Warwick (Chicago, IL: Irwin Professional Publishing, 1996) , p. 16. Reprinted with permission.

Implications of EMH Violations

There are several implications of the existence of weak and semistrong EMH violations. First, such a discovery would validate the acceptance of technical analysis as a useful forecasting tool. This process may already be starting—after the publication of recent academic studies that discussed evidence on inefficiencies, there was very little negative reaction by other researchers loyal to the EMH.[19]

The second implication has to do with our opinions of market participants. One of the tenets of the EMH is that traders act rationally to releases of information, and that securities prices reflect this by fluctuating randomly around an expected fair value—the so-called "random walk theory." Weak-form inefficiencies such as price patterns and market trends refute the idea of a random walk. If such inefficiencies do exist, then the extent of rational behavior exhibited by traders must be re-examined.

Lastly, the existence of inefficiencies validates the use of another tool of the speculator—crowd psychology. The presence of market trends and usable price patterns may function best as indications for impending crowd behavior. As Gustave Le Bon wrote in his classic book *The Crowd:*

> When defining crowds, we said that one of their general characteristics was an excessive suggestibility, and we have shown to what an extent suggestions are contagious in every human agglomeration; a fact which explains the rapid turning of the sentiments of a crowd in a definite direction. However indifferent it may be supposed, a crowd, as a rule, is in a state of expectant attention, which renders suggestion easy. The first suggestion formulated which arises implants itself immediately by a process of contagion in the brains of all assembled, and the identical bent of the sentiments of the crowd is immediately an accomplished fact.[20]

Inefficiencies and Portfolio Management

How might the possibility of market inefficiencies affect the modern portfolio manager? If there are ways to identify and exploit nonrandom market behavior, then a trader could add value to the investment process if he increased the return of the portfolio without increasing its risk profile (or by reducing the portfolio's risk profile while keeping return constant). Further, the portfolio's systematic risk could be reduced if inefficiencies were exploited in markets different from those in the original portfolio (i.e., managed futures combined with a portfolio of equity and debt securities). The introduction of additional markets has been shown to be an effective risk management tool during volatile conditions.[21] If the proper statistical techniques are used, market participants who can identify and exploit market inefficiencies can add value to the investment process.

REFERENCES

1. Jensen, M.L. "Some Anomalous Evidence Regarding Market Efficiency: An Editorial Introduction." *Journal of Financial Economics* 9, 1978, pp. 95–101.
2. Ibid, p. 97.
3. Examples of research that supports the efficient markets hypothesis include the following:

   Galai, D. "Tests of Market Efficiency of the Chicago Board Options Exchange." *Journal of Business* 50 (April 1977) pp. 421–42.

   Labys, W.C., and C.W. Granger. *Speculation, Hedging, and Commodity Price Forecasts.* Lexington, MA: Heath Lexington Books, 1970.

   Samuelson, P.A. "Proof that Properly Anticipated Prices Fluctuate Randomly." *Industrial Management Review* 6, 1965, pp. 41–49.
4. Brinegar, C.S. "A Statistical Analysis of Speculative Price Behavior." *Food Research Institute Studies* 9, Supplement 1970.
5. Cargill, T.F., and G.C. Rausser. "Temporal Price Behavior in Commodity Futures Markets." *Journal of Finance* 30, 1975, pp. 1043–53.
6. Taylor, S.J. "The Behavior of Prices over Time." *Applied Economics* 17, 1985, pp. 713–34.
7. Lukac, L., Wade Brorsen, and Scott H. Irwin. *A Comparison of Twelve Technical Trading Systems.* Greenville, SC: Traders Press, Inc., 1990.
8. Neftci, Salih N. "Naive Trading Rules in Financial Markets and Wiener-Kolmogorov Prediction Theory: A Study of Technical Analysis." *Journal of Business* 64, 1991, pp. 549–71.
9. Irwin, S.H., and B. Wade Brorsen. "A Note on the Factors Affecting Technical Trading System Returns." *Journal of Futures Markets* 7, 1987, pp. 591–95.
10. Leuthold, R.M. "An Analysis of the Futures-Cash Price Basis for Live Beef Cattle." *North Central Journal of Agricultural Economics* 1, 1979, pp. 47–52.
11. Brock, W., Blake LeBaron, and Joseph Lakonishok. "Simple Technical Trading Rules and the Stochastic Properties of Stock Returns," *Journal of Finance* 12, 1992.
12. Taylor, Stephen J. "Trading Futures Using a Channel Rule: A Study of the Predictive Power of Technical Analysis with Currency Examples." *The Journal of the Futures Markets* 14, 1994, pp. 215–35.

13. Blume, Lawrence, D. Easley, and M. O'Hara. "Market Statistics and Technical Analysis: The Role of Volume," *The Journal of Finance* 49, 1994, pp. 153–81.

14. Houtakker, H.S. "Systematic and Random Elements in Short-Term Price Movements." *American Economic Review* 51, 1961, pp. 164–72.

15. Stevenson, R.A., and R.M. Bear. "Commodity Futures: Trends or Random Walk?" Reprinted in *Peck* (1977), pp. 279–94.

16. Rendelmen, Richard J., C. Jones, and H. Latane. "Empirical Anomalies Based on Unexpected Earnings and the Importance of Risk Adjustments." *Journal of Financial Economics* 10, 1982, pp. 269–87.

17. Larson, Arnold. "Measurement of a Random Process in Futures Prices." *Food Research Institute Studies* 1, no. 3 (1960).

18. Schneeweis, Tom. "Capital Market Efficiency in Fixed Income Securities." *Review of Business and Economic Research,* Winter 1980 pp. 34–42.

19. Hulbert, Mark. "Don't Throw Away Your Charts." *Forbes* 10, 1995, p. 140.

20. Le Bon, Gustave. *The Crowd.* Greenville, SC: Traders Press, 1994 (originally published in 1897).

21. Bodie, Z. "Commodity Futures as a Hedge against Inflation." *The Journal of Portfolio Management,* Spring 1983.

CHAPTER 18

MANAGEMENT SUMMARY

Title: "Dependence in Commodity Prices"

Publication: *The Journal of Futures Markets* 12, no. 4, pp. 429–46 (1992).

Authors: Richard L. Peterson, Texas Tech University
             Christopher K. Ma, Texas Tech University
             Robert J. Ritchey, Texas Tech University

Data: Daily prices for 17 commodities from 1969 to 1987.

Synopsis: The study found that the time-variance relationship does not hold for returns of short- and longer-term holding periods, in violation of the random walk hypothesis. This implies that the returns are not independent. The evidence further indicates that there is a positively correlated random component over the intermediate time frames for many commodities. In the short run, a negative serial correlation may result from price overreactions that cause realized daily returns to exhibit a mean-reverting process for some of the commodities. However, when the holding horizon is longer, the realized returns exhibit positive serial correlation for almost all commodities tested.

Dependence in Commodity Prices

Richard L. Peterson

Christopher K. Ma

Robert J. Ritchey

INTRODUCTION

In recent years, the time-series properties of speculative prices have been given renewed attention. Two key issues involve the shape of the distribution that generates price changes and the relationship of price changes across time. The random walk hypothesis incorporates both of these elements by specifying that price changes in all nonoverlapping periods be independent and possess the same stationary distribution. Moreover, the concept of market rationality, which is consistent with the random walk theory, asserts that assets are priced by traders who use all available information to make unbiased predictions of future prices. The collective wisdom from earlier studies [Working (1934); Kendall (1953); Roberts (1959); Alexander (1961); Fama (1965)] generally supports the notion that speculative prices do follow a random walk, based on tests of serial correlation between successive price changes. Recent studies, however, reveal contradictory evidence regarding the nature of asset price changes over

The authors appreciate comments from participants in the Research Seminar of Texas Tech University and those of the two referees of the Journal. The remaining errors are, of course, the authors' responsibility.

Richard L. Peterson is the I. Wylie and Elizabeth Briscoe Professor of Bank Management and Professor of Finance at Texas Tech University.

Christopher K. Ma is an Associate Professor of Finance at Texas Tech University.

Robert J. Ritchey is an Associate Professor of Finance at Texas Tech University.

The Journal of Futures Markets 12, no. 4, pp. 429–46 (1992).

different time horizons. In particular, monthly and annual security returns have been shown to exhibit negative serial correlation [Fama and French (1988); Lehmann (1988); Poterba and Summers (1987); Cecchetti, Lam, and Mark (1989)]. Daily and weekly *individual* security returns appear to be negatively autocorrelated [French and roll (1986); Lo and MacKinlay (1988)], while weekly *portfolio* returns reflect positive serial correlation [Conrad and Kaul (1988); Lo and Mackinlay (1988)]. The common conclusion from this evidence suggests a violation of the random walk hypothesis in many financial markets, implying that there are information components in past prices, beyond a general trend, that can be used by the technical analyst to predict future prices.

Perhaps more interesting is the attempt recent studies have made to suggest economic rationales either supporting or refuting the random walk hypothesis. These studies include "memory" in speculative prices caused by fads [Lehmann (1988); De Long et al. (1987, 1988, 1989)], rational bubbles [Behzad and Grossman (1987)], overreactions [DeBondt and Thaler (1985)], preference reversals [Slovic and Lichtenstein (1983)], production smoothing [Fair (1989)], consumption smoothing [Black (1989)], dividend smoothing [Shiller (1989)], market learning [Turner, Startz, and Nelson (1989)], time-varying risk perception [Friedman and Kuttner (1988)], small sample bias [Kim, Nelson, and Startz (1988)], and nonsynchronous trading [Lo and MacKinlay (1989)].

The relevance of time-series properties of speculative price movements is intensified by the recent debate on market volatility. Shiller (1981) argues that nonrandom stock price movements may be causing return volatility which is "excessive" in that it cannot be fully explained by volatility of the underlying fundamentals. French and Roll (1986) also show that the return variance in trading time periods is significantly higher than that in nontrading time periods. They argue that this phenomenon is at least partially due to noise form traders' overreaction to previous trades.

Compared with the financial markets literature, limited evidence exists on price behavior in real asset markets. Pindyck and Rotemberg (1988) show that prices of largely unrelated raw commodities have a tendency to move together. The excess comovement amount commodity prices is puzzling since the correlation of prices cannot be fully accounted for by correlation of underlying common fundamentals. It has been hypothesized that the excess cross-sectional correlation is due to "herd" behavior, or fads, in markets—either bullish or bearish trading on all commodities for no explainable economic reason. Moreover, this seemingly irrational behavior could be explained if excess correlation is attributed to pooling of the aggregate fundamentals, thereby providing more information than the fundamental price determinants for each individual asset analyzed separately. The commonality among movements in raw commodity prices is further supported by evidence that the changes in commodity prices are often indicators of future inflation [Boughton and Branson (1988)].

Ma (1989) shows that daily cash commodity prices often exhibit reversals immediately following the arrival of significant information. While this evidence is consistent with the overreaction hypothesis, his findings cannot be generalized since they apply only to price behavior after significant events. Similarly, as Frankel (1986) points out, if commodity prices are flexible but other goods prices are sticky, a decline in the nominal money supply will raise the real interest rate and depress real commodity prices in the short run. Commodity prices would then overshoot their equilibrium levels to generate an expectation of future appreciation sufficient to offset the higher interest rate. When the real rate effects eventually vanish, the price will revert to its true long-run equilibrium.

This study seeks to test directly the random walk hypothesis in the cash prices of 17 commodities. Three theoretical components of commodity price series are identified: a systematic component reflecting price drift or the expected arrival of information, a negatively autocorrelated component that is attributed to the bid-ask spread of marketmakers, and a noise term that represents the pricing of unexpected information. Using the variance ratio test of Lo and MacKinlay (1988), the random walk hypothesis is rejected for daily commodity prices since many short-term realized returns exhibit either positive or negative persistence over different time horizons. Furthermore, the positive serial correlation between successive price changes goes beyond the structure of the underlying fundamentals. For many commodities, particularly grains and other crops, there is some evidence that positive serial correlation exists in price changes over short and intermediate time horizons. These results indicate that many daily commodity prices appear not to react to unexpected information in a rational fashion in that either the adjustment process to new information is not instantaneous, possibly because of transaction costs, or because new information is revealed in a serially correlated fashion that is not properly anticipated. In other markets, such as livestock and gold, evidence of short-term price reversals appears. Such price reversals may occur because farmers and ranchers alter their near-term marketing plans in response to recent price changes, or because central banks try to stabilize gold price markets in the short run. Longer-term positive price trends (possibly due to inflation changes) are apparent in gold prices, while price reversals (possibly due to cobweb cycle effects) appear in livestock markets.

Finally, in some markets such as silver and soybeans, no significant violations of random walk assumptions are observed.

EMPIRICAL DESIGN

Variance Ratio Tests

Before investigating the nature or random walks, Working (1934) and Larson (1960) make the distinction between anticipatory and random elements in a price series. As pointed out by Houthakker (1934), the randomness of a process can only be defined as the absence of any systematic pattern. The importance of the distinction between the anticipatory component and the random component is also empirically demonstrated by Conrad, Kaul, and Nimalendran (1989), who show that the individual components in the stock return series exhibit different time-series properties. As the short-horizon realized return shows negative dependence due to the bid-ask spread, an incorrect conclusion may be reached with respect to the time-series property of the true underlying return process. Others argue that the systematic structure of the time series, if expected, should be deterministic. Therefore, the testing of the random walk hypothesis should only be relevant with respect to the random component in the price series.[1]

The basic idea behind variance ratio tests is that price changes following a stable random walk will have a random variance component that increases linearly with time. Thus, if a commodity price series tends to vary up or down with a random variance of 0.1 over a one-day interval, the random variance component of price changes would, on average, be 0.2 over a two-day interval and 0.5 over a five-day interval, etc. Of course, estimates of variances over each interval would not be precise if they were made from random samples of data. For instance, the one-day random price change might be computed to be 0.09 and the five-day random price change variance might be computed to be 0.475. Thus, it is necessary to use a test-statistic to determine whether ratios of variances computed over different intervals are consistent with the linear variance characteristics of a random walk process or differ significantly from the results that would ordinarily be generated by a random walk process. Lo and MacKinlay (1988) have developed appropriate "variance ratio" test statistics for investigating the random walk properties of price series. Their test statistics are used to analyze the random walk properties of commodity price data. The procedures are described in Appendix A.

The variance ratio test in Appendix A is conducted over q-day intervals versus one-day intervals. However, the test is robust for various interval length combinations. For instance if q is designated as the number of lags and the basic interval length is designated i, variance ratio tests can be conducted for various combinations of q and i. Thus, for values of $i = 1$, i.e., for one-day price changes, variance ratio tests re run for (lag) values of $q = 2$, i.e., for price changes over two days, 4, i.e., for price changes over four consecutive trading days, or one trading week, 8, and 16. Values for i of 4 are used also (to measure the variance of price changes over approximately a one-month, or four-week period). When, for instance, variance ratio tests are computed for $i = 16$ and $q = 2$, the variance of price changes over 32 trading days is compared to the variance of price changes over 16 days.

All price changes are measured as log price relatives, i.e., as In (P_t/P_{t-qi}) where P_t is the closing price on day t and p_{t-qi} is the closing price of qi days earlier. If a stable random walk process holds, once the price change series is detrended and other regularities in price movements are taken into account, the random variance of the price change series should grow linearly with the length of time over which the price changes are computed.

However, if the error component of price changes tends to cumulate rather than to vary randomly over some specific time interval, then the variance of the price change over large intervals would be greater than expected. The expected long interval price change variance should equal the variance of the short-interval price change multiplied by q (the number of short intervals in the long interval). However, if random price movements are positively correlated so prices move continuously in the same direction, the price change would cumulate in that direction, and would not be systematically offset by random walk movements in the opposite direction. One factor that could cause cumulative price movements would be a failure of the market to incorporate all new information in current prices instantaneously. Thus, prices might move in the same direction for several days or weeks in a row. Another factor generating price trends could be the sequential release of information that is not fully anticipated. For instance, in a drought, it may rain on any given day, yet, each day that goes by without rain will cause escalating crop damage at some point. As the next day comes and goes without rain, prices may continue to adjust to the ever-increasing possibility that crop damage will be severe. Conversely, every day in the fall that goes by without frost may increase the chances for obtaining a bumper crop. As the weather information is revealed day by day, crop prices may continue to adjust in the same direction to reflect new supply possibilities.

Conversely, price changes may also move inversely over various time intervals. For instance, high hog prices one year may cause farmers to breed more hogs for the next market season, at which point prices are likely to fall. Similarly, high cattle prices one day may induce more farmers to ship their cattle to market in the next day or two so cattle prices will fall. Corn-hog cycles and cobweb cycles are well known in agriculture and cause large price changes over one interval to be offset by significant reversals over longer intervals. Such processes also violate random walk assumptions since random price changes in one period are inversely correlated with price changes over a longer interval rather than being independent. If such phenomena exist, the variance of price changes over long intervals will be less than would be expected if short interval price changes are merely extrapolated to the longer period. Thus, if the variance ratio tests are significantly negative, evidence exists that the random walk hypothesis is rejected in a manner that would be expected if price reversals occurred. However, if variance ratio tests are significantly positive, this will be consistent with the evidence of persistence in price movements.

Return Adjustments for Holidays, Weekends, and Nontrading Periods

Before performing the variance ratio tests as described in the previous section, the sample must be examined to determine the transaction type of the daily prices (bid, ask, or variable transaction prices), then trading, and the impact of nontrading periods. Each of these issues is relevant for the current topic. For example, if actual transaction prices are used, a seemingly negative autocorrelation may be produced since actual transaction prices often fluctuate between bid and ask prices. For this reason, the daily prices in the sample are obtained from dealer's offering quotes or ask prices. The selection of prices of the same type allows elimination of the bias on variance ratios from the negatively correlated component in the transaction price series—if the process of the bid-ask spread is stationary. A further bias in estimates of serial correlation can be introduced if the prices are taken from thin or nonsynchronized trading. This is mainly attributed to the fact that for a less actively traded instrument, the price may reflect new information after a lag. However, the slower adjustment speed to information, while it may exhibit nonrandom walks, does not suggest opportunities for profit since the instrument is not often traded. Lehmann (1980), recognizing both the problem of bid-ask spreads and of thin trading, suggest that using weekly returns from Thursday to Thursday may significantly reduce both biases. This is due to the fact that the impact of bid-ask spreads or infrequent trading will be insignificant when returns are computed over a longer time horizon. Therefore, to reduce the possible biases, the variance ratios over price changes are measured on longer time horizons as well as short horizons.

Since the variance ratio test is used to compare return variances, computed over periods of different lengths of time, the ratio will be biased if the time-series used is non homogeneous in terms of time periods covered for every price change. Whenever there are many types of institutional nontrading periods, such as holidays and weekends, the price change will cover more than the standard daily period, i.e., one day trading session and one evening nontrading session. Thus, the variance ratio specified by equation (4) will be biased. Another subtle but significant issue with respect to uneven lengths of time periods over which price changes are computed results form the fact that return variances are higher in the trading session than in the nontrading session [French and Roll (1986)]. For instance, the Friday close to Monday close seemingly does not cover three standard daily periods, since there is only one day trading session and two day nontrading sessions in that period.

Therefore, it is important to adjust for both the uneven length of time and the uneven mix of trading and nontrading periods over a given interval. This can be conducted by first computing the daily return series, R_t, by the difference of logarithms of the original daily price series, P_t, i.e.,

$$R_t = \text{Log}(P_t / P_{t-1}) \tag{1}$$

Note that while the time horizon of R_t generally covers one day trading session and one night nontrading session, it may also include more than one trading and nontrading periods if day t is a day following a nontrading day session, e.g., weekday holidays or Monday. To assure that the price series being tested is homogeneous in terms of the length of trading/nontrading periods, the daily returns immediately following a nontrading day session are excluded from the sample. That is, all Monday returns and returns following holidays are discarded. Using the rest of the sample, the revised price series P_t' can be generated by

$$P_i' = P_o\left(1 + \exp\prod_{t=0}^{t}(1 + R_j) - 1\right) \tag{2}$$

where P_o is the base price on the first day of the sample. Equation (2) computes a revised price based on the continuously compounded daily returns from a base price. This way, daily prices are generated based on daily returns that all have the same length of trading and nontrading periods. Thus, the simulated time series of daily prices, P'_t, has the property that each price change from the previous one covers the same number of trading and nontrading hours. Since all Monday returns are taken from the sample, the weekly return (Tuesday to Tuesday return) measured over the P'_t series is equivalent to Lehmann's (1988) weekly return adjusted for bid-ask spread and thin trading, and four trading days comprise one week.

EMPIRICAL RESULTS

The sample includes daily cash prices for 17 commodity prices. The data used in the sample are described in Appendix B. All commodities have futures contracts traded during the same sample periods. Most commodities have more than 4,000 daily observations that range over at least 15 years. To eliminate weekend and holiday effects, all price series are modified, as shown in equation (2), to eliminate returns ascribable to trading days that immediately following a trading halt. Thus, each daily return represents only on full day's return. Based on the procedure described in the previous section, the variance ratios and their test statistics for various trading intervals and lags 2 through 60 ($q = 2$ to 60) are computed for each price series. For the sake of brevity, only the variance ratios of daily returns for selected lags with representative values are reported in Table 18-1.[2]

The intervals over which returns are calculated for Table 18-1 include daily returns, with lags approximately equal to one week (four trading days), two weeks (eight trading days), and four weeks (16 days). Because holidays also are omitted, a month of trading contains approximately 16 trading days, and a year of trading contains between 12 and 13 such "months." The use of lags and intervals of approximately one week, one month, etc. in length should help reduce or eliminate possible systematic price patterns that recur on regular calendar-day intervals. Regarding the variance ratios presented in Table 18-1, for all commodity price series combined, more than half of the variance ratios are significantly different from one at the 10 percent level or better, as indicated by the Z values in parentheses. The data suggest that the random walk hypothesis is rejected for the daily price movements of most commodities since at least one variance ratio is significantly different from zero at the 10 percent confidence level for every commodity except silver and soybeans. The variance ratio for lag 2 can be approximated by $1-\gamma$, where γ is the first-order autocorrelation. For example, a variance ratio of 1.014 for soybean oil implies a 1.4 percent positive serial correlation between successive daily prices.

Therefore, based on the one- to two-day variance ratios, with an interval of one day and a lag of 2 reported in Table 18–1, the (log-) prices of soybean meal, oats, coffee, sugar, heating oil, pork bellies, and copper are positively autocorrelated, and the day-to-day price changes of corn, feeder cattle, live hogs, and gold are negatively autocorrelated.

Over longer periods of time, from one week to one month, most of the commodity price changes exhibit positive persistence. For instance, when price changes are compared over one- to four-day intervals, thereby roughly comparing weekly to monthly price changes, price changes for soybean oil, wheat, cotton, coffee, sugar, heating oil, live cattle, live hogs, and copper all exhibit significantly positive serial correlation, while only pork bellies exhibit significantly negative serial correlation. A large proportion of the 17 commodities analyzed also show positive serial correlation when the variance of daily price changes is compared over four-, eight-, or 16-day intervals, or when four-day price changes are compared over two consecutive four-day periods. These results suggest that trending prices frequently occur in commodity markets; thus, there may be some validity to using trend-following technical analysis techniques in various commodity markets.

However, several commodities exhibit significantly negative serial correlation. Feeder cattle price changes usually exhibit significantly negative correlation patterns, while pork bellies also exhibit decreasing variance ratio patterns except for very short intervals. In addition, gold exhibits negative serial correlation over relatively short intervals but positive serial correlation over longer periods, as variances computed over 2 to 12 lags are compared for 16-day return intervals. A possible explanation for these results might be that there might still be some systematic component remaining when the price series are differenced using small q's. Thus, variance ratios different from unity, observed at the shorter lags, may only reflect the serial correlation of the underlying systematic process of the commodity prices rather than the structure of the noise component per se. However, if the noise component, ϵ_t, truly follows a random walk, the variance ratio should follow a U (or a reversed U) shape as the level of q increases.[3] That is, $\lambda(q)^* = 1$ when $q = 1$ and q^*, and that does not appear to be the case. Thus, it is also possible that some markets do not respond efficiently to short-run random price shocks. For instance, farmers may bring more or less livestock to market with a lag, in response to past price increases or decreases, respectively, thereby causing negative correlation in price changes. Also, central banks may move to stabilize gold prices after sharp short-run price changes occur in gold's dollar price, etc.

TABLE 18–1

Variance Ratios for Different Interval Lengths and Lags

Length of Interval Number of Lags	1 2	1 4	1 8	1 16	4 2	4 4	16 2	16 12
Corn	0.970[a] (−1.884)	0.990 (−0.376)	1.048 (1.074)	1.111 (1.598)	1.030 (0.930)	1.070 (1.265)	1.174[b] (2.742)	1.203 (0.856)
Oats	1.120[b] (6.545)	1.274[b] (8.579)	1.395[b] (7.594)	1.486[b] (6.053)	1.027 (0.735)	1.094 (1.480)	0.968 (−0.429)	0.681 (−1.158)
Wheat	0.983 (−1.090)	0.959 (−1.505)	0.982 (−.409)	1.102 (1.478)	0.986 (−0.447)	1.125[b] (2.268)	1.059 (0.929)	1.008 (0.035)
Soybeans	0.984 (−1.014)	0.993 (−0.256)	0.939 (−1.350)	0.937 (−0.912)	1.041 (1.275)	1.024 (0.442)	0.951 (−0.776)	0.711 (−1.215)
Bean oil	1.014 (0.872)	1.079[b] (2.874)	1.147[b] (3.282)	1.239[b] (3.453)	1.066[b] (2.079)	1.142[b] (2.582)	1.129[a] (2.031)	1.088 (0.370)
Soybean meal	1.072[b] (4.511)	1.139[b] (5.068)	1.104[b] (2.319)	1.095 (1.373)	1.032 (1.017)	1.034 (0.622)	0.932 (−1.074)	0.754 (−1.035)
Cotton	0.974 (−1.521)	0.971 (−0.953)	0.999 (0.016)	1.087 (1.145)	1.069 (0.137)	1.168[b] (2.796)	1.067 (0.970)	0.938 (−0.239)
Heating oil	1.043[a] (1.892)	1.080[b] (2.033)	1.184[b] (2.864)	1.265[b] (2.668)	1.081[a] (1.773)	1.158[b] (2.008)	0.953 (−5.17)	0.695 (−0.892)
Coffee	1.093[b] (5.181)	1.284[b] (9.120)	1.590[b] (11.619)	1.992[b] (12.670)	1.190[b] (5.286)	1.475[b] (7.630)	1.143[b] (1.990)	1.641[b] (2.381)

TABLE 18–1 *(continued)*

Variance Ratios for Different Interval Lengths and Lags

Length of Interval Number of Lags	1 2	1 4	1 8	1 16	4 2	4 4	16 2	16 12
Sugar	1.056[b] (3.229)	1.085[b] (2.812)	1.137[b] (2.785)	1.251[b] (3.314)	1.049 (1.404)	1.147[b] (2.450)	1.014 (0.197)	1.292 (1.123)
Gold	0.889[b] (−5.925)	0.908[b] (−2.835)	0.910[a] (−1.708)	1.019 (0.233)	0.918[b] (−2.193)	1.045 (0.595)	1.125[b] (1.666)	1.595[b] (2.122)
Silver	0.989 (−0.644)	1.036 (1.240)	1.026 (0.555)	1.115 (1.571)	0.949 (−1.521)	1.058 (0.859)	1.013 (0.192)	0.998 (0.007)
Copper	1.100[b] (5.793)	1.220[b] (7.318)	1.343[b] (6.987)	1.511[b] (6.757)	1.094[b] (2.706)	1.274[b] (3.956)	1.082 (1.178)	0.749 (0.965)
Feeder cattle	0.908[b] (−4.115)	0.841[b] (−4.089)	0.787[b] (−3.355)	0.723[b] (−2.830)	0.941 (−1.304)	0.871 (−1.437)	0.847[a] (−1.695)	0.464 (−1.588)
Live cattle	0.974 (−1.638)	0.960 (−1.468)	1.038 (0.834)	1.212[b] (3.061)	1.032 (1.002)	1.231[b] (3.633)	0.990 (−0.164)	0.413[b] (−2.467)
Live hogs	0.850[b] (−9.399)	0.742[b] (−9.357)	0.821[b] (−3.984)	0.992 (−0.121)	1.061[a] (1.922)	1.354[b] (5.563)	1.044 (0.684)	0.616 (−1.610)
Pork bellies	1.046[b] (2.930)	1.018 (0.672)	1.012 (0.262)	0.871[a] (−1.867)	1.009 (0.282)	0.816[b] (−2.903)	0.855[b] (−2.281)	0.523[a] (−2.007)

[a] Significant at the 10% level.
[b] Significant at the 5% level.

Overall, in the cash price series of most of 17 commodities analyzed, most series exhibit autocorrelated random components. A few commodities exhibit a negatively correlated component over some variance intervals. Positive trends may reflect serially correlated releases of unexpected information—such as the unanticipated worsening of potential supply shortages or of droughts over time. Negative serial correlation might reflect the unanticipated lagged effect of supply adjustments or storage adjustments in response to previous price changes as, for instance, when more feeder cattle are sent to the meat packer rather than being kept on feed if prices are temporarily high, and the market does not anticipate the increased supply.

The findings of this study sharply contrast with other evidence in financial markets. Conrad, Kaul, and Nimalendran (1989); Ma (1989); Fama and French (1987); Lehmann (1987); and Lo and MacKinlay (1987) all show that the daily, weekly, and monthly realized returns for stocks are negatively serially correlated. However, Conrad, et. al (1989) find that while the bid-ask spread exhibits negative serial correlation, the expected return component is positively autocorrelated. To the contrary, this study suggests that the noise term, which represents the price reaction to unexpected information, exhibits positive long-term serial correlation for many commodities, particularly for most agricultural crops, heating oil, and gold and silver.

The empirical evidence also suggest that the long-term price dependence between successive daily commodity prices is significant enough to reject the random walk hypothesis. The level of serial correlation indicates that there is a component in the prior prices that can be used to predict future prices. If asset returns reflect the arrival of information, the systematic component represents market pricing with respect to the expected component of the information set, and the noise term represents the reaction to the unexpected information arrival. Consequently, the evidence of a positively autocorrelated random component for most commodities, and negatively correlated price changes for some other, suggest that the dependence between successive prices goes beyond the level expected by the market.

Under the current structure, one can only speculate on the sources of the nonrandom walks. One possibility is that information may arrive sequentially, so that market participants are not equally informed at the same point of time [Copeland (1976)]; or, given the same information set, the analytical ability differs among market participants [Heiner (1983); DeLong et al. (1987)]. Either explanation, although seriously challenging the basic assumption of market efficiency, does not necessarily reject economic efficiency because trading costs are not considered. The finding also provide a strong argument for the possibility of market irrationality, since the market price does not fully adjust to unexpected information instantaneously. This may be a result of fads or trading noises, as suggested by previous authors. Undoubtedly the design of this study is unable to provide a direct test on the causes of nonrandomness in commodity prices.

Potential traders may be able to use random walk tests to determine which commodities tend to exhibit random walk behavior, and which do not. More intensive studies using trend-following trading rules may be justified for markets that exhibit positive price change persistence over some intervals, while trading systems that try to exploit price reversals might be usefully investigated if negative price persistence (significantly low variance ratios) is found to exist. However, even if random walk conditions are violated, it is possible that no trading rules will be able to exploit such "inefficiencies" profitably if market monitoring (information) and trading costs are high. This may particularly be the case with cash markets, which are investigated here. The findings only suggest that market inefficiencies exist, but evidence is not sufficient to show that excess profits can be earned as a result.

In particular, caution should be exercised in concluding that significant statistical relationships necessarily imply significant excess economic profit. Predictable relationships in time series can be stable and significant by some statistical criteria, but not meaningful in obtaining economic profit. The necessary requirements to achieve significant economic profit depend on more than the identification of predictable and repetitive patterns. Further, the statistical relationship needs to be specific enough to suggest operational trading rules and the profit generated must be high enough to cover both transaction costs and the risk premium associated with trading. Therefore, the mere evidence of serially correlated price changes does not guarantee the existence of excess economic profit.

CONCLUSIONS

In this study, the random walk hypothesis in the cash prices of 17 commodities is tested. Using variance ratio tests, it is found that the time-variance relationship generally does *not* hold for returns of short- and longer-term holding periods, as expected by the random walk hypothesis. This implies that the returns are not independent and intertemporally uncorrelated. The evidence further indicates that there is a positively autocorrelated random component over intermediate time intervals for many commodities. In the short run, a negative serial correlation may result from price overreactions that cause realized daily returns to exhibit a mean-reverting process for some of the commodities. However, when the holding horizon is longer, the realized returns exhibit positive serial correlation for almost all commodities except some livestock-related commodities.

The implication from the findings suggests that in the price series there is a component, independent of the underlying fundamentals, that can be used to predict future prices. This implies the possibility of market irrationality since positive dependence of prices may be a result of fads in the market. This may also reflect some type of market rigidity in the form of traders' noninstantaneous adjustment to unexpected information, the speed of information releases, serial correlation in information disclosures that are not fully anticipated, or institutional restrictions that prevent the market from being cleared immediately. The sources of non-random walks are left for future research.

Practical implications of nonrandom walks are not absent, however. In particular, in a market characterized by positive serial correlation in price movements, trend-following technical analysis may provide traders with useful insights into future market direction. Also, in such a market, option prices may need to be increased for more distant options to allow for the possibility that accelerating price trends may develop over time. Conversely, in markets characterized by overreaction in daily price changes or long-term negative serial correlation, fair prices for long-term options may be somewhat lower than prices determined by employing a variance measure calculated from the standard deviation of log price changes over daily intervals or other short-term (weekly) intervals—as is commonly done.

APPENDIX A

VARIANCE RATIO TESTS

To separate the random component in the price change from the systematic component reflecting the changes of an underlying economic model, the variance ratio test first developed by Tintner (1940) is used, as well as the corresponding test statistics developed by Lo and MacKinlay (1988). Specifically, let P_t represent the asset price at time t, and L_t be the natural logarithm of price. The continuously compounded return, R_t, which is the difference in successive log-prices, should contain two components: a systematic component, ϕ_t, which is differentiable with respect to time and determined by the underlying price trend and systematic price movement fundamental of the asset, and the random innovation, ϵ_t, generated by unexpected random causes. Therefore,

$$\text{Log}(P_t/P_t-1) = \phi_t + \epsilon_t \tag{A1}$$

where $\text{cov}(\phi_t, \epsilon_t) = 0$, and $\text{E}(\epsilon_t) = 0$. In equation (A1), it should be noted, however, that the systematic component can be serially correlated due to the nature of the economic determinants, which may be time-path dependent. That is, $\text{cov}(\phi_t, \phi_{t-1})$ is not necessarily equal to zero. Based on the specification in equation (A1), the ϵ_t are said to follow a Gaussian *random walk* if and only if the noise component is independent of time, and normally distributed with an expected value of zero and variance equal to σ^2.

It is necessary, therefore, to isolate the noise component from the entire series. This can be accomplished by taking finite differences of the price series. When a lag, q, is used to finite difference the log of the price series, any systematic pattern of ϕ_t that exists between P_t and P_{t-q} should be irrelevant in determining the variance ratios. For instance, a constant geometric (percentage) drift at rate pt will merely cause the mean of the log relative, log (P_t/P_{t-q}), to be adjusted by a constant term equal to $q*$ in p, but will not affect the variance of the log relative. Furthermore, for systematic price behavior that follows a regular cyclical pattern, as the time interval, q, lengthens, regular harmonic processes such as day of the week effects will tend to net out and, therefore, have less effect on variance measures. Thus, the finite differencing of a lagged price series will eliminate drift effects and either eliminate or, at least, reduce the importance of other systematic components without also eliminating the random component [Powers, (1971)]. On the other hand, the random component of a price series over various differencing intervals cannot be reduced by finite differencing since it is not ordered in time.

Variance ratio tests are often considered superior to traditional white-noise tests or autocorrelation tests for random walks, since they do not require that the underlying economic model, ex ante, be specific. The traditional autocorrelation method assumes either that there is no systematic component in the underlying process (Martingale), or that the economic model be specified ad hoc to distinguish the random component ϵ_t for testing. In either case, the hypothesis is always a joint test for both the validity of the model and the independence of the ϵ_t.

However, the finite difference method can effectively eliminate a large number of functional forms as possible candidates for the underlying systematic component without actually specifying the true relationship.[4] Equation (A1) produces the familiar stochastic differential equation:

$$dL(t) = \mu_\phi \, dt + (\sigma + \sigma_\phi) \, dZ(t) \qquad \text{(A2)}$$

where $dZ(t)$ is a Wiener process with mean of zero and variance equal to t. μ_ϕ and $\sigma^2{}_\phi$ are the mean and variance of the systematic component, ϕ_t. Two important properties of equation (A2) are first, that the "drift" in log-price over a given time interval is proportional to the length of the interval, i.e., a drift of $\mu_\phi \Delta t$ and second, that the variance of the random error term, $\sigma^2 \Delta t$ is also proportional to the elapsed time. The variance ratio test will facilitate the testing of the time-variance property implied by a random walk—if the elapsed time between observations is Δt and the variance of the associated noise term is σ^2, then doubling the time between observations will imply a variance equal to $2\sigma^2$, tripling, a variance of $3\sigma^2$, and so on. This can be demonstrated by the qth differencing of equation (A1) where there exists a strictly positive integer, q such that the ϕ, systematic component vanishes from the variance calculation after the differencing. Since the bid-ask spread is not time additive over longer time periods, the left-hand side becomes Log (P_j/P_{j-q}), which represents the holding period return over q periods, and is equal to the sum of the random component, ϵ_t, from $t = j - q$ to $t = j$, the net drift components at time t and $t - q$ that is,

$$\text{Log}(P_t/P_{t-q}) \approx \sum_{k=0}^{q} \epsilon_{t-k} + q \ln \mu_\phi$$

and the variance of the q-period return is:

$$V(R_q) \approx \sum_{k=0}^{q} V(\epsilon_{t-k}) + \sum_{i=0}^{q}\sum_{j=0}^{q} \text{Cov}(\epsilon_{t-i}, \epsilon_{t-j})$$

$$\text{where } i \neq j.$$

The random walk hypothesis would require that the ϵ_t be independent and identically distributed (i.i.d.). Therefore,

$$V(R_q) = qV(\epsilon_t) \qquad \text{(A3)}$$

which reduces to $V(R_q) \approx qV(\epsilon_t) \approx q\sigma^2$. Thus, the familiar unit-root variance ratio, and the following necessary condition for random walks must hold:

$$\lambda(q) = V(q)/[V(1)q] = 1 \qquad \text{(A4)}$$

where $\lambda(q)$ represents the variance ratio of the finite difference log-price series, $V(q)$ equals the variance over an interval of length, q, and $V(1)$ represents the variance over an interval of unit length. The variance ratio test compares the variance of a q-period return to that of the product of q and the variance of a one-period turn.

To test the null hypothesis that the time-variance relationship in equation A4 holds, finding $\lambda(q)$ significantly different from unity is sufficient to reject the random walk hypothesis. Lo and MacKinlay (1988) derive efficient estimators for $V(q)$ as well as the asymptotic distribution of $\lambda(q)$. Their test is more powerful than similar previous tests since they allow the use of overlapping data, which results in significantly larger sample sizes, particularly for large q^*. Therefore, consider the observed log-price series $L_o, L_1,...L_n$, where the total number of observations equals $n + 1$. Define the unbiased estimators of μ, $V(1)$, and $V(q)$ as $u, v(1)$, and $v(q)$, respectively. Then

$$u = 1/(n - 1) \sum_{k=1}^{n}(L_k - L_{k-1})$$

$$v(1) = 1/(n - 1) \sum_{k=1}^{n}(L_k - L_{k-1} - u)^2$$

$$v(q) = 1/[(n - q + 1)(1 - q/n)] \sum_{k=1}^{n}(L_k - L_{k-q} - qu)^2$$

As shown by Lo and MacKinlay (1988), the test statistic, $z(q)$, is asymptotically normal with a mean of zero and variance of unity with the following:

$$z(q) = n^{1/2}(\lambda(q) - 1)(2(2q - 1)(q - 1)/3q)^{-1/2}$$

where the variance ratio is estimated by

$$\lambda^*(q) = v(q)/[v(1)q]$$

The estimations on the variance ratios of different lags, $\lambda(q)$, and their associated test statistics $z(q)$ allows one to determine whether the variance ratios are significantly different from unity. The random walk hypothesis will be rejected if $\lambda^*(q)$ is significantly different from unity. Furthermore, an estimate of $\lambda(q)$ greater (less) than 1 for $q = 2$ would suggest significantly positive (negative) serial correlation between prices.[5]

To determine whether a nondrift systematic component in the original price series is contributing to the price dependence measured by the variance ratios, the length of the differencing interval, q, may need to be large. However, the variance ratio would start from one ($q = 1$) and exhibit deviations from one as q becomes larger, and eventually resolves back to one when q equals q^*, where q^* is the number of differences needed to eliminate all systematic effects and randomize the original series. As q^* is unknown if the underlying model is not first estimated, the evidence of deviations from unity for a given q only indicates the rejection of random walks *relative to* the holding period being investigated.

The variance ratio tests can also be modified by altering the "unit" interval over which price changes are calculated. Then, q refers to the number of such intervals used in the analysis. For instance, this study uses the "unit" interval lengths of one day, four days, and 16 days. Thus, when $q = 12$, for a 16-day interval, the variance of price changes over 192 trading days is compared to the variance of price changes over a 16-trading-day interval.

BIBLIOGRAPHY

Alexander, S. "Price Movements in Speculative Markets: Trends or Random Walks." *Industrial Management Review* 2 (1961), pp. 7–26.

Black, F. "Mean Reversion and Consumption Smoothing," *NBER Working Paper No. 2946,* 1989.

Boughton, J., and W. Branson. "Commodity Prices as a Leading Indicator of Inflation," *NBER Working Paper No. 2750,* October 1988.

Campbell, J., and R. Shiller "Cointegration and Tests of Present Value Models," *Journal of Political Economy* 95, 1987, pp. 1062–88.

Campbell, J., and R. Shiller. "Stock Prices, Earnings and Expected Dividends." *NBER Working Paper No. 2511,* February 1988.

Cecchetti, S., P. Lam, and N. Mark. "Mean Reversion in Equilibrium Asset Prices." *Working Paper,* Ohio State University, Columbus, OH, 1989.

Chan, K. "On the Return of the Contrarian Investment Strategy," *Journal of Business* 61 (1988), pp. 147–63.

Choi, J., D. Salandro, and K. Shastri. "On the Estimation of Bid-Ask Spreads: Theory and Evidence." *Journal of Financial and Quantitative Analysis* 23 (1988), pp. 219–30.

Conrad, J., and G. Kaul. "Time-Variation in Expected Returns," *Journal of Business* 61 (1988), pp. 147–63.

Conrad, J., G. Kaul, and M. Nimalendran. "Components of Short-Horizon Individual Security Returns," *Working Paper,* University of North Carolina, Chapel Hill, NC., 1989.

Copeland, T. "A Model of Asset Trading under the Assumption of Sequential Information Arrival." *Journal of Finance* 31 (1976), pp. 1149–68.

Cutler, D., J. Poterba, and L. Summers. "What Moves Stock Prices." *NBER Working Paper No. 2538,* March 1988.

DeBondt, W.E., and R. Thaler. "Does the Stock Market Overreact?" *Journal of Finance* 40 (1985), pp. 793–804.

DeLong, J., A. Shleifer, L. Summers, and R. Waldmann. "The Economic Consequences of Noise Traders." *Working Paper,* Boston University and NBER, 1987.

DeLong, J., A. Schleifer, L. Summers, R. Waldmann. "The Size and Incidence of the Losses From Noise Trading," *NBER Working Paper No. 2875,* March 1989.

APPENDIX B

Sample Description: Daily Spot Commodity Prices

Spot Commodity	Description	Unit	Sample Period	Daily Obs.
Pork bellies	12-14 lb., mid-U.S.	lb.	Jun. 69-Dec. 87	4706
Soybeans	No. 1 yellow, cent. Ill.	bu.	Jun. 69-Dec. 87	4706
Live cattle	Tex.-Okla.	cwt.	Jun. 69-Dec. 87	4706
Coffee	Brazilian, N.Y.	lb.	Jun. 69-Dec. 87	4706
Sugar	Cane, raw, world,	lb.	Jun. 69-Dec. 87	4706
Corn	No. 2 yellow, cent. Ill.	bu.	Jun. 69-Dec. 87	4706
Cotton	1 1-16 in. str. lw.-md., Memphis	lb.	Jun. 69-Dec. 87	4706
Feeder cattle	Feeder, Okla. City avg.	cwt.	Jun. 69-Dec. 87	4706
Heating oil	No. 2 N.Y.	gal.	Sep. 79-Dec. 87	3104
Hogs	Omaha avg.	cwt.	Jun. 69-Dec. 87	4706
Wheat	No. 2 hard, Kansas City	bu.	Jun. 69-Dec. 87	4706
Soymeal	Decatur, Ill.	ton.	Jun. 69-Dec. 87	4706
Oats	No. 2 milling, Minneapolis	bu.	Jun. 69-Dec. 87	4706
Soybean oil	Crd., Decatur, Ill.	lb.	Jun. 69-Dec. 87	4706
Gold	London fixing AM	oz.	Jun. 69-Dec. 87	4706
Silver	London fixing AM	oz.	Jun. 69-Dec. 87	4706
Copper	Cathodes	lb.	Jun. 69-Dec. 87	4706

Source: *The Wall Street Journal*, provided by MJK Commodity Data Services.

DeLong, J., A. Schleifer, L. Summers, R. Waldmann. "The Survival of Noise Traders in Financial Markets," *NBER Working Paper No. 2715,* September 1988.

Dornbush, R. "Expectations and Exchange Rate Dynamics," *Journal of Political Economy* 84 (1976), pp. 1161–76.

Edmister, R., and H. Merriken. "Pricing Efficiency in the Mortgage Market," *AREUEA Journal* 16 (1988), pp. 50–62.

Eichenbaum, M. "Rational Expectations and the Smoothing Properties of Inventories of Finished Goods," *Journal of Monetary Economics* 14 (1984), pp. 71–96.

Fair, R.C. "The Production Smoothing Model is Alive and Well." *NBER Working Paper No. 2877,* March 1989.

Fama, E., and K. French. "Permanent and Temporary Components of Stock Prices," *Journal of Political Economy*, 1988.

Frankel, J. "Expectations and Commodity Price Dynamics: The Overshooting Model," *American Journal of Agricultural Economics* 68 (1986), pp. 344–48.

French, K., and R. Roll. "Stock Return Variances: The Arrival of Information and the Reaction of Traders," *Journal of Financial Economics* 17 (1986), pp. 5–26.

Friedman, B., and K. Kuttner. "Time-Varying Risk Perceptions and the Pricing of Risky Assets," *NBER Working paper No. 2694,* August 1988.

Gau, G.W. "Efficient Real Estate Markets: Paradox or Paradigm," *AREUEA Journal* 15 (1987), pp. 1–12.

Gau, G.W. "Weak Form Tests of the Efficiency of Real Estate Investment Markets," *Financial Review* 19 (1984), pp. 301–20.

Grether, D.M., and C.R. Plott. "Economic Theory of Choice and the Preference Reversal Phenomenon," *American Economic Review* 69 (1979), pp. 623–38.

Grossman, S., and R. Shiller. "The Determinants of the Variability of Stock Market Prices," *American Economic Review* 71 (1981), pp. 222–27.

Haubrich, J., and A. Lo. "The Sources and Nature of Long-Term Memory in the Business Cycle." *NBER Working Paper No. 2951,* April 1989.

Heiner, R. "The Origin of Predictable Behavior," *American Economic Review* 83 (1983), pp. 560–95.

Houthakker, H. "Systematic and Random Elements in Short-Term Price Movements," *Journal of the American Statistical Association* 29 (1934), pp. 164–72.

Kahneman, D., and A. Tversky. "Intuitive Prediction: Biases and Corrective Procedures," in *Judgement Under Uncertainty: Heuristics and Biases*, Kahneman, D., Slovic, P., and Tversky, A. (eds). Cambridge, UK: Cambridge University Press, 1981.

Kendall, M. "The Analysis of Economic Time-Series, Part I: Prices," *Journal of the Royal Statistical Society* 96 (1953), pp. 11–25.

Kim, M.J., C. Nelson, and R. Startz. "Mean Reversion in Stock Prices? A Reappraisal of the Empirical Evidence." *NBER Working Paper No. 2795,* December 1988.

Lehmann, B. "Fads, Martingales, and Market Efficiency," *Quarterly Journal of Economics*, 1988.

Lo, W., and C. MacKinlay. "Stock Market Prices Do Not Follow Random Walks: Evidence from a Simple Specification Test," *Review of Financial Studies* 1 (1988), pp. 41–66.

Lo, W., and C. MacKinlay. "An Econometric Analysis of Nonsynchronous Trading." *NBER Working Paper No. 2960,* May 1989.

Lo, W. "Long Term Memory in Stock Market Prices," *NBER Working Paper No. 2984,* May 1989.

Locke, S. "Real Estate Market Efficiency," *Land Development Studies* 3 (1986), pp. 171–78.

Ma, C. "Overreactions in Commodity Prices." Working paper, 1989.

MacKinlay, C., and K. Ramaswamy. "Index-Futures Arbitrage and the Behavior of Stock Index Futures Prices," *Review of Financial Studies* 1 (1988), pp. 137–58.

Niederhoffer, V., and M. Osboirne. "Market Making and Reversal on the Stock Exchange," *Journal of American Statistical Association* 61 (1966), pp. 897–916.

Paterba, J., and L. Summers. "Mean Reversions in Stock Prices: Evidence and Implications," *NBER Working Paper No. 2343,* August 1987.

Pindyck, R., and J. Rotemberg. "The Excess Co-Movement of Commodity Prices," *NBER Working Paper No. 2671,* July 1988.

Pommerehne, W., F. Schneider, and P. Zweifel. "Economic Theory of Choice and Preference Reversal Phenomenon: A Reexamination." *American Economic Review* 72 (1982), pp. 569–74.

Powers, M. "Does Futures Trading Reduce Price Fluctuations in the Cash Markets?" *American Economic Review* 61 (1971), pp. 460–64.

Roberts, H. "Stock Market 'Pattern' and Financial Analysis" Methodological Suggestions," *Journal of Finance* 14 (1959), pp. 1–10.

Roll, R. "A Simple Measure of the Effective Bid-Ask Spread in an Efficient Market," *Journal of Finance* 39 (1984), pp. 1127–39.

Samuelson, P. "Proof that Properly Anticipated Prices Fluctuate Randomly," *Industrial Management Review* 6 (1965), pp. 41–49.

Shefrin, H., and M. Statman. "Noise Trading and Efficiency in Behavioral Finance." *Working Paper,* Santa Clara University, Santa Clara, CA, 1989.

Shiller, R. "Do Stock Prices Move too Much to Be Justified by Subsequent Changes in Dividends?" *American Economic Review* 71 (1981), p. 421.

Shiller, R. "Comovements in Stock Prices and Comovements in Dividends," *NBER Working Paper No. 2846,* February 1989.

Slovic, P., and S. Lichtenstein. "Preference Reversals: A Broader Perspective," *American Economic Review* 83 (1983), pp. 596–606.

Stein, J. "Overreactions in the Options Market," *Journal of Finance,* September 1989.

Summers, L. "Does the Stock Market Rationally Reflect Fundamental Values?," *Journal of Finance* 41 (1986), pp. 591–601.

Tintner, G. *The Difference Method,* Bloomington, IN, 1940.

West, K.D. "Bubbles, Fads and Stock Price Volatility Tests: A Partial Evaluation," *NBER Working Paper No. 2574,* December 1987.

Working, H. "A Random Difference Series for Use in the Analysis of Time Series," *Journal of the American Statistical Association* 29 (1934), pp. 11–24.

ENDNOTES

1. The serial correlation computed over the original price series may reflect mainly the time-series property of the underlying systematic structure expected by the market.

2. Only a few variance ratios of the 59 are reported for each of the commodities. The other results may be obtained from the authors upon request.

3. As pointed out by Fama and French (1986); the variance ratios would follow a U-shape if the underlying return generating process is composed of a random process and a mean-reverting process. The duration of the U-curve depends on the relative magnitude of each process.

4. The finite difference method cannot eliminate all possible forms of the systematic structure. For example, if S_t follows a recurring format, such as a sine or cosine function, the variance ratios will also follow a U-shape repetitively with respect to the lags for the differences. However, typical patterns (daily, weekly, monthly, seasonalities, or trends), that are related to fundamentals or institutional arrangements, can be removed by finite differences.

5. Lo and MacKinlay (1988) demonstrate the relationship between variance ratios and n-order serial correlations.

CHAPTER 19

MANAGEMENT SUMMARY

Title: "Naive Trading Rules in Financial Markets and Wiener-
                Kolmogorov Prediction Theory: A Study of Technical
                Analysis"

Publication: *Journal of Business* 64, no. 4, pp. 549–71 (1991).

Author: Salih N. Neftci, City University of New York

Data: Price data from the Dow Jones Industrial Average, 1911-76.

Synopsis: The study attempts to discover if an objective basis for the use
                of technical analysis exists. Technical analysis is shown as
                ineffective in predicting future prices in a linear process.
                However, if the process is nonlinear, technical analysis might
                capture some information ignored by traditional Wiener-
                Kolmogorov prediction theory.

                Tests done using the Dow Jones Industrials suggested that
                this may be the case for the moving average rule.

Naive Trading Rules in Financial Markets and Wiener-Kolmogorov Prediction Theory: A Study of "Technical Analysis"

Salih N. Neftci*
Graduate School, City University of New York

The attention that technical analysis receives from financial markets is somewhat of a puzzle. According to Wiener-Kolmogorov prediction theory, time-varying vector autoregressions (VARs) should yield best forecast of a stochastic process in the mean square error (MSE) sense. Yet, quasitotality of traders use technical analysis in day-to-day forecasting although it bears no direct relationship to Wiener-Kolmogorov prediction theory. In fact, technical analysis is a broad class of prediction rules with unknown statistical properties, developed by practitioners without reference to any formalism.

This article attempts a formal study of technical analysis, which is a class of informal prediction rules, often preferred over Wiener-Kolmogorov prediction theory by participants of financial markets. Yet Wiener-Kolmogorov prediction theory provides optimal linear forecasts. This chapter investigates two issues that may explain this contradiction. First, the article attempts to devise formal algorithms to represent various forms of technical analysis in order to see if these rules are well defined. Second, the article discusses under which conditions (if any) technical analysis might capture those properties of stock prices left unexploited by linear models of Wiener-Kolmogorov theory.

*The author is professor of economics at the Graduate School and University Center of the City University of New York. I would like to thank Chris Sims for his comments. I also would like to thank Jonathan Sampson.
Journal of Business 64, no. 4 (1991).

371

This chapter investigates statistical properties of technical analysis in order to determine if there is any objective basis to the popularity of its methods. Broadly, there are two issues of interest. First, can one devise formal algorithms that can generate buy and sell signals identical to the ones given by technical analysis—that is, are any of these rules (mathematically) well defined? The second issue is the extent to which well-defined rules of technical analysis are useful in prediction over and above the forecasts generated by Wiener-Kolmogorov prediction theory.

Normally, just the resources spent on using and developing new forms of technical analysis should provide sufficient motivation for this chapter. However, a series of interesting papers makes such a study more relevant. For example, Brockett, Hinich, and Patterson (1985) and Hinich and Patterson (1985) have argued that several times series, among them asset prices, are stochastically nonlinear. Thus any method that can capture the nonlinearity of asset prices can potentially improve forecasts generated by the Wiener-Kolmogorov prediction theory. For example. Wiener-Kolmogorov theory will not utilize the information contained in higher-order moments of nonlinear processes. It is possible that, in developing technical analysis, practitioners have informally attempted to use the information contained in higher-order moments of asset prices. In fact, it appears that since the October 19, 1987, crash of financial markets, traders have shown more interest in technical analysis—possibly because a crash of that magnitude is a nonlinear event, and the framework provided by the Wiener-Kolmogorov theory would fail to handle it properly.

In particular, linear models are incapable of describing at least two types of plausible stock market activity that are of interest to participants in financial markets. First is the problem of how to issue sporadic buy and sell signals. By nature, this problem is nonlinear. The decision maker observes some indicators, and at random moments, issues signals. VARs cannot explicitly generate such signals. The second example involves "patterns" that may exist in observed time series. Linear models such as VARs can handle these patterns only if they can be fully characterized by the first- and second-order moments. This basically involves any pattern with smooth curvatures. A speculative bubble, which generates a smooth trend and then ends in a sudden crash, cannot be handled easily by linear models.

This article shows that most patterns used by technical analysts need to be characterized by appropriate sequences of local minima and/or maxima and will lead to nonlinear prediction problems. It is well known that the theory of the minima and maxima of stochastic processes can be very tedious [Leadbetter, Lindgren, and Rootzen (1983)]. Under these circumstances, technical analysis may serve as a practical way of using the information contained in such statistics. At the least, this is a possibility that needs to be investigated.[1]

To the best of my knowledge, there is no formal study of the predictive power of technical analysis. Existing studies are mostly directed toward practical applications, informal treatments of which Pring (1980) is a good example. One of the first illustrations of technical analysis is the discussion of Dow theory in Rhea (1932). Although not directly related to any form of technical analysis, the survey by Tong (1983) and the pioneering work of Granger and Andersen (1978) provide some of the tools used here.[2]

The chapter is organized as follows. First, I discuss some reasons behind conducting such a study. In the next section I introduce the notion of Markov times and show that a rule of technical analysis has to generate Markov times in order to be well defined. I then discuss results that can help in deciding whether a rule generates Markov times or not. I show under what conditions well-defined forms of technical analysis can be useful over and above the Wiener-Kolmogorov prediction theory. Finally, I provide examples using the Dow-Jones industrials from 1792 to 1976.

CAN TECHNICAL ANALYSIS BE FORMALIZED?

Pring (1980) introduces "technical analysis" and related methods as follows:

> The technical approach to investment is essentially a reflection of the idea that the stock market moves in trends which are determined by changing attitudes of investors to a variety of economic, monetary, political and psychological forces. The art of technical analysis, for it is an art, is to identify changes in such trends at an early stage and to maintain an investment posture until a reversal of that trend is indicated. . . . By studying the nature of previous market turning points, it is possible to develop some characteristics which can help identify major market tops and bottoms. Technical analysis is therefore based on the assumption that people will continue to make the same mistakes that they made in the past.[3]

Clearly, technical analysis covers a broad category of highly subjective forecasting rules. To simplify the discussion, I first adopt a preliminary classification. A survey of the literature suggests three major classes to group various forms of technical analysis.

Letting $\{X_t, t = 0, 1, ..\}$ represent asset prices, the first class of rules issues signals market turning points using level crossings of the X_t process. The level is almost always defined using various local maxima or minima of $\{X_t\}$. It is the choice of the level that differentiates one rule from another. Figures 19–1a and 19–1b illustrate two examples. The bull (bear) markets are signaled as the Dow-Jones industrials cross trend lines determined by appropriate local maxima (minima). We label this class of rules the trend-crossing method.

Figure 19–2 displays a second major category labeled moving average method. Various moving averages of an observed series are obtained and the intersections of these averages are interpreted as buy and sell signals.

The third group consists of various patterns, whose occurrence is claimed to signal particular types of future behavior by $\{X_t\}$. Some of these patterns are shown in Figure 19–3. This chapter agues that, in principle, all these patterns can be fully characterized using appropriate local minima and maxima. Hence, any pattern can potentially be formalized. However, I show that formal identification of local minima and maxima that can accomplish this is likely to be quite tedious.

Thus, the first step of the analysis is to quantify and formalize, wherever possible, these three categories of technical analysis. I proceed in two stages. First, I prove that any method that relates to crossings of moving averages constitutes a well-defined prediction methodology. Second, I show that patterns or trend crossings used in obtaining market signals are almost always related to some sequences of local minima and maxima, and more important, are generally ill defined in their current formulation. I discuss these points using the important notion of Markov times. In fact, one contribution this chapter makes is to recognize the importance of Markov times as a tool to pick well-defined rules for issuing signals at market turning points.

MARKOV TIMES

Let $\{X_t\}$ be an asset price observed by decision makers. Let $\{I_t\}$ be the sequence of information sets (sigma-algebras) generated by the X_t and possibly by other data observed up to time t.

Definition

We say that a random variable τ is a Markov time if the event

$$A_t = \{\tau < t\}$$

is I_t-measurable—that is, whether or not τ is less than t can be decided given I_t. According to this definition, Markov times are random time periods, the

F I G U R E   19–1a

The Trend-Crossing Method

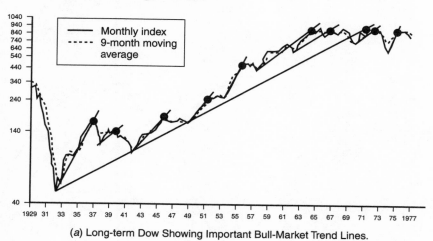

(*a*) Long-term Dow Showing Important Bull-Market Trend Lines.

F I G U R E   19–1b

The Trend-Crossing Method

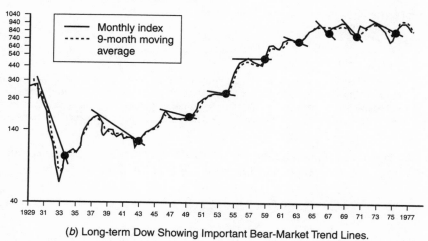

(*b*) Long-term Dow Showing Important Bear-Market Trend Lines.

Source: Pring (1980).

FIGURE 19-2

The Moving Average Method, Dow-Jones Industrials, 1973-79.

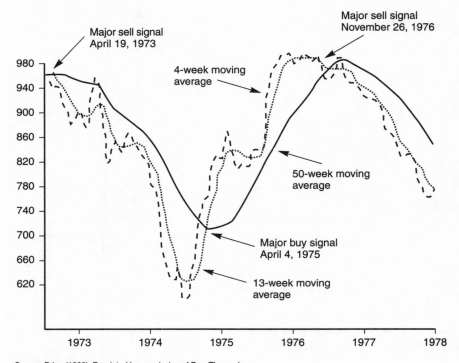

Source: Pring (1980). Reprinted by permission of Dow Theory, Inc.

value of which can be determined by looking at the current information set. Thus, Markov times cannot depend on future information. In order to see the distinction between Markov times and non-Markov times better, and to emphasize the importance of this concept in studying methods of technical analysis, two examples are discussed.

Example 1. Let τ_1 denote the date at which a process $\{X_t\}$, observed continuously, shows a 10 percent jump for the first time during $t \in [0, \infty)$:

$$\tau_1 = \inf_t \{t \in [0, \infty) : d(\ln X_t)/dt > .1\}. \tag{1}$$

Then τ_1 is a Markov time since, by looking at the current information set, it is possible to tell whether such a jump in X_t has occurred or not.

FIGURE 19–3a

Head and Shoulders Dow Jones Transportation Average, 1976

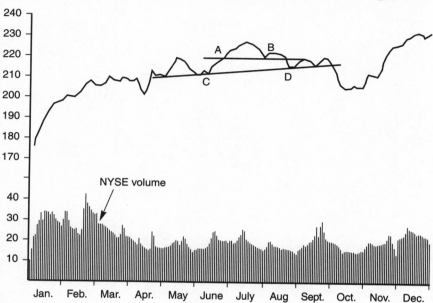

Source: Ping (1980).

Example 2. Let τ_2 denote the beginning date of a business cycle or a stock market uptrend. Then τ_2 is not a Markov time since, in order to know whether $\tau_2 = t$, one needs to have access to I_{t+s}, $s > 0$. In fact, suppose one is at time t and that an uptrend started at time $\tau_2 = t - 2$. In general, one has to wait more than 2 months to be sure that an upturn is under way. Thus, one needs I_{t+s} 3, 4, . . . before one knows $\{\tau_2 < t\}$—that is, future information is needed before deciding which value τ_2 has assumed.

Clearly, any well-defined technical analysis rule has to pass the test of being a Markov time since any buy or sell signal should, in principle, be an announcement based on data available at time t. If a rule generates a sequence of buy and sell orders that fail to be Markov times, then the procedure would be using future information in order to issue such signals. The procedure would anticipate the future. This implies a signaling decision based on considerations that are not part of the available information at time t. These are often the subjective feelings of the forecaster or information not available to the general public.

FIGURE 19–3b

Triangles, Dow Jones Industrial Average, 1938

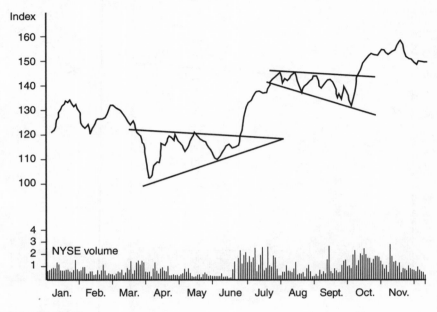

Source: Pring (1980).

It is surprising that such infeasible rules of technical analysis may look perfectly reasonable when illustrated on a chart displaying past data. In using charts, an investigator may implicitly use "future" information while defining a procedure. For example, note that, on a chart displaying observed data, the beginning dates of any uptrend can easily be identified, yet these dates are not Markov times as example 2 demonstrates. Graphic methods are not the best ways of determining classes of Markov times that are useful in prediction. Yet, more often than not, this is how technical analysis rules are defined. Hence the importance of developing formal algorithms that can duplicate the buy and sell signals given by technicians.

This discussion suggests that any method that exploits the current inflection point of a series will fail to generate Markov times since these latter are not I_t-measurable. At the same time, several popular forms of technical analysis use past local maxima (minima) and these are I_t-measurable.

We now have a criterion to determine which rules of technical analysis can be quantified. Indeed, if one can show that signals generated by a

FIGURE 19–3c

Various Gaps

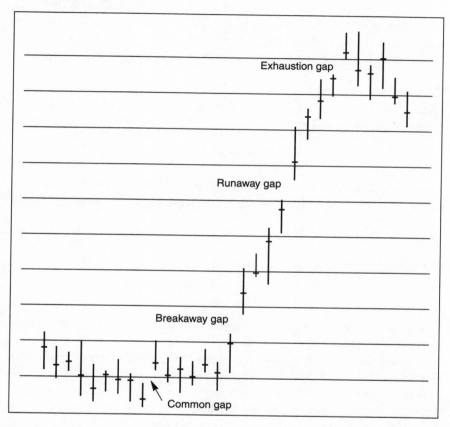

rule of technical analysis are Markov times, then this would simultaneously imply (1) that the method can be quantified, (2) that it is feasible,
and (3) that one can investigate its predictive power using formal statistical models.

The following theorem is important in sorting out Markov times.

THEOREM. Let $\{X_t\}$ be a random process assuming values on the
real line R. Let B be the set of all intervals belonging to R, and I_t be the
information set at time t. Then the times $\{\tau_A^s\}$,

$$\tau_A^s = \inf_t \{t < s : X_t \in A, A \in B\}, \tag{2}$$

are Markov times (Shiryayev 1985).

Basically, this theorem states that the first entry of X_t in an interval A is always a Markov time. The interval in question can, for example, be $[0,\infty)$ or $(-\infty,0]$; but it can also depend on the I_t itself since, if $X_t \in A_t$, we can define $Y_t = X_t - f(A_t)$ such that $Y_t \in [0,\infty]$, as long as A_t is I_t measurable. For example, suppose that a forecaster intends to issue a sell signal as soon as observed price X_t crosses, from above, a trend line $f(I_t, t)$:

$$f(I_t, t) = a_t t + b_t,$$

where a_t and b_t are I_t-measurable slope and intercepts of the trend line. Then a signal is issued at:

$$\tau = \inf_t \{t : X_t < f(I_t, t)\}.$$

This signal deals with the first entry of X_t in a time-dependent set $A_t = [0, f(I_t, t)]$. The time dependence of A_t can easily be eliminated by redefining

$$Y_t = X_t - f(I_t, t)$$

and issuing a signal at the first entry on Y_t in $(-\infty, 0)]$:

$$\tau = \inf_t \{t : Y_t < 0\}.$$

Hence the above theorem can be applied to first entries of X_t in I_t-measured sets as well.

Also, the fact that the theorem deals with the first entry is not a real restriction. The same theorem can be proven for nth entry of X_t into A. The important restriction is that n be known a priori by the forecaster. In fact, I intend to show below that most methods of technical analysis are ill defined precisely because they do not set this parameter n a priori. Below is shown which of the broad forms of technical analysis can be formulated as Markov times.

Characterizing Moving Average Crossings

Figure 19–2 illustrated an example of how moving average crossings are used to signal turning points. To formalize these moving average crossings I first define

$$Z_t = \left[(1/n) \sum_{s=0}^{n-1} X_{t-s} \right] - \left[(1/m) \sum_{s=0}^{m-1} X_{t-s} \right]. \tag{3}$$

The "moving average" rule of technical analysis then uses sign changes in Z_t to generate the times $\{\tau_i\}$ sequentially as

$$\tau_i = \inf_t \{t : t > \tau_{i-1}, Z_t Z_{t-1} < 0\}, \tag{4}$$

with τ_0 defined as zero.

Now consider what (3) and (4) say in words. I basically calculate two moving averages of the X_t process. Assuming that $n > m$, the first moving average will be smoother than the second one in the sense of having relatively more power at low frequencies. Then, as soon as Z_t, $\tau_{i-1} < t$ changes sign, the rule in (4) will assign the value of t to τ_i. These latter are signals of major market downturns and upturns according to the moving average method of technical analysis.

I now show that the $\{\tau_i\}$ are Markov times, and that they constitute a well-defined method of prediction. Clearly, the product $Z_{t-1} Z_t$ is measurable with respect to I_t—that is, given I_t, the value of $Z_{t-1} Z_t$ is known. The τ_i are then defined as the first entry of $Z_{t-1} Z_t$ in the interval $(-\infty, 0) \in R$. Thus the τ_i are Markov times according to the theorem above. This makes the moving average method a statistically well-defined procedure. We should, in principle, be able to evaluate the contribution of the $\{\tau_i\}$ in predicting market turning points using formal tools.

Characterizing Trend Crossings

Methods that use crossings of observed data with trend lines, defined in a variety of ways, constitute the most common form of technical analysis. In contrast to the moving average method, it is not possible to determine a unique definition that would encompass all trend crossing rules. The notion of a moving average immediately suggests a mathematical formulation, whereas trend crossings appear to be based on arbitrary hand-drawn trends in charts illustrating historical data. Figure 19–1 displays an example. The main idea behind trend crossing methods is to determine two linear trends, one above, the other below, that would envelop the portion of the data observed since the last turning point. Then, upcrossings (downcrossings) of the upper (lower) envelope are taken as signals of market strength (weakness).

It is clear that all trend lines that envelop observed data can be defined by using only two extrema of the portion of the series under consideration. In order to obtain an upper envelope, the two highest local maxima are used. Two lowest local minima define, similarly, a lower envelope. Thus, the theory of local minima (maxima) of time series will play an important role in investigating this type of technical analysis.

I first show that most signals generated using trend lines are not Markov times. Let t_1 and t_0 be the times of onset of the two lowest (highest) local minima (maxima) of X_t during the period $(\tau_{i-1}, t]$, where τ_{i-1} is assumed to be known. Let X_1 and X_0 be the values of these minima (maxima). Consider the trend line $T(t)$,

$$T(t) = [(X_1 - X_0)/(t_1 - t_0)](t) + [(X_0 t_1 - X_1 t_0)/(t_1 - t_0)], \qquad (5)$$

for $t_1 > t_0 > \tau_{i-1}$. This function defines a straight line that goes through the two lowest (highest) local minima (maxima) observed during the interval (τ_{i-1}, t). As in the previous case, we obtain the times $\{\tau_i\}$ using

$$Z_t = X_t - T(t), \qquad (6)$$

and

$$\tau_i = \inf_t \{t : t > \tau_{i-1}, Z_t Z_{t-1} < 0\}. \qquad (7)$$

I now show that the times $\{\tau_i\}$ generated by this algorithm will not be Markov times.

It is clear that if the Z_t defined by (6) is I_t-measurable, and if we adopted the rule (7) to determine the $\{\tau_i\}$, then this would be the first entry in the interval $[0, \infty)$ by an I_t-measurable random variable, and the τ_i would be Markov times. But it turns out that, in general, Z_t is not I_t-measurable since t_1 and t_0 are never specified as the times of onset of the first two (or the nth) local minima (maxima) during $\tau_{i-1} < t$. In practice, the t_0 and t_1 are simply said to be two lowest (highest) local minima (maxima) that occur after some predetermined time τ_{i-1}. But such an event is not I_t-measurable since, before it can be decided whether a local maxima is highest or second highest, one needs to know the levels of subsequent maxima. Figure 19–4 illustrates this point. None of the trend lines shown here utilize the first two local maxima in determining the $T(t)$. There were several local maxima between the selected t_1 and t_0, and these were ignored in obtaining the trend lines of Figure 19–4. Two of these are shown on Figure 19–4 as dotted lines.

Thus we see that trend crossing techniques will not generate Markov times unless one specifies an I_t-measurable mechanism for ignoring the local minima (maxima) between t_1 and t_0.

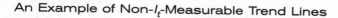

FIGURE 19-4

An Example of Non-I_t-Measurable Trend Lines

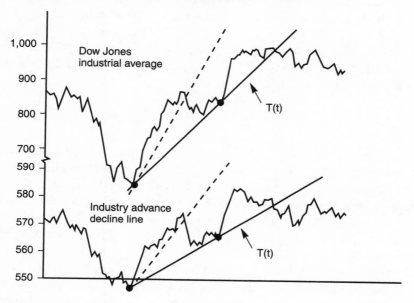

Characterization of Patterns

The third class of procedures used by technical analysts utilizes the occurrence of various patterns to issue signals. Some of these patterns are shown in Figures 19–3a–c. The theorem above suggests that, if these patterns are well-defined signals of upcoming events, one should be able to formulate them as first entries of an I_t-measurable random process in a set $A \in R$. In this chapter, the two most popular patterns are considered, namely, "triangles" and "head and shoulders." I first show that, in principle, these patterns can be formally defined using particular sequences of local minima and maxima. Second, I claim that, in their current formulation, these patterns are not I_t-measurable events.

An example of head and shoulders is shown in figure 19–3a. According to this figure, a head and shoulders pattern is observed whenever the trendlines that envelop the date behave as a step function: two sets of local minima with similar heights, separated by some higher local minima during the interval (τ_{i-1}, t). Let the mutually exclusive sets,

$$\{t_0 < \ldots < t_k\}, \quad \{t_{k+1} < \ldots < t_m\}, \quad \{t_{m+1} < \ldots < t_n < t\}, \quad (8)$$

denote the times of onset of three sets of (lowest) consecutive local minima up to time t. To obtain a head and shoulders pattern, the heights of the local minima in the first and third sets must be (approximately) the same, say M^*. In addition, the levels of the local minima in the second set must be significantly higher, say M^{**}. Then a (sell) signal is issued the first time X_t falls below M^* once such a pattern takes shape. That is to say,

$$\tau_i = \inf_t \{X_t < M^*, t > t_n).$$

Since $\{\tau_i < t, i = 1, \ldots, k\}$, the local minima defined in (8) are I_t-measurable. Hence an event describing head and shoulders becomes I_t-measurable once a formal way of subdividing the three sets of local extrema shown in (8) is selected. Such criterion is needed in order to decide when the local minima in the middle exceed significantly the local minima in the first and third sets. This requires an a priori selection of a lower bound on the difference $M^{**} - M^*$, although the levels of M^* and M^{**} need not be specified individually. If all these conditions are met, a head and shoulders pattern becomes I_t-measurable.

This construction shows that actual signals generated using observed head and shoulders patterns are not Markov times. For example, in Figure 19–3, the first occurrence of such an event is illustrated by the line AB rather than the suggested head and shoulders pattern CD selected by technicians. The only way one would select CD is if one anticipated that a local minimum such as D would occur at time t. Accordingly, in this example, the decision of whether $\tau = t$ or not depends on future values of the underlying series. The stopping time illustrated in Figure 19–3a cannot be a Markov time.

Further, head and shoulders patterns defined formally as above are likely to be probability-zero events if one insists that the minima in the first and second sets have the same height M^*. Conversely, removing this requirement will impose further a priori restrictions on the sets of local minima shown in (8).

Figure 19–3b illustrates a triangle. In principle, this pattern can also be defined using consecutive local minima and maxima. To generate such a triangle, consecutive local maxima have to be in descending, and consecutive local minima in ascending order. Thus let

$$\{t_{\max,1} < \ldots < t_{\max,k}\} \text{ and } \{\text{Max}_1 > \text{Max}_2 > \ldots > \text{Max}_k\} \quad (9)$$

represent the times of onset and the heights of k consecutive local maxima of X_t during $\tau_{i-1} < t$. Similarly, let $\{t_{\min,1} < \ldots < t_{\min,k}\}$ and $\{\text{Min}_1 < \ldots < \text{Min}_k\}$ be the times of onset and heights of k lowest local minima during the same period. Then, a buy or sell signal is generated as soon as observed X_t exceeds the last local maxima or falls below the latest local minima (see Figure 19–3b). More precisely,

$$\tau_i = \inf_t \{\text{Max}_1 > \ldots > \text{Max}_k < X_t \text{ or Min}_1 < \ldots < \text{Min}_k > X_t\}, \quad (10)$$

for $\tau_{i-1} < t$.

Clearly, this is an I_t-measurable event, hence a prediction method using triangles defined this way will generate Markov times. Yet this does not mean that, in practice, the signals generated using triangles are nonanticipatory. In fact, what makes the above signals I_t-measurable is the a priori specification of the parameter k, namely, the number of minima or maxima that one has to observe before the crossing occurs. If this information is omitted from the definition, the use of triangles will cease to generate Markov times. Without this parameter, even two consecutive local extrema can generate a triangle. Clearly, this is not what technical analysts have in mind, as shown in Figure 19–3b. If two extrema are not sufficient, then how may does one need? Obviously, the answer to these questions necessitates a priori selection of some parameter such as k.

Finally, in Figure 19–3c, we show another pattern, namely gaps in daily price ranges. In contrast to other patterns, the use of gaps does generate Markov times since a signal is issued the first time three consecutive gaps are observed. This constitutes a first entry into an interval and leads to Markov times.

A CRITERION ON PRACTICAL USE

Suppose a method of technical analysis is known to generate Markov times $\{\tau_i\}$ as signals of market turning points. A forecaster may, in addition, want to know the size of the probability $p(\tau_i < \infty)$, $i = 1, 2, \ldots$ before investing resources in applying this rule. Indeed, if this probability is less than one, then the rule may never give a signal. This may be uneconomical. Yet, in terms of formal statistical criteria, there is nothing wrong with a Markov time that fails to be finite. In this section, I discuss which categories of technical analysis are likely to yield finite Markov times.

Definition

We say that a Markov time τ is *finite* if

$$P(\tau < \infty) = 1. \tag{11}$$

It is clear that a Markov time that is not finite may fail to be a financial rewarding method of forecasting since it may never give a positive or negative signal in spite of being well defined.

It turns out that only in very few cases the $\{\tau_i\}$ generated by technical analysis will be finite, hence usable, in the sense above. The major exception is the method of moving averages. I show below the conditions under which the moving average method generates finite Markov times.

PROPOSITION 1. If the observed process $\{X_t\}$ is stationary and m-dependent, all moving average methods characterized by (3)–(4) generate finite Markov times.

Proof. Let Z_t be given by (3). If X_t is stationary, then Z_t and $Z_t Z_{t-1}$ are stationary (e.g., Breiman 1968, proposition 6.6). Also note that, due to stationarity $E[Z_t] = 0$, hence $0 < P(Z_t \geq 0) < 1$, unless $Z_t = 0$ almost surely. Let

$$Y_t = Z_t Z_{t-1}, \quad t = 0, 1 \ldots .$$

Clearly, $P(Y_t \geq 0) < 1$. Now, I apply the theorem provided in the Appendix. Consider

$$P(Y_t \leq 0, \text{ at least once for } t \leq n) = 1 - P(Y_0 > 0, Y_1 > 0, \ldots Y_n > 0).$$

The theorem in the Appendix requires this probability be one, as n goes to infinity. To show that this is indeed true, note that, if X_t is m-dependent, the Y_t's sufficiently apart will also be independent. Thus, select an integer u so that Y_t and Y_{t+u} are independent. We utilize such Y_t's sufficiently apart to write, for large n,

$$P(Y_0 > 0, \ Y_1 > 0, \ldots Y_n > 0) \leq P(Y_0 > 0)P(Y_u > 0) \ldots P(Y_{ku} > 0)$$
$$\leq P(Y_0 > 0)^k$$

by stationarity and m-dependence. As we let k $\to \infty$,

$$P(Y_0 > 0)^k \to 0,$$

since $P(Y_0 > 0) < 1$, as shown above. Thus,

$$P(Y_n \leq 0 \text{ at least once}) = 1.$$

Hence, all conditions of the theorem supplied in the Appendix are satisfied and Markov times $\tau_1, \tau_2, \ldots, \tau_n$ are finite.

Note that assumptions such as stationarity and mixing, a simple form of which is m-dependence, are needed to obtain this result. This might seem unnecessary, but without similar assumptions, one cannot guarantee the finiteness of these Markov times. Indeed, if the process X_t is explosive enough, then a moving average method may not generate finite Markov times.[4]

One implication of this is that trend crossing methods of technical analysis might not always yield finite Markov times—even after a precise definition is adopted. To illustrate this, note that a trend line $T(s)$ such as the one shown in Figure 19–5, will admit the representation,

$$T(s) = a_t + b_t s \quad s > t, \tag{12}$$

where a_t and $b_t > 0$ are I_t-measurable intercept and slope. Now, the difference,

$$D_s = X_s - a_t - b_t s, \quad s > t,$$

is clearly not stationary. So the assumptions of proposition 1 are not satisfied for $D_s, s > t$. Hence, even with stationary and m-dependent $\{X_t\}$ as s goes to infinity, $P(X_s - a_t - b_t s \leq 0)$ may equal one, and X_s may never cross the trend line $T(s)$ again. Under these conditions, implied Markov times may be infinite even though they are well defined. For example, this may be the case if X_t is given by

$$X_t = \epsilon_t + .5\epsilon_{t-1}$$

where the distribution of the independently and identically distributed (i.i.d) errors $\{\epsilon_t\}$ has finite support:

$$P(\epsilon_t \geq \alpha) = 0 \quad 0 < \alpha < \infty.$$

REMARK. Note that, even if a rule generates signals that are finite with high probability, with, say, $P(\tau_i < \infty) = .9$, this may still create major problems for practical users. In fact, such a probability implies that one out of every 10 signals may be infinite—assuming that the signals are sufficiently apart, and that they are not correlated. For a forecaster working in real time, a long waiting period then implies either a large (but finite) τ_i or, with smaller probability, an outcome where no signal will be given. In this latter case, the forecaster should switch to other rules. Since technical analysis never specifies how one rule should be abandoned in favor of others, the requirement that $P(\tau_i < \infty) = 1$ is less trivial than it seems at the outset.

FIGURE 19–5

An Infinite Markov Time

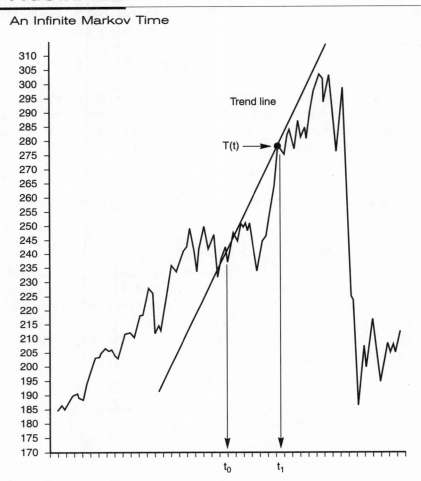

PREDICTIVE POWER OF TECHNICAL ANALYSIS

The fact that some methods of technical analysis admit a formal definition is important. Yet well-defined sequences of finite Markov times $\{\tau_i\}$ may still have no predictive value. Thus, the next question is, Under what conditions (if any) would the well-defined procedures of technical analysis be useful in prediction over and above the standard econometric models?

There are two results. The first deals with the usefulness of technical analysis under the assumption that observed data can be characterized as linear processes. I adopt the following definition of linearity.

Definition

A process $\{X_t\}$, $E[X_t] < \infty$ is said to be linear, or has the linear regression property, if, for $s \geq 0$,

$$E[X_{t+s}|X_{t-1}, X_{t-2}, \ldots, X_{t-k}] = \alpha_1 X_{t-1} + \ldots + \alpha_k X_{t-k}.$$

That is, the process is linear if expectations of X_t given finite past X's are linear in the latter. In particular, Gaussian processes are linear. In fact, the class of processes that have the linearity property is identical to the sub-Gaussian processes [Hardin (1982)]. However, our definition of linearity is not identical to the one given in Hardin (1982), who does not discriminate between past and future X's as conditioning factors.

REMARK. It is interesting to note that the definition of linearity that we have here is not equivalent to $E[X_t|X_{t-1}, X_{t-2}, X_{t-3} \ldots\}$ being a linear combination of past X_t's. It is possible to construct finite moving average (MA) processes with infinite autoregressive representations, that are not linear according to the definition used here.[5]

I now show that nonlinearity of asset prices is a necessary condition for the usefulness of technical analysis.

PROPOSITION 2. If the X_t process is linear in the sense above, then no sequence of Markov times obtained from a finite history of $\{X_t\}$ can be useful in prediction over and above (vector) autoregressions.

Proof. If $\{\tau_i\}$ are Markov times obtained from a finite history of $\{X_t\}$, they must be measurable with respect to $\{X_t, X_{t-1}, \ldots, X_{t-k}\}$, some finite k. This means that

$$E[X_{t+s}|\{X_t, X_{t-1}, \ldots, X_{t-k}\}, \{\tau_i : \tau_i < t\}]$$
$$= E[X_{t+s}|\{X_t, X_{t-1}, \ldots, X_{t-k}\}]$$
$$= \alpha_0 X_t + \alpha_1 X_{t-1} + \ldots + \alpha_k X_{t-k},$$

due to the linearity of $\{X_t\}$.

This proposition may have important implications for technical analysis. First of all, it can be seen that one necessary condition for the usefulness of any technical analysis rule is the requirement that asset prices be nonlinear in the sense of the definition above. For example, if a rule is well defined and yet stock prices are Gaussian, then, due to proposition 2, we immediately know that the rule is useless as a prediction technique. If, however, there is some evidence that stock prices are nonlinear, technical analysis may be useful in prediction—that is, it may be a simple way of taking such nonlinearities into account. Under these conditions, the question of whether technical analysis rules have any predictive power becomes an empirical issue.

Recent work such as Hinich and Patterson (1985) and Diebold (1989) provide evidence on the nonlinearity of data from financial markets. Yet because notions of linearity and nonlinearity used in these papers and here are not identical, these empirical results do not necessarily imply that there are forms of technical analysis useful in prediction. For example, Diebold (1989) shows that taking nonlinearities into consideration does not improve forecasts of exchange rates, although there appears to be a great deal of evidence that these latter are nonlinear.

Since Martingales are linear processes, a corollary to proposition 2 is the following:

COROLLARY. If the X_t process is a Martingale, then no sequence of finite Markov times $\{\tau_i\}$, calculated from a finite history of $\{X_t\}$, can be useful in prediction over and above linear regressions.

The point is that, if some technical analysis rules are indeed useful in prediction, then this should rule out a Martingale representation for the series under consideration. Using these propositions we provide some empirical results.

Empirical Results. To illustrate how one can test the predictive value of technical analysis, I select the method claimed to work the best according to participants in financial markets. "Although technical analysts caution that investors should consider a variety of factors in trying to discern the market's direction, they say the single, clearest factor is probably the 150-day moving average. History has shown that when the (Dow-Jones) index rises decisively above its moving average the market is likely to continue on an upward trend. When it is below the average it is a bearish signal."[6]

The moving average method was one of the few rules that generated Markov times. Also, these Markov times were easy to quantify. This, plus one other consideration, made me choose stock prices as the X_t in (3), and the 150-day moving average as the $X_t{}^*$. We then use the algorithm in (4) to obtain sequence of Markov times $\{\tau_i\}$. The last consideration for making these selections was the availability of a long sample for the Dow-Jones index. In fact, when using Dow-Jones industrials it is possible to go all the way to 1792 and work with almost a 200-year-long monthly data series. This greatly facilitates investigating the predictive power of technical analysis since on-and-off prediction rules are likely to yield relatively few signals compared to regular monthly data.

Proposition 2 and the corollary that follows it provide the necessary framework to do the empirical work. According to these, we need to show that, given a long autoregression, the addition of Markov times to the right-hand side does not improve forecasts of Dow-Jones industrials. If this is the case, then the rule in question will have no predictive value.

Thus I let

$$X_{t+\mu} = \sum_{i=1}^{k}\alpha_i X_{t-i} + \sum_{i=1}^{n}\beta_i D_{t-i} + \epsilon_{t+\mu} \quad \mu > 0, \; n < k, \tag{13}$$

where

$$D_t = \begin{cases} 1 \text{ if } X_t > X_t^* \text{ has occurred at } t \text{ given } X_{t-1} < X_{t-1}^*, \\ -1 \text{ if } X_t < X_t^* \text{ has occurred at } t \text{ given } X_{t-1} > X_{t-1}^*, \\ 0 \text{ otherwise}, \end{cases}$$

and where the disturbances $\{\epsilon_t\}$ form an innovation sequence with respect to the finite history of X_t,

$$E[\epsilon_{t+\mu}|X_{t-1}, \ldots, X_{t-k}] = 0.$$

According to this, $\epsilon_{t+\mu}$ measures all unpredictable events between t and $t + \mu$. The $\{\beta_i\}$ represents the contribution of the Markov times $\{\tau i\}$ in explaining $X_{t+\mu}$ over and above the own past of the series. To the extent the D_t's are obtained from $\{X_{t-1}, \ldots, X_{t-k}\}$, they should have no contribution to forecasting $X_{t+\mu}$ beyond the finite history of X_t if this latter is a linear process.

There is an important point that concerns inference with equation (13). Note that (13) requires a sufficiently long autoregressive component (i.e., a large k). Otherwise, if k is small, then some D_{t-i}'s may become significant simply because they are calculated from a more distant past of $\{X_t\}$.

The parameter μ in (13) determines how many periods ahead one is forecasting. It captures the claim that the moving average method detects changes in long-run trends, and that it is not necessary useful for 1-period-ahead forecasts. Hence the value of μ should be selected as greater than 1 or 2 months. In the empirical work reported below, I selected μ (arbitrarily) as 12 months. The results remain qualitatively similar for μ greater than 12. Inference with the equation shown in (13) appears to be straightforward at the outset. However, if $\mu > 1$, the errors of equation (13) will be serially correlated, and this needs to be taken into account. In fact, the error structure in these equations will always be given by a $(\mu - 1)$th-order MA process:

$$\epsilon_t = v_t + a_1 v_{t-1} + a_2 v_{t-2} + a_3 v_{t-3} + \ldots + a_{\mu-1} v_{t-\mu-1}, \tag{14}$$

where the $\{v_t\}$ are the innovations in the X_t process.

I corrected for the serial correlation shown in (14) using Hannan's efficient procedure. In fact, the $\{\epsilon_t\}$ can be consistently estimated by applying ordinary least squares to (13). The periodogram of these (first-stage) residuals is then calculated. The Fourier transform of X_t is divided by the corresponding entries of the square root of the periodogram of residuals. This series is then transformed back to the time domain. Equation (13) is estimated with these transformed data.

Empirical results are provided in Tables 19–1 to 19–3. The results are interesting. The F-tests on the D_t are insignificant for the subperiods 1795–1851, and 1852–1910. However, they are highly significate for the period 1911–76. Thus the particular moving average rule of 150 days seems to have a significant predictive power for the latter part of the sample. It is interesting to note that any general belief by market participants that such a rule is useful would be self-fulfilling and would lead to significant $\{\tau_i\}$.

For this last period, all lags of the dummy variable that indicates buy (+1), sell (−1), and no action (0) signals are significant. Furthermore, the signs are in the right direction, in that they are all positive. It is also interesting to note that the coefficients of the dummy variable have a nice reverse V shape, with the peak occurring at lag 23 (Table 19–1).

Hence, the moving average method does seem to have some predictive value beyond the own lags of Dow-Jones industrials. In fact, the results displayed in these tables remained qualitatively similar when different values were used for μ, except for $\mu = 1$, where the 150-day moving average turned out to be insignificant in all equations.[7]

CONCLUSIONS

This chapter discussed some criteria that one can apply in evaluating the set of ad hoc prediction rules widely used in financial markets and generally referred to as technical analysis. I showed that a few of these rules generate well-defined techniques of forecasting. Under the hypothesis, economic time series are Gaussian, and even well-defined rules were shown to be useless in prediction.

At the same time, the discussion indicated that if the processes under consideration were nonlinear, then the rules of technical analysis might capture some information ignored by Wiener-Kolmogorov prediction theory.

Tests done using the Dow-Jones industrials for 1911-76 suggested that this may indeed be the case for the moving average rule.

TABLE 19–1

Dow-Jones Industrials, 1792:1-1851:12

Label and Lag	Coefficient	t-statistic
Dow Jones industrials:		
18	.83	3.8
19	−.14	−.45
20	.03	.05
21	.02	.03
22	.03	.05
23	−.03	−.09
24	−.05	−.15
25	−.01	−.04
26	.01	.04
27	−.05	−.15
28	.01	.05
29	.01	.05
30	−.05	−.15
31	.01	.04
32	.26	1.34
Dummy:		
18	.45	1.16
19	.63	1.39
20	.67	1.35
21	.58	.92
22	.61	1.06
23	.50	.71
24	.32	.69
Constant	1.51	7.12

NOTE.—R^2 = .73; sum of square residuals = 3592; F-statistic = .46. 1792:1 = January 1792.

TABLE 19–2

Dow-Jones Industrials, 1852:12–1910:12

Label and Lag	Coefficient	t-statistic
Dow Jones industrials:		
18	.86	4.60
19	.00	.01
20	−.08	−.31
21	.04	.17
22	−.21	−.80
23	−.09	−.34
24	.08	.29
25	−.06	−.20
26	−.04	−.16
27	.07	.27
28	−.16	−.66
29	−.06	−.24
30	.06	.23
31	−.01	−.02
32	.55	3.15
Dummy:		
18	.53	.67
19	.85	1.0
20	1.1	1.3
21	1.5	1.9
22	1.9	2.4
23	1.8	2.3
24	1.2	1.8
Constant	4.1	5.4

NOTE.—R^2 = .72; sum of square residuals = 36120.202; F-statistic = .050330. 1852:12 = December 1852.

TABLE 19-3

Dow-Jones Industrials, 1911: 1-1976:12

Label and Lag	Coefficient	t-statistic
Dow Jones industrials:		
18	.19	2.34
19	−.04	−.39
20	.01	.05
21	.18	1.36
22	.05	.34
23	.04	.25
24	.19	1.31
25	.12	.78
26	.01	.04
27	.09	.61
28	.02	.13
29	.07	.48
30	.02	.14
31	−.01	−.05
32	.09	1.11
Dummy:		
18	26.9	2.9
19	28.3	2.9
20	28.4	2.9
21	28.2	2.9
22	30.1	3.1
23	30.8	3.2
24	21.8	2.4
Constant	19.6	4.6

NOTE.—R^2 = .91; sum of square residuals = 6521516; F-statistic = 3.71. 1911:1 = January 1911.

APPENDIX

PROPOSITION (Breiman 1968). Let the process $\{Y_t\}$ be stationary, such that

$$P(Y_n \geq 0 \text{ at least once}) = 1;$$

then the τ_i $I = 1, 2,...$are finite almost surely and on the sample space $\{w: Y_0 \geq 0\}$ they form a stationary sequence under the probability $p(\cdot|Y_0 \geq 0$, and

$$E[\tau_1|Y_0 \geq 0] = 1/p(Y_0 \geq 0).$$

BIBLIOGRAPHY

Breiman, L. *Probability*. Reading, Mass.: Addison-Wesley, 1968.

Brockett, P. L., M. L. Hinich, and D. Patterson. Bispectral based tests for the detection of Gaussianity and linearity in time series. Manuscript. University of Texas at Austin, 1985.

Diebold, F., and J. M. Nason. Nonparametric exchange rate prediction? Manuscript. Washington, D.C.; Federal Reserve Board of Governors, 1989.

Granger, C. W., and A. Andersen. *An Introduction to Bilinear Time Series Models*. Göttingen; Vandenhoeck & Ruprecht, 1978.

Hardin, C. D. On the linearity of regressions. *Zeitschrift fur Wahrscheinlichkeits-theorie* 61 1982, pp. 291–302.

Hinich, M. L., and D. M. Patterson. Evidence of nonlinearity in daily stock returns. *Journal of Business and Economic Statistics* 3 (January 1985) pp. 69–77.

Leadbetter, M. R., G. Lindgren, and H. Rootzen. *Extremes and Related Properties of Random Sequences and Processes*. New York: Springer-Verlag, 1983.

Pring, M. J. *Technical Analysis Explained*. New York: McGraw-Hill, 1980.

Rhea, R. *Dow Theory*. New York: Barron's, 1932.

Shiryayev, I. *Probability*. New York: Springer-Verlag, 1985.

Tong. H. *Threshold Models in Non-linear Time Series Analysis*. New York: Springer-Verlag, 1983.

ENDNOTES

1. The popularity of technical analysis admits a second explanation. If markets are efficient, asset prices would behave (approximately) as Martingales. Then, VARs would yield trivial-looking forecasts, such as $\{X_{t+\tau} = X_t, \tau = 1, 2 \ldots\}$. Finding it unattractive to report such forecasts that remain constant over the forecasting horizon, traders might use (irrationally) techniques that give them nontrivial-looking forecasts, even though they are suboptimal. This interpretation requires that financial markets continue to allocate significant resources on a practice that has negative returns.

2. A recent example of the popularity of technical analysis is the following, "Starting today The *New York Times* will publish a comprehensive three-column market chart every Saturday. . . . History has shown that when the S&P index rises decisively above its (moving) average the market is likely to continue on an upward trend. When it is below the average that is a bearish signal." [*New York Times*, March 11, 1988]

3. Pring (1980), p. 2.

4. Here is an example provided by the referee. Let X_t be generated by an explosive AR(1) model:

$$X_t = \beta X_{t-1} + \epsilon_t, \quad t = 1, 2, \ldots$$

where $\beta > 2$, and ϵ_t are independently and identically distributed random variables with uniform distribution over the interval $[-1, 1]$. Note that the event $E = \{X_t$ is always larger than 1 and tends to $\infty\}$ has positive probability. Now, consider two moving averages with 1 and 2 terms, respectively. Then Z_t defined by formula (3) is equivalent to

$$Z_t = (1/2)[(\beta - 1)X_{t-1} + \epsilon_t].$$

With this Z_t, we have $\tau = \infty$ on the event E.

5. An interesting example provided by the referee is the following: Let ϵ_t be i.i.d. and

$$\epsilon_t = \begin{cases} -1 \text{ with probability } 2/3 \\ \\ 2 \text{ with probability } 1/3. \end{cases}$$

Construct the process X_t using

$$X_t = \epsilon_t + .5\epsilon_{t-1}.$$

Clearly, X_t has an infinite autoregressive representation, hence, is a linear combination of all past X_t's. Yet $E[X_t|X_{t-1}]$ cannot be linear in X_{t-1}. To see this, note that $E[X_t|X_{t-1}=0]$ can be directly calculated to be $-1/2$, yet if $E[X_t|X_{t-1}=0]$ were linear to X_{t-1} in the sense of our definition, $E[X_t|X_{t-1}=0]$ would have to equal zero. This contradiction implies that the X_t process cannot have a linear regression property as defined here.

6. *The New York Times* (March 11, 1988).

7. Estimates of the same equation with $\mu = 1$ yields no significant lags for the dummy variable in consideration. This supports the contention that the method predicts longer-run behavior of the X_t.

CHAPTER 20

MANAGEMENT SUMMARY

Title: "Trading Futures Using a Channel Rule: A Study of the Predictive Power of Technical Analysis with Currency Examples"

Publication: *Journal of Futures Markets* 14, No. 2, pp. 215–35 (1994).

Author: Stephen J. Taylor, Lancaster University, England

Data: Daily futures prices for the German Mark, Swiss Franc, Japanese Yen, and British Pound from 1981–87.

Synopsis: A simple channel rule was tested to determine if the systematic use of technical analysis techniques could produce profits in the currency markets. The author constructed an ARIMA model to replicate the price action of currency futures. He found that the channel rule was a better predictor of price movements than a traditional ARIMA prediction method, and that the channel rule produced surprisingly robust results at many different lookback periods.

Trading Futures Using a Channel Rule: A Study of the Predictive Power of Technical Analysis with Currency Examples

Stephen J. Taylor
Professor of Finance at Lancaster University, England

INTRODUCTION

The channel rule of Irwin and Uhrig (1984) is a simple, technical trading rule. A long futures position is replaced by a short position when the price is less than the minimum price during the preceding L days. Likewise, a short futures position is replaced by a long position when the price is more than the maximum price during the preceding L days. The integer L is the only parameter. This chapter uses theoretical methods to show that the channel rule can be surprisingly profitable when market prices almost follow random walks. The adjective *channel* here refers to two lines drawn parallel to the time-axis, one through the minimum closing price during the preceding L days and the other through the maximum closing price. Only closing prices are considered in this chapter. All intra-day prices are ignored when channels are defined and decisions made.

 Lukac, Brorsen, and Irwin (1986, 1988) found that the channel rule performed best in their ex ante study of several technical trading systems, including the filter rule of Alexander (1961). They concluded that the channel rule should be preferred in academic studies of futures trading and market efficiency. Taylor (1992a) recently showed that the channel rule gives remarkably profitable results (after transactions costs) for ex ante currency futures trades, from December 1981 to November 1987. The channel rule outperformed decision rules based upon ARIMA predictions during this period. A theory of short-run disequilibrium, developed by Beja and Goldman (1980) and discussed by Lukac, Brorsen, and Irwin (1988), might explain the success of trend-following systems such as the channel rule.

The prediction rules, called technical analysis by Neftci (1991), include rules like the channel rule. Neftci (1991, p. 550) remarked: "To the best of my knowledge, there is no formal study of the predictive power of technical analysis." Presumably Neftci considered that the many published trading rule studies lacked a formal prediction methodology, although several studies apply a rigorous methodology for testing the efficient market hypothesis. See, for example, Sweeney (1986); Lukac, Brorsen, and Irwin (1988); Lukac and Brorsen (1990); and Taylor (1992a). The recent article by Brock, Lakonishok, and LeBaron (1992) shows that technical trading rules have predictive power for the Dow Jones Index.

The major contribution of this study is a theoretical explanation of why the channel rule can be successful compared with ARIMA decision rules when futures prices do not follow random walks. It is shown that when prices are generated by a particular ARIMA(1,1,1) model there are several values of L for which the channel rule correctly identifies the sign of conditional expected returns with probability well above 0.5. The probabilities attained by the channel rule are close to the best possible probabilities given by ARIMA predictions. The expected payoff from the channel rule as a function of L is shown to vary little in a fairly wide interval around the optimal value. The channel rule appears to do well in ex ante studies because it has a high probability of selecting a value for the single parameter L within a satisfactory interval even when very few contracts are available to guide the choice. Appropriate ARIMA rules, however, usually require the estimation of at least one AR and one MA parameter [Taylor (1988, 1992b)].

The next section provides definitions of the gross and net payoffs from the channel rule, which are used throughout the chapter. The third section describes an ARIMA(1,1,1) model that can give a good description of the futures price process at some markets. The fourth and fifth sections give the results of Monte Carlo studies of the channel rule, showing how expected payoffs vary with L and the number of daily futures prices available when Choosing L. The sixth section summarizes new results for currency futures trades using the channel rule applied to daily closing prices.

PAYOFFS FROM CHANNEL RULE TRADES

Assumptions

The channel rule alternates between long and short futures positions and is never neutral. A method for summarizing the net payoff from a set of decisions for a single futures contract has been described in Taylor (1988, 1992a) and this method is used throughout this chapter. Several assumptions are made about a representative trader. First, the trader can deposit U.S. Treasury bills as margin. Second, the futures price of goods traded equals a particular T-bill price whenever a trade commences. Losses during a trade can only exceed the price of the margin security if a short position is taken and the futures price more than doubles. Third, transaction costs are taken to be a constant proportion of the futures price of goods traded.

The investment used to finance futures trades is assumed to be the capital required to purchase the T-bill, which is used as a margin security. All definitions of the investment capital required for futures trading are arbitrary to some degree. An alternative definition might define the investment to be the maximum drawdown but a rigorous ex ante definition of the maximum is problematic.

Measuring Trading Performance

First, suppose the channel rule generates N trades in some futures contract between times t_1 and t_2, with trade j begun at the price P_j and concluded at Q_j. The times t_1 and t_2 are defined ex ante. To distinguish between long and short positions, let $\pi_j = 1$ for the former and $\tau_j = -1$ for the latter.

Second, suppose there is a T-bill that trades at both times t_1 and t_2. Let B_1 be the price of the T-bill at time t_1 and let one futures contract be for F units of the relevant goods. It is assumed that when trade j commences, the quantity traded is $B_1/(FP_j)$ contracts. Thus B_1 is both the dollar price of the contracts when any trade starts and the price of the T-bill when the first trade commences.

Third, suppose transaction costs for one round-trip in these contracts are a constant proportion c of B_1.

The *gross payoff* from the N trades is defined to be:

$$G = \sum_{j=1}^{N} \pi_j \frac{(Q_j - P_j)}{P_j} \tag{1}$$

The *net payoff* from the trades is defined to be

$$R = G - Nc \tag{2}$$

For example, if

1. t_1 is May 31st when a long position is commenced at 5000,
2. The long position is reversed to short at 5100 on July 10th, and
3. The short position is closed out at 5049 on November 30th, which is t_2, then $N = 2$, $\pi_1 = 1$, $\pi_2 = -1$ and G is

$(5100 - 5000)/5000 - (5049 - 5100)/5100 = 0.03$ or 3 percent

When the proportional trading cost c is 0.2 percent the value of R is 2.6 percent.

The quantity R is simply the aggregate net trading profit divided by the futures price of goods at the commencement of trades. As the initial futures price of goods is the price of the T-bill at time t_1, it follows that R equals the return on capital used to purchase a T-bill, which is then used as margin collateral for the futures trades minus the return when an identical T-bill is purchased and not used as collateral. This interpretation allows R to be called an *excess return*. Further details are given in Taylor (1988, 1992a) where the relationship between return and risk is also discussed in a general portfolio context.

Currency Results to November 1987

The average value of R is 3.93 percent over 6 months for ex ante pound, mark, Swiss franc, and yen channel rule trades using daily futures closing prices from December 1981 to November 1987, with trading costs c equal to 0.2 percent per trade [Taylor (1992a), Table 1]. All trades are executed at the close. No intraday prices are considered. The assumed average trading cost is slightly more than \$100 per contract, which is more than the total trading costs of a typical retail customer.

The channel parameter L is optimized over eight June and December contracts up to November 1981 to obtain a value for trading the June 1982 contract; then L is optimized again but over nine contracts to obtain a value to trade the December 1982 contract, etc. with separate optimizations for each currency. Averaging R across currencies gives one average value for each of the 12 June and December delivery months from June 1982 until December 1987. From these 12 averages the figure above of 3.93 percent is computed. The null hypothesis that the average excess return is zero is rejected at the 1 percent significance level. Taylor (1992a) claims that risk cannot explain the significant average value of R. The high average value of R provides the motivation for the research reported in this chapter.

Decisions based upon ARIMA decision rules are less successful than those generated by the channel rule although the differences in performance between these rules are not statistically significant.

A PRICE MODEL FOR MONTE CARLO SIMULATIONS

To learn more about why the channel rule has the potential to give net payoffs whose expectations are positive, it is necessary to perform Monte Carlo simulations. The simulations require a time series model for daily futures prices that is consistent with the statistical evidence about prices. Daily changes in futures prices are known to be almost random and to display conditional heteroscedasticity. Consequently, a model is simulated that has very small positive correlations between price changes and also has changes in the conditional variances of price changes. As will be seen the small correlations are sufficient for the channel trading rule to obtain positive expected net returns.

The Model

Simulated futures prices f_t are obtained after first simulating logarithmic differences x_t defined by

$$x_t = \ln(f_t) - \ln(f_{t-1}) \tag{3}$$

The prices are given by $f_t = f_{t-1} \exp(x_t)$. The logarithmic differences x_t are called returns in this chapter, for convenience, even though capital is not necessary to trade futures. Futures prices would be a random walk if returns were uncorrelated at all lags; so $\mathrm{cor}(x_t, x_{t+\tau}) = 0$ for all positive τ. Positive dependence between returns will create trend effects in prices and the possibility of trading profits—a set of positive returns will be more likely than a set of negative returns to be followed by positive returns. Evidence for positive autocorrelation among exchange rate returns can be found in Hodrick and Srivastava (1987); Mark (1988); and Taylor (1986, 1992b).

Positive dependence at all lags can be obtained by letting returns be the sum of two stationary and independent processes, the first an AR(1) component μ_t and the second a white noise component e_t, thus:

$$x_t = \mu_t + e_t \tag{4}$$

$$\mu_t = p\mu_{t-1} + v_t, \quad 1 > p > 0 \tag{5}$$

and $\quad\quad \text{cor}(v_t, v_{t+\tau}) = \text{cor}(e_t, e_{t+\tau}) = 0, \quad \tau > 0 \tag{6}$

Then, for $\tau > 0$,

$$\text{cor}(x_t, x_{t+\tau}) = Ap^\tau, \quad A = \text{var}(\mu_t)/\text{var}(x_t) \tag{7}$$

The term μ_t can be interpreted in several ways. A risk premium interpretation is one possibility but the predictable component might be attributable to inefficient pricing. As prices are at least very like random walks, only values for A, which are almost zero, can be considered.

Returns are conditionally heteroscedastic for exchange rates, stocks, and many other assets; therefore, $h_t = \text{var}(x_t I_{t-1})$ is a function of past returns $I_{t-1} = \{x_{t-1}, x_{t-2}, \ldots\}$. Recent reviews of empirical evidence and appropriate model specifications can be found in Bollerslev, Chou, and Kroner (1992) and Taylor (1994). The residual e_t must display conditional heteroscedasticity. An interesting issue is whether or not μ_t also displays conditional heteroscedasticity. There is certainly evidence that the conditional autocorrelations of returns decrease toward zero as the conditional variance of returns increases [Taylor (1986) and Kim (1989) for currencies, and LeBaron (1992) and Sentana and Wadhwani (1990) for stocks]. These studies support models in which the conditional variance of μ_t is independent of past, present, and future residuals e_s.

A Gaussian AR(1) process is simulated for μ_t. This process has mean 0, variance $A\sigma^2$ and autoregressive parameter p. The simulated process for e_t has unconditional variance $(1 - A)\sigma^2$ so that the unconditional variance of returns x_t is equal to σ^2. To simulate conditional heteroscedasticity effects, it is supposed that e_t is the product of a stochastic volatility variable V_t and an i.i.d. term ϵ_t; thus,

$$e_t = V_t \epsilon_t, \tag{8}$$

and also

$$\ln(V_t) - \alpha = \phi[\ln(V_{t-1}) - \alpha] + \eta_t, \tag{9}$$

with

$$\epsilon_t \sim \text{i.i.d. } N(0, 1 - A), \quad \text{and} \quad \eta_t \sim \text{i.i.d. } N(0, \beta^2(1 - \phi^2)) \tag{10}$$

Similar equations have been specified in Taylor (1986, 1994); Chesney and Scott (1989); Melino and Turnbull (1990); and Harvey, Ruiz, and Shephard (1994). The innovation processes $\{v_t\}$, $\{\epsilon_t\}$ and $\{n_t\}$ are assumed to be stochastically independent.

Plausible Parameter Values

To perform the simulations it is necessary to select values for A, p, α, ß, and ϕ. All the values chosen in this study are intended to be reasonable for the prices of exchange rate futures observed daily. Values for A and p should then satisfy two criteria. First, A and p should be consistent with observed sample autocorrelations for daily currency returns. Following Taylor (1986, 1992b), this suggests selecting $0 < A \leq 0.04$ and $0.9 \leq p < 1$. Second, the values must give a first-lag autocorrelation for monthly sums of daily returns, which is consistent with the literature about returns from one-month forward contracts. Mark (1988) gives monthly, first-lag, auto-correlations that range from 0.08 to 0.19. Satisfactory choices for both criteria are given by $A = 0.02$ and $p = 0.95$. The maximum autocorrelation between returns is then a mere 0.019, but the sum of the autocorrelations over all positive lags is 0.38.

Choices for the remaining parameter, α, ß, and ϕ, can be made by estimating the parameters of stochastic volatility models from time series of daily exchange rates. The "base case" simulations use values motivated by the DM futures results in an early draft of Taylor (1994). These values are $\alpha = -5.15$, ß $= 0.422$, and $\phi = 0.973$.

It might at first be assumed that ARIMA decision rules would be better than the channel rule if prices are generated by the ARIMA(1,1,1) model implied by eqs. (3) to (10). The results of a small Monte Carlo study in Taylor (1992a) show that this is not so when the trading rule parameters are chosen by ex ante optimizations over a small number of simulated contracts. The average values of R are indistinguishable between the channel and ARIMA rules when 4 to 10 years of simulated daily prices are used to select decision and forecast parameters.

TRADING RESULTS AS A FUNCTION OF *L*

Assumptions

Daily prices f_t are simulated by using a reliable random number algorithm to generate values for the normally distributed residual terms in (5), (8), and (9). Every price should be interpreted as the price when the market closes. For each simulated contract, the time t runs from 1 to 189 (9 months, assuming 252 trading days in 1 year). Each contract is traded for 6 months, commencing when $t = 63$. The prices before time 63 are used only when they are needed for the calculation of minimum and maximum prices in an L-day period commencing before time 63. For a hypothetical June contract, one could associate $t = 1$, 63, and 189 with March 1st, May 31st, and November 30th.

The prices for one contract cannot be simulated without considering other contracts that would exist at the same time. Consequently, when 189 prices are generated for each of a series of contracts, each traded for 6 months, it is assumed that prices are equal across contracts during the overlapping 3-month periods, i.e., when $t < 64$, the price f_t for contract i equals the price f_{t+126} for contract $i - 1$; similarly, equal trend and volatility terms are assumed in (5) and (9). The assumption of perfect contemporaneous correlation between returns, across contracts, is satisfactory in a currency context because real market returns move closely together. They do this because futures returns are spot returns plus a relatively small term for changes in interest rates.

A long, short, or neutral position is held by the channel rule at the end of each day. Neutral positions only occur for days 1 to 62, inclusive, and day 189. The choice of a long or short position on day 63 is made by selecting the position that would have been held on day 189 for the previous contract if further trading in that contract is allowed. From day 64 onwards, the previous contract is ignored in all the calculations. Of course the trading positions from days 63 to 188 depend on the channel length L.

Expected Payoffs

The price model given in the third section is simulated for 500,000 contracts using the price parameter values given in that section. The financial consequences of channel rule trading decisions are calculated for all channel lengths L from 2 to 60 days inclusive. Table 20–1 summarizes the average gross payoff $\overline{G}$, the average number of trades $\overline{N}$, and the average net payoff $\overline{R}$ when transaction costs are 0.2 percent per round-trip.

The best choice of L is between 12 and 15, inclusive, when there are no transaction costs. The expected value of G is then estimated to be 3.81 percent. This estimate implies that when T-bills return 3 percent over 6 months, an average return of 6.81 percent can be obtained over 6 months

TABLE 20-1

Channel Trading Results as the Channel Length *L* Varies

L Days	$\bar{G}$ %	$\bar{N}$	$\bar{R}$ %	P %
2	2.44	35.68	−4.69	57.96
3	2.85	24.87	−2.12	59.35
4	3.13	19.08	−0.69	60.28
5	3.32	15.50	0.23	60.95
6	3.47	13.08	0.85	61.44
7	3.58	11.35	1.31	61.82
8	3.66	10.04	1.66	62.09
9	3.73	9.02	1.92	62.29
10	3.76	8.21	2.12	62.43
11	3.79	7.55	2.28	62.52
12	3.81	7.01	2.41	62.58
13	3.80	6.55	2.49	62.60
14	3.81	6.15	2.58	62.60
15	3.81	5.81	2.65	62.57
16	3.79	5.51	2.69	62.53
17	3.77	5.25	2.72	62.47
18	3.76	5.02	2.75	62.40
19	3.73	4.81	2.77	62.33
20	3.71	4.63	2.78	62.23
21	3.68	4.46	2.79	62.14
22	3.66	4.31	2.79	62.04
23	3.63	4.17	2.80	61.94
24	3.60	4.04	2.79	61.84
25	3.56	3.93	2.78	61.73
26	3.53	3.82	2.77	61.61
27	3.50	3.72	2.76	61.50
28	3.47	3.63	2.74	61.38
29	3.43	3.54	2.73	61.27
30	3.40	3.46	2.71	61.15
31	3.37	3.39	2.69	61.04
32	3.33	3.32	2.67	60.92
33	3.30	3.25	2.65	60.80
34	3.27	3.19	2.63	60.68
35	3.24	3.13	2.61	60.57
36	3.20	3.07	2.59	60.45

TABLE 20–1 *(concluded)*

L Days	$\bar{G}$ %	$\bar{N}$	$\bar{R}$ %	P %
37	3.16	3.02	2.56	60.35
38	3.13	2.97	2.54	60.23
39	3.10	2.92	2.51	60.11
40	3.06	2.88	2.49	60.00
41	3.03	2.84	2.46	59.89
42	3.00	2.80	2.44	59.78
43	2.97	2.76	2.42	59.67
44	2.94	2.72	2.40	59.58
45	2.91	2.69	2.37	59.48
46	2.88	2.65	2.35	59.37
47	2.85	2.62	2.32	59.27
48	2.82	2.59	2.30	59.17
49	2.79	2.56	2.28	59.07
50	2.76	2.53	2.26	58.97
51	2.74	2.50	2.24	58.88
52	2.71	2.47	2.21	58.79
53	2.68	2.45	2.19	58.70
54	2.65	2.42	2.17	58.61
55	2.63	2.40	2.15	58.51
56	2.60	2.38	2.13	58.42
57	2.58	2.35	2.10	58.34
58	2.55	2.33	2.09	58.26
59	2.53	2.31	2.06	58.18
60	2.50	2.29	2.04	58.10

The numbers tabulated are the average gross payoff $\bar{G}$, the average number of trades $\bar{N}$, the average net payoff $\bar{R}$ when transactions costs c are 0.2%, and the probability P of taking the correct trading decision. These figures are calculated by simulating 500,000 contracts, each for 6 months. The correlation between daily futures returns on different days is always positive. The maximum correlation of 0.019 occurs when the time lag is 1 day.

on capital used to purchase T-bills, which are then used as margin collateral, always assuming that market prices are generated by the rules used for the simulations and that traders know the optimal range for L. The estimated standard deviation of G is 8.68 percent for the best L. The values of G have minimal autocorrelation (e.g., 0.008 for adjacent contracts) so the standard error of $\bar{G}$ is estimated to be 0.01 percent.

Figure 20–1 shows plots of $\overline{G}$ and $\overline{R}$ against L. It is striking how slowly $\overline{G}$ decreases as L is moved away from the optimal range. The expected value of G is within 90 percent of its maximum value whenever L is in the interval from 6 to 29.

The definition of the channel rule implies that the number of trades is a decreasing function of L. Very approximately, the number of trades is halved when L is doubled. There is about one trade per month, on average, when L maximizes the average gross payoff.

As transaction costs increase, so too does the optimal value of L. The optimal range is 21 to 24 when costs are 0.2 percent per trade. The estimated expected value of R is then 2.79 percent (standard error 0.01 percent) and 90 percent or more of the optimal expected net payoff can be obtained when L is in the interval from 14 to 38. At the optimum L, one-quarter of the gross payoff is lost to transaction costs and the number of trades over 6 months averages 4.2 and has standard deviation equal to 1.5. Figure 20–1 shows that $\overline{R}$ decreases sharply as L falls below 10 due to the rapidly increasing number of trades.

Small positive expected net payoffs can be obtained even for transaction costs as high as 1 percent per trade, providing L is at least 32.

Probabilities of Correct Trading Decisions

Trading rules aim to take long [short] positions when the futures price is expected to rise [fall]. The success of a trading rule applied to the simulated price process depends on how often long [short] positions are taken when the unobservable AR(1) component μ_t in returns x_t is positive [negative]. Trading rules use the returns history, $I_{t-1} = \{x_{t-1}, x_{t-2},...\}$, to implicitly provide forecasts of the sign of μ_t. The accuracy of a rule's sign forecasts can be measured by defining

$$d_t = 1 \text{ if long from close } t - 1 \text{ to close } t$$

$$= -1 \text{ if short...} \tag{11a}$$

$$s_t = \text{sign}(\mu_t) = 1 \text{ if } \mu_t > 0$$

$$= -1 \text{ if } \mu_t < 0 \tag{11b}$$

and then estimating

$$P = \text{Prob}(d_t = s_t) \tag{12}$$

FIGURE 20-1

Gross and Net Average Percentage Payoffs. Vertical Axis: Average Percentage Payoff. Horizontal Axis: Channel Length L (days)

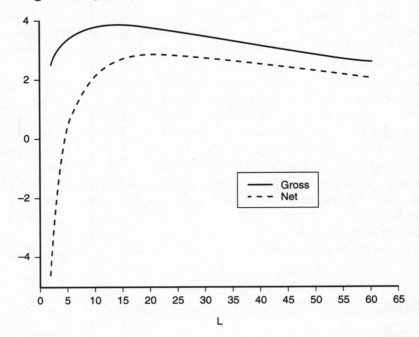

Table 20–1 shows estimates of the probability P as a function of L. Not surprisingly, the highest probabilities occur for the same L values that give the maximum expected gross payoff. The maximum probability of making the correct trading decision is 62.6 percent and the probability is more than 60 percent for any L between 4 and 39, inclusive; here correct means being long [short] when μ_t is positive [negative]. There is an almost linear relationship between $\overline{G}$ and P. For all L considered, $100\overline{G}/(P - 0.5)$ is between 30 and 31.

Returns follow an ARMA(1,1) process for the model simulated. An ARMA trading rule would use a forecast $\hat{x}_t$ of x_t, made at time $t - 1$ using I_{t-1}, as in Taylor (1988, 1992a, b). Let $d_t^* = \text{sign}(\hat{x}_t)$. It is of interest to compare

$$P^* = \text{Prob}(d_t^* = s_t) \tag{13}$$

with P. The usual optimal linear forecast, which ignores the ARCH effects in the simulated returns, achieves $P* = 63.6$ percent when the correct AR and MA parameters are used to define the forecasts. This is similar to the theoretical probability (62.1 percent), which can be calculated for a Gaussian ARIMA process when the price volatility is constant ($\beta = 0$). Revising the forecasts to take account of conditional heteroscedasticity is possible in several ways. The best sign forecasts obtained have $P* = 63.8$ percent compared with $P = 62.6$ percent. It is concluded that the channel rule is only slightly inferior to ARMA forecasts when predicting the sign of the unobservable AR(1) component μ_t.

Sensitivity to Price Model Parameter Changes

All the results summarized in Table 20–1 are for the chosen price process with the five parameters given by: $A = 0.02$, $p = 0.95$, $\alpha = -5.15$, $\beta = 0.422$, and $\phi = 0.973$. Table 20–2 summarizes further results when one or two parameters are changed. The price follows a random walk when $A = 0$ and, not surprisingly, $\overline{G}$ is almost zero for all L, while $\overline{R}$ is negative and is maximized by making L as large as possible.

The remaining variations are evaluated for 20,000 contracts, using the same sequence of random numbers to generate the prices for all these variations. The first set of variations only change the value of A, which is defined in (7). The optimal average gross payoff is very roughly a constant times A over the range $0.005 \leq A \leq 0.03$. Likewise, the optimal average net payoff has an approximate linear relationship with A, although the intercept is obviously negative and the best L decreases as A increases. The second set of variations only change the value of p, which is defined in (5). Now the optimal average gross payoff is approximately a constant times $\ln(1 - p)$. From the first and second sets of variations, a general result about the optimal expected gross payoff from the channel rule may be conjectured: when the returns process has autocorrelations p_τ satisfying $p_\tau > p_{\tau+1} > 0$ for all positive lags $_\tau$, then the optimal expectation is approximately some constant times the following function f of ρ_1 and $\rho\Sigma = \Sigma_{\tau=1}^{\infty} \rho_\tau$:

$$f = \rho_1 \rho\Sigma \left[\frac{\ln(\rho\Sigma) - \ln(\rho_1)}{\rho\Sigma - \rho_1} \right] \qquad (14)$$

The multiplicative constant will depend primarily upon the unconditional standard deviation of the returns.

TABLE 20–2

Selected Channel Trading Results for Different Price
Process Parameters

Variation	$\bar{G}$ %	Best L	$\bar{R}$ %	Best L	$\bar{P}$ %
None	3.81	14	2.80	23	62.6
Random walk	0.05	5	−0.48	60	50.0
$A = 0.005$	1.16	19	0.43	40	57.1
$A = 0.01$	2.13	14	1.28	26	59.6
$A = 0.03$	5.43	14	4.36	18	64.6
$p = 0.8$	2.10	4	0.25	19	56.7
$p = 0.9$	2.93	10	1.52	19	59.4
$p = 0.975$	4.84	24	4.17	31	66.2
$\phi = 0.95$	3.83	13	2.81	24	62.5
$\phi = 0.99$	3.92	14	2.96	24	62.8
$\beta = 0.3,$ $\alpha = -5.062$	3.64	14	2.71	27	61.8
$\beta = 0.7,$ $\alpha = -5.462$	4.64	12	3.50	18	65.5

Sensitivity of (a) the maximum average gross payoff $\bar{G}$ and the best L; (b) the maximum average net payoff $\bar{R}$ and the best L when transactions costs c are 0.2%; and (c) the probability P of taking the correct trading decision for the best L in (a), to changes from the simulation parameters used to produce Table 20–1.
The first row of the table is the base case defined by:

$$A = 0.02, p = 0.95, \alpha = -5.15, \beta = 0.422, \text{ and } \phi = 0.973.$$

The averages are calculated from 60,000 contracts for the random walks, 20,000 contracts for each of the other variations, and 500,000 contracts for the base case.

Table 20–2 also shows that the results are not sensitive to ϕ which measures how quickly volatility is expected to revert towards its median level. The final two rows of the table are for changes in both α and ß, which leave the unconditional standard deviation unchanged. The price volatility varies more through time as β increases and then the channel rule becomes slightly more profitable.

TRADING RESULTS WHEN *L* IS CHOSEN FROM PAST PRICES

Assumptions

The usual ex ante methodology for evaluating trading rules requires parameters to be chosen by optimization over some learning period. The average net payoff for contract $C + 1$ in a series of contracts is now estimated as a function of the amount of information, C contracts, used to choose L. The learning period ranges from $C = 1$ to $C = 30$ contracts inclusive, each traded for 6 months. The trading parameter L is chosen to be that value which maximizes the average net payoff during the learning period. Transaction costs are assumed to be 0.2 percent per trade. The choice of initial position on day 63 for the first contract in the learning period is arbitrary; a long position is always selected.

The price process of the third section is simulated with the parameters given in that section. It is therefore assumed that the process and the parameters do not change during the learning period and any subsequent ex ante evaluations.

Expected Net Payoffs

Prices for 30 consecutive contracts are simulated to give choices for L as C increases from 1 to 30. Three thousand replications are used to estimate the probability $p(l,C)$ of choosing $L = l$ when C contracts are used to make the choice. From Table 20–1 one knows the expected net payoff for any contract when $L = l$. Call this $E(R|l)$. The unconditional expected net payoff for contract $C + 1$ is then:

$$E(\text{R} \mid \text{learn from } C \text{ contracts}) = \sum_{l=2}^{60} p(C, l)E(R|l) \qquad (15)$$

Table 20–3 lists the estimates of the unconditional expected net payoff for contract $C + 1$ based upon learning from C contracts. The ultimate limit of these expectations, as $C \to \infty$, is 2.80 percent from Table 20–1. It can be seen from Table 20–3 that what can be learned from past prices is learned remarkably quickly. Fifteen years of prices would give an expected net payoff of 2.49 percent; but 2.19 percent is expected if only 2 years of prices are used. More than two-thirds of the expected payoff from an infinite price history can be achieved from only 1 year of prices!

Other Criteria

Table 20–3 also gives the expected gross payoff and the probability of taking the correct trading decision (as discussed in the fourth section) when learning from C contracts. These numbers are almost constant. There is, of course, no reason why either the gross expectation or the probability should quickly improve when the objective is to maximize the net expectation.

The chance of making the correct decision is 61.2 percent when seeking to use a few contracts to learn how to maximize net payoffs. This is close to the 61.9 percent attainable from an infinite learning set. It is conjectured that ARMA decision rules need more contracts to achieve a similar proportion of their predictive potential. If true, this could explain why channel and ARMA rules have comparable expected payoffs when learning from a moderate number of contracts with ARMA rules only superior for very long learning periods.

The Distribution of Choices for L

Some information about the distribution of the optimized choices for L is provided in Table 20–3. The average value chosen for L varies between 25 and 27 when the learning period is between 5 and 30 contracts. As $C \to \infty$, the average converges to 23. The final two columns show that the interquartile ranges of the distributions are considerable. Learning from 4 years of prices would give half the choices for L either below 12 or above 38. Figure 20–2 shows how often the optimized channel length equals the possible integers between 2 and 60 when $C = 2$ and $C = 20$. From Figure 20–1 it is clear that the channel rule will be most successful when small channel lengths L are avoided. Figure 20–2 shows that small values of L are often chosen when $C = 2$, but are infrequently chosen when $C = 20$.

FURTHER TRADING RESULTS FOR CURRENCY FUTURES

It is important to report the results of all trading rule evaluations; otherwise there is the possibility of biased conclusions with the direction of the bias depending on the inclination of the researcher either for or against the efficient market hypothesis. Taylor (1992a) gives channel results for IMM currency futures up to November 1987. The channel results are here extended to November 1990.

TABLE 20-3

Channel Trading Results When L Depends on Past Prices

Learning Period C	Expected Net Payoff %	Expected Gross Payoff %	Chance Correct Decision %	Choice for L		
				Average	Q1	Q3
1	1.73	3.45	61.34	18.48	7	26
2	1.98	3.42	61.25	21.88	8	32
3	2.09	3.41	61.21	23.41	9	34
4	2.19	3.41	61.19	24.68	11	36
5	2.20	3.39	61.15	25.25	11	37
6	2.25	3.40	61.16	25.71	11	38
7	2.31	3.39	61.15	26.31	12	38
8	2.31	3.40	61.16	26.34	12	38
9	2.31	3.39	61.15	26.41	12	38
10	2.34	3.40	61.17	26.49	12	38
11	2.35	3.40	61.16	26.83	13	39
12	2.37	3.40	61.15	27.05	13	39
13	2.38	3.40	61.17	27.04	13	39
14	2.40	3.40	61.18	27.02	14	38
15	2.41	3.41	61.19	27.07	14	38
16	2.42	3.39	61.15	27.57	14	39
17	2.42	3.40	61.18	27.26	14	38
18	2.43	3.40	61.19	27.34	14	38
19	2.44	3.41	61.21	27.22	14	38
20	2.46	3.41	61.22	27.27	14	38
21	2.46	3.41	61.20	27.52	14	38
22	2.46	3.41	61.19	27.62	14	38
23	2.46	3.41	61.21	27.38	14	38
24	2.47	3.42	61.22	27.35	14	38
25	2.47	3.41	61.21	27.47	14	38
26	2.48	3.42	61.22	27.46	14	37
27	2.48	3.42	61.22	27.48	14	37
28	2.48	3.42	61.24	27.31	14	37
29	2.49	3.42	61.23	27.53	15	38
30	2.49	3.42	61.23	27.54	15	37
infinity	2.80	3.63	61.94	23	23	23

Expected net and gross payoffs when C contracts are used to choose the value of L for the next contract by maximizing the average net payoff for the C contracts. The expectations are estimated from 3,000 replications of the learning process.

F I G U R E 20-2

Distribution of Optimized Channel Length (Learning from 2
and 20 Contracts). Vertical Axis: Frequency. Horizontal
Axis: Channel Length L (Days)

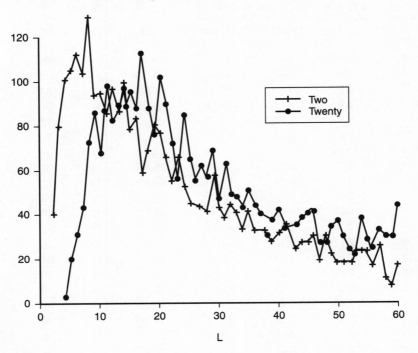

ARIMA trading rules would have given positive net returns for
Sterling, Deutschemark, and Swiss Franc futures from December 1978 to
November 1981 (contracts delivered in 1979–81) according to Taylor
(1986, p. 220). That methodology was different from the one applied here;
although the results suggest an annual, average, net payoff of about 7 percent. Both technical and ARIMA trading rules would have been profitable
from December 1981 to November 1987 (contracts delivered in 1982–87)
as discussed in the second section. Now consider whether positive average
net payoffs persist into more recent years.

Channel trading results are calculated for March, June, September, and
December contracts delivered in 1982–90, with each contract traded for the
3 months preceding the delivery month. These trading periods are chosen to
avoid any problems of relatively illiquid trading many months from delivery.

Results are obtained for sterling, deutschemark, yen, and Swiss franc futures using daily closing prices. The choice of L for a contract is given by optimizing the average net payoff using all previous contracts for the currency, commencing with the March 1980 contract. Transaction costs are assumed to be 0.2 percent of the futures price of the currencies traded. This is a conservative figure: most nonfloor traders would pay less than 0.2 percent in costs. The initial position for each contract, long or short, is determined using the method described in the fourth section.

The average net payoff, over 3 months, is calculated for 3-year periods by averaging across 48 contracts, 12 for each of the four currencies. To calculate a standard error for a 3-year average, across currency averages are calculated for each of the 12 delivery months and these averages are assumed to be a random sample from some distribution. The conventional t-ratio used to test the null hypothesis that the average net payoff is at most zero is given by dividing the average net payoff by its estimated standard error. The results for the three 3-year periods and all 9 years are as follows:

Delivery Months	Average Net Payoff %	Standard Error %	t-ratio
1982–84	0.63	0.59	1.06
1985–87	2.92	1.43	2.05
1988–90	1.63	1.80	0.91
1982–90	1.73	0.82	2.11

During the most recent period, 1988–90, the average net payoff is positive, but statistically insignificant. Nevertheless, these results extend the sequence of profitable 3-year periods from three such periods (1979 –81,...,1985–87) to four (1979–81,...,1988–90). It can be seen that net payoffs are more volatile during 1988–90 than during the other two periods.

The channel results for all 9 years, 1982–90, give an average net payoff equal to 6.9 percent per annum. A standard 95 percent confidence interval for this average is from 0.3 percent to 13.6 percent. A one-tail test is appropriate when seeking to decide whether the channel rule is worthless (the null hypothesis) or profitable on average (the alternative hypothesis).

The null is then rejected at the 2.5 percent significance level. It is obvious that the best trading opportunities occur during the period 1985–87 and this period alone can explain the significant t-ratio for all 9 years. Systematic equity risk cannot explain technical trading profits for currencies [LeBaron (1991); Taylor (1992a)].

The average net payoffs for real currency futures can be compared with the average figures obtained from the Monte Carlo simulations, but it must be remembered that the averages for real prices have high standard errors. The 9-year average of 6.9 percent per annum can be compared with 5.6 percent per annum for the best L in Table 20–1. The Monte Carlo study might never have taken place if the results for 1982–87 had not been so encouraging. A comparison of 1988–90 with the Monte Carlo results from learning over 8 years may, therefore, be more objective. This gives 6.5 percent per annum for 1988–90 compared with 4.8 percent expected from Table 20–3. These figures are not far apart considering the standard errors involved.

CONCLUSIONS

Technical analysis often deserves unflattering criticism and its popularity has puzzled many researchers. Neftci (1991, p. 549) aptly commented that "The attention that technical analysis receives from financial markets is somewhat of a puzzle," and "...traders use technical analysis in day to day forecasting although it bears no direct relationship to Wiener–Kolmogorov prediction theory." The theoretical results presented in this chapter for the channel trading rule show that technical analysis can be constructive in certain circumstances and is not necessarily inferior to ARIMA prediction methodology. Indeed, the channel rule may be superior when a trading objective is evaluated because it may require less information to learn about a satisfactory value for its one parameter than an ARIMA rule needs to find satisfactory estimates of its AR and MA parameters. The channel rule does not provide predictions of future prices. It only predicts the sign of price changes, positive or negative; but this is sufficient to make net trading profits when the sign prediction is frequently correct. As shown in the fourth and fifth sections, more than 60 percent of the sign predictions can be correct for the channel rule even when the maximum correlation between returns on different days is less than 0.02.

Currency futures prices have not followed random walks [Taylor (1986, 1992b)] and there have been several studies that support the idea that technical rules can make net profits at currency markets. Some of these studies are Sweeney (1986); Bilson (1990); LeBaron (1991); and Taylor (1992a). The results of this study for an extended period for currency futures from 1988 to 1990 are not decisive, yet they give more credibility to the notion that the channel rule makes net profits. Net trading profits for currency futures transactions are now reported for four consecutive 3-year periods. These results may be explained by risk, by the activities of central banks, or by an inefficient market.

BIBLIOGRAPHY

Alexander, S.S. "Price Movements in Speculative Markets: Trends or Random Walks?," *Industrial Management Review* 2 (1961), pp. 7–26.

Beja, A., and M.B. Goldman. "On the Dynamic Behavior of Prices in Disequilibrium," *Journal of Finance* 34 (1980), pp. 235–47.

Bilson, J.F.O. "Technical Currency Trading," in *The Currency-Hedging Debate*, Thomas, L.R. (ed.), London: IFR Publishing Ltd., 1990, pp. 257–75.

Bollerslev, T., R.Y. Chou, and K.F. Kroner. "ARCH Modeling in Finance: A Review of the Theory and Empirical Evidence," *Journal of Econometrics* 52 (1992), pp. 5–59.

Brock, W., J. Lakonishok, and B. LeBaron. "Simple Technical Trading Rules and the Stochastic Properties of Stock Returns," *Journal of Finance* 47 (1992), pp. 1731–64.

Chesney, M., and L.O. Scott. "Pricing European Currency Options: A Comparison of the Modified Black–Scholes Model and a Random Variance Model," *Journal of Financial and Quantitative Analysis* 24 (1989), pp. 267–84.

Harvey, A.C., E. Ruiz, and N.G. Shephard. "Multivariate Stochastic Variance Models," *Review of Economic Studies*, forthcoming.

Hodrick, R.J., and S. Srivastava. "Foreign Currency Futures," *Journal of International Economics* 22 (1987), pp. 1–24.

Irwin, S.H., and J.W. Uhrig. "Do Technical Analysts Have Holes in Their Shoes?" *Review of Research in Futures Markets* 3 (1984), pp. 264–77.

Kim, C.M. "Volatility Effect on Time Series Behavior of Exchange Rate Changes," Working Paper, University of Chicago and Korea Institute for International Economic Policy, 1989.

LeBaron, B. "Technical Trading Rules and Regime Shifts in Foreign Exchange," Working Paper, Social Systems Research Institute, University of Wisconsin, 1991.

LeBaron, B. "Some Relations between Volatility and Serial Correlations in Stock Market Returns," *Journal of Business* 65 (1992), pp. 199–219.

Lukac, L.P., B.W. Brorsen, and S.H. Irwin. "A Comparison of Twelve Technical Trading Systems with Market Efficiency Implications," Unpublished manuscript, Department of Agricultural Economics, Purdue University, 1986.

Lukac, L.P., B.W. Brorsen, and S.H. Irwin. "A Test of Futures Market Disequilibrium Using Twelve Different Trading Systems," *Applied Economics* 20 (1988), pp. 623–39.

Lukac, L.P., and B.W. Brorsen. "A Comprehensive Test of Futures Market Disequilibrium," *Financial Review* 25 (1990), pp. 593–622.

Mark, N.C. "Time-Varying Betas and Risk Premia in the Pricing of Forward Foreign Exchange Contracts," *Journal of Financial Economics* 22 (1988), pp. 335–54.

Melino, A., and S.M. Turnbull. "Pricing Foreign Currency Options with Stochastic Volatility," *Journal of Econometrics* 45 (1990), pp. 239–65.

Neftci, S.N. "Naive Trading Rules in Financial Markets and Wiener–Kolmogorov Prediction Theory: A Study of Technical Analysis," *Journal of Business* 64 (1991), pp. 549–71.

Sentana, E., and S. Wadhwani. "Feedback Traders and Stock Return Autocorrelations: Evidence from a Century of Daily Data," Working Paper, London School of Economics, 1990.

Sweeney, R.J. "Beating the Foreign Exchange Market," *Journal of Finance* 41 (1986), pp. 163–82.

Taylor, S.J. *Modelling Financial Time Series*. Chichester: Wiley, 1986.

Taylor, S.J. "How Efficient are the Most Liquid Futures Contracts?—A Study of Treasury Bond Futures," *The Review of Futures Markets* 7 (1988), pp. 574–92.

Taylor, S.J. "Rewards Available to Currency Futures Speculators: Compensation for Risk or Evidence of Inefficient Pricing?," *Economic Record* 68 (Supplement) (1992a), pp. 105–16.

Taylor, S.J. "Efficiency of the Yen Futures Market at the Chicago Mercantile Exchange," in *Rational Expectations and Efficiency in Futures Markets*, Goss, B.A., (ed.), London: Routledge, 1992b, pp. 109–28.

Taylor, S.J. "Modelling Stochastic Volatility," *Mathematical Finance,* forthcoming.

CHAPTER 21

MANAGEMENT SUMMARY

Title: "Market Statistics and Technical Analysis: The Role of Volume"

Publication: *Journal of Finance* 49 (1994) pp. 153–81.

Author: Lawrence Blume, Cornell University
             David Easley, Cornell University
             Maureen O'Hara, Cornell University

Synopsis: The study investigates how technical analysis could be valuable to traders in an economy in which the only uncertainty arises from the underlying information structure. The model shows that technical analysis is valuable because current market statistics may be sufficient to reveal some information, but not all.

             The study also shows that volume can play a role in assessing the quality of information traders use to make decisions.

Market Statistics and Technical Analysis: The Role of Volume

Lawrence Blume
David Easley
Maureen O'Hara*

Technical analysis of market data has long been a pervasive activity in both security and futures markets. Technical analysts believe that price and volume data provide indicators of future price movements, and that by examining these data, information may be extracted on the fundamentals driving returns.[1] If markets are efficient in the sense that the current price impounds all information, then such activity is clearly pointless. But if the process by which prices adjust to information is not immediate, then market statistics may impound information that is not yet incorporated into the current market price. In particular, volume may be informative about the process of security returns.

In this chapter we investigate the informational role of volume. That volume may play an important role in markets has long been a subject of empirical research [see, for example, Gallant, Rossi, and Tauchen (1992); Karpoff (1987) provides an excellent review of previous research]. This research has documented a remarkably strong relation between volume and the absolute value of price changes in both equity markets and futures markets. But why such a pattern exists or even how volume evolves in

---

*Blume and Easley are from the Department of Economics, Cornell University, and O'Hara is from the Johnson Graduate School of Management, Cornell University. We would like to thank David Brown, Sanjeev Goyal, Matt Spiegel, and seminar participants at Cornell, Duke, Harvard, Rutgers, the Stockholm School of Economics, Vanderbilt, the Western Finance Association meetings, the European Finance Association meetings, and the Winter Finance Research Conference for helpful comments. We also appreciate the helpful comments of an anonymous referee and the editor, René Stulz.

426 PART 3 Evidence Regarding Market Inefficiencies

markets is not clear. Our goal in this research is to determine how the statistical properties of volume relate to the underlying value of the asset and to the behavior of market prices. By establishing these properties, we hope to show what traders could learn from volume and how this could provide one explanation for the use of volume-based technical analysis in markets.

A natural starting place for our research would seem to be the recently developed models looking at the information content of price sequences. In particular, Brown and Jennings (1989) and Grundy and McNichols (1989) consider rational expectations models in which single price does not reveal the underlying information but a sequence of security prices does. These papers demonstrate that technical analysis of price patterns may be valuable because it facilitates the learning ability of traders. But adapting such models to investigate the role of volume reveals an immediate problem: In standard rational expectations models with aggregate supply uncertainty, volume plays the role of adding noise to the model. Allowing traders to observe volume essentially allows them to know the aggregate supply and this results in a fully revealing single price. In this framework, the informational role of volume is large, but vacuous. With no role to play other than noise, volume in these models can never provide insights into underlying economic fundamentals or give guidance to the process by which information is impounded into the price.

In this chapter, therefore, we develop an alternative equilibrium approach for studying the behavior of security markets. Our model is standard in that some fundamental is unknown to all traders and traders receive signals that are informative of the asset fundamental. However, in our model aggregate supply is fixed. The source of noise is the quality of the information; specifically the precision of the signal distribution. Prices alone cannot provide full information on both the magnitude of the signals and their precision. We show that volume provides information about the quality of traders' information that cannot be deduced from the price statistic. We also show how sequences of volume and prices can be informative, and demonstrate that traders who use information contained in the market statistic will do "better" than traders who do not. In our model, technical analysis arises as a natural component of the agents' learning process.

This property of traders using the information contained in volume is a unique and important feature of our model. In other models of volume [see for example Campbell, Grossman, and Wang (1991), Harris and Raviv (1991) and Wang (1991)], volume is interesting for its correlation with other variables, but in itself is unimportant: Traders never learn from volume nor use volume in any decision making. By contrast, in our model volume enters traders' learning problems because they use the specific volume statistic in updating their beliefs. Consequently, volume matters in our model because it affects the behavior of the market, rather than merely describing it.

Our construction of sequences of price and volume also allows us to make predictions about the equilibrium properties of price, price changes, and volume. Our model demonstrates why volume and the absolute value of price changes are positively correlated, and provides interesting comparative static predictions of the effects of information precision and dispersion on the price-volume relationship. Such predictions may be useful to researchers interested in a wide variety of issues in accounting and finance. From a time series perspective, our model provides an intriguing result on the equilibrium behavior of volume. We show that although all traders will learn the asset's value, and prices will thus converge to the full information or strong-form efficient price, volume does not converge to zero. In fact, volume has a limit distribution that is nondegenerate. This demonstrates that markets do not shut down as beliefs converge and has the important implication that the "no-trade" equilibrium results so prevalent in the literature may not describe the limit behavior of equilibrium models with learning. Finally, our model also shows why technical analysis of price and volume data can be valuable and provides predictions regarding the type of firms for which it will be particularly useful. Thus, we provide one explanation for the paradoxical existence of technical analysis in seemingly efficient markets.

The paper is organized as follows. In Section I we consider how allowing agents to condition on both prices and volume affects the equilibrium in the standard rational expectations random supply framework. Our purpose in doing so is to demonstrate why such models fail in the presence of volume, and to delineate what must be changed if volume is to be incorporated (and analyzed) in an economically meaningful way. We then investigate in Section II what information is provided by price and volume statistics in a new model in which agents condition on prior market outcomes and there is no aggregate supply uncertainty. Section III examines how the sequence of price and volume statistics reveals information, and provides results on the time series of price and volume. Section IV shows how technical analysis based on price and volume can make agents better off. The paper's final section is a conclusion.

I. PRICE, VOLUME, AND TECHNICAL ANALYSIS

We begin our analysis by examining the role of volume and trade information in the standard rational expectations framework typically employed to investigate how market clearing prices reflect underlying information, and how agents, in turn, learn from prices. Our approach in this section is to investigate simplified versions of models developed by Brown and Jennings and Grundy and McNichols that address the role of price data in technical analysis. These models share a common rational expectations approach, but introduce aggregate supply uncertainty in different ways. As we show, this difference results in major differences in equilibria when volume data are introduced. After investigating the role of volume and trade information in the Brown and Jennings model and then in the Grundy and McNichols framework, we summarize the problems revealed in the standard approach, and detail how theoretical models must be changed to provide a meaningful analysis of price and volume data.

In the standard approach [see Grossman and Stiglitz (1980)], a collection of agents, indexed by $i = 1,...,I$, trade a risky asset and a riskless asset in a single market. Both Brown and Jennings and Grundy and McNichols consider the limit case where the number of agents I is infinite. In this standard model, trades may occur at time 1 and at time 2. We analyze only time 1 and so do not include time indexes. At the end of trading, the riskless asset pays a known dividend of 1 and the risky asset pays a liquidating dividend given by the random variable ψ. Traders begin with the identical beliefs about the payoff ψ, which are represented by a normal distribution $N(\psi_0, 1/\rho_0)$.

Traders maximize negative exponential utility functions defined on final wealth (or consumption) of the form

$$U(w_i) = -\exp[-w_i] \tag{1}$$

where w_i is agent i's terminal wealth (we have fixed the coefficient of absolute risk aversion at one). Final period wealth depends on the agents' trading decisions and the assets' payoffs, and so can be written as $w_i = d_i\psi + n_i$, where d_i is agent i's demand for the risky assets and n_i is the number of units of the riskless asset that have a price normalized to one.

Before the start of period 1, each trader receives an endowment of n_0 units of the riskless asset. Each trader also receives a private signal, y_i, on the value of the risky asset which is given by

$$y_i = \psi + e_i \tag{2}$$

where the distribution each e_i is $N(0, 1/\rho)$. Because the signals' errors are assumed normally distributed with finite variances and are independent across traders, it follows that the average signal, $\bar{y} = \sum_{i=1}^{I} y_i/I$, converges to ψ with probability 1 as the number of traders grows large.

In the Brown and Jennings framework, there is an exogenous supply of the random asset given by the random variable X, with per capita supply X/I, denoted x. As is the case with all random variable in the model, x is normally distributed and is independent of any private signals. Equilibrium requires that

$$x = \sum_{i=1}^{I} d_i/I \tag{3}$$

or simply that per capita demand equal per capital supply.

In rational expectations models of the form considered here, equilibrium involves a set price and demand functions that satisfy the following properties. First, given their information sets H^i (to be specified later) agents conjecture the equilibrium price function. Based on these price functions and an observation of the equilibrium price, traders determine their demands for the risky asset. In an equilibrium, these price conjectures will be correct and per capita demand will equal per capita supply.

To construct such an equilibrium, suppose that each trader conjectures that the price of the risky asset, p, is a linear function of aggregate information $\bar{y}$ and per capita supply (x):

$$p = \alpha\psi_0 + \beta\bar{y} - \gamma x. \tag{4}$$

Then, the posterior distribution of ψ given $H^i = (y_i, p)$ is normal with mean $E[\psi|H^i]$ and variance Var $[\psi|H^i]$. Trader i's demand is then

$$d_i = \frac{E[\psi|H^i] - p}{\text{Var }[\psi|H^i]} . \tag{5}$$

Using the equilibrium condition (3), Brown and Jennings then solve for the equilibrium price. They show that it is linear as conjectured and that the coefficient on x is not zero. Thus, prices are not revealing. This allows Brown and Jennings to demonstrate how a sequence of prices could provide information that a single price observation could not, and thus provides a role for technical analysis.

Now, we suppose that contemporaneous volume data is publicly available.[2] Volume is typically defined as the number of shares of the risky asset that are traded. Since every trade involves a buyer and a seller, volume could be calculated by simply adding up all buy orders or all sell orders. An equivalent approach in a Walrasian equilibrium is to sum the absolute value of traders' demands and divide by two.[3]

If traders do know volume in the Brown and Jennings framework, then the role for technical analysis dissipates. What causes this to happen is that, if traders use the information conveyed by volume and their own trading behavior, there is revealing equilibrium. Consequently, with all information revealed to traders, there is no benefit to considering the sequence of prices. To see why this occurs, suppose we let traders condition on per capita volume and the direction of their own trade (i.e., either a buy or a sell).[4] Their information set is now $H^i = (p, y_i, V, J)$ where J is an indicator variable denoted by whether the trader buys or sells, and (per capita) volume is defined by $V = \frac{1}{2I}(\sum_{i=1}^{I}|d_i| + |X|)$. Further, let traders conjecture that the equilibrium price function is given by (4) and that price and volume together will be revealing. In this case, each trader's demand function is given by[5]

$$d_i = (\psi_0\rho_0 + \bar{y}I\rho) - p(\rho_0 + I\rho) \qquad (6)$$

and the price function is given by

$$p = (\psi_0\rho_0 + \bar{y}I\rho - x) / (\rho_0 + I\rho). \qquad (7)$$

To show that these equations describe an equilibrium, we need to show that the traders' conjectures are correct and that the market clears. First, note that in a revealing equilibrium, every trader will demand the same amount of the risky asset, i.e., $d_i = d_j = d$ for all i and j. So per capita volume will be $\frac{1}{2}(|d| + |x|)$. Now market clearing yields $d = -x$, so $V = |x|$. Thus, each trader infers that $x = -V$ if he is a buyer, i.e., $d_i > 0$, or $x = V$ if he is a seller, i.e., $d_i < 0$.[6] Using this inferred value for x and the market price, p, each trader inverts the price equation (7) to solve for $\bar{y}$. Given knowledge of $\bar{y}$, the optimal demand for any trader is given by (6). It is easy to check that the price given by (7) clears the market when demands are given by (6). Thus, traders have equal demands and their conjectures are correct. Once you know volume, therefore, you can infer the underlying supply uncertainty, prices are revealing, and technical analysis has no role.

Interestingly, the opposite conclusion arises from the Grundy-McNichols approach: volume is devoid of any useful information whatever. The reason for this lies in the uncertainty structure of their model. Unlike the random aggregate supply feature of the Brown and Jennings model, Grundy and McNichols introduce uncertainty by assuming that each of the I traders in the market receives a random endowment of the risky asset. These endowments, x_i, are assumed independently and identically normally distributed with mean μ_x, and variance $\sigma_x^2 I$. In this model, some traders receive negative quantities of the risky asset, some receive positive quantities, and trade presumably arises in part to rebalance portfolios.

To ensure that individual traders' endowments carry no information about per capita supply x, Grundy and McNichols consider only the limit economy. In this economy, the variance of x is infinite and the Law of Large Numbers cannot be applied. Note that this assumption of the limit economy (infinite traders) is fundamental to their approach. If we consider the finite economy, then there is a finite variance and endowments must provide some information. Each trader also receives a private signal $y_i = \psi + w + \epsilon_i$ where ψ is the per unit payoff from the risky asset, w is a common error, and ϵ_i is an idiosyncratic error.

If we examine per capita volume in the limit economy we find the distracting feature that it is infinite. In particular, per capita trading volume is

$$\frac{1}{2} \lim_{I \to \infty} \frac{1}{I} \sum_{i=1}^{I} |d_i - x_i| \tag{8}$$

where d_i is trader i's equilibrium demand and x_i is his endowment. Asymptotically, d_i and x_i are uncorrelated, but x_i has infinite variance. Thus, per capita volume is infinite and it provides no information about the value of the asset.[7]

The fundamental difficulty is the underlying supply structure. Whether supply is introduced by an exogenous random supply or by random endowments, if volume reveals anything it reveals the supply. Consequently, if we allow traders to condition on contemporaneous volume, it is essentially allowing them to remove the "noise" in the pricing equation.[8] With prices then depending only on private signals, the only known equilibrium is one in which price reveals the underlying information.

In this context, volume provides no useful information about any fundamentals relating to the asset but rather is exogenously determined. It seems more reasonable to believe that the volume statistic should capture some endogenous aspect of the trading process not necessarily incorporated in prices. In particular, since volume arises from individual demands, it may be the case that volume reflects aspects of the information structure that traders might wish to know.[9]

But a second difficulty arises in investigating this role. This is the problem created by conditioning on contemporaneous information. Even if volume has some meaningful economic role, when traders use the information conveyed by contemporaneous volume, the only revealing equilibrium is the anomalous one in which volume actually has no information. To see why this is so, consider a Grossman-Stiglitz-style model without the modelling device of random endowments or random supply. Suppose that traders have common preferences and endowments and receive payoff-relevant signals. Now, suppose that there exists a revealing rational expectations equilibrium with conditioning on price and volume. In this equilibrium, traders have common information and they all choose the same trade. But the only such trade that is consistent with market clearing is no trade, and so regardless of the signals, volume is zero—and carries no information.[10] Alternatively, there could be nonrevealing equilibria in which traders condition on price and volume. However, as volume is a sum of absolute values it cannot be normally distributed. So although such an equilibrium might exist there seems to be no hope of constructing it, and hence no hope of using a contemporaneous data approach to study volume.

One way to avoid these difficulties is to allow traders to condition on all information up to but not including the market statistic resulting from their desired trade. This approach, first suggested by Hellwig (1982), avoids the simultaneity problem noted above while retaining the ability to learn from market information. Blume and Easley (1984) use this approach to examine the information content of past market prices. In this paper, we use such conditioning on existing market statistics to investigate the role of price and volume.

This approach, like the approach of conditioning on contemporaneous data, is an abstraction. We offer two justifications for it. First, traders who submit market orders do not know the price at which their order will execute until after the trade occurs. Even traders who use limit orders cannot condition their quantity perfectly on price unless they use incredibly and unrealistically complex orders. But unless traders know the price at which they will trade, and use the information the price contains in selecting their trade, the usual rational expectations approach is not valid. Hence, actual market settings are not consistent with contemporaneous conditioning requirements, but are compatible with the conditioning requirement we consider. Second, asset markets such as the New York Stock Exchange are never in a Walrasian equilibrium: The market is a dynamic process in which continual adjustments occur. The fiction of a Walrasian equilibrium is itself an approximation to workings of the market. Whether this oversimplified description is best constructed with conditioning on past or contemporaneous data depends on how well each model serves its intended purpose.

Conditioning on predetermined rather than contemporaneous information has another advantage. If traders can condition on contemporaneous price information, they can also condition on the information contained in their own net trade.[11] If we include his own net trade in each individual's information set, the conventional equilibrium remains as an equilibrium. But there are others as well. Jordan (1983) has shown that with these information sets there always exists a revealing equilibrium.[12] Furthermore, the revealing equilibrium is in a sense more natural as it is robust to the model specification (i.e., exponential utilities and normal distributions) whereas the conventional equilibrium is not robust. Analyses with conditioning on contemporaneous information thus finesse a delicate equilibrium selection problem, which does not arise when traders use past information.

In the next section, we investigate how traders learn from market information by developing a Walrasian model in which traders are allowed to use the information conveyed by all past prices and volumes. In our model, price and volume data each convey information about the underlying asset value but the type of information they convey differs. As we demonstrate, this provides a role for technical analysis in which both price and volume data are useful. It should be noted that by technical analysis we do not mean using market statistics from the previous period to infer information from that period. As we do not allow conditioning on current endogenous data, this use of past data occurs by assumption. By technical analysis we mean the use in period t of market statistics from periods $t-1, t-2,...,$ to make inferences about the future value of assets.

II. THE INFORMATION CONTENT OF VOLUME

We consider a repeated asset market in which agents can trade a risk-free and a risky asset. All trade is between the agents we model; there is no exogenous supply of any asset. Each agent maximizes a negative exponential utility function of the form defined in equation (1). The asset's eventual value is given by the random variable ψ, where ψ is normally distributed with mean ψ_0 and variance $1/\rho_0$. All traders initially have $N(\psi_0, 1/\rho_0)$ as their (common) prior on asset value. We make the usual assumption that all random variables in the model are independent.

Our interest is in the market statistics that arise in a competitive economy with a large number of traders. We develop these statistics by analyzing a market with N traders and providing results as $N \to \infty$. We refer to results obtained by taking the limit as the number of traders grows large as results for the large economy. Because traders are risk averse, movements in the price elicit portfolio rebalancing trades. In addition, trade may also occur in response to new information on the asset's true value. Each trader in our economy receives an informative signal in every period. We divide the traders into two groups, with $N_I = \mu N$ traders in group 1 and $N_u = (1 - \mu)N$ in group 2. The traders in each group receive signals from a common distribution, but there are different distributions for the two groups. Formally, each informed trader i in group 1, $i = 1,...,$ N_I, receives a signal at date t of $y_t^i = \psi + w_t + e_t^i$ where w_t is a common error term distributed $N(0,1/\rho_w)$. The e_t^i represents an idiosyncratic error which is distributed $N(0,1/\rho_t^1)$. Similarly, trader i in group 2, $i = N_I + 1,..., N$, receives signal $y_t^i = \psi + w_t + \epsilon_t^i$ where each $\epsilon_t^i \sim N(0, 1/\rho^2)$. We keep ρ^2 fixed (and known) to reduce the complexity of our presentation.

The precision of group 1's signals (the ρ_t^1) are random variables.[13] All parameters other than the ρ_t^1's are known to all traders, but each ρ_t^1 is known only to traders in group 1. This randomness in precisions means that the "quality" of signals varies over time. Consequently, the underlying information structure is complex, in that both the level and quality of signals are unknown.

Each trader begins with zero endowment of the risky asset and some exogenous endowment, N_0, of the riskless asset. For simplicity, we set the price of the riskless asset at one. As the utility function is negative exponential and the asset's eventual payoff has a normal distribution, it is well known that a trader's demands for the risky asset will be independent of his wealth. Our interest is in the Walrasian equilibrium price and volume of the risky asset. To calculate these equilibrium statistics, we need only find traders' demands for the risky asset and find the price that clears the market (i.e., makes excess demand zero).

To make it easier to write asset demands, note that for traders in group 1 each signal y_t^i is distributed $N(\psi, 1/\rho_t^{s1})$ where $\rho_t^{s1} = \rho_w \rho_t^1/(\rho_w + \rho_t^1)$.[14] Similarly, for traders in group 2 each y_t^i is distributed $N(\psi, 1/\rho^{s2})$ where $\rho^{s2} = \rho_w \rho^2/(\rho_w + \rho^2)$. Conditional on w_t each y_t^i is distributed $N(\theta_t, 1/\rho_t^1)$ for traders in group 1 and $N(\theta_t, 1/\rho^2)$ for traders in group 2, where $\theta_t = \psi + w_t$. So by the Strong Law of Large Numbers, the mean signal in each group, $\bar{y}_t^1$ and $\bar{y}_t^2$, converges almost surely to θ_t as $N \to \infty$. In the large economy, the mean signal is almost surely equal to the true value plus the common error.

Initially, we consider a two-period version of the model, and then extend our results to the multiperiod version. Following Brown and Jennings, we assume that traders have myopic, or naive, demands so that each trader chooses his demand to maximize expected utility on a period-by-period basis.[15] Denoting the price of the risky asset by p_1, the first period demand for the risky asset for each trader i in group 1 is given by

$$\rho_0(\psi_0 - p_1) + \rho_1^{s1}(y_1^i - p_1) \qquad (9)$$

and by

$$\rho_0(\psi_0 - p_1) + \rho_1^{s2}(y_1^i - p_1) \qquad (10)$$

for each trader i in group 2. The equilibrium first-period price for an economy with N traders is then given by

$$p_1 = \frac{\rho_0 \psi_0 + \mu \rho_1^{s1} \bar{y}_1^1 + (1 - \mu) \rho^{s2} \bar{y}_1^2}{\rho_0 + \mu \rho_1^{s1} + (1 - \mu) \rho^{s2}} \qquad (11)$$

By the Strong Law of Large Numbers we know that in the large economy,

$$p_1 = \frac{\rho_0 \psi_0 + (\mu \rho_1^{s1} + (1 - \mu) \rho^{s2}) \theta_1}{\rho_0 + \mu \rho_1^s + (1 - \mu)\rho^{s2}}. \qquad (12)$$

An important property of this equilibrium price is that it is not revealing. Because traders in group 2 do not know ρ_1^s they cannot infer the signal θ_1 from the equilibrium price. Hence, although prices reflect the aggregated value of the underlying signals, these traders do not have enough information to discern what this value is. The conditional distribution of θ_1 given price is not normal, so any multiperiod analysis with conditioning on price alone would be quite complex. Traders in group 1, however, do know ρ_1^{s1} and ρ_1^{s2}, so observing the equilibrium price tells them θ_1, which is everything that can be known about the underlying asset.

Because traders in group 2 cannot recover θ_1 from price alone, there is a reason for them to look at volume. The first period volume can be found by summing the absolute values of demands at price p_1 and dividing by 2. As it will be easier to consider per capita volume, we define this as

$$V_1 = \frac{1}{2} \frac{1}{N} \left(\sum_{i=1}^{N_I} | \rho_0(\psi_0 - p_1) + \rho_1^{s1}(y_1^i - p_1)| \right.$$

$$\left. + \sum_{i=N_I+1}^{N} | \rho_0(\psi_0 - p_1) + \rho^{s2}(y_1^i - p_1)| \right). \qquad (13)$$

Inspection of the volume definition in equation (13) reveals an immediate problem in analyzing the properties of this market statistic.

Because volume is based on absolute values of the demands defined in equations (9) and (10), its distribution is complicated. Unfortunately, while demands involve normally distributed random variables, volume per se cannot be normally distributed. Consequently, if we are to understand the market information conveyed by the volume statistic we must find a way to describe its statistical properties. Proposition 1 provides this characterization of the volume statistic.

PROPOSITION 1: *In the large economy, given θ_1, per capital volume, V_1, is given by*

$$\frac{\mu}{2}\left[2\,\frac{\rho_1^{s1}}{(\rho_1^1)^{1/2}}\,\phi\left(\frac{\delta^1(\rho_1^1)^{1/2}}{\rho_1^{s1}}\right) + \delta^1\left(\phi\left(\frac{\delta^1(\rho_1^1)^{1/2}}{\rho_1^{s1}}\right) - \phi\left(\frac{-\delta^1(\rho_1^1)^{1/2}}{\rho_1^{s1}}\right)\right)\right]$$

$$+ \frac{(1-\mu)}{2}\left[2\,\frac{\rho^{s2}}{(\rho^2)^{1/2}}\,\phi\left(\frac{\delta^2(\rho^2)^{1/2}}{\rho^{s2}}\right)\right.$$

$$\left. + \delta^2\left(\phi\left(\frac{\delta^2(\rho^2)^{1/2}}{\rho^{s2}}\right) - \phi\left(\frac{-\delta^2(\rho^2)^{1/2}}{\rho^{s2}}\right)\right)\right]$$

where ϕ is the standard normal density, ϕ is the standard normal cumulative distribution function and $\delta^i = \rho_0(\psi_0 - p_1) + \rho_1^{si}(\theta_1 - p_1)$, $i = 1,2$.

Proof: All proofs are given in the Appendix.

From Proposition 1 and equation (12) we know the market statistics for price and volume in period 1. The question of interest is what information do these market statistics provide? We know from our earlier discussion that price alone is not revealing, so traders cannot infer the noisy signal value θ_1 from just the market price. However, if traders observe both the price and the volume, then potentially the volume information can provide sufficient additional information about θ_1.

To determine the value of looking at volume, we need to separate out the information generated by prices from that generated by volume. From the volume equation it is apparent that the volume statistic includes both θ_1 and ρ_1^1. Using the equilibrium price equation we know that

$$\theta_1 - p_1 = \rho_0(p_1 - \psi_0) / (\mu\rho_1^{s1} + (1 - \mu)\,\rho^{s2}). \tag{14}$$

Substituting for θ_1 allows us to write the volume statistic as

$$\frac{\mu}{2}\left[2\, \frac{\rho^{s1}}{(\rho_1^1)^{1/2}}\, \phi\left(\frac{\hat{\delta}_1^1(\rho_1^1)^{1/2}}{\rho_1^{s1}}\right) + \hat{\delta}_1^1\left(\phi\left(\frac{\hat{\delta}_1^1(\rho_1^1)^{1/2}}{\rho_1^{s1}}\right) - \phi\left(\frac{-\hat{\delta}_1^1(\rho_1^1)^{1/2}}{\rho_1^{s1}}\right)\right)\right]$$

$$+ \frac{(1-\mu)}{2}\left[2\, \frac{\rho^{s2}}{(\rho^2)^{1/2}}\, \phi\left(\frac{\hat{\delta}_1^2(\rho^2)^{1/2}}{\rho^{s2}}\right)\right.$$

$$+ \hat{\delta}_1^2\left(\phi\left(\frac{\hat{\delta}_1^2(\rho^2)^{1/2}}{\rho^{s2}}\right) - \phi\left(\frac{-\hat{\delta}_1^2(\rho^2)^{1/2}}{\rho^{s2}}\right)\right)\right] \qquad (15)$$

where

$$\hat{\delta}_1^j = \rho_0(p_1 - \psi_0)\left(\frac{\rho_1^{sj}}{\mu\rho_1^{s1} + (1-\mu)\,\rho^{s2}} - 1\right), \text{ for } j = 1, 2.$$

Using this expression for volume, we now investigate how volume is related to the underlying parameters in the market. We show that given price, volume conveys information about signal quality, ρ_1^1, which can then be used in the price equation to make an inference about θ_1.

Calculation shows that if $\rho_1^1 \in (\rho^2, \rho_w)$, then volume is increasing the precision of group 1's signal. To explain why this relationship occurs, and how traders use it, we focus on the simple case where $p^2 = 0$ and $\rho_1^1 > 0$. As a first property note that given a price p_1, the effect of changing the precision, ρ_1^1, on volume is given by

$$\partial V_1/\partial \rho_1^1 = \frac{\mu}{2}\, \phi\left(\hat{\delta}_1\, \frac{(\rho_w + \rho_1^1)}{\rho_w(\rho_1^1)^{1/2}}\right)\left(\frac{\rho_w}{(\rho_1^1)^{1/2}}\right)\frac{(\rho_w - \rho_1^1)}{(\rho_w + \rho_1^1)^{1/2}}. \qquad (16)$$

Thus, for any price, p_1, per capita volume is increasing in the precision, ρ_1^1, of group 1's signal for $\rho_1^1 < \rho_w$ and decreasing in ρ_1^1 for $\rho_1^1 > \rho_w$.

The intuition for this result can be seen by considering what happens when group 1 receives low-quality signals, i.e., ρ_1^1 near 0. In this case, traders in group 1 received very dispersed signals, but place little confidence in them. At the extreme value of $\rho_1^1 = 0$, there are no useful signals and the only possible equilibrium occurs at $p_1 = \psi_0$ and volume of zero. Alternatively, if ρ_1^1 is large, i.e., $\rho_1^1 > \rho_w$, then volume is again low, but for the opposite reason. Now, group 1 receives high-quality signals, but they are also highly correlated. As $\rho_1^1 \to \infty$, group 1 traders all receive the same signal and so do not trade with each other. Now the only trade occurs between group 1 and group 2. This suggests that simple linear predictions of the correlation between information and volume are seriously misspecified; low volume may be as indicative of new information as is high volume. Volume is related to dispersion of beliefs, and the link between dispersion and information is complex.

This relationship between price, volume, and the quality of information can perhaps best be investigated by examining the actual equilibrium outcomes for a specific economy. Because our model provides closed-form solutions, it is possible to graph these outcomes for a specific set of parameter values. As a starting point, let the initial prior mean $\psi_0 = 1$, and let the fraction of traders in group 1, μ, be 0.5. For simplicity, let both the precision of the common error in the signal, ρ_w, and the precision of the prior, ρ_o, be 0.5. Finally, let $\rho^2 = 0$, so we know that $\rho_1^1 > \rho^2$. Figure 21–1 is generated by selecting, for each ρ_1^1 in a grid, various θ's and then calculating the equilibrium price and per capita volume.

Slices of Figure 21–1 for fixed precision, ρ_1^1, suggest a convex relationship between price and volume. This is in fact true generally, not just for the specific economy graphed in Figure 21–1. Volume is convex in price with its minimum at price equal to the prior expected value of the asset.

PROPOSITION 2: *In equilibrium volume, V_1 is strictly convex in price and achieves its minimum at $p_1 = \psi_0$.*

This convexity result in Proposition 2 follows from the fact that the second derivative of volume with respect to price is positive everywhere and that the first derivative is zero at $p = \psi_0$. To see why this occurs, first note that $p = \psi_0$ can happen only if $\theta_1 = p = \psi_0$, so that on average traders posterior means are unchanged from their prior mean. Trade occurs as individuals have differing signals, but it is limited. As the mean signal, θ_1, moves away from ψ_0, and thus price moves away from ψ_0, on average posterior means are changed and the first term in the demand equations (9) and (10) adds to trade. This term reflects portfolio rebalancing in which even a trader with no new information (i.e., $\rho_1^{si} = 0$) will engage. This convex, or V-shaped, relationship can be seen from slices of the curve in Figure 21–1, but it is even more vividly illustrated in Figure 21–2, which provides a plot of equilibrium per capita volume against equilibrium price. This figure is drawn for an economy in which $\psi_0 = \psi = 1$, $\rho_0 = \rho_w = 2$, $\rho^2 = 0$, $\mu = 0.5$ and ρ_1^1 is uniformly distributed on $(0, 1)$. The graph was then constructed by drawing 500 pairs of (θ_1, ρ_1^1) from their distributions and calculating the equilibrium for each pair.

FIGURE 21–1

The Relation of Volume to Equilibrium Price and
Information Precision

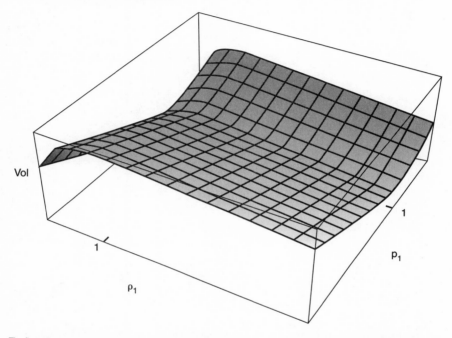

The figure is constructed for an economy with the prior mean $\psi_0 = 1$, $\rho_w = \rho_0 = 1$, $\rho^2 = 0$, and the fraction of traders receiving information $\mu = 0.5$. The graph is generated from equation (15), which shows per capita volume (*vol*) as a function of the precision of group 1's signals (ρ_1) and the equilibrium (p_1).

Interpreting the prior mean ψ_0 as the previous price, this graph also illustrates the obvious positive correlation between volume and the absolute value of price changes. Figure 21–3 shows this with a plot of volume against the absolute value of price change for the observations in Figure 21–2. As is apparent, large price changes (either positive or negative) tend to be associated with large volume. Hence, it is the case that absolute price movements and volume are positively related.

What is particularly intriguing about these results is their remarkable similarity to the findings of empirical researchers. As reported by Karpoff (1987), a V-shape has been found by virtually all empirical investigators of the price-volume relation in equity markets. Moreover, the relation between absolute price changes and volume has been established for both

F I G U R E   21–2

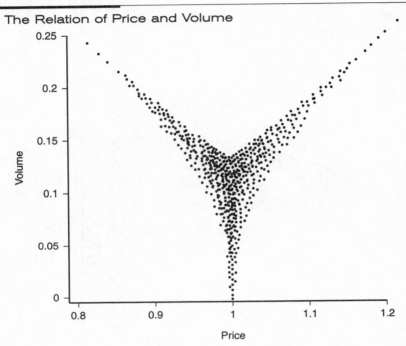

The Relation of Price and Volume

The figure is drawn for parameter values $\psi_0 = \psi = 1$, $\rho_0 = \rho_w = 2$, $\rho^2 = 0$, and $\mu = 0.5$ and $\rho_1^1 \in [0, 1]$. The figure is constructed by drawing 500 pairs of (θ_1, ρ_1^1) from their distributions and calculating the resulting equilibrium. Each point corresponds to the resulting equilibrium price and volume for a single draw.

equity and futures markets. In more recent work, Gallant, Rossi, and Tauchen (1991) use time-series data to demonstrate the V-shaped pattern between price and volume, and also report that the dispersion of the distribution of the price changes increased uniformly with volume. Although the consistency of these results is impressive, what is not well established is why these relations exist. A related question is how, if at all, these phenomena are related to the existence of information.

These issues can be addressed for our sample economy by examining how both the quality (the precision) and the quantity (the dispersion) of information affect the price-volume relation. Figure 21–4 depicts the resulting price-volume equilibrium outcomes for three different information precisions. What is most striking is that while greater information quality (i.e., larger precision) reduces the dispersion of the points, it does not change the general V-shape of the relation. Indeed, the graph suggests that as the precision

FIGURE 21–3

The Relation of Volume to the Absolute Value of
Price Changes

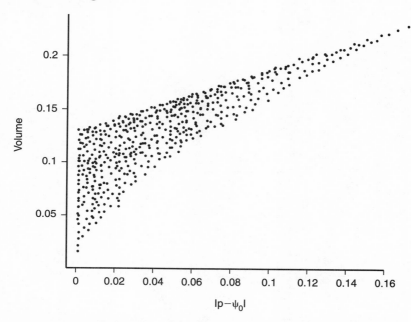

The figure is drawn for parameter values $\psi_0 = \psi = 1$, $\rho_0 = \rho_w = 2$, $p^2 = 0$, and $\mu = 0.5$ and $\rho_1^1 \in [0, 1]$. The figure is constructed by drawing 500 pairs of (θ_1, ρ_1^1) from their distributions and calculating the resulting equilibrium.

approaches its limit, the price-volume relation is characterized by a simple V-shape. These results on information quality suggest a remarkable robustness to the V-shape reported by empirical researchers, but are not consistent with the dispersion results reported by Gallant, Rossi and Tauchen.

The effect of the quantity of information is perhaps even more interesting. Figure 21–5 plots the price-volume outcomes for three scenarios corresponding to 10 percent of the traders being in the high-precision group, 50 percent of the traders being in this group, and 90 percent of the traders being in this group. As information is more widely disseminated, the top of the distribution flattens out, with the V-shape noted earlier virtually disappearing. The dispersion of points, however, increases dramatically, corresponding quite closely to the time series relation depicted in Gallant, Rossi, and Tauchen. In the 90 percent high-precision scenario, it is still the case that the absolute value of prices changes and volume are

FIGURE 21–4

The Relation of Price and Volume for Different Information Quality

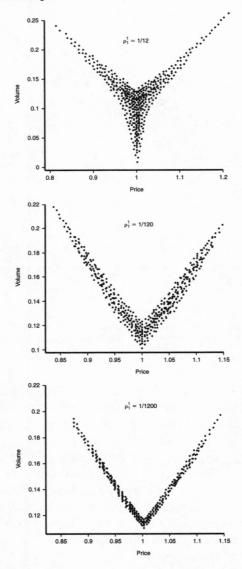

The figures are drawn for parameter values $\psi_0 = \psi = 1$, $\mu = 0.5$, $\rho_0 = \rho_w = 2$, $\rho^2 = 0$. The top panel sets $\rho_1^1 = \frac{1}{12}$, the middle panel sets $\rho_1^1 = \frac{1}{120}$, and the bottom panel sets $\rho_1^1 = \frac{1}{1200}$. Each panel is constructed by drawing 2,000 pairs of (θ_1, ρ_1) from their distributions and calculating the resulting equilibrium. The greater the precision, the better is the information, so the bottom panel corresponds to greater information quality.

FIGURE 21–5

The Relation of Price and Volume for Different Levels of Information Dissemination.

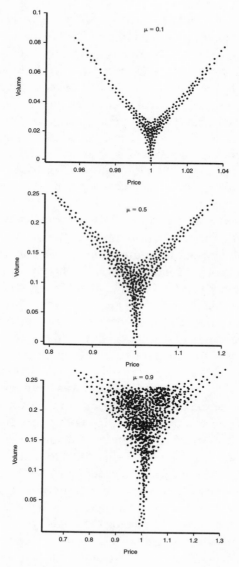

The figures are drawn for parameter values $\psi_0 = \psi = 1$, $\rho_0 = \rho_w = 2$ and $\rho^2 = 0$, and $\rho_1^1 = \frac{1}{12}$. In the top panel, $\mu = 0.1$, in the middle panel, $\mu = 0.5$ and in the bottom panel, $\mu = 0.9$. Each panel is constructed by drawing 2,000 pairs of (θ_1, ρ_1^1) from their distributions and calculating the resulting equilibrium. The higher the μ, the greater the information dispersion, so the bottom panel corresponds to the most information dispersion.

positively related. What our results suggest, however, is that the sensitivity of this relationship (the slope) is greatly affected by the extent of information dissemination. We intend to explore these information quality effects further in future work.

Given this role for volume, it now becomes apparent why observing price and volume together is more informative than observing price alone. A trader observing only a high price is unable to determine whether the price is high because of a high average signal (the θ_1) or an average signal with a high quality ρ_1^1. In fact, he is left with a curve of (θ_1, ρ_1^1) that is consistent with the price. Volume picks up the quality of the signal in a way different from price because, unlike price, volume is not normally distributed. In our model, as Figure 21–1 and equation (15) suggest, there are two (θ_1, ρ_1^1) pairs that are consistent with an observation of price and volume. One pair has $\rho_1^1 > \rho_w$ and a low θ_1, the other has $\rho_1^1 < \rho_w$ and a high θ_1. So looking at volume in addition to price reduces the range of possible values of θ_1 to only two points.

The role of volume as a signal of the precision of beliefs means that the volume statistic provides information to the market that is not conveyed by price. Moreover, this information is related to information about the asset value and not exogenous liquidity or supply shocks. This role for volume is remarkably similar to that claimed by proponents of technical analysis. For example, Pring (1991) explains that "Most indicators [of market movements] are a statistical deviation from price data. Since volume indicators are totally independent of price, they offer a more objective view of the quality of the price trend." In our model, this "independence" of volume is also what allows the quality of information to be inferred from market statistics. It becomes natural to watch volume because it complements the information provided by price. A trader watching only prices cannot learn as much as a trader watching both prices and volume and so faces an unnecessary penalty if he ignores the volume statistic.[16]

In the next section, we extend our model to a multiperiod setting in order to investigate the time series properties of price and volume. To make this analysis tractable, we want the equilibrium in each period to be revealing. (Otherwise, traders will have priors, which are mixtures of normals and are thus not normal.) Equation (15) and Figure 21–1 suggest that, given price, volume will reveal ρ_1^1 as long as $\rho_1^1 > \rho^2$ and ρ_1^1 is known to be above ρ_w or known to be below ρ_w. We assume that $\rho_t^1 \in (\rho^2, \rho_w)$ for all t.

PROPOSITION 3: *If* $\rho_t^1 \in (\rho^2, \rho_w)$, *that in the large economy* (ρ_1^1, θ_1) *is revealed by* (p_1, V_1).

The proposition demonstrates that under our assumptions market statistics are revealing. Of course, the value of the asset is not known to anyone with certainty because of the common error term, and so it cannot be revealed by these market statistics. Nonetheless, by observing volume in conjunction with price, traders can infer all the information available in the market. However, since traders do not know the true asset value (the ψ) it is not the case that the price and the volume reveal complete information. This lack of perfect revelation means that all traders face a learning problem in determining the value of the underlying asset. Since new signals arrive every period, it may be that the sequence of price and volume statistics provides information to all market participants. If this is the case, then technical analysis of past market statistics can be valuable. In the next section we begin our investigation of this role of technical analysis by extending our model to a multiperiod setting.

III. EQUILIBRIUM PRICE-VOLUME TIME SERIES

To examine the time series of price and volume we extend the asset market model of Section II to multiple periods. Period one price and volume reveal θ_1 so upon entering the second trading period, traders again have a common prior on the asset's eventual value. The prior is, by Bayes's rule, a normal with mean $(\rho_w \theta_1 + \rho_0 \psi_0)/(\rho_w + \rho_0)$ and variance $(\rho_w + \rho_0)^{-1}$. Traders in group 1 then receive signals $y_2^i = \psi + w_2 + e_2^i$ where the precision of the e_2^i distribution is ρ_2^1. Similarly, traders in group 2 receive signals $y_2^i = \psi + w_2 + \epsilon_2^i$ where the precision of the ϵ_2^i distribution is ρ^2. The market proceeds as in period one with the only differences being the new common prior, the new randomly drawn precision, the new randomly drawn signals, and the fact that endowments are now equilibrium, period one demands. All traders are engaging in technical analysis in the sense that their behavior is influenced by their prior, which in turn depends on past market statistics. At this point, however, the use of past data is dictated by our timing convention on when market data are available. It is more interesting to examine the effect of data from more than one previous period.

Our argument for revelation of information through market statistics is constructed inductively. Suppose that market statistics through period $t - 1$ are revealing. Then upon entering trading period t, the traders' common prior is a normal with mean

$$\bar{\theta}_{t-1} = \left[\rho_w \sum_{\tau=1}^{t-1} \theta_\tau + \rho_0 \psi_0 \right] \bigg/ [(t-1) \cdot \rho_w + \rho_0] \qquad (17)$$

and variance $(\hat{\rho}_{t-1})^{-1} = [(t-1) \cdot \rho_w + \rho_0]^{-1}$. The traders' gross demands for the risky asset are then given by

$$\hat{\rho}_{t-1}(\bar{\theta}_{t-1} - p_t) + \rho_t^{s1}(y_t^i - p_t) \qquad (18)$$

for each trader i in group 1, and by

$$\hat{\rho}_{t-1}(\bar{\theta}_{t-1} - p_t) + \rho^{s2}(y_t^i - p_t) \qquad (19)$$

for each trader i in group 2.

An application of the analysis in Section III shows that for the large economy the equilibrium period t price is given by

$$P_t = \frac{\hat{\rho}_{t-1}\bar{\theta}_{t-1} + (\mu\rho_t^{s1} + (1-\mu)\rho^{s2})\theta_t}{\hat{\rho}^{t-1} + \mu\rho_t^{s1} + (1-\mu)\rho^{s2}}. \qquad (20)$$

Per capita volume in period t for the large economy is

$$V_t = E\left[\frac{\mu}{2} \mid \hat{\rho}_{t-1}(\bar{\theta}_{t-1} - p_t) + \rho_t^{s1}(y_t^1 - p_t) - \hat{\rho}_{t-2}(\bar{\theta}_{t-2} - p_{t-1}) \right.$$

$$- \rho_{t-1}^{s1}(y_{t-1}^1 - p_{t-1}) \mid + \frac{(1-\mu)}{2} \mid \hat{\rho}_{t-1}(\bar{\theta}_{t-1} - p_t) + \rho^{s2}(y_t^2 - p_t)$$

$$\left. - \hat{\rho}_{t-2}(\bar{\theta}_{t-2} - p_{t-1}) - \rho^{s2}(y^2_{t-1} - p_{t-1}) \mid \right] \qquad (21)$$

where the expectation is with respect to the conditionally independent random variables $y_t^1 \sim N(\theta_t, 1/\rho_t^1)$, $y_{t-1}^1 \sim N(\theta_{t-1}, 1/\rho_{t-1}^1)$, $y_t^2 \sim N(\theta_t, 1/\rho^2)$, and $y_{t-1}^2 \sim N(\theta_{t-1}, 1/\rho^2)$.[17]

This volume expression differs from that in period one because traders now have endowments that are their equilibrium period $t-1$ demands. Traders do not know each individual's equilibrium period $t-1$ demands but they do know p_{t-1} and our induction hypothesis is that they have inferred ρ_t^s-1, $\hat{\rho}_{t-2}$ and $\bar{\theta}_{t-2}$ from past market statistics. So everything in the per capita volume expression other than y_t^1, y_{t-1}, y_t^2, y_{t-1}^2 and p_t^s is known. Calculation similar to that in the proof of Proposition 1 shows that per capita volume in period t for the large economy is

$$V_t = \frac{\mu}{2} \left[2(x_t^1)^{-1} \, \phi \, (\delta_t^1 x_t^1) + \delta_t^1 (\Phi(\delta_t^1 x_t^1) - \Phi(-\delta_t^1 x_t^1)) \right]$$

$$+ \frac{(1-\mu)}{2} \left[2(x^2)^{-1} \, \phi \, (\delta_t^2 x^2) + \delta_t^2 (\Phi(\delta_t^2 x^2) - \Phi(-\delta_t^2 x^2)) \right], \quad (22)$$

where

$$x_t^1 = \left(\frac{(\rho_t^{s1})^2}{\rho_t^1} + \frac{(\rho_{t-1}^{s1})^2}{\rho_{t-1}^1} \right)^{-1/2}, \; x^2 = \left(\frac{2(\rho^{s2})^2}{\rho^2} \right)^{-1/2}$$

$$\delta_t^1 = \hat{\rho}_{t-1}(\bar{\theta}_{t-1} - p_t) + \rho_t^{s1}(\theta_t - p_t) - \hat{\rho}_{t-2} \, (\bar{\theta}_{t-2} - p_{t-1}) - \rho_{t-1}^{s1}(\theta_{t-1} - p_{t-1}),$$

and

$$\delta_t^2 = \hat{\rho}_{t-1}(\bar{\theta}_{t-1} - p_t) + \rho^{s2}(\theta_t - p_t) - \hat{\rho}_{t-2}(\bar{\theta}_{t-2} - p_{t-1}) - \rho^{s2}(\theta_{t-1} - p_{t-1}).$$

Given our induction hypothesis, the only unknowns in p_t and V_t are ρ_t^1 and θ_t. Now, an argument parallel to that in Proposition 3 shows that (p_t, V_t) reveals (ρ_t^1, θ_t). So, if past market statistics have revealed past information, current market statistics will reveal current information. As a result, the price and per capita volume given above are equilibrium marked statistics.

PROPOSITION 4: *Suppose* $\rho_t^1 \in (\rho^2, \rho_w)$ *for all t. In the large economy, the equilibrium price and per capita volume time series are given by (20) and (22).*

In this economy, the equilibrium price converges almost surely to ψ. This occurs because all traders are using price-volume data to infer a sequence of θ_t's each of which is normally distributed with mean ψ. So, by the Strong Law of Large Numbers each individual's posterior mean, $\bar{\theta}_t$ is converging to ψ and the posterior variance is converging to zero. In the limit economy, everyone knows ψ, price is ψ and no trade occurs.[18]

One would be tempted to conjecture from this that trade vanishes, i.e., volume goes to zero, as time proceeds. This conjecture is false: Volume in the limit economy is zero, but the limit of volume as time proceeds is not zero. So the limit economy is not a good approximation to an economy after many periods.

The behavior of the price and volume time series for an economy with $\psi_0 = \psi = 1$, $\rho_0 = \rho_w = 2$, $\rho^2 = 0$, $\mu = 0.5$ and ρ_t^1 uniformly and independently distributed on $(0, 1)$ is illustrated in Figure 21–6. The equilibrium time series was constructed by drawing a sequence of 1,000 pairs of θ_t

FIGURE 21–6

The Time-Series Behavior of Volume and Price

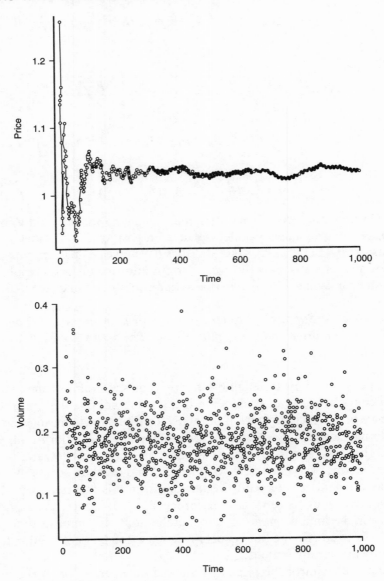

The figures are constructed for an economy with $\psi_0 = \psi = 1$, $\rho_0 = \rho_w = 2$, $\rho^2 = 0$, and $\mu = 0.5$ and ρ_t^i uniformly and independently distributed on $(0, 1)$. The equilibrium time series was constructed by drawing a sequence of 1,000 pairs of θ and ρ_t^i and constructing the equilibrium at each date given the draws in the sequence up to that date. Each point depicts the equilibrium actions at that date.

and ρ_t^1 and constructing the equilibrium at each date given the draws in the sequence up to that date. For this economy, price converges to $\psi = 1$ and volume has a nondegenerate limit distribution.

Trade does not disappear because although traders' beliefs are converging to a common belief, their precisions are diverging at the same rate. Intuitively, these effects can be explained by noting that in early periods traders may receive information indicating a wide discrepancy of price from true value, but because they are not very sure of the true value (i.e., their precision is low), they take limited positions. In later periods, when prices are close to true values, traders are more confident (precisions are high) and hence take large positions to exploit even small price discrepancies. Our results on the distribution of volume dictate that these two effects essentially offset. Thus, volume converges to a limit distribution, which is very different from volume in the limit economy.

IV. TECHNICAL ANALYSIS

Traders in the multiperiod economy developed in Section III are engaging in technical analysis. Their demands depend on past market statistics through their dependence on the sufficient statistic $\bar{\theta}_{t-1}$. Further, knowledge of the past helps in interpreting current market statistics. A trader who does not engage in technical analysis, and thus does not know $\hat{\rho}_{t-1}$ and $\bar{\theta}_{t-1}$ cannot fully infer current information from the current market statistics. Here traders need to remember the past; they cannot glean everything from current data.

To make the value of technical analysis more precise, let d_i^* $(p_t^*, \hat{\psi}, \hat{\rho})$ be uninformed trader i's demand for the risky asset at time t give equilibrium price p_t^*, prior mean $\hat{\psi}$ and prior precision $\hat{\rho}$.[19] Then give a wealth of w_t^i at the beginning of date t, trader i's date $t + 1$ random wealth (assuming that the period $t + 1$ the asset finally pays off) will be

$$w_{t+1}^i(p_t^*, \hat{\psi}, \hat{\rho}, \psi) = w_t^i + d_t^i(p_t^*, \hat{\psi}, \hat{\rho} \, [\psi - p_t^*], \tag{23}$$

where the predicted distribution of ψ is $N(\hat{\psi}, 1/\hat{\rho})$. Thus trader i's equilibrium expected utility is

$$E_\psi\left[-\exp\left[-w_{t+1}^i\left(p_t^*, \hat{\psi}, \hat{\rho}, \psi\right)\right]\right]. \tag{24}$$

Note that this expected utility depends on the trader's beliefs because of its explicit dependence on $\hat{\psi}$ and $\hat{\rho}$ and because the expectation is taken using the distribution $N(\hat{\psi}, 1/\hat{\rho})$.

A technical analyst believes $\hat{\psi} = \bar{\theta}_{t-1}$ and $\hat{\rho} = \hat{\rho}_{t-1}$. A trader who does not use past data believes $\hat{\psi} = \psi_0$ and $\hat{\rho} = \rho_0$. This divergence in beliefs allows us to calculate the value of technical analysis at time t:

$$E\left[E_\psi\left[-\exp\left[-w_{t+1}^i\left(p_t^*, \bar{\theta}_{t-1}, \hat{\rho}_{t-1}, \psi\right)\right]\middle|\bar{\theta}_{t-1}, \hat{\rho}_{t-1}\right]\right]$$
$$-E_\psi\left[-\exp\left[-w_{t+1}^i\left(p_t^*, \psi_0, \rho_0, \psi\right)\right]\right]. \tag{25}$$

The first expected value in equation (25) is the prior expected value of the ability to condition demand on the data revealed by market statistics through period $t - 1$, whereas the second expected value is simply the expected utility when the trader does not learn from the past. The difference between these expected values is thus the amount that an uninformed trader would be willing to pay at date t to know all past market statistics. (In this calculation we assume that this trader will have no effect on prices as he is one of the countable infinity of traders). This value is clearly non-negative because the trader can always ignore the data if they are not useful. In our economy, the value will be strictly positive as $\bar{\theta}_{t-1}$ is a consistent estimator of ψ. Proposition 5 demonstrates that the value of technical analysis depends on the quality of information.

PROPOSITION 5: *The value of technical analysis at time t is $1/2(t - 1)^{-1}\rho_w[(\psi_0 - p_t^*)^2 + 1/\rho_0] > 0$. This value is increasing in ρ_w and decreasing in ρ_0.*

One aspect of our results that should be stressed is that technical analysis is valuable not because of volume or any other specific statistic but rather because there is some underlying uncertainty to be learned in the economy. Technical analysis is valuable for all traders in our model. Where volume matters is in affecting the benefits of technical analysis. Though traders gain from watching prices, they do better still by watching prices and volume.

That technical analysis is more valuable if past market statistics, impound higher-quality information (i.e., ρ_w is large), and is less valuable if there is less to be learned from market data (i.e., ρ_0 is large) is an interesting result of our analysis. Because technical analysis helps traders interpret current information, watching the sequence of market statistics allows traders to correctly update beliefs. It seems reasonable that the value of doing so depends on the properties of the information structure. If traders already know a lot about the asset (their prior precision ρ_0 is large) or information in general is not very good (ρ_w small) then watching the market is not very valuable.

The properties of technical analysis derived above suggest that it may be particularly appropriate for small, less widely followed stocks. Such firms tend to have greater uncertainty about their future prospects and hence have a low prior precision. Moreover, such stocks may be more affected by private rather than public information, meaning that the effect of private signals may be higher. For such stocks, technical analysis of market statistics may play an important role in providing information to the market and, consequently, efficiency to the price.

V. CONCLUSIONS

We have investigated how technical analysis can be valuable to traders in an economy in which the only uncertainty arises from the underlying information structure. In our model, technical analysis is valuable because current market statistics may be sufficient to reveal some information, but not all. Because the underlying uncertainty in the economy is not resolved in one period, sequences of market statistics can provide information that is not impounded in a single market price.

Where we believe our results are most interesting is in delineating the important role played by volume. In our model, volume provides information in a way distinct from that provided by price. As is true in most rational expectations models, price impounds information about the average level of trader's private information. But unique to our model is the feature that volume captures the important information contained in the quality of traders' information signals. Because the volume statistic is not normally distributed, if traders condition on volume they can sort out the information implicit in volume from that implicit in price. We have shown that volume plays a role beyond simply being a descriptive parameter of the trading process.

Our focus on quality, or precision, of information suggests that the value of particular market statistics may vary depending upon characteristics of the information structure. While we have discussed the potential applications of technical analysis for small, thinly followed stocks, it seems likely that even (or perhaps, especially) in active markets volume may play an important role. The existence of the Dow-Jones "Rumor Wire" suggests that even "bad" (in the sense of imprecise) information can affect stock prices, so that using the information conveyed by volume may be particularly useful to traders operating in such volatile markets. Indeed, one criticism of program trading voiced by professional traders is that it distorts the information typically provided by trading volume. As our analysis here suggests, introducing trading volume unrelated to the underlying information structure would surely weaken the ability of uninformed traders to interpret market information accurately.

APPENDIX

Proof of Proposition 1: We first provide a useful lemma.

LEMMA 1: *Let* y ~ $N(\theta, 1/\rho)$, *then*

$$E[|\gamma y + a|] = 2\frac{\gamma}{\sqrt{2\pi\rho}} \exp\left[-\frac{1}{2}\left(\frac{\delta\rho^{1/2}}{\gamma}\right)^2\right] + \delta\left[\Phi\left(\frac{\delta\rho^{1/2}}{\gamma}\right) - \Phi\left(\frac{-\delta\rho^{1/2}}{\gamma}\right)\right],$$

for $\delta = a + \gamma\theta$, *and* Φ *the cumulative normal.*

Proof of Lemma 1: Note that $\Pr(|\gamma y + a| \leq \alpha) = \Pr(-\alpha \leq \gamma y + a \leq \alpha) =$

$$\Pr\left(\frac{\rho^{1/2}}{\gamma}(-\alpha - \gamma\theta - a) \leq z \leq \frac{\rho^{1/2}}{\gamma}(\alpha - \gamma\theta - a)\right)$$

$$= \Phi\left(\frac{\rho^{1/2}}{\gamma}(\alpha - a - \gamma\theta)\right) - \Phi\left(\frac{\rho^{1/2}}{\gamma}(-\alpha - a - \gamma\theta)\right),$$

for z a standard normal. Thus, the density of the random variable $|\gamma y + a|$ is $f(\alpha) = \rho^{1/2}/\gamma[\phi((\rho^{1/2}/\gamma)(\alpha - a - \gamma\theta)) + \phi((\rho^{1/2}/\gamma)(-\alpha - a - \gamma\theta))]$, for ϕ the standard normal density. The claim in the lemma now follows by computing the integral $\int_0^\infty \alpha f(\alpha)d\alpha$. Q.E.D.

Rewriting equation (13) we have:

$$V_1 = \frac{\mu}{2}\left[\frac{1}{N_I}\sum_{i=1}^{N_I}\left|\rho_0(\psi_0 - p_1) + \rho_1^{s1}(y_1^i - p_1)\right|\right]$$

$$+ \frac{(1 - \mu)}{2}\left[\frac{1}{N_u}\sum_{i=N_I+1}^{N}\left|\rho_0(\psi_0 - p_1) + \rho^{s2}(y_1^i - p_1)\right|\right].$$

By the Strong law of large numbers as $N \to \infty$ this sequence of random variables converges almost surely to

$$\frac{\mu}{2} \; E\left[\left| \rho_0(\psi_0 - p_1) + \rho_1^{s1}(y^1 - p_1)\right|\right]$$

$$+ \; \frac{(1-\mu)}{2} \; E\left[\left| \rho_0(\psi_0 - p_1) + p^{s2}(y^2 - p_1)\right|\right]$$

where

$$y^1 \sim N(\theta_1, \, 1/\rho_1^1) \text{ and } y^2 \sim N(\theta_1, \, 1/\rho^2).$$

Using Lemma 1 we have limit per capita volume almost surely equal to the expression given in Proposition 1.

Proof of Proposition 2: Differentiating volume, equation (15) in the text, with respect to p_1 yields

$$\frac{\partial V_1}{\partial p_1} = \frac{\mu}{2} \frac{\partial \hat{\delta}_1^1}{\partial p_1} \left[\Phi\left(\frac{\hat{\delta}_1^1 (\rho_1^1)^{1/2}}{\rho_1^{s1}}\right) - \Phi\left(-\frac{\hat{\delta}_1^1 (\rho_1^1)^{1/2}}{\rho_1^{s1}}\right)\right]$$

$$+ \; \frac{(1-\mu)}{2} \; \frac{\partial \hat{\delta}_1^2}{\partial p_1}\left[\Phi\left(\frac{\hat{\delta}_1^2 (\rho^2)^{1/2}}{\rho^{s2}}\right) - \Phi\left(-\frac{\hat{\delta}_1^2 (\rho^2)^{1/2}}{\rho^{s2}}\right)\right].$$

At $p_{1 \,=\,} \psi_0$ we have $\hat{\delta}_1^1 = \hat{\delta}_1^2$. Thus, $\partial V_1/\partial p_1 = 0$ at $p_1 = \psi_0$.
The second derivative of volume with respect to price is

$$\frac{\partial^2 V_1}{\partial p_1^2} = \mu\left(\frac{\partial \hat{\delta}_1^1}{\partial p_1}\right)^2 \frac{(\rho_1^1)^{1/2}}{\rho_1^{s1}} \; \phi\left(\frac{\hat{\delta}_1^1 (\rho_1^1)^{1/2}}{\rho_1^{s1}}\right)$$

$$+ \; (1-\mu)\left(\frac{\partial \hat{\delta}_1^2}{\partial p_1}\right)^2 \frac{(\rho^2)^{1/2}}{\rho^{s2}} \; \phi\left(\frac{\hat{\delta}_1^2 (\rho^2)^{1/2}}{\rho^{s2}}\right) > 0.$$

Thus, volume is convex in p_1 and achieves its minimum at $p_1 = \psi_0$.

Proof of Proposition 3: Differentiating volume, equation (15) in the text, with respect to ρ_1^1 yields

$$\frac{\partial V_1}{\partial \rho_1^1} = \frac{\mu}{2}\left[\left(\frac{\rho_w(\rho_w - \rho_1^1)}{\rho_1^1(\rho_w + \rho_1^1)^2}\right)\phi\left(\frac{\hat{\delta}_1^1(\rho_w + \rho_1^1)}{\rho_w(\rho_1^1)^{1/2}}\right) + \left(\frac{\partial \hat{\delta}_1^1}{\partial \rho_1^1}\right)\left\{\Phi\left(\frac{\hat{\delta}_1^1(\rho_w + \rho_1^1)}{\rho_w(\rho_1^1)^{1/2}}\right)\right.$$

$$-\Phi\left(-\frac{\hat{\delta}_1^1(\rho_w + \rho_1^1)}{\rho_w(\rho_1^1)^{1/2}}\right)\right\}\right] + \frac{(1-\mu)}{2}\left(\frac{\partial\hat{\delta}_1^2}{\partial\rho_1^1}\right)\left[\Phi\left(\frac{\hat{\delta}_1^2(\rho_w + \rho^2)}{\rho_w(\rho^2)^{1/2}}\right)\right.$$

$$-\Phi\left(-\frac{\hat{\delta}_1^2(\rho_w - \rho^2)}{\rho_w(\rho^2)^{1/2}}\right)\right].$$

The term involving the normal density, ϕ, is positive if $p_w \geq \rho_1^1$. The terms involving the differences of cumulative normals are also positive as $\partial\hat{\delta}_1^i/\partial\rho_1^1$ the difference of the cumulative normals always have the same sign as long as $\rho_1^1 > \rho^2$. Thus, $\partial V_1/\partial\rho_1^1 > 0$ for $\rho_1^1 \in (\rho^2, \rho_w)$.

So, given the price of p_1 and the equilibrium pricing equation, the only unknown in volume is ρ_1^1 and volume is strictly increasing in ρ_1^1. Thus, given p_1 volume reveals ρ_1^1. Then θ_1 is revealed by the pricing equation (12). Q.E.D.

Proof of Proposition 4: Given the induction hypothesis the proof that (ρ_1^1, θ_t) is revealed by (p_t, V_t) follows directly from the proof of Proposition 3. We know by Proposition 3 that (ρ_1^1, θ_1) is revealed by (p_1, V_1). This completes the induction argument. Now the fact that (20) and (22) describe period t equilibrium follows from the calculations in the text.

Proof of Proposition 5: The calculation shows that the value of technical analysis given by equation (25) is

$$\frac{1}{2}(t-1)^{-1}\rho_w\left[(\psi_0 - p_t^*)^2 + 1/\rho_0\right].$$

This value is strictly positive, increasing in ρ_w and decreasing in ρ_0.

BIBLIOGRAPHY

Bhattacharya, Utpal, and Matthew Spiegel. "Are Noisy Prices Caused by Noisy Traders? Theory and Evidence." Working paper, Columbia University, 1991.

Blume, Lawrence, and David Easley. "Rational Expectations Equilibrium: An Alternative Approach," *Journal of Economic Theory* 34 (1984), pp. 116–29.

———. "Implementation of Walrasian Equilibria." *Journal of Economic Theory* 51 (1990), pp. 207–27.

Brown, David, and Robert Jennings, "On Technical Analysis," *Review of Financial Studies* 2, 1989, pp. 527–51.

Brock, William, Josef Lakonishok, and Blake LeBaron. "Simple Technical Trading Rules and the Stochastic Properties of Stock Returns," *Journal of Finance* 47 (1992), pp. 1731–64.

Campbell, J., S. Grossman, and J. Wang. "Trading Volume and Serial Correlations in Stock Returns." Working paper, M.I.T., 1991.

Conrad, Jennifer; Allaudeen Hameed; and Cathy Niden. "Volume and Autocovariance in Short Horizon Individual Security Returns." Working paper, University of North Carolina, 1992.

DeGroot, Morris. *Optimal Statistical Decisions* New York: McGraw-Hill, 1970.

Easley, David, and Maureen O'Hara, "Time and the Process of Security Price Adjustment," *Journal of Finance* 47 (1992), pp. 577–605.

Edwards, R.D., and John Magee. *Technical Analysis of Stock Trends* Springfield, Mass.: J. Magee, 1957.

Gallant, A. Ronald; Peter E. Rossi; and George Tauchen. "Stock Prices and Volume," *Review of Financial Studies* 5 (1992), pp. 199–242.

Grossman, Sanford, and Joseph Stiglitz. "On the Impossibility of Informationally Efficient Markets," *American Economic Review* 70 (1980), pp. 393–408.

Grundy, Bruce, and Maureen McNichols. "Trade and the Revelation of Information through Prices and Direct Disclosure," *Review of Financial Studies* 2 (1989), pp. 495–526.

Harris, Milton, and Artur Raviv. "Differences of Opinion Make a Horse Race." Working paper, Northwestern University, 1991.

Hellwig, Martin. "Rational Expectations Equilibrium with Conditioning on Past Prices: A Mean-Variance Example," *Journal of Economic Theory* 26 (1982), pp. 279–312.

Jordan, James. "'On the Efficient Markets Hypothesis," *Econometrica* 51 (1983), 1325–44.

Karpoff, Jonathan. "The Relation between Price Changes and Trading Volume: A Survey," *Journal of Financial and Quantitative Analysis* 22 (1987), pp. 109–26.

Neftci, S.N.. "Naive Trading Rules in Financial Markets and Weiner-Kolmogorov Prediction Theory: A Study of Technical Analysis," *Journal of Business* 64 (1991), pp. 549–71.

Pring, Martin J., *Technical Analysis Explained*, 3rd ed. (McGraw-Hill, New York) 1991.

Randner, Roy. "Rational Expectations Equilibrium: Generic Existence and the Information Revealed by Prices," *Econometrica* 47 (1979), pp. 665–78.

Wang, Jiang. "A Model of Competitive Stock Trading Volume." Working paper, M.I.T., 1991.

ENDNOTES

1. The classic work on technical analysis is generally regarded as Edwards and Magee (1957). A more recent work that also details the explicit role of volume in technical analysis is Pring (1991). Neftci (1991) and Brock, Lakonishok, and LeBaron (1992) provide empirical testing of some common rules used in technical analysis of price changes. The latter paper suggests that positive returns may accrue to at least some price-based technical strategies.

2. We conduct a Walrasian analysis and so do not ask how such equilibria could be attained. This is a problem even for rational expectations equilibria

without conditioning on volume. Blume and Easley (1990) show that absent some restrictive conditions there does not exist a mechanism that would implement rational expectations equilibria. We view equilibria with conditioning on contemporaneous market statistics as one of several possible approximations to actual market processes. In Section III, we explore an alternative approximation that we find more appealing.

3. We consider Walrasian equilibria. There is no market maker, so we do not worry about inventory affecting the total quantity traded. If traders have endowments of the risky asset then we need to sum the absolute value of the trader's net demands (see equation (8)).

4. If traders are not allowed to condition on the direction of their own trade, or if they have differing endowments so that they cannot infer the sign of x from their trade, then the only equilibrium would be nonrevealing. However, the distribution of ψ given their information could not be normal, so finding this equilibrium would be a formidable task.

5. Those expressions are for any finite economy. The limit economy is degenerate with $p = \psi$. Grundy and McNichols consider the limit to avoid the computational difficulties that arise when individual endowments carry information. That is not a problem here as price and volume are already fully informative. In any case, the limit would be no problem in any economy in which the aggregate signal $\bar{y}$ was not perfect. For example, the common error model used in Brown and Jennings would work.

6. Obviously, a trader could also infer x from his own demand. We address this possibility later in this section.

7. Our analysis applies to first-period volume, but would apply equally well to volume in any period in which new endowments were distributed as they were in period one. Grundy and McNichols consider volume in period two where no new endowments arrive, and so per capita volume is not infinite. They provide some interesting results on when the "no-trade" equilibrium results break down and volume, per se, is positive. They do not consider the possibility of conditioning on volume, which is the focus of our concern here.

8. An interesting analysis of the role of noise in noisy rational expectations models is given by Bhattacharya and Spiegel (1991).

9. In a market microstructure model, Easley and O'Hara (1992) demonstrate that volume may provide information on the existence of new information. In their model, however, trades occur sequentially, so that the information content of volume differs from the role it plays in a call market, rational expectation framework.

10. The assumption that preferences and endowments are identical is not necessary. Suppose traders have constant absolute risk aversion utility functions of the form $-\exp(-R_i w_i)$ and endowments y_i. If price and volume are revealing, then volume must be

$$\frac{1}{2}\Sigma_i \left| \frac{\Sigma_j y_j}{R_i \Sigma_j (1/R_j)} - y_i \right|.$$

But this does not depend on private information. So unless price alone was revealing, price and volume cannot be revealing.

11. Note that this information includes not only the direction of the trade, but its magnitude as well.

12. It is easy to calculate this revealing equilibrium in the Grundy-McNichols and Brown-Jennings models. If each trader conjectures that price and his own net trade is revealing, then his demand depends only on the mean signal. His demand and price then reveal the per capita supply as well as the mean signal.

13. At this point, we place no assumption on the p_t stochastic process. In the following section some additional structure will be needed.

14. This is the exogenous distribution of trader i's signal from trader i's point of view. He knows that the signal has unknown mean ψ and known variance $1/\rho_t^s$. Using standard Bayesian updating [see DeGroot (1970)], the expected value of the asset given signal y_t^i is $(\rho_0 \psi_0 + \rho_t^s y_t^i)(\rho_0 + \rho_t^s)^{-1}$.

15. Ideally, each trader would predict the stochastic process of prices, given his current information, and then solve the intertemporal decision problem taking potential capital gains into account. This problem is tractable if and only if future prices are normally distributed. When precisions are known, this occurs and we have solved the resulting dynamic programming problems. In this case, the value function is negative exponential in wealth, so the only change from the analysis in the text is a change of parameters in demands and thus prices. With random precisions we cannot obtain a closed-form solution to the decision problem and we have thus chosen the approximation of myopic demands.

16. This complementary role of price and volume is also characteristic of technical analysis techniques. Pring (1991) notes: "It is therefore essential to relate the movement of the volume oscillator (or moving average) to the prevailing movement in price." For a discussion of techniques involving volume see Pring, chapter 18.

17. The expression $\hat{\rho}_{t-2}(\bar{\theta}_{t-2} - p_{t-1}) + \rho_{t-1}^{si}(y_{t-1} - p_{t-1})$ is a random variable representing the period t endowment of group i traders. Traders do not know any individual's endowment, but they do know the distribution of endowments.

18. Of course any discussion of the limit is straining our story of an asset with an eventual value of ψ a bit too much. But this is intended to be a discussion of the general tendencies of price and volume.

19. This is the demand by a trader who does not receive a signal at date t. The calculation for a trader who has received a signal is similar but more complex.

CHAPTER 22

MANAGEMENT SUMMARY

Title: "Evidence of Chaos in Commodity Futures Prices"

Publication: *The Journal of Futures Markets* 12, no. 3, pp. 291–305.

Authors: Gregory P. DeCoster, Bowdoin College
             Walter C. Labys, West Virginia University
             Douglas W. Mitchell, West Virginia University

Data: Daily futures data representing 4,462 observations for sugar; 5,297 observations for silver; 5,308 for copper; and 4,087 observations for coffee. The data were extracted from 1969 to 1989.

Synopsis: The study shows the presence of chaotic structure in all markets tested. The evidence of structure raises further questions about the efficient market hypothesis, since it creates the possibility that profitable, nonlinear-based trading rules may exist.

Evidence of Chaos in Commodity Futures Prices

Gregory P. DeCoster
Walter C. Labys
Douglas W. Mitchell

INTRODUCTION

The analysis and modeling of commodity futures price behavior continues to be an important issue. Much of this research centers on the following issues [Kamara, (1982)]: (1) Forecasting performance—is the futures price an unbiased predictor of the spot price at maturity, or are there explainable systematic biases? (2) Stochastic or structural character of futures prices—can they be explained by some linear or nonlinear model, or some form of random walk? (3) Distribution of futures prices—do they follow a normal distribution; if not, what other form? (4) Equilibrium pricing of futures contracts within the capital market—how are they related to the prices of other risky assets?

This study is concerned with the second issue; specifically, whether there exists nonlinear dynamic structure and, in particular, chaotic structure in the behavior of futures prices.[1] Chaotic dynamic systems are capable of generating a rich variety of time-series patterns, and such time series are often random-appearing. Yet, if such structure can be shown to exist, the implication would be that the empirical validity of simple, early versions of the efficient markets hypothesis [e.g. Fama (1970)] which imply a

The authors are grateful to Curt Taylor for his excellent and extensive programming assistance, and
to Rachel Connelly, Dan Gijsbers, and John Georgellis for their generous help.
Gregory P. DeCoster is an Assistant Professor of Economics at Bowdoin College.
Walter C. Labys is a Professor of Resource Economics at West Virginia University.
Douglas W. Mitchell is a Professor of Economics at West Virginia University.

random walk for asset prices is called into question.[2] This would indicate that future research should be directed toward the difficult task of identifying the specific form of the underlying price structure. When that is accomplished, a better understanding of the economic behavior underlying the markets, and the potential for improved short-term (though not long-term) predictions will result.[3]

The search for nonlinear structure in financial and economic time series has become widespread in the past few years. Of particular note in the context of commodity prices are the works of Frank and Stengos (1989), who find evidence of nonlinear structure in gold and silver rates of return, and of Blank (1990), who finds nonlinear structure in soybean futures prices. Other examples include Scheinkman and LeBaron (1989a) and Hinich and Patterson (1985) on stock returns; Blank (1990) on stock futures prices; Barnett and Chen (1988) and DeCoster and Mitchell (1991b) on monetary aggregates and components; Hsieh (1989) on exchange rates; and Frank and Stengos (1988b), Frank, Gencay, and Stengos (1988), Brock and Sayers (1988), and Scheinkman and LeBaron (1989b) on macroeconomic data. These studies collectively suggest that chaotic dynamics may be of considerable importance in financial and economic data.

A technique commonly used in these articles is the correlation dimension technique of Grassberger and Procaccia (1983). The purpose of the present article is to use the correlation dimension technique to search for chaotic structure in daily futures price data for each of four commodities: sugar, coffee, silver, and copper. This study finds that, for all four futures prices series, there is strong evidence of nonlinear structure, and possibly, chaos. The results are not explained by the alternative hypothesis of an ARCH model. As pointed out by Barnett and Hinich (forthcoming), this evidence can be interpreted as a failure to reject the null hypothesis of chaos in the data. It should be noted that all the data series contain in excess of 4,000 observations (far more than in most previous correlation dimension studies in economics). Thus, although there is some question as to the effectiveness of this technique in very small samples [Ramsey, Sayers, and Rothman (1988)], the use of the technique is strongly justified by the sizes of this study's data sets. The concern in DeCoster and Mitchell (1991a) about possible insufficient ability to detect chaos in samples of the present size is not important in the present context.

MODELING FUTURES PRICES

The ideal that futures prices might follow a random walk is initially found in Working (1958), who postulates that the continuous flow of many different kinds of information into the market causes frequent price changes, which might be nearly random. Still this model allows for some gradualness of price changes, and thus, for some degree of a very short-term predictability. Samuelson (1965) further developed this model by postulating that futures prices follow a Martingale process. That is, futures prices, insofar as they constitute unbiased estimates of future spot prices, can be described by a stochastic process in which the expected price in the next period equals the current price.

Most of the empirical tests of the random walk and Martingale processes search for the existence of serial correlation and trends, since both require price changes to be independent. In practice, even when systematic dependencies in price changes are detected, it is very difficult to determine whether their magnitude and frequency are sufficient to violate the random walk model. Previous findings in this regard are well known and need not be mentioned except briefly. Trend deviations from random walk were first discovered for wheat and corn by Houthakker (1961), and for soybeans by Smidt (1965). Their results based on filter or trading rules are questioned by Cargill and Rausser (1975). Rocca (1969), Labys and Granger (1970), and Cargill and Rausser (1972) in performing spectral analysis of more than 20 futures price series find some evidence for a modified random walk process, mostly resembling the Martingale process. Such studies test for the existence of a linear model; yet it is possible that some form of nonlinear model might underlie the price fluctuations in question. Stevenson and Bear (1970) and Leuthold (1972) employing filter rules confirm positive and negative price dependence to cast doubt on the validity of the random walk model.

Another approach of interest deals with the testing of the weak form and semi-strong form efficient market models. Even though the Martingale model may be rejected in empirical tests of futures price behavior, this does not constitute a rejection of the efficient market model underlying that behavior. A market can be said to use information efficiently if no way exists to use available information to increase expected wealth by frequent trading. This implies that trading rules are worthless and price information cannot indicate the best opportunities to buy and sell. Regarding the efficient market hypothesis, it can be said to be true if the risk-adjusted return net of all costs from the best trading rule is not more than the comparable figure, when assets are traded infrequently [Jensen (1978); Taylor (1986)]. The interpretation of this hypothesis in a commodity futures price context is sometimes confusing: (1) trading rules do not replicate real trading possibilities; (2) it is difficult to find benchmarks for return comparisons; (3) insufficient information is available about the distribution of filter returns to confirm the significance of a distribution; and (4) retrospective optimization of the parameters or structure of a filter is dubious [see Taylor (1986)]. Danthine (1977) finds confusion in linking Martingale processes and efficiency in commodity markets for other reasons. In particular, the possibility of shortages may lead to above-normal expected profits, and a diminishing marginal rate of transformation over time may cause a severe correlation of price changes, even in an efficient market.

Guimaraes, Kingsman, and Taylor (1989) attempt to reappraise the efficiency hypothesis. Taylor's (1980) approach evaluates a futures price model that resembles a random walk yet includes a price-trend term for which formal stochastic processes are conjectural. This model, used on tests of 10 commodity futures contracts traded in London, identifies a "price drift," which can be associated with the weak form of the efficient market model. Gross (1988) is concerned also about whether futures prices fully incorporate all publicly available information at the time of contracting. Based on a study of LME futures prices for copper and aluminum, he finds that the efficiency hypothesis cannot be rejected for these metals. Gupta and Mayer (1981), in performing efficiency tests for sugar, cocoa, and coffee prices as well as tin prices, also confirm the efficiency hypothesis. Both tests involve the more rigorous semi-strong form of the hypothesis. Among studies that have difficulty in confirming the hypothesis, MacDonald and Taylor (1988), also employing LME futures prices, confirm the hypothesis for copper and lead but not for zinc. They employ a more rigorous vector autoregressive methodology using appropriate stationarity-inducing transformations. Brorsen et al (1984) cannot confirm the hypothesis for cotton futures prices representing contract funding in New York.

Although most of the above studies are based on linear models, a more recent approach to futures price modeling considers the possibility that other deviations from random processes may exist. That approach involves the use of nonlinear equations generating chaotic behavior. Interestingly, the application of the concept of chaos to commodity futures price behavior can be found in an earlier work by Mandelbrot.

Drawing upon Houthakker's (1961) analysis of cotton prices, Mandelbrot (1963a and b) developed a model of price behavior by replacing Gaussian probability laws with those termed "stable Paretian." His approach represented an attempt to discover orderly behavior within what appeared to be a random series of price fluctuations. It is in this context that Frank and Stengos (1989) investigated the Martingale hypothesis using an approach of Sims (1984) as well as a chaos-based approach.

Although Frank and Stengos were not able to reject the Martingale hypothesis in a series of standard econometric tests involving daily and weekly silver and gold prices, they did provide correlation dimension-based evidence of the presence of nonlinear structure. Note that such structure can be consistent with efficient markets. This article follows Frank and Stengos in investigating whether nonlinear structure exists in futures price data for four commodities.

THE CORRELATION DIMENSION TECHNIQUE

The correlation dimension technique was originally developed by the physicists Grassberger and Procaccia (1983).[4] The technique is intended to detect the presence of chaotic structure in data by embedding overlapping subsequences of the data in m-space for various embedding dimensions, m. Purely random data are infinite-dimensional, and thus will "fill" a region of m-space for any finite m. On the other hand, data generated by a deterministic system will have a finite dimension, which will be no greater than the number of independent state variables in the system and which may be a noninteger. Thus, for sufficiently large m, one will be able to detect structure in deterministic data.

Specifically, suppose a deterministic system $y_t = f(y_{t-i})$ where y is an n-dimensional vector of (possibly unobserved) state variables. Suppose further a time series of a scalar variable, x, generated by $x_t = g(yt)$ for some observer function, g. Then Takens' (1980) embedding theorem states that $m \geq 2n + 1$ is a sufficiently large embedding dimension to detect the structure. Since n is not known, an increasing sequence of m values must be tried.

For any value of m, one computes the correlation dimension of a stationary series $\{x_t\}$ by first computing the correlation integral $C(\epsilon,m)$ for various values of a critical distance, ϵ. $C(\epsilon,m)$ is defined to be the fraction of pairs of m-dimensional points $(x_i x_{i+1} \cdots x_{i+m-1})$, $(x_j x_{j+1} \cdots x_{j+m-1})$ whose distance from each other is no greater than ϵ. The distance is measured according to the commonly used sup norm, defined as:

$$||(x_i x_{i+1} \cdots x_{i+m-1}), (x_j x_{j+1} \cdots x_{j+m-1})|| \equiv \max_{k\in[0,_{m-1}]}\{|x_{i+k} - x_{j+k}|\}$$

One computes the correlation integral for a variety of ϵ equally spaced on a log scale, so that $C(\epsilon,m)$ ranges from near zero to unity.

The correlation dimension for a given m is the elasticity of $C(\epsilon,m)$ with respect to ϵ. Thus, one needs to run a linear regression of $\log C(\epsilon,m)$ on $\log \epsilon$ with an intercept. To prepare for this regression, one first plots $\log C(\epsilon,m)$ against $\log \epsilon$, and visually inspects the plot. While, in principle, the plot should be linear throughout, in practice, the presence of noise in data is likely to result in a separate and relatively steep region at low values of ϵ; and finiteness of the data set may cause a choppy appearance in the plot as well as curvature at high values of ϵ. Therefore, one must judgmentally determine the linear range over which to run the regression. The slope estimate from this regression is the correlation dimension estimate for this value of m.

This procedure is repeated for a sequence of increasing values of m. If the data are purely random, then in infinite samples, the correlation dimension will equal m for all m. In practice, with a finite data set, the correlation dimension estimate may be substantially below m and may rise with m at less than a one-for-one rate [Frank and Stengos (1988b, 1989); Ramsey and Yuan (1987)]. If the data are deterministic, the slope estimates should "saturate" at some m, not rising any more as m is further increased; this saturation value of the slope is the correlation dimension estimate for the unobserved structure that generates the data. In practice, the slope estimates may never completely stop rising. Thus, the process of determining whether saturation has occurred, and structure has been detected, can, in general, be rather judgmental.[5] However, in all the cases reported in this study, the evidence that structure is detected is strong. The slope estimates are usually well under one-third of the respective m values used to generate them, and they rise only slowly with m.

The data for which this procedure is conducted must be stationary. Since the raw data, as described below, are futures prices, the data are rendered stationary by taking the first difference of the logs of the price data. Thus, the transformed data re rates of return.

To make sure that the detected structure is nonlinear rather than linear, Brock's (1986) residual test is employed. The stationary data are delinearlized by replacing the data with residuals from an autoregression of the data. If nonlinear structure is present, this procedure should, in principle, make no difference for the estimated correlation dimensions. However, in practice [Brock and Sayers (1988, p. 84)] the correlation dimension estimates rise with the number of terms in the autoregression. Therefore, this procedure should be used cautiously. The following procedure is utilized. Simple autocorrelations of rates of return are computed for lags 1–24. Then, an autoregression is run for the rate of return including any lags for which the simple autocorrelation is significant at the 1 percent level. The residuals from this autoregression serve as the AR-transformed data. Thus, the correlation dimension technique is performed for each commodity price series on both the rate of return data and on the AR-transformed data.

The shuffle test is also appropriate, given the tendency of finite sets of both noise and structured data to depart from the idealized behavior in their correlation dimension estimates. The shuffle test of Scheinkman and LeBaron (1989a) tests the hypothesis that a given correlation dimension estimate can come from a data series of noise with the same data distribution as that exhibited by the actual data. For the AR residuals of each of the four rate of return series, 20 artificial noise series with the same length and distribution as the AR residuals are created by sampling with replacement from those residuals. Then the correlation dimension is estimated for each artificial series, at the previously determined saturation embedding dimension and also at the highest embedding dimension (40). If at least 95 percent of these correlation dimension estimates for noise are above the corresponding estimates for the unshuffled data, the hypothesis that the unshuffled data are noise is rejected and the alternative hypothesis of nonlinear structure is accepted.

Finally, financial market data frequently appear to have a time-varying variance, which could produce correlation dimension estimates suggestive of deterministic nonlinear structure even if there are no deterministic components in the data. A time-varying variance could be generated by either a (stochastic) ARCH process or a deterministic process. Therefore, an ARCH filter is used to see if it is possible to rule out an ARCH process as an alternative explanation of the data. The same AR structure is used as before, and an ARCH(10) test is employed. Correlation dimension estimates are calculated for the standardized ARCH residuals and shuffle tests are conducted for each series at the saturation embedding dimension and at the highest embedding dimension.

DATA AND RESULTS

Daily data series of near futures prices for sugar, silver, copper, and coffee are used. These series have, respectively, 4,462, 5,297, 5,308, and 4,087 observations beginning between January 1968 and October 1972 and ending in March 1989. Further details appear in the Appendix.

As previously indicated, the data are transformed into first differences of logs of futures prices. The AR-transformed data, derived as described above, involve AR regressions with lags at 1 and 21 for sugar; at 3 and 15 for silver; at 2, 3, and 6 for copper. and at 1, 16, and 17 for coffee.

The correlation integral graphs, computed for embedding dimension values 4–40 by increments of 4, all look very similar to each other. For the non-AR-transformed data, a typical correlation integral graph, that of copper, is shown in Figure 22–1 for embedding dimensions 28–40 by increments of 4. Figure 22–2 shows a blow-up of the nearly linear region for ϵ values 0.020258 through 0.027296. The curves appear close to parallel, suggesting saturation.

Table 22–1 shows the correlation dimension estimates for the four rate of return series for embedding dimensions 4–40 by increments of 4. The correlation dimensions are always far below the corresponding embedding dimensions, and never rise above 11. The most striking results are for coffee. The correlation dimension is always below 6, strongly suggesting nonlinear structure with a relatively low state dimension. The other three series show strong evidence of structure as well.

The information provided by the level of the correlation dimension estimates is confirmed by the data in Table 22–2, which shows how fast these estimates rise with the embedding dimension. This rate of rise is measured by $H \equiv \Delta$ (correlation dimension)$/\Delta m$, where the increment Δmm is always 4. By the time an embedding dimension of 20 is reached, the H values for the four series are 0.16, 0.25, 0.21, and 0.13, and for higher embedding dimensions they drop even lower. In each case, these are much closer to the theoretical value of zero for pure structured, noiseless data than to the theoretical value of unity for structureless noise; thus, these results effectively approximate saturation, implying the presence of noisy structure. So the results for both the level and the saturation of the correlation dimension support a hypothesis of structure in the data. Note again that any inference of the specific saturation embedding dimension would necessarily be very imprecise; the point is simply that there is strong evidence for saturation and thus for the presence of structure.

To make sure that this structure is not linear, the residual test as described above is performed. Correlation dimension estimates computed for the autoregressive residuals are reported in Table 22–3. The results in Table 22–3 are very close to those in Table 22–1 for non-AR-transformed data, thereby supporting the notion that the structure detected is nonlinear rather than linear. H values for Table 22–3 estimates are presented in Table 22–4.

While these results strongly suggest the presence of nonlinear structure, it is prudent to check further the possibility that pure noise data could have generated these results in samples of these sizes. As discussed above, the shuffle test for the AR-transformed data for each commodity is performed using 20 shuffles at each of $m = 40$ and the m value for which H (taken out to three decimal places) is minimized (thus showing the

F I G U R E 22–1

Correlation Integral, Copper

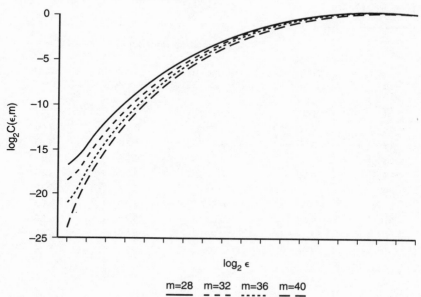

F I G U R E 22–2

Linear Region, Correlation Integral, Copper

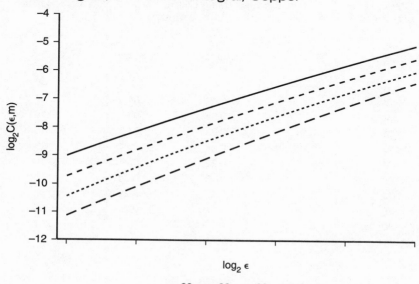

TABLE 22-1

Correlation Dimension Estimates for Daily Rate of
Return Data

| m | Correlation Dimension | | | |
	Silver (N = 5297)	Copper (N = 5308)	Sugar (N = 4462)	Coffee (N = 4087)
4	1.65	2.16	1.80	1.51
8	2.73	3.84	3.14	2.46
12	3.58	5.23	4.18	3.23
16	4.28	6.39	5.06	3.84
20	4.90	7.37	5.89	4.34
24	5.46	8.26	6.71	4.75
28	6.03	8.96	7.52	5.06
32	6.61	9.64	8.39	5.35
36	7.18	10.33	9.36	5.62
40	7.76	10.99	10.29	5.88

TABLE 22-2

H Values for Daily Rate of Return Data: $[H \equiv$ (Correlation
Dimension for This Embedding Dimensions Minus That for
the Next Lower Embedding Dimension) Divided by 4

m	Silver	Copper	Sugar	Coffee
4	—	—	—	—
8	0.27	0.42	0.34	0.24
12	0.21	0.35	0.26	0.19
16	0.18	0.29	0.22	0.15
20	0.16	0.25	0.21	0.13
24	0.14	0.22	0.21	0.10
28	0.14	0.18	0.20	0.08
32	0.15	0.17	0.22	0.07
36	0.14	0.17	0.24	0.07
40	0.15	0.17	0.23	0.07

TABLE 22-3

Correlation Dimension Estimates for AR Residuals

	Correlation Dimension			
m	Silver (N = 5282)	Copper (N = 5302)	Sugar (N = 4441)	Coffee (N = 4070)
4	1.75	2.18	1.90	1.77
8	2.90	3.89	3.30	2.92
12	3.80	5.31	4.68	3.80
16	4.55	6.50	5.30	4.50
20	5.22	7.51	6.16	5.06
24	5.83	8.41	7.01	5.51
28	6.46	9.12	7.85	5.92
32	7.10	9.80	8.81	6.33
36	7.73	10.48	9.94	6.75
40	8.36	11.16	11.07	7.16

TABLE 22-4

H Values for AR Residuals: [H ≡ (Correlation Dimension for This Embedding Dimension Minus That for the Next Lower Embedding Dimension) Divided by 4]

m	Silver	Copper	Sugar	Coffee
4	—	—	—	—
8	0.29	0.43	0.35	0.29
12	0.23	0.36	0.27	0.22
16	0.19	0.30	0.23	0.18
20	0.17	0.25	0.22	0.14
24	0.15	0.23	0.21	0.11
28	0.16	0.18	0.21	0.10
32	0.16	0.17	0.24	0.10
36	0.16	0.17	0.28	0.11
40	0.16	0.17	0.28	0.10

strongest saturation). For each set of 20 shuffles, Table 22–5 gives the mean, the high, and the low values of the estimated correlation dimension, and compares them to that of the corresponding unshuffled series.

Table 22–5 shows that, out of a total of 160 shuffle correlation dimension estimates computed, not a single one is as low as the corresponding nonshuffle estimate. Thus one can reject, with high confidence, the possibility that the data reflect simply structureless noise masquerading as structured data.

Finally, to test for an ARCH explanation of the data, an ARCH(10) test is run on the above AR specifications, standardizing the ARCH residuals to remove the time-varying aspect of their variance, estimating the correlation dimensions of the standardized residuals, and conducting shuffle tests. The correlation dimension estimates, H values, and shuffle results appear in Tables 22–6, 22–7, and 22–8, respectively (note that for three commodities the lowest H value occurs at the highest embedding dimension—40—so for those commodities only one shuffle test is needed.

A comparison of Table 22–6 with Table 22–3 shows that the ARCH filtering process increases the estimated correlation dimensions, as would be expected of any filtering process with finite data. However, the increases are not very large. The H values are also increased, as shown by Table 22–7 in comparison with Table 22–4, but they still reach minima much closer to the theoretical deterministic value of zero than to the theoretical noise value of one. The shuffle tests on the ARCH residuals uniformly confirm the earlier shuffle results. All 100 correlation dimension estimates for shuffled series of ARCH residuals are higher than the corresponding unshuffled correlation dimension estimate. This result is striking in light of the substantial filtering the data undergo, and it provides strong evidence for the proposition that there is some nonlinear process with a deterministic component underlying these data series.

CONCLUSIONS

This study applies the correlation dimension technique, along with the associated AR and ARCH residual tests and shuffle test, to rate of return series for the futures prices of four commodities. The results for the rate of return data and for their autoregressive and ARCH residuals, both in regard to the level and saturation of the correlation dimension estimates, strongly suggest the presence of structure in the data. The fact that the results are relatively unchanged by the use of AR residuals implies that this structure is nonlinear in nature, and the fact that the results hold up

TABLE 22–5

Shuffle Results, AR Residuals: Mean, High, and Low Values of Correlation Dimension Estimates over 20 Shuffles

Silver		Sugar	
$m = 24$	Mean = 7.42	$m = 28$	Mean = 9.27
	Low = 5.97		Low = 8.08
	High = 10.43		High = 10.69
	Unshuffled = 5.83		Unshuffled = 7.85
$m = 40$	Mean = 12.74	$m = 40$	Mean = 13.32
	Low = 10.02		Low = 11.72
	High = 17.54		High = 15.72
	Unshuffled = 8.36		Unshuffled = 11.07
Copper		**Coffee**	
$m = 32$	Mean = 12.74	$m = 28$	Mean = 8.42
	Low = 11.75		Low = 7.46
	High = 14.75		High = 10.62
	Unshuffled = 9.80		Unshuffled = 5.92
$m = 40$	Mean = 16.01	$m = 40$	Mean = 12.20
	Low = 14.77		Low = 10.78
	High = 18.36		High = 15.83
	Unshuffled = 11.16		Unshuffled = 7.16

TABLE 22–6

Correlation Dimension Estimates for Standardized
Arch Residuals

| | Correlation Dimension | | | |
| | Silver
($N = 5262$) | Copper
($N = 5282$) | Sugar
($N = 4421$) | Coffee
($N = 4050$) |
m				
4	1.57	1.59	1.56	1.57
8	3.15	3.23	3.10	3.01
12	4.64	4.93	4.61	4.45
16	5.99	6.55	6.00	5.83
20	7.22	8.08	7.28	7.07
24	8.36	9.53	8.55	8.09
28	9.46	10.84	9.70	9.00
32	10.54	12.04	10.85	9.87
36	10.55	13.23	12.07	10.63
40	12.55	14.40	13.31	11.32

TABLE 22–7

H Values for Standardized Arch Residuals

m	Silver	Copper	Sugar	Coffee
4	—	—	—	—
8	0.40	0.41	0.39	0.36
12	0.37	0.43	0.38	0.36
16	0.34	0.41	0.35	0.35
20	0.31	0.38	0.32	0.31
24	0.29	0.36	0.32	0.26
28	0.28	0.33	0.29	0.23
32	0.27	0.30	0.29	0.22
36	0.26	0.30	0.31	0.19
40	0.24	0.29	0.32	0.17

TABLE 22-8

Shuffle Results, Standardized Arch Residuals: Mean, High and Low Values of Correlation Dimension Estimates over 20 Shuffles

Silver		Sugar	
$m = 40$	Mean = 16.04	$m = 28$	Mean = 10.79
	Low = 13.10		Low = 9.85
	High = 19.95		High = 13.84
	Unshuffled = 12.55		Unshuffled = 9.70
		$m = 40$	Mean = 15.28
			Low = 14.09
			High = 18.99
			Unshuffled = 13.34
Copper		**Coffee**	
$m = 40$	Mean = 16.32	$m = 40$	Mean = 13.97
	Low = 14.64		Low = 12.46
	High = 19.31		High = 17.05
	Unshuffled = 14.40		Unshuffled = 11.32

under ARCH filtering shows that the apparent structure does not simply reflect heteroskedasticity. Further, the fact that the shuffle tests are passed with "flying colors" implies that the results are not a fluke that could have been achieved misleadingly, with unstructured data. It is worth noting that, since the data series had in excess of 4,000 observations, the procedures employed are stronger than they would be with the much smaller data series commonly used with these procedures by economists.

A noise explanation of the data as well as a linear-structure-plus-noise explanation are rejected. Thus, the hypothesis of nonlinear structure is accepted. As Barnett and Hinich (1989) point out, this acceptance is necessary but not sufficient for the presence of chaos in the data. If chaos is viewed as the null hypothesis, this study fails to reject it. Evidence for the presence of chaos is provided, but, as Barnett and Hinich say, "further research is needed before we can confirm or reject the discovery of chaos." In any event, if chaos is present, it is probably accompanied by noise, so even if the chaos is exactly identified, an incentive for risk-averse agents to engage in hedging behavior still exists.

The evidence of structure in futures prices raises further questions about the efficient markets hypothesis, since it creates the possibility that profitable, nonlinearity-based trading rules may exist. Clearly then, an important area for future research is to identify more precisely the nature of the nonlinearity in the data. Only then can it be established what, if any, profitable trading rules exist. Moreover, identification of the structure would establish whether prediction beyond some horizon is precluded, due to the sensitive dependence on initial conditions inherent in chaotic systems. Another important area for future research is to further develop equilibrium models of financial markets, which can give rise to dynamic structure in rates of return. Previous work in this vein includes van der Ploeg (1986) and Lucas (1978). Perhaps this substrand of literature could further clarify the relation between market efficiency and nonlinear dynamics.

APPENDIX

Daily futures price data are gathered for four major commodities traded on exchanges in New York: (1) The Coffee "C" contract at the Cocoa, Sugar, and Coffee Exchange, Inc., in ¢/100 lbs.; (2) The Sugar No. 11 contract at the Cocoa, Sugar, and Coffee Exchange, Inc., in ¢/100 lbs., (3) The Silver .999 Fine contract at the Commodity Exchange, Inc. in ¢/10 troy oz.; and (4) The Refined copper contract, at the Commodity Exchange, Inc. in ¢/100 lbs. The data are in the form of settlement prices and are from the Center for the Study of Futures Markets, Graduate Business School, Columbia University, New York.

The typical structure of commodity futures price series is that they are quoted for selected months of the year for which contracts are traded. The terms of these contracts are spaced from the near months to the more distant months. The accepted practice [Labys and Granger (1970); Taylor (1986)] is followed to compile the near future price series. These series adopt prices from the contract nearest to the present or spot data; a jump is made to the prices of the successive contract at the beginning of the month in which the near contract comes to maturity. The series for silver and copper begin in January 1968; the series for sugar begins in January 1971; and the series for coffee begins October 1972. All series end in March 1989.

ENDNOTES

1. Chaos refers to deterministic dynamic behavior which is bounded and neither periodic nor asymptotically periodic. Some nonlinear dynamic equations generate chaos, while some generate periodic behavior (repeating sequences).

Accessible introductions to the mathematics of chaos are to be found in Savit (1988), Gabisch (1987), Kelsey (1988), Baumol and Quandt (1985), Baumol and Benhabib (1989), and Frank and Stengos (1988a).

2. Van der Ploeg (1986) presents a model in which asset prices can evolve according to the logistic equation, which admits chaos, implying that rates of return would not be white noise. Lucas (1978) give another model with structure in rates of return.

3. Long-term prediction of a chaotic system is impossible even if the form and paramaterization of the system are perfectly known. This is because chaotic systems have sensitive dependence on initial conditions, meaning that the minute errors in the observation of the state of the system when predictions are made get translated into increasingly large errors in the predicted state of the system as the predictions go farther into the future. However, short-term prediction remains feasible.

4. See also Brock (1986) and Barnett and Chen (1988) for descriptions of this technique.

5. Note that the slope estimate for given m can be quite sensitive to the choice of the linear range over which to run the regression. Thus numerical estimates of the correlation dimension must be regarded with caution. However, the judgment of whether saturation has occurred tends to be insensitive to the choice of linear range.

BIBLIOGRAPHY

Barnette, W. A. and P. Chen. "The Aggregation-Theoretic Monetary Aggregates Are Chaotic and Have Strange Attractors." In *Dynamic Econometric Modeling,* Barnett, W., Berndt, E., and White, H. (eds.). Cambridge, UK: Cambridge University Press, 1988.

Barnette, W. A. and M. J. Hinich. "Has Chaos Been Discovered with Economic Data?" In *Evolutionary Dynamics and Nonlinear Economics,* P. Chen and R. Day (eds.). Oxford: Oxford University Press, (forthcoming).

Baumol, W., and J. Benhabib. "Chaos: Significance, Mechanism, and Economic Applications," *Journal of Economic Perspectives* 3 (1989), pp. 77–105.

Baumol, W., and R. Quandt. "Chaos Models and Their Implications for Forecasting," *Eastern Economic Journal* 11 (1985), pp. 3–15.

Blank, S. "'Chaos' in Futures Markets? A Nonlinear Dynamical Analysis," Columbia Business School Center for the Study of Futures Markets, Working Paper #204. Columbia University, New York, January 1990.

Brock, W. "Distinguishing Random and Deterministic Systems: Abridged Version," *Journal of Economic Theory* 40 (1986), pp. 168–95.

Brock, W. and C. Sayers. "Is the Business Cycle Characterized by Deterministic Chaos?" *Journal of Monetary Economics* 22 (1988), pp. 71–90.

Brorsen, B. W., D. Von Bailey, and J. W. Richardson. "Investigation of Price Discovery and Efficiency for Cash and Futures Cotton Prices," *Western Journal of Agricultural Economics* 9 (1984), pp. 170–76.

Cargill, T. F., and G. C. Rausser. "Time and Frequency Domain Representation of Futures Prices as a Stochastic Process," *Journal of the American Statistical Association* 67 (1972), pp. 23–30.

Cargill, T. F., and G. C. Rausser. "Temporal Price Behavior in Commodity Futures Markets," *Journal of Finance* 30 (1975), pp. 1043–53.

Danthine, J. P. "Martingale, Market Efficiency and Commodity Prices." *European Economic Review* 10 (1977), pp. 1–17.

DeCoster, G. P. and D. W. Mitchell. "The Efficacy of the Correlation Dimension Technique in Detecting Determinism in Small Samples," *Journal of Statistical Computation and Simulation* 39 (1991a), pp. 221–29.

DeCoster, G. P., and D. W. Mitchell. "Nonlinear Monetary Dynamics," *Journal of Business and Economic Statistics* 9 (1991b), pp. 455–61.

Fama, E. "Efficient Capital Markets: Review of Theory and Empirical Work," *Journal of Finance* 25 (1970), pp. 383–417.

Frank, J. R. Gencay, and T. Stengos. International Chaos?" *European Economic Review* 32 (1988), pp. 1569–84.

Frank, M. and T. Stengos. Chaotic Dynamics in Economic Time-Series," *Journal of Economic Surveys* 2 (1988a), pp. 103–33.

Frank, M. and T. Stengos. "Some Evidence Concerning Macroeconomic Chaos," *Journal of Monetary Economics* 22 (1988b), pp. 423–38.

Frank, M. and T. Stengos. "Measuring the Strangeness of gold and Silver Rates of Return," *Review of Economic Studies* 56 (1989), pp. 553–67.

Gabisch, G. "Nonlinearities in Dynamic Economic Systems," *Atlantic Economic Journal* 15 (1987), pp. 22–31.

Grassberger, P., and I. Procaccia. "Measuring the Strangeness of Strange Attractors," *Physica* 9D (1983), pp. 189–208.

Gross, M. "A Semi-Strong Test of the Efficiency of the Aluminum and Copper Markets at the LME," *Journal of Futures Markets* 8 (1988), pp. 67–77.

Guimaraes, R. M., B. G. Kingsman, and S. J. Taylor. *A Reappraisal of the Efficiency of Financial Markets*. Berlin: Springer–Verlag, 1989.

Gupta, S., and T. Mayer. "A Test of the Efficiency of Futures Markets in Commodities," *Weltwirtschaftliches Archives* 117 (1981), pp. 661–71.

Hinich, M. J., and D. M. Patterson. "Evidence of Nonlinearity in Daily Stock Returns," *Journal of Business and Economic Statistics* 3 (1985), pp. 69–77.

Houthakker, H. "Systematic and Random Elements in Short-Term Price Movements," *American Economic Review* 51 (1961), pp. 164–72.

Hsieh, D. A. "Testing for Nonlinear Dependence in Daily Foreign Exchange Rates," *Journal of Business* 62 (1989), pp. 339–68.

Jensen, M. C. "Some Anomalous Evidence Regarding Market Efficiency: An Editorial Introduction," *Journal of Financial Economics* 6 (1978), pp. 95–101.

Kamara, A. "Issues in Futures Markets: A Survey," Working Paper CSFM-30, Center for the Study of Futures Markets, Columbia University, New York, 1982.

Kelsey, D. "The Economics of Chaos or the Chaos of Economics," *Oxford Economic Papers* 40 (1988), pp. 1–31.

Labys, W. C. and C. W. J. Granger. *Speculation, Hedging and Commodity Price Forecasts*. Lexington, MA: Heath Lexington Books, 1970.

Leuthold, R. M. "Random Walk and Price Trends: The Live Cattle Futures Market," *Journal of Finance* 27 (1972), pp. 879–89.

Lucas, R. E. "Asset Prices in an Exchange Economy," *Econometrica* 46 (1978), pp. 1429–45.

MacDonald, R., and M. P. Taylor. "Testing Rational Expectations and Efficiency in the London Metal Exchange," *Oxford Bulletin of Economics and Statistics* 50 (1988), pp. 41–52.

Mandelbrot, B. "New Methods in Statistical Economics," *Journal of Political Economy* 41 (1963b), pp. 421–43.

Mandelbrot, B. "The Variation of Certain Speculative Prices," *Journal of Business* 36 (1963b), pp. 394–429.

Ploeg, F. van der "Rational Expectations, Risk and Chaos in Financial Markets," *Economic Journal* 96 (suppl.) (1986), pp. 151–62.

Ramsey, J. B.; C. L. Sayers; and P. Rothman. "The Statistical Properties of Dimension Calculations Using Small Data Sets: Some Economic Applications," Research Report #88-10, C. V. Starr Center, New York University, 1988.

Ramsey, J. B., and H. J. Yuan. "The Statistical Properties of Dimension Calculations Using Small Data Sets," Research Report #87-20, C. V. Starr Center, New York University, 1987.

Rocca, L. H. "Time Series Analysis of Commodity Futures Prices," Ph.D. dissertation, University of California, Berkeley, 1969.

Samuelson, P. "Proof that Properly Anticipated Prices Fluctuate Randomly," *Industrial Management Review* 6 (1965), pp. 41–49.

Savit, R. "When Random is Not Random: An Introduction to Chaos in Market Prices," *Journal of Futures Markets* 8 (1988), pp. 271–89.

Scheinkman, J. A., and B. Lebaron. "Nonlinear Dynamics and Stock Returns," *Journal of Business* 62 (1989a), pp. 311–37.

Schienkman, J. A. and B. LeBaron. "Nonlinear Dynamics and GNP data," in *Economic Complexity,* Barnett, W., Geweke, J., and Shell, K. (eds.) Cambridge, UK: Cambridge University Press, 1989b.

Sims, C. A. "Martingale-Like Behavior of Prices and Interest Rates," Discussion Paper No. 205, Department of Economics, University of Minnesota, Minneapolis, 1984.

Smidt, S. "A test of the Serial Independence of Price Changes in Soybean Futures," as reprinted in *Selected Writings on Futures Markets,* Peck, A. (ed.). Chicago: Chicago Board of Trade, 1965/1977, pp. 257–77.

Stevenson, R. A., and R. M. Bear. "Commodity Futures: Trends or Random Walk?", as reprinted in *Selected Writings on Futures Markets,* Peck, A. (ed.). Chicago Board of Trade, 1970/1977, pp. 279–94.

Takens, F. "Detecting Strange Attractors in Turbulence," in *Dynamical Systems and Turbulence: Lecture Notes in Mathematics* #898, Rand, D. and Young, L. (eds.). Berlin: Springer-Verlag, 1980, pp. 366–82.

Taylor, S. J. "Conjectured Models for Trends in Financial Prices: Tests and Forecasts," *Journal of the Royal Statistical Society A* 143 (1980), pp. 338–62.

Taylor, S. J. *Modeling Financial Time Series.* Chichester, UK: Wiley, 1986.

Working, H. "A Theory of Anticipatory Prices," as reprinted in *Selected Writings of Holbrook Working.* Chicago: Chicago Board of Trade, 1958/1977.

CHAPTER 23

MANAGEMENT SUMMARY

Title: "A Note on the Factors Affecting Technical Trading System Returns"

Publication: *Journal of Futures Markets* 7, no. 5, pp. 591–95.

Author: Scott H. Irwin, Ohio State University
                B. Wade Brorsen, Pardue University

Data: Futures fund returns from 1978 through 1984.

Synopsis: This chapter seeks to explain the wide variation in technical trading system returns. The results show a positive association between economic uncertainty (inflation) and technical returns, suggesting traders may expect lower returns during periods of low uncertainty (low inflation). This also suggests that inflation-induced uncertainty reduces the efficiency of futures price movements. No relationship was found between the relative amount of system trading and technical returns.

A Note on the Factors Affecting Technical Trading System Returns

Scott H. Irwin

B. Wade Brorsen

In recent years, technical trading in futures markets by large managed accounts has increased dramatically.[1] Irwin and Brorsen (1985) reported that the equity of technically managed public futures funds increased from $5.0 million to $315.2 million over the January 1978—March 1984 period. However, judging by the performance of public futures funds during the 1980s [Murphy (1986); Elton, Gruber, and Rentzler (1987)], the returns to technical trading have been poor. The low returns in recent years may be due to increased use of trading systems. Another possibility is that commodity prices may have become more stable due to changes in macroeconomic policies.

In sum, technical trading system returns have varied widely over time [Irwin and Uhrig (1984)]. Technical traders may benefit if they have a greater awareness concerning the factors associated with the wide variation in returns. In addition, analysis of the factors associated with trading system returns may yield new insights concerning the process generating futures price movements. The purpose of this chapter is to report research relating two factors—uncertainty and the relative size of technical system usage—to technical trading system returns.

Scott H. Irwin is an Assistant Professor in the Agricultural Economics and Rural Sociology
    Department at The Ohio State University.
B. Wade Brorsen is an Assistant Professor in the Agricultural Economics Department at Purdue
    University.

Conceptual background and procedure are discussed in the next section. Results based on linear regression are then presented. The final section presents conclusions based on the regression results.

Disequilibrium models [Black (1976); Beja and Goldman (1980)] are useful starting points for identifying factors affecting technical trading system returns.[2] The basic premise of disequilibrium models is that prices do not adjust instantaneously to supply and demand imbalances. Thus, markets experience short-run periods where it is profitable for traders to act on price trends signaled by technical analysis. Information may not be acted upon instantaneously for a variety of reasons: uncertainty, transaction costs, taxes, costs of acquiring and evaluating information, and lags in obtaining information.

While disequilibrium factors should be positively related to trading system returns, the same returns could be limited by the total amount of technical trading in the market. The logic can be traced to the efficient market hypothesis [Fama (1970)], which implies that speculative markets are self-regulating. If a system is profitable for a period of time, it is doomed to be self-defeating. As more and more traders adopt the profitable system, nontechnical traders are likely to learn the workings of the system and buy or sell in anticipation of the technical traders. As a result, trading system profits are reduced to a level consistent with market efficiency.[3]

The previous discussion suggests technical trading system returns are a function of disequilibrium factors and the number of system users. Of the possible disequilibrium factors discussed, only uncertainty is likely to vary significantly over time. This leads to the following model:

$$\text{Technical Trading System Returns} = f(\text{Uncertainty, Usage}) \qquad (1)$$

Carlton (1983), among others, has argued that general uncertainty is directly related to inflation, due to the positive relationship between price variance and inflation.[4] Therefore, inflation, as measured by the percent change in the Consumer Price Index, will be used as a measure of general uncertainty. Two specific measures of how inflation may generate uncertainty are used: (a) the absolute value of the inflation rate, and (b) the square of the inflation rate. The total dollar equity in technically managed public futures funds is used as a measure of the total usage of technical trading systems in U.S. futures markets. Because the proportion of total trading conducted by technical traders is the true variable of interest, the equity of futures funds was normalized by dividing by the total open interest in 21 of the largest futures markets.

The first measure of technical returns is the aggregate return of public futures funds that Irwin and Brorsen (1985) identified as relying solely on technical trading systems. Because fund returns represent a mix of technical trading systems that has probably changed over time, a simulated return series was also used as a measure of technical returns. The technical trading system simulated was a one-parameter channel system. The simulation was based on a set of assumptions that mirrored the operation of a futures fund.[5] All returns were net of transaction costs and the result of out-of-sample trading.

The sample period is the first quarter of 1978 through the fourth quarter of 1984. All equations are estimated in linear form via ordinary least squares.

RESULTS AND ANALYSIS

Regression results are reported in Table 23–1. The R^2 values ranged from .15 to .31, indicating the two specified factors explain only a small portion of return variability. Inflation rate coefficients were positive and significant in all four models, suggesting technical trading was more profitable during periods of high uncertainty. The measure of trading system usage had an unexpected positive sign in all four equations. However, none of the estimated coefficients were significant. The unexpected results may be due to measurement problems. Futures fund equity may be a poor measure of the usage of technical trading systems.

In spite of the likely data problems, all the estimated equations suggest that increased uncertainty, related to high levels of inflation (in absolute terms), is favorable to technical trading systems. Knowledge of the relationship of technical returns to inflation may help traders increase profits by decreasing or stopping system trading during low inflation periods and increasing system trading during high inflation periods. The results also suggest that futures price movements are less efficient during periods of high inflation. Finally, the results do not indicate that system traders should be overly concerned with recent increases in system usage.

SUMMARY AND CONCLUSIONS

This chapter sought to explain the wide variation in technical trading system returns over time. Two factors were proposed to explain returns, uncertainty and the relative amount of systems trading in futures markets. Uncertainty was measured by the inflation rate, and trading activity was

TABLE 23-1

Regressions of Technical Trading System Returns against the Inflation Rate and Technical Trading System Use*

		Independent Variables			
Dependent Variable (Estimation Period)	Intercept	Absolute Value of the Inflation Rate	Square of the Inflation Rate	Normalized Futures Fund Equity	R^2
Futures fund returns	−15.62*	6.14*		0.01	.24
(1978I-1984IV)	(−2.09)	(2.81)		(1.59)	
	−11.68*		1.61*	0.01	.31
	(−2.09)		(3.36)	(1.73)	
Simulated returns	−16.29	9.05*		0.02	.15
(1978I-1984IV)	(−1.80)	(2.05)		(0.95)	
	−8.29		2.12*	0.01	.15
	(−0.73)		(2.09)	(0.86)	

*Asterisks denote significance at the 5% level using two-tailed t-test. Values in parentheses are t-values.

measured by public futures fund equity in relation to open interest. The results show a strong positive association between uncertainty and technical returns, suggesting traders may expect lower returns during periods of low uncertainty (low inflation), and may partially explain the recent decrease in returns to technical trading. This also suggests that inflation-induced uncertainty reduces the efficiency of futures price movements. No relationship was found between the relative amount of system trading and technical returns. However, the previous result may be due to the lack of precision in measuring the relative amount of system trading.

ENDNOTES

1. Technical trading systems forecast price movements based on historical prices and/or volume and open interest.
2. The research findings of Nawrocki (1984) and Lukac, Brorsen, and Irwin (1986) suggest disequilibrium models are useful descriptions of short-run price behavior in speculative markets.

3. Jensen (1986) argues that trading returns in an efficient market will not exceed a normal economic level, where normal returns are adjusted for risk and net of all costs.

4. See Fisher (1981) for documentation of the effect of inflation on price variance.

5. See Irwin and Brorsen (1984) for a complete description of the simulation model.

BIBLIOGRAPHY

Beja, A. and M.B. Goldman. "On the Dynamic Behavior of Prices in Disequilibrium." *Journal of Finance* 32 (1980), pp. 235–47.

Black, S.W. "Rational Response to Shocks in a Dynamic Model of Capital Asset Prices." *American Economic Review* 66 (1976), pp. 767–79.

Carlton, D.W. "Futures Trading, Market Interrelationships and Industry Structures." *American Journal of Agricultural Economics* 65 (1983), 380–87.

Elton, E.J., M.J. Gruber, and J.C. Rentzler. "Professionally Managed, Publicly Traded Commodity Funds." *Journal of Business* 60 (1987), pp. 175–99.

Fama, E.F. "Efficient Capital Markets: A Review of Theory and Empirical Work." *Journal of Finance* 25 (1970), pp. 383–417.

Fisher, S. "Relative Shocks, Relative Price Variability, and Inflation." Brookings Paper on Economic Activity, no. 2, 1981, pp. 381–431.

Irwin, S.H., and B.W. Brorsen. "An Economic Evaluation of Technical Analysis." Staff Paper No. 84-7, Department of Agricultural Economics, Purdue University, 1984.

Irwin, S.H. and B.W. Brorsen. "Public Futures Funds." *Journal of Futures Markets* 5 (1985), pp. 463–85.

Irwin, S.H., and J.W. Uhrig. "Do Technical Analysts Have Holes in Their Shoes?" *Review of Research in Futures Markets* 3 (1984), pp. 264–77.

Jensen, M.L. "Some Anomalous Evidence Regarding Market Efficiency: An Editorial Introduction." *Journal of Financial Economics* 9 (1978), pp. 95–101.

Lukac, L.P., B.W. Brorsen, and S.H. Irwin. "A Comparison of Twelve Technical Trading Systems with Market Efficiency Implications." Station Bulletin No. 495, Department of Agricultural Economics, Agricultural Experiment Station, Purdue University, 1986.

Murphy, J.A. "Futures Fund Performance: A Test of the Effectiveness of Technical Analysis." *Journal of Futures Markets* 6 (1986), pp. 175–85.

Nawrocki, D. "Adaptive Trading Rules and Dynamic Disequilibrium." *Applied Economics* 16 (1984), pp. 1–14.

INDEX

489